MW00736871

Two Gentlemen
of Verona

SHAKESPEARE CRITICISM
VOLUME 15
GARLAND REFERENCE LIBRARY OF THE HUMANITIES
VOLUME 1645

E.Edwards.del.   *M.Liart.sculp*

Ruffian let go that rude uncivil Touch –

Publish'd according to Act of Parl.t May 1.1774. by John Bell, Strand.

The Two Gentlemen of Verona *Act 5, Scene 4. By Edward Edwards.*
By permission of the Folger Shakespeare Library.

TWO GENTLEMEN OF VERONA
CRITICAL ESSAYS

EDITED BY
JUNE SCHLUETER

GARLAND PUBLISHING, INC.
NEW YORK AND LONDON
1996

Library of Congress Cataloging-in-Publication Data

Two gentlemen of Verona : critical essays / edited by June Schlueter.
     p.   cm. — (Garland reference library of the humanities ; v.
1645. Shakespeare criticism ; v. 15)
   Includes bibliographical references.
   ISBN 0-8153-1020-X (alk. paper)
   1. Shakespeare, William, 1564–1616.   Two gentlemen of Verona.
2. Comedy.   I. Schlueter, June.   II. Series: Garland reference
library of the humanities ; vol. 1645.   III. Series: Garland
reference library of the humanities.   Shakespeare criticism ; v. 15.
PR2838.T96   1996
822.3'3—dc20   95–45741
                                       CIP

Cover illustration: The Two Gentlemen of Verona Act 5, Scene 4. By Edward
Edwards. By permission of the Folger Shakespeare Library.

Printed on acid-free, 250-year-life paper
Manufactured in the United States of America

CONTENTS

General Editor's Introduction

The continuing goal of the Garland Shakespeare Criticism series is to provide the most influential historical criticism, the most significant contemporary interpretations, and reviews of the most influential productions. Each volume in the series, devoted to a Shakespearean play or poem (e.g., the sonnets, *Venus and Adonis,* the *Rape of Lucrece*), includes the most essential criticism and reviews of Shakespeare's work from the seventeenth century to the present. The series thus provides, through individual volumes, a representative gathering of critical opinion of how a play or poem has been interpreted over the centuries.

A major feature of each volume in the series is the editor's introduction. Each volume editor provides a substantial essay identifying the main critical issues and problems the play (or poem) has raised, charting the critical trends in looking at the work over the centuries, and assessing the critical discourses that have linked the play or poem to various ideological concerns. In addition to examining the critical commentary in light of important historical and theatrical events, each introduction functions as a discursive bibliographic essay that cites and evaluates significant critical works—essays, journal articles, dissertations, books, theatre documents—and gives readers a guide to the research on a particular play or poem.

After the introduction, each volume is organized chronologically, by date of publication of selections, into two sections: critical essays and theatre reviews/documents. The first section includes previously published journal articles and book chapters as well as original essays written for the collection. In selecting essays, editors have chosen works that are representative of a given age and critical approach. Striving for accurate historical representation, editors include earlier as well as contemporary criticism. Their goal is to include the widest possible range of critical approaches to the play or poem, demonstrating the multiplicity and complexity of critical response.

In most instances, essays have been reprinted in their entirety, not butchered into snippets. The editors have also commissioned original essays (sometimes as many as five to ten) by leading Shakespearean scholars, thus offering the most contemporary, theoretically attentive analyses. Reflecting some recent critical approaches in Shakespearean studies, these new essays approach the play or poem from many perspectives, including feminist, Marxist, new historical, semiotic, mythic, performance/staging, cultural, and/or a combination of these and other methodologies. Some volumes in the series even include bibliographic analyses that have significant implications for criticism.

The second section of each volume in the series is devoted to the play in performance and, again, is organized chronologically, beginning with some of the earliest and most significant productions and proceeding to the most recent. This section, which ultimately provides a theatre history of the play, should not be regarded as different from or rigidly isolated from the critical essays in the first section. Shakespearean criticism has often been informed by or has significantly influenced productions. Shakespearean criticism over the last twenty years or so has usefully been labeled the "Age of Performance." Readers will find information in this section on major foreign productions of Shakespeare's plays as well as landmark productions in English. Consisting of more than reviews of specific productions, this section also contains a variety of theatre documents, including interpretations written for the particular volume by notable directors whose comments might be titled "The Director's Choice," histories of seminal productions (e.g., Peter Brook's *Titus Andronicus* in 1955), and even interviews with directors and/or actors. Editors have also included photographs from productions around the world to help readers see and further appreciate the way a Shakespearean play has taken shape in the theatre.

Each volume in the Garland Shakespeare Criticism series strives to give readers a balanced, representative collection of the best that has been thought and said about a Shakespearean text. In essence, each volume supplies a careful survey of essential materials in the history of criticism for a Shakespearean text. In offering readers complete, fulfilling, and in some instances very hard to locate materials, volume editors have made conveniently accessible the literary and theatrical criticism of Shakespeare's greatest legacy, his work.

PHILIP C. KOLIN
UNIVERSITY OF SOUTHERN MISSISSIPPI

INTRODUCTION

With the notable exceptions of brief commentaries by William Hazlitt (1817), Algernon Charles Swinburne (1880), and Edward Dowden (1890), the documentary record on *The Two Gentlemen of Verona* through 1900 is an editorial one, with compilers of Shakespeare's works offering occasional critical remarks on the play. In fact, it is only with Alexander Pope's 1723 edition—which followed Heminge and Condell (1623, 1632, 1663–64, 1685) and Nicholas Rowe (1707)—that critical commentary on *Two Gentlemen* appears. Tellingly, Pope identifies the crux that has most stubbornly resisted accommodation into a hospitable reading of the play, particularly in contemporary times: the ending. Of Valentine's offer of "all that was mine in Silvia" to his friend, Pope observes, it is "very odd to give up his mistress thus at once," an opinion endorsed and extended by Thomas Hanmer (1743–44), who thought it impossible "that Valentine would act so out of character and Silvia would remain silent."

Lewis Theobald, who edited the works in 1733, is generally without charity, judging the play "one of Shakespeare's worst." Pope, however, notes that "the style of this comedy is less figurative, and more natural and unaffected than the greater part of this author's," a comment which Samuel Johnson quotes and endorses in the preface to his own 1765 edition. In response to Upton's judgment that the play must "seek for its parent elsewhere," Johnson agrees that *Two Gentlemen* lacks "diversities of character" and "striking delineations of life" and is not among Shakespeare's "most powerful effusions," but he is not prepared to disown it: the play, he discovers, reflects the "language and sentiments of Shakespear." With a rhetorical restraint characteristic of criticism of the time, John Bell's 1774 edition concludes that *Two Gentlemen* "is very far from a bad piece, and much less distant from merit; tolerable judgment and genius would make it a living entertainment."

In addition to occasional commentary in editions—Charles Knight's (1843) and W.J. Craig's (1892), for example—the nineteenth century produced the first independent critical assessments of the play, each within a larger study of Shakespeare. Hazlitt's *Characters of Shakespeare's Plays* (1817) is in large part a reaction to Johnson's preface, which remains the most influential of eighteenth-century commentaries on Shakespeare. Though Johnson had faulted the playwright for the individuality of his characters, preferring the general representation of human nature, Hazlitt celebrates the "life and variety of character" and devotes his study to individual analyses of the principal characters of the plays. Quoting extensively from Schlegel's *Lectures on Drama* (1808), Hazlitt praises the German critic for his stimulating account of Shakespeare's work. In his two-page commentary on *Two Gentlemen*, Hazlitt reacts to Pope's expression of editorial despair over the play's second scene: the eighteenth-century compiler had regretted that "This whole scene, like many others in these plays (some of which I believe were written by Shakespear, and others interpolated by the players) is composed of the lowest and most trifling conceits, to be accounted for only by the gross taste of the age he lived in." In return, Hazlitt, though admitting that the play is "little more than the first outlines of a comedy loosely sketched in," speaks of "passages of high poetical spirit" and "inimitable quaintness of humour" and of moments of "sweetness of sentiment and expression." In particular, he praises the style of the play's "familiar" parts, noting the drollery and invention of the fourth act scene with Launce and Crab.

In *A Study of Shakespeare* (1880), Swinburne similarly registers reservations, judging the play deficient in the "elegiac beauty" of the earlier plays and the "exalted eloquence" of the later, yet he sees in this "slight" play of "swift . . . execution" an "even sweetness." And, with Hazlitt, he celebrates Launce, claiming the comic character and his dog were worth "all the bright fantastic interludes of Boyet and Adriano, Costard and Holofernes; worth even half the sallies of Mercutio, and half the dancing doggrel or broad-witted prose of either Dromio." Dowden, too, is restrained in his praise of the play, but he credits *Two Gentlemen* with being an advance over the earlier comedies and a starting point for the romantic love story told in dramatic form, with Julia prefiguring Juliet, Viola, Portia, Rosalind, and Imogen.

The first four decades of the twentieth century saw a number of critical editions of the complete works, including George Lyman Kittredge's in 1936. More important for criticism, individual editions of plays began to appear, inviting editors to offer extended introductions to the play. Editions by R. Warwick Bond (Arden, 1906), John Dover Wilson and Arthur Quiller-Couch (New Cambridge, 1921), Karl Young (Yale Shakespeare, 1924), and M.R. Ridley (New Temple Shakespeare, 1935) provided valuable information and judgments on dating, sources, textual variations, performances, and authorship.

More important still, these years engendered book-length critical studies of Shakespeare's plays and individual critical essays, enabling more focused attention. Representative books included George Baker's *The Development of Shakespeare as a Dramatist* (1907), which, in a chapter on "Early Experimentation in Plotting and Adaptation," analyzes technique in *Two Gentlemen*, concluding that this early work is weak in exposition and plotting; Victor Oscar Freeburg's *Disguise Plots in Elizabethan Drama* (1915), which discusses the female page, including Julia; E.K. Chambers' *Shakespeare: A Survey* (1925), which devotes a chapter to *Two Gentlemen*, characterizing the play as an immature dramatic effort and connecting it thematically with the sonnets; G. Wilson Knight's *The Shakespearean Tempest* (1932), which devotes a chapter to the romantic comedies and speaks of sea images in *Two Gentlemen*; Caroline Spurgeon's *Shakespeare's Imagery and What It Tells Us* (1935), which includes a short discussion of patterns of imagery in the play; and H.B. Charlton's *Shakespearian Comedy* (1938), which offers an extended analysis of romantic conventions in *Two Gentlemen*.

The first individual essay to concern itself primarily with *Two Gentlemen*, S. Asa Small's "The Ending of *The Two Gentlemen of Verona*," appeared in *PMLA* in 1933. Taking his cue from Alwin Thaler's "Shakespeare and the Unhappy Happy Ending" (*PMLA*, 1927) (which attributes Silvia's silence to her breathlessness following the struggle), Small explores the ending of *Two Gentlemen* in the context of romantic conventions, particularly the competing claims of love and friendship. The ending, he concludes, fails artistically because it does not respect the convention: Valentine, who otherwise acts thoughtfully, as a friend/lover should, does not acknowledge his affront to Silvia.

It is clear from this sampling of early twentieth-century criticism that such assessments of the play reflected the same critical ambiguity registered in earlier centuries: critics were ready to acknowledge the poetic and dramatic effectiveness of the play's parts, but all fell short of admiration for this underdeveloped and flawed apprentice work.

The 1940s and 1950s brought translations of the complete works into Russian, Italian, Turkish, Romanian, Armenian, French, Spanish, German, Japanese, Portuguese, Frisian, Polish, and Dutch (all listed in D'Orsay W. Pearson's annotated bibliography). Some ten new editions of the complete plays or the complete works were published, the most familiar of these being George B. Harrison's for Harcourt, Brace & World (1948) and Hardin Craig's Scott, Foresman edition (1951). Three individual editions of *Two Gentlemen* also appeared: George B. Harrison (Penguin, 1956), Charles J. Sisson (Laurel Shakespeare, 1958), and John Dover Wilson (Cambridge Pocket Shakespeare, 1958). Interesting commentary appeared in Oscar James Campbell's *Shakespeare's Satire* (1943), which suggests that Launce was the first clown role Shakespeare designed for Will Kempe; Sister Miriam Joseph's *Shakespeare's Use of the Arts of Language* (1947), which identifies rhetorical figures throughout the canon; T.W. Baldwin's structural analysis in *Shakspere's Five-Act Structure* (1947), which analyzes Shakespeare's dramatic strategies in *Two Gentlemen* and three other early plays; Hardin Craig's chapter on *Two Gentlemen* in *An Interpretation of the Works of Shakespeare* (1948), which evaluates the play within the context of Shakespeare's later work, with special reference to his treatment of women; Harold C. Goddard's *The Meaning of Shakespeare* (1951), which proposes that *Two Gentlemen* be read ironically; Northrop Frye's still influential "The Argument of Comedy" (1948), which identifies the pattern of death and revival characteristic of "green world comedy," including *Two Gentlemen*; and Volume 1 of Geoffrey Bullough's *Narrative and Dramatic Sources of Shakespeare* (1957), which surveys and reprints sources and analogues.

Two important *PMLA* essays appearing in the 1950s were Ralph M. Sargent's "Sir Thomas Elyot and the Integrity of *The Two Gentlemen of Verona*" (1950) and Karl F. Thompson's "Shakespeare's Romantic Comedies" (1952). Both writers attempt to reclaim the play, Sargent by comparing Shakespeare's treatment of romantic love and friendship with that of Elyot and others, Thompson by placing the play within the literary tradition of courtly love. A third essay, Thomas A. Perry's "Proteus, Wry-Transformed Traveller," which appeared in *Shakespeare Quarterly* (1954), examines the travel motif in *Two Gentlemen*, and Mario Praz's "Shakespeare's Italy," published in *Shakespeare Survey* (1954), treats the Italianate context of several of Shakespeare's plays.

Scholarship on *The Two Gentlemen of Verona*, and, even more so, on Shakespeare's more popular plays, burgeoned in the 1960s. Editions of the collected works included Charlton Hinman's Norton Facsimile of the First Folio (1968), as well as Alfred Harbage's Complete Pelican Shakespeare (1964); *Two Gentlemen* was edited individually by Bertrand Evans (Signet Classic, 1964), Berners A. W. Jackson (Pelican, 1964), Louis B. Wright and Virginia A. LaMar (Folger, 1964), Norman Sanders (New Penguin, 1968), George L. Kittredge (revised by Irving Ribner, 1969), and Clifford Leech

(Arden, 1969). The decade saw several new books on the comedies, among them Bertrand Evans' *Shakespeare's Comedies* (1960), Derek Traversi's *The Early Comedies* (1960), John Dover Wilson's *Shakespeare's Happy Comedies* (1962), Robert Grams Hunter's *Shakespeare and the Comedy of Forgiveness* (1965), E.M.W. Tillyard's *Shakespeare's Early Comedies* (1965), and Peter G. Phialias' *Shakespeare's Romantic Comedies: The Development of Their Form and Meaning* (1966). The freshest of these is Evans, who explores discrepant levels of awareness as a comic device, isolating moments of ignorance and their effect not simply on the progress of the play but on audience reception. Evans illustrates ways in which Shakespeare's plays exploit the audience's privileged position, or its ignorance, to achieve their effect, providing numerous examples in *Two Gentlemen*, including the circumstance of Julia's disguise.

Essays in the 1960s were legion, many reinforcing earlier observations and several focusing their analyses on the play's imagery, its neoplatonism, its rhetoric, structure, or theatrical conventions. John Vyvyan's analysis of *Two Gentlemen* in *Shakespeare and the Rose of Love* (1960) highmindedly attempts to restyle this troubling play as Platonic allegory. William Leigh Godshalk, in "The Structural Unity of *Two Gentlemen of Verona*" (1969), also tries to reclaim the play: structural recurrence, he suggests, as well as classical and mythical allusion, creates unity and a masterfully designed play. William E. Stephenson, in "The Adolescent Dream World of *The Two Gentlemen of Verona*" (1966), proposes that the play might be better understood as youthful fantasy. The more practical Stanley Wells, in "The Failure of *The Two Gentlemen of Verona*" (1963), willingly reconsiders critical objections to the play but concludes, without apology, that the play is flawed. Two important essays on the play's comic elements also appeared in the 1960s. Harold F. Brooks' "Two Clowns in a Comedy (to say nothing of the Dog): Speed, Launce (and Crab) in *The Two Gentlemen of Verona*" (1963) identifies parodic parallels between the clown scenes and other parts of the play. And Robert Weimann's "Laughing with the Audience: *The Two Gentlemen of Verona* and the Popular Tradition of Comedy" (1969) offers insights into the aside and the direct address, comic devices in *Two Gentlemen* that do not derive from the popular tradition.

The 1970s, though producing two major editions of the complete works, by Hardin Craig and David Bevington (1973, a revision of Craig's 1951 edition) and by G. Blakemore Evans (*The Riverside Shakespeare*, 1974) (as well as Denis Carey's Folio Society edition of *Two Gentlemen* [1974]), proved a lean period for *Two Gentlemen* criticism. Books on Shakespeare's comedies or the early plays—Larry S. Champion's *The Evolution of*

Shakespeare's Comedy (1970), Roland M. Frye's *Shakespeare: The Art of the Dramatist* (1970), John Arthos' *Shakespeare: The Early Writings* (1972), Patrick Swinden's *An Introduction to Shakespeare's Comedies* (1973), Robert Turner's *Shakespeare's Apprenticeship* (1974), and Kenneth Muir's *Shakespeare's Comic Sequence* (1979), for example—continued the motifs of earlier full-length studies and did little to rescue *Two Gentlemen* from the judgment of history. As Isaac Asimov put it in *Asimov's Guide to Shakespeare* (1970), of the early works, *Two Gentlemen* is "the most forgettable." Alexander Leggatt offered characteristically perceptive insights on the play in *Shakespeare's Comedy of Love* (1974), arguing that *Two Gentlemen* had a comic and a rhetorical quality of modest value and noting that the various styles and points of view came together in the character of Julia; Ralph Berry, in *Shakespeare's Comedies: Explorations in Form* (1972), credited the work as an experiment in behavioral conventions; and Thomas F. Van Laan, in *Role-playing in Shakespeare* (1978), focused attention on that device in each of the plays, including *Two Gentlemen*.

The decade saw only a few essays dedicated to the play; the best of these were Inga-Stina Ewbank, "'Were man but constant, he were perfect': Constancy and Consistency in *Two Gentlemen of Verona*" (1972), which explores the play's inconsistencies and makes a case for connecting *Two Gentlemen* and Sonnet 40; Thomas E. Scheye, "Two Gentlemen of Milan" (1974), which examines the three worlds of the play (Verona, Milan, the forest) in terms of the characters' search for identity; and Peter Lindenbaum, "Education in *The Two Gentlemen of Verona*" (1975), which explores the motif of the perfect gentleman within the tradition of Christian fallibility.

A critical breakthrough in Shakespeare criticism came in the 1970s with a spate of publications that questioned assumptions about sexuality and gender and focused attention on Shakespeare's women. Charles Brooks' "Shakespeare's Heroine-Actresses" (1960) and Anne Righter's *Shakespeare and the Idea of the Play* (1962) had secured the emphasis on identity, role-playing, and theatricality that informs much contemporary criticism. In addition, the Brooks essay, in renewing interest in the disguised heroine, prefigured more theoretically sophisticated studies of gender relations, gender identity, and gender/genre ideology (see Philip C. Kolin's *Shakespeare and Feminist Criticism: An Annotated Bibliography and Commentary* [1991]). Among the earliest of these were Juliet Dusinberre's *Shakespeare and the Nature of Women* (1975), Marianne Novy's "Shakespeare's Female Characters as Actors and as Audience" (1977), Robert Speaight's "Shakespeare's Heroines" (1977), and Kezia Sproat's "Sisterhood in Shakespeare" (1978). These were followed, in the 1980s, by Angela Pitt's *Shakespeare's Women*

(1981), Marilyn French's *Shakespeare's Division of Experience* (1981), Linda Woodbridge's *Women and the English Renaissance: Literature and the Nature of Womankind, 1540–1620* (1984), Marianne Novy's *Love's Argument: Gender Relations in Shakespeare* (1984), and an influential collection of essays that galvanized the political underpinnings of the inquiry: Carolyn Ruth Swift Lenz, Gayle Greene, and Carol Thomas Neely's *The Woman's Part: Feminist Criticism of Shakespeare* (1980). The collective impact of these publications on Shakespeare studies was to extend—and to revise—the field of critical play. Traditional essays on courtly conventions, thematic motifs, and structural features of the early comedies still appeared, but the moral and critical imperative of feminism became increasingly evident. For *Two Gentlemen*, this meant that Julia and Silvia began a critical upstage of their male counterparts.

The past fifteen years have brought their share of book-length studies of Shakespeare's plays and of new editions. The 1980s began with the publication of David Bevington's *The Complete Works of Shakespeare*, third edition, to be followed in 1992 by the fourth. Other major editions of the complete works included Stanley Wells and Gary Taylor's Oxford Shakespeare (1986, compact edition 1988), as well as Michael J.B. Allen and Kenneth Muir's facsimile edition of *Shakespeare's Plays in Quarto* (1981). *The Illustrated Stratford Shakespeare* (1982) and *The Globe Illustrated Shakespeare*, which reprints Howard Staunton's 1857–60 texts (1983), also appeared. Among the several individual editions of *Two Gentlemen* to be published were the BBC TV performance text (1984), which contains an introduction by John Wilders and production notes by Henry Fenwick; Tony Bareham's Longman edition (1983), and A.L. Rowse's edition in the Contemporary Shakespeare Series (1986). The most helpful of the new editions is Kurt Schlueter's New Cambridge Shakespeare (1990), which provides a lengthy introduction that is especially strong on the stage history of the play.

In the 1980s and 1990s, the inventory of books on the comedies is considerable. These include Ruth Nevo, *Comic Transformations in Shakespeare* (1980); Jack A. Vaughn, *Shakespeare's Comedies* (1980); Edward Berry, *Shakespeare's Comic Rites* (1984); William C. Carrol, *The Metamorphoses of Shakespearean Comedy* (1985); Karen Newman, *Shakespeare's Rhetoric of Comic Character* (1985); Richard A. Levin, *Love and Society in Shakespearean Comedy* (1985); W. Thomas MacCary, *Friends and Lovers: The Phenomenology of Desire in Shakespearean Comedy* (1985); Robert Ornstein, *Shakespeare's Comedies: From Roman Farce to Romantic Mystery* (1986); Linda Anderson, *A Kind of Wild Justice: Revenge in Shakespeare's Comedies* (1987); David Richmond, *Laughter, Pain and Wonder:*

Shakespeare's Comedies and the Audience in the Theater (1990); Roger L. Cox, *Shakespeare's Comic Changes: The Time-Lapse Metaphor as Plot Device* (1991); Ejner J. Jensen, *Shakespeare and the Ends of Comedy* (1991); Anthony J. Lewis, *The Love Story in Shakespearean Comedy* (1992); and Gary Waller's edited collection, *Shakespeare's Comedies* (1991).

Recent books of special interest are David Bevington's *Action Is Eloquence: Shakespeare's Language of Gesture* (1984), which treats the stage properties and business of Shakespeare's plays, including letters, Julia's ring, and the grieving gesture in *Two Gentlemen*; Keir Elam's *Shakespeare's Universe of Discourse* (1984), a semiotic approach to the plays that provides special insight into Launce's lines; and John Drakakis' edited volume, *Alternative Shakespeares* (1985), which offers a range of rereadings, including Catherine Belsey's "Disrupting Sexual Difference: Meaning and Gender in the Comedies," which uses Julia as an example of the instability of gender categories.

Several essays particular to *Two Gentlemen* reflect a sustained interest in dramatic form, sources and analogues, and thematic motifs. These include William Rossky's "*The Two Gentlemen of Verona* as Burlesque" (1982), which suggests that the spirit of the play is that of a Gilbert and Sullivan operetta; Camille Wells Slights' "*The Two Gentlemen of Verona* and the Courtesy Book Tradition" (1983), which deepens the connection between Castiglione's *The Courtier* and the conduct of Shakespeare's gentlemen; Frederick Kiefer's "Love Letters in *The Two Gentlemen of Verona*" (1986), which examines the many texts within the text; and René Girard's "Love Delights in Praises: A Reading of *The Two Gentlemen of Verona*" (1989), which offers a stimulating interpretation of the play in terms of symmetry and mimetic desire. Individually and collectively, these essays suggest that new critical approaches may engender new readings.

Indeed, the section of this volume representing the 1990s, with several newly written essays included, offers evidence of renewed thinking about *The Two Gentlemen of Verona*. Charles A. Hallett's "'Metamorphising' Proteus: Reversal Strategies in *The Two Gentlemen of Verona*" builds on his and Elaine S. Hallett's 1991 book, *Analyzing Shakespeare's Action: Scene Versus Sequence*, in its analysis of textual and performance units of action. Kathleen Campbell, in "Shakespeare's Actors as Collaborators: Will Kempe and *The Two Gentlemen of Verona*," sees *Two Gentlemen* as a case study in staging, using Elizabethan stage conventions to speculate on the casting of Crab. John Timpane's "'I am but a foole, looke you': Launce and the Social Functions of Humor" deepens Campbell's perspective on the comic characters, noting how improvisational invitations are built into the text. Two essays on performance complete this section, the first, Michael Friedman's "'To be slow in words is a woman's only virtue': Silence and Satire in *The Two Gentlemen of Verona*" explores contemporary staging possibilities; the second, Patty S. Derrick's "Feminine 'Depth' on the Nineteenth-Century Stage," connects stage history and cultural perceptions of female character.

These recent essays reflect a growing interest in Shakespeare's plays as scripts for the stage. Though the stage history of *Two Gentlemen* is lean, the earliest record of its production being 139 years after its publication in the First Folio, contemporary directors, working within a postmodern critical context, have seen the play, and particularly the final scene, as a production challenge. Indeed, it was not until William Charles Macready's 1841 Drury Lane production that Shakespeare's textual ending, or at least Valentine's offer of Silvia to Proteus, was restored. The 1762 production at Garrick's Drury Lane theatre followed an adapted text by Benjamin Victor, which rearranged, conflated, and interpolated speeches and scenes and omitted the troubling gesture that continues to vex critics who would like to defend the play. Subsequent performances—Covent Garden in 1784 (with Mrs. Stephen Kemble as Silvia and Mr. Wroughton as Proteus); in Drury Lane in 1790 (by John Philip Kemble, with Mrs. Kemble and Mr. Wroughton in their 1784 roles and Mr. Barrymore as Valentine); in Covent Garden in 1808 (again by John Philip Kemble, with Kemble playing Valentine); and in Covent Garden in 1821 (apparently extravagant)—took textual liberties. In his New Cambridge edition of the play (1990), Kurt Schlueter offers commentary on each of these early productions, along with an analysis of how various textual changes affected interpretation. The casting of actors older than one would expect for this youthful play may well have influenced staging decisions: in 1762, the thirty-four-year-old Mrs. Yates played Julia; in 1784, the thirty-eight-year-old Mrs. Mattocks played Julia; and in 1808, the fifty-year-old John Philip Kemble played Valentine (with Julia played by the twenty-five-year-old Mrs. Goodall).

Macready's production, featuring Macready himself as Valentine, was taken to New York in 1846 and revived at the Haymarket, London, in 1848, by Charles Kean, with Mr. and Mrs. Kean as Valentine and Julia. The play was also produced in the nineteenth century at the Olympic Theatre (1849), by Samuel Phelps at Sadler's Wells (1857), by Osmond Tearle at Stratford (1890), and at Daly's Theatre (1895).

The first half of the twentieth century saw productions by Harley Granville Barker (1904) and William Poel (1910), the latter staged at Sir Herbert Beerbohm Tree's invitation at His Majesty's Theatre, London. The Old Vic mounted productions in 1916 and 1923 (Robert Atkins) and again in 1952 (the Bristol Old Vic in London, directed by Denis Carey), and 1956 (directed by Michael Langham). The Carey production, with John Neville as Valentine and Laurence Payne as Proteus, won the approval of the *Times* reviewer who felt it would "make audiences wonder why it is not done more often"; the Langham production, set in the nineteenth century, with Keith Mitchell as a Byronic Proteus, was hailed by Muriel St. Clare Byrne as "a producer's and designer's triumph with a much neglected play."

Over the years, England's Royal Shakespeare Company has regularly returned to *Two Gentlemen*, offering stagings in 1890, by Tearle; 1910, by Frank Benson; 1925, by William Bridges-Adams; 1938, by Iden Payne; 1960, by Peter Hall; 1970, by Robin Phillips; 1981, by John Barton (in a curious pairing with *Titus Andronicus*)—all described in Kurt Schlueter's informative survey—and 1991, by David Thacker.

In the United States, Shakespeare festivals across the country have staged the play: the New York Shakespeare Festival, for example, in 1957 and 1994 and the Oregon Shakespeare Festival in 1957, 1974, and 1981; the Folger Theatre staged the play in 1977, The Acting Company, on tour, in 1990 (to name just a few). The Stratford Festival in Ontario, Canada, offered productions in 1975, directed by Robin Phillips; in 1984, directed by Leon Rubin; in 1988, directed by Robert Beard; and in 1992, directed by Marti Maraden. The Rubin mounting, highly controversial among Canadian critics, featured punk haircuts that developed bright pink streaks signalling when the character was smitten by love.

Even as contemporary Shakespearean directors sought new ways to mount familiar texts, BBC TV and Time Life Productions were preparing the plays for television. Under the direction of Don Taylor, *The Two Gentlemen of Verona* entered the BBC Television Shakespeare series in the 1983–84 season. Though not among the more memorable of the play's stagings, the production assumes a place within a series that has become virtually canonical for teachers of Shakespeare.

On its own, however, *Two Gentlemen* has yet to redeem itself from a largely scornful—even patronizing—critical history, which, from the start, characterized the play as the work of a crude, unpolished youth, who had thematic ideas and dramatic ideals he was as yet unable to realize. Yet productions of the play in recent years have been delightfully engaging: I think of the RSC revival of its palm court setting, a production that handled the ending more intelligently than any other I've seen; the punk version in Stratford, Ontario, which frankly admitted its youth; the Acting Company's circus romp, in which Milan was dressed like the Wild West; the New York Shakespeare Festival's production in Central Park, alongside a lake that fed into an onstage river; and a Pennsylvania Stage Company production in which Crab, a forlorn-looking beagle, howled on cue. Those who know Shakespeare measure this early effort against his mature achievements, and the play necessarily comes up short. Still, over the centuries, grudging acknowledgments of its successes, including Launce and Crab, have punctuated the criticism, which, even in its most uncharitable form, never fully dismisses the play. As one who was prompted to compile this volume by a stubborn attraction to this early work, I retain an open eye. For despite implausibilities, inconsistencies, and a hurried and painfully sexist ending (at least to twentieth-century minds), the play in contemporary production is almost always spirited, resonant, and fun.

Those who shared in the fun of helping me prepare this volume include my husband, Paul Schlueter; Lafayette College's Skillman Library staff; and Nancy Williams, who ably—and patiently—typed what began as a manuscript twice this size. Offstage partners in this project were D'Orsay W. Pearson and Kurt Schlueter, whose annotated bibliography and New Cambridge Shakespeare introduction, respectively, gave helpful direction. To their unrivaled merit, I thus subscribe.

WORKS CITED

Allen, Michael J.B. and Kenneth Muir, eds. *Shakespeare's Plays in Quarto: A Facsimile Edition of Copies Primarily from the Henry E. Huntington Library.* Berkeley: University of California Press, 1981.

Anderson, Linda. *A Kind of Wild Justice: Revenge in Shakespeare's Comedies.* Newark: University of Delaware Press, 1987.

Arthos, John. *Shakespeare: The Early Writings.* London: Bowes and Bowes, 1972.

Asimov, Isaac. *Asimov's Guide to Shakespeare.* 2 vols. Garden City: Doubleday, 1970.

Baker, George. *The Development of Shakespeare as a Dramatist.* New York: Macmillan, 1907.

Baldwin, T.W. *Shakspere's Five-Act Structure.* Urbana: University of Illinois Press, 1947, pp. 719–41.

Bareham, Tony, ed. *The Two Gentlemen of Verona.* Harlow: Longman, 1983.

Bell, John, ed. *Bell's Edition of Shakespeare's Plays, as they were performed at the Theatres Royal in London.* 8 vols. London, John Bell, 1774.

Belsey, Catherine. "Disrupting Sexual Difference: Meaning and Gender in the Comedies." In *Alternative Shakespeares.* Ed. John Drakakis, pp. 166–90.

Berry, Edward. *Shakespeare's Comic Rites.* Cambridge: Cambridge University Press, 1984.

Berry, Ralph. *Shakespeare's Comedies: Explorations in Form.* Princeton: Princeton University Press, 1972.

Bevington, David, ed. *The Complete Works of Shakespeare*, 3rd ed. Glenview: Scott, Foresman, 1980; 4th ed. New York: HarperCollins, 1992.

Bevington, David. *Action is Eloquence: Shakespeare's Language of Gesture.* Cambridge: Harvard University Press, 1984.

Bevington, David and Hardin Craig, eds. *The Complete Works of William Shakespeare*, rev. ed. Glenview: Scott, Foresman, 1973.

Bond, R. Warwick, ed. *The Two Gentlemen of Verona* (Arden Edition). London: Methuen, 1906.

Brooks, Charles. "Shakespeare's Heroine-Actresses." *Shakespeare Jahrbuch* 96 (1960): 134–44.

Brooks, Harold F. "Two Clowns in a Comedy (to say nothing of the Dog): Speed, Launce (and Crab) in *The Two Gentlemen of Verona.*" *Essays and Studies* 16 (1963): 91–100 [present volume, pp. 71–78].

Bullough, Geoffrey. *Narrative and Dramatic Sources of Shakespeare.* 8 vols. London: Routledge and Kegan Paul; New York: Columbia University Press, 1957–1975.

Campbell, Kathleen. "Shakespeare's Actors as Collaborators: Will Kempe and *The Two Gentlemen of Verona*" [present volume, pp. 179–87].

Campbell, Oscar James. *Shakespeare's Satire.* London: Oxford University Press, 1943.

Carey, Denis, ed. *The Two Gentlemen of Verona* (Folio Society Edition). London: The Folio Society, 1974.

Carrol, William C. *The Metamorphoses of Shakespearean Comedy.* Princeton: Princeton University Press, 1985.

Chambers, E.K. *Shakespeare: A Survey.* London: Sidgwick & Jackson, 1925.

Champion, Larry S. *The Evolution of Shakespeare's Comedy: A Study in Dramatic Perspective.* Cambridge: Harvard University Press, 1970.

Charlton, H.B. *Shakespearian Comedy.* London: Methuen, 1938.

Cox, Roger L. *Shakespeare's Comic Changes: The Time-Lapse Metaphor as Plot Device.* Athens: University of Georgia Press, 1991.

Craig, Hardin, ed. *The Complete Works of William Shakespeare.* Chicago: Scott, Foresman, 1951.

Craig, Hardin. *An Interpretation of the Works of Shakespeare.* New York: Citadel Press, 1948.

Craig, Hardin and David Bevington, eds. *The Complete Works of Shakespeare,* rev. ed. Glenview: Scott, Foresman, 1973.

Craig, W.J., ed. *The Complete Works of William Shakespeare.* Oxford Edition. London: H. Frowde, 1892.

Derrick, Patty S. "Feminine 'Depth' on the Nineteenth-Century Stage" [present volume, pp. 259–62].

Dowden, Edward. *Shakespere* (Literature Primers). New York: American Book Company, 1890.

Drakakis, John, ed. *Alternative Shakespeares.* London: Methuen, 1985.

Dusinberre, Juliet. *Shakespeare and the Nature of Women.* London: Macmillan Press, 1975.

Elam, Keir. *Shakespeare's Universe of Discourse: Language-Games in the Comedies.* Cambridge: Cambridge University Press, 1984.

Evans, Bertrand, ed. *The Two Gentlemen of Verona* (Signet Classic Shakespeare). New York: New American Library, 1964.

Evans, Bertrand. *Shakespeare's Comedies.* Oxford: Clarendon, 1960 [excerpt in present volume, pp. 59–69].

Evans, G. Blakemore, ed. *The Riverside Shakespeare.* Boston: Houghton Mifflin, 1974.

Ewbank, Inga-Stina. "'Were man but constant, he were perfect': Constancy and Consistency in *Two Gentlemen of Verona.*" In *Shakespearean Comedy* (Stratford-upon-Avon Studies 14). Ed. Malcolm Bradbury and David Palmer. New York: Crane, Russak, 1972, pp. 31–57 [present volume, pp. 91–114].

Freeburg, Victor Oscar. *Disguise Plots in Elizabethan Drama: A Study in Stage Tradition.* New York: Columbia University Press, 1915 [excerpt in present volume, pp. 13–20].

French, Marilyn. *Shakespeare's Division of Experience.* New York: Summit Books, 1981.

Friedman, Michael. "'To be slow in words is a woman's only virtue': Silence and Satire in *The Two Gentlemen of Verona.*" *Selected Papers from The West Virginia*

Shakespeare and Renaissance Association 17 (1994): 1–9 [present volume, pp. 213–22].

Frye, Northrop. "The Argument of Comedy." In *English Institute Essays, 1948.* Ed. D.A. Robertson. New York: Columbia University Press, 1949, pp. 58–73.

Frye, Roland M. *Shakespeare: The Art of the Dramatist.* Boston: Houghton Mifflin, 1970.

Girard, René. "Love Delights in Praises: A Reading of *The Two Gentlemen of Verona.*" *Philosophy and Literature* 13.2 (October 1989): 231–47.

Globe Illustrated Shakespeare, The: The Complete Works. Annotated. New York: Greenwich House, 1983.

Goddard, Harold C. *The Meaning of Shakespeare.* Chicago: University of Chicago Press, 1951.

Godshalk, William Leigh. "The Structural Unity of *Two Gentlemen of Verona.*" *Studies in Philology* 66 (1969): 168–81.

Hallett, Charles A. "'Metamorphising' Proteus: Reversal Strategies in *The Two Gentlemen of Verona*" [present volume, pp. 153–77].

Hallett, Charles A. and Elaine S. Hallett. *Analyzing Shakespeare's Action: Scene Versus Sequence.* Cambridge: Cambridge University Press, 1991.

Hanmer, Thomas, ed. *The Works of Shakespeare in Six Volumes.* Oxford: Printed at the Theatre, 1743–44.

Harbage, Alfred, ed. *William Shakespeare: The Complete Works* (The Complete Pelican Shakespeare). New York: The Viking Press, 1969.

Harrison, George B., ed. *The Two Gentlemen of Verona.* Baltimore: Penguin, 1956.

Harrison, George B., ed. *Shakespeare: The Complete Works.* New York: Harcourt, Brace & World, 1948.

Hazlitt, William. *Characters of Shakespear's Plays* [1817]. London: Oxford University Press, 1934, pp. 219–21 [present volume, pp. 7–9].

Heminge, John and Henry Condell, eds. *The First Folio of Shakespeare.* London: Isaac Jaggard and Ed. Blout, 1623.

Hinman, Charlton, ed. *The Norton Facsimile: The First Folio of Shakespeare.* London: Paul Hamlyn, 1968.

Hunter, Robert Grams. *Shakespeare and the Comedy of Forgiveness.* New York: Columbia University Press, 1965.

Illustrated Stratford Shakespeare, The. London: Chancellor Press, 1982.

Jackson, Berners A.W., ed. *The Two Gentlemen of Verona* (The Pelican Shakespeare). Baltimore: Penguin, 1964.

Jensen, Ejner J. *Shakespeare and the Ends of Comedy.* Bloomington: Indiana University Press, 1991.

Johnson, Samuel, ed. *The Plays of William Shakespeare.* 8 vols. London: Tonson, Woodfall, Rivington, et al., 1765 [excerpt in present volume, pp. 3–5].

Joseph, Sister Miriam. *Shakespeare's Use of the Arts of Language.* New York: Columbia University Press, 1947.

Kiefer, Frederick. "Love Letters in *The Two Gentlemen of Verona.*" *Shakespeare Studies* 18 (1986): 65–85 [present volume, pp. 133–52].

Kittredge, George L., ed. *The Two Gentlemen of Verona,* revised by Irving Ribner. Waltham: Blaisdell, 1969.

Kittredge, George Lyman, ed. *The Complete Works of William Shakespeare.* Boston: Ginn, 1936.

Knight, Charles, ed. *The Comedies, Histories, Tragedies and Poems of William Shakespeare,* 2nd ed. 11 vols. London: Charles Knight, 1843.

Knight, G. Wilson. *The Shakespearean Tempest.* London: Oxford University Press, 1932.

Kolin, Philip C. *Shakespeare and Feminist Criticism: An Annotated Bibliography and Commentary.* New York: Garland Publishing, 1991.

Leech, Clifford, ed. *The Two Gentlemen of Verona* (The Arden Shakespeare). London: Methuen, 1969.

Leggatt, Alexander. *Shakespeare's Comedy of Love*. London: Methuen & Co., 1974.

Lenz, Carolyn Ruth Swift, Gayle Greene, and Carol Thomas Neely, eds. *The Woman's Part: Feminist Criticism of Shakespeare*. Urbana: University of Illinois Press, 1980.

Levin, Richard A. *Love and Society in Shakespearean Comedy: A Study of Dramatic Form and Content*. Newark: University of Delaware Press, 1985.

Lewis, Anthony J. *The Love Story in Shakespearean Comedy*. Lexington: University Press of Kentucky, 1992.

Lindenbaum, Peter. "Education in *The Two Gentlemen of Verona*." *Studies in English Literature* 15 (1975): 229–44.

Muir, Kenneth. *Shakespeare's Comic Sequence*. New York: Barnes & Noble, 1979.

Nevo, Ruth. *Comic Transformation in Shakespeare*. London: Methuen, 1980.

Newman, Karen. *Shakespeare's Rhetoric of Comic Character: Dramatic Convention in Classical and Renaissance Comedy*. London: Methuen, 1985.

Novy, Marianne. *Love's Argument: Gender Relations in Shakespeare*. Chapel Hill: The University of North Carolina Press, 1984.

Novy, Marianne. "Shakespeare's Female Characters as Actors and as Audience" [1977]; In *Shakespearean Metadrama*. Ed. John W. Blanpied. Rochester: University of Rochester, 1977, pp. 17–39; reprinted in *The Woman's Part*. Ed. Carolyn Ruth Swift Lenz et al., pp. 256–70.

Ornstein, Robert. *Shakespeare's Comedies: From Roman Farce to Romantic Mystery*. Newark: University of Delaware Press, 1986.

Pearson, D'Orsay W., comp. *"Two Gentlemen of Verona": An Annotated Bibliography*. New York: Garland Publishing, 1988.

Perry, Thomas A. "Proteus, Wry-Transformed Traveller." *Shakespeare Quarterly 5* (1954): 33–40 [present volume, pp. 49–58].

Phialias, Peter G. *Shakespeare's Romantic Comedies: The Development of Their Form and Meaning*. Chapel Hill: University of North Carolina Press, 1966.

Pitt, Angela. *Shakespeare's Women*. Newton Abbot, Devon, UK: David & Charles; Totowa NJ: Barnes & Noble, 1981.

Pope, Alexander, ed. *The Works of Mr. William Shakespeare*. 6 vols. London: Jacob Tonson, 1723–25.

Praz, Mario. "Shakespeare's Italy." *Shakespeare Survey* 7 (1954): 95–106.

Richmond, David. *Laughter, Pain and Wonder: Shakespeare's Comedies and the Audience in the Theater*. Newark: University of Delaware Press, 1990.

Ridley, M.R., ed. *The Two Gentlemen of Verona* (New Temple Shakespeare). London: Dent; New York: Dutton, 1935.

Righter, Anne. *Shakespeare and the Idea of the Play*. London: Chatto and Windus, 1962.

Rossky, William. "*The Two Gentlemen of Verona* as Burlesque." *English Literary Renaissance* 12 (1982): 210–19.

Rowe, Nicholas, ed. *The Works of Mr. William Shakespeare in Six Volumes*. London: Jacob Tonson, 1707.

Rowse, A.L., ed. *"The Two Gentlemen of Verona": Modern Text with Introduction* (Contemporary Shakespeare Series). Lanham: University Press of America, 1986.

Sanders, Norman, ed. *The Two Gentlemen of Verona* (New Penguin Shakespeare). Harmondsworth: Penguin, 1968.

Sargent, Ralph M. "Sir Thomas Elyot and the Integrity of *The Two Gentlemen of Verona*." *PMLA* 65 (December 1950): 1166–80 [present volume, pp. 33–48].

Scheye, Thomas E. "Two Gentlemen of Milan." *Shakespeare Studies* 7 (1974): 11–23.

Schlegel, August Wilhelm. *Lectures on Dramatic Art and Literature* [1808], trans. John Black. London: George Bell, 1815.

Schlueter, Kurt, ed. *The Two Gentlemen of Verona* (The New Cambridge Shakespeare). Cambridge: Cambridge University Press, 1990.

Sisson, Charles J., ed. *The Two Gentlemen of Verona* (The Laurel Shakespeare). New York: Dell, 1958.

Slights, Camille Wells. "*The Two Gentlemen of Verona* and the Courtesy Book Tradition." *Shakespeare Studies* 16 (1983): 13–31 [present volume, pp. 115–32].

Small, S. Asa. "The Ending of *The Two Gentlemen of Verona*." *PMLA* 48 (1933): 767–76 [present volume, pp. 21–32].

Speaight, Robert. "Shakespeare's Heroines." In *Essays by Divers Hands*. New Series 39. London: Oxford University Press, 1977, pp. 146–62.

Sproat, Kezia. "Sisterhood in Shakespeare." *Shakespeare and Renaissance Association of West Virginia: Selected Papers* 2.3 (1978): 8–19.

Spurgeon, Caroline. *Shakespeare's Imagery and What It Tells Us*. New York: Macmillan; Cambridge: Cambridge University Press, 1935.

Stephenson, William E. "The Adolescent Dream-World of *The Two Gentlemen of Verona*." *Shakespeare Quarterly* 17 (1966): 165–68.

Swinburne, Algernon Charles. *A Study of Shakespeare*. London: Chatto and Windus, 1880, pp. 48–49 [present volume, p. 11].

Swinden, Patrick. *An Introduction to Shakespeare's Comedies*. London: Macmillan, 1973.

Thaler, Alwin. "Shakespeare and the Unhappy Happy Ending." *PMLA* 42 (1927): 736–61.

Theobald, Lewis, ed. *The Works of Shakespeare in Seven Volumes*. London: Bettesworth, Hitch, Tonson, et al., 1733.

Thompson, Karl F. "Shakespeare's Romantic Comedies." *PMLA* 67 (1952): 1079–93.

Tillyard, E.M.W. *Shakespeare's Early Comedies*. New York: Barnes & Noble, 1965.

Timpane, John. "'I am but a foole, looke you': Launce and the Social Functions of Humor" [present volume, pp. 189–211].

Traversi, Derek. *Shakespeare: The Early Comedies*. London: Longmans, Green, 1960.

Turner, Robert. *Shakespeare's Apprenticeship*. Chicago: University of Chicago Press, 1974.

Van Laan, Thomas F. *Role-playing in Shakespeare*. Toronto: University of Toronto Press, 1978.

Vaughn, Jack A. *Shakespeare's Comedies*. New York: Frederick Ungar, 1980.

Vyvyan, John. *Shakespeare and the Rose of Love: A Study of the Early Plays in Relation to the Medieval Philosophy of Love*. New York: Barnes & Noble, 1960.

Waller, Gary, ed. *Shakespeare's Comedies*. London: Longman, 1991.

Weimann, Robert. "Laughing with the Audience: *The Two Gentlemen of Verona* and the Popular Tradition of Comedy." *Shakespeare Survey* 22 (1969): 35–42 [present volume, pp. 79–89].

Wells, Stanley. "The Failure of *The Two Gentlemen of Verona*." *Shakespeare Jahrbuch* 99 (1963): 161–73.

Wells, Stanley and Gary Taylor, eds. *William Shakespeare: The Complete Works* (The Oxford Shakespeare). Oxford: Clarendon Press, 1986 (Compact Edition, 1988).

Wilders, John, intro. *The Two Gentlemen of Verona* (The BBC TV Shakespeare). London: British Broadcasting Corporation, 1984.

Wilson, John Dover, ed. *The Two Gentlemen of Verona* (The Cambridge Pocket Shakespeare). Cambridge: Cambridge University Press, 1958.

Wilson, John Dover. *Shakespeare's Happy Comedies*. London: Faber and Faber, 1962.

Wilson, John Dover and Arthur Quiller-Couch, eds. *The Two Gentlemen of Verona* (New Cambridge Edition). Cambridge: Cambridge University Press, 1921.

Woodbridge, Linda. *Women and the English Renaissance: Literature and the Nature of Womankind, 1540–1620*. Urbana: University of Illinois Press, 1984.

Wright, Louis B. and Virginia A. LaMar, eds. *The Two Gentlemen of Verona*. (The Folger Library General Reader's Shakespeare). New York: Washington Square Press, 1964.

Young, Karl, ed. *The Two Gentlemen of Verona* (The Yale Shakespeare). New Haven: Yale University Press, 1924.

PART I
CRITICISM

Excerpt from His Edition of The Plays of William Shakespeare (1765)

Samuel Johnson

> *It is observable (I know not for what cause) that the stile of this comedy is less figurative, and more natural and unaffected than the greater part of this author's, tho' supposed to be one of the first he wrote.*—Pope.

To this observation of Mr. *Pope*, which is very just, Mr. *Theobald* has added, that this is one of *Shakespear's worst plays, and is less corrupted than any other*. Mr. *Upton* peremptorily determines, *that if any proof can be drawn from manner and style, this play must be sent packing and seek for its parent elsewhere. How otherwise*, says he, *do painters distinguish copies from originals, and have not authors their peculiar style and manner from which a true critick can form as unerring a judgment as a Painter?* I am afraid this illustration of a critick's science will not prove what is desired. A Painter knows a copy from an original by rules somewhat resembling these by which criticks know a translation, which if it be literal, and literal it must be to resemble the copy of a picture, will be easily distinguished. Copies are known from originals even when the painter copies his own picture; so if an authour should literally translate his work he would lose the manner of an original.

Mr. *Upton* confounds the copy of a picture with the imitation of a painter's manner. Copies are easily known, but good imitations are not detected with equal certainty, and are, by the best judges, often mistaken. Nor is it true that the writer has always peculiarities equally distinguishable with those of the painter. The peculiar manner of each arises from the desire, natural to every performer, of facilitating his subsequent works by recurrence to his former ideas; this recurrence produces that repetition which is called habit. The painter, whose work is partly intellectual and partly

Reprinted from *Johnson on Shakespeare*. Ed. Walter Raleigh. Oxford: Oxford University Press, 1908, pp. 72–75.

manual, has habits of the mind, the eye and the hand, the writer has only habits of the mind. Yet, some painters have differed as much from themselves as from any other; and I have been told, that there is little resemblance between the first works of *Raphael* and the last. The same variation may be expected in writers; and if it be true, as it seems, that they are less subject to habit, the difference between their works may be yet greater.

But by the internal marks of a composition we may discover the authour with probability, though seldom with certainty. When I read this play I cannot but think that I discover both in the serious and ludicrous scenes, the language and sentiments of Shakespear. It is not indeed one of his most powerful effusions, it has neither many diversities of character, nor striking delineations of life, but it abounds in γνῶμαι beyond most of his plays, and few have more lines or passages which, singly considered, are eminently beautiful. I am yet inclined to believe that it was not very successful, and suspect that it has escaped corruption, only because being seldom played it was less exposed to the hazards of transcription.

ACT I. SCENE ii.

That this, like many other Scenes, is mean and vulgar, will be universally allowed; but that it was interpolated by the players seems advanced without any proof, only to give a greater licence to criticism.

ACT II. SCENE vii. (II.iv.137–9)

> Love's a mighty lord:
> And hath so humbled me as, I confess,
> There is no woe to his correction.

No misery that *can be compared to* the punishment inflicted by love. *Herbert* called for the prayers of the *Liturgy* a little before his death, saying, *None to them, none to them.*

In this play there is a strange mixture of knowledge and ignorance, of care and negligence. The versification is often excellent, the allusions are learned and just; but the author conveys his heroes by sea from one inland town to another in the same country; he places the Emperour at *Milan* and sends his young men to attend him, but never mentions him more; he makes *Protheus*, after an interview with *Silvia*, say he has only seen her picture, and, if we may credit the old copies, he has by mistaking places, left his scenery inextricable. The reason of all this confusion seems to be, that he took his story from a novel which he sometimes followed, and sometimes forsook, sometimes remembred, and sometimes forgot.

EXCERPT FROM *CHARACTERS OF SHAKESPEAR'S PLAYS* (1817)

William Hazlitt

This is little more than the first outlines of a comedy loosely sketched in. It is the story of a novel dramatised with very little labour or pretension; yet there are passages of high poetical spirit, and of inimitable quaintness of humour, which are undoubtedly Shakespear's, and there is throughout the conduct of the fable a careless grace and felicity which marks it for his. One of the editors (we believe Mr. Pope) remarks in a marginal note to the *Two Gentlemen of Verona*—

> It is observable (I know not for what cause) that the style of this comedy is less figurative, and more natural and unaffected than the greater part of this author's, though supposed to be one of the first he wrote.

Yet so little does the editor appear to have made up his mind upon this subject, that we find the following note to the very next (the second) scene.

> This whole scene, like many others in these plays (some of which I believe were written by Shakespear, and others interpolated by the players) is composed of the lowest and most trifling conceits, to be accounted for only by the gross taste of the age he lived in: *Populo ut placerent.* I wish I had authority to leave them out, but I have done all I could, set a mark of reprobation upon them, throughout this edition.

It is strange that our fastidious critic should fall so soon from praising to reprobating. The style of the familiar parts of this comedy is indeed made up of conceits—low they may be for what we know, but then they are not

Reprinted from *Characters of Shakespear's Plays* [1817]. London: Oxford University Press, 1934, pp. 219–21.

poor, but rich ones. The scene of Launce with his dog (not that in the second, but that in the fourth act) is a perfect treat in the way of farcical drollery and invention; nor do we think Speed's manner of proving his master to be in love deficient in wit or sense, though the style may be criticised as not simple enough for the modern taste.

> *Valentine.* Why, how know you that I am in love?
> *Speed.* Marry, by these special marks: first, you have learned, like
>   Sir Protheus, to wreathe your arms like a malcontent, to
>   relish a love-song like a robin-red-breast, to walk alone like
>   one that had the pestilence, to sigh like a school-boy that
>   had lost his ABC, to weep like a young wench that had buried her grandam, to fast like one that takes diet, to watch
>   like one that fears robbing, to speak puling like a beggar at
>   Hallowmas. You were wont, when you laughed, to crow
>   like a cock; when you walked, to walk like one of the lions;
>   when you fasted, it was presently after dinner; when you
>   looked sadly, it was for want of money; and now you are
>   metamorphosed with a mistress, that when I look on you, I
>   can hardly think you my master.

The tender scenes in this play, though not so highly wrought as in some others, have often much sweetness of sentiment and expression. There is something pretty and playful in the conversation of Julia with her maid, when she shews such a disposition to coquetry about receiving the letter from Protheus; and her behaviour afterwards and her disappointment, when she finds him faithless to his vows, remind us at a distance of Imogen's tender constancy. Her answer to Lucetta, who advises her against following her lover in disguise, is a beautiful piece of poetry.

> *Lucetta.* I do not seek to quench your love's hot fire,
>   But qualify the fire's extremest rage,
>   Lest it should burn above the bounds of reason.
> *Julia.* The more thou damm'st it up, the more it burns;
>   The current that with gentle murmur glides,
>   Thou know'st, being stopp'd, impatiently doth rage;
>   But when his fair course is not hindered,
>   He makes sweet music with th' enamell'd stones,
>   Giving a gentle kiss to every sedge
>   He overtaketh in his pilgrimage:

And so by many winding nooks he strays,
With willing sport, to the wild ocean.
Then let me go, and hinder not my course;
I'll be as patient as a gentle stream,
And make a pastime of each weary step,
Till the last step have brought me to my love;
And there I'll rest, as after much turmoil,
A blessed soul doth in Elysium.

If Shakespear indeed had written only this and other passages in the *Two Gentlemen of Verona*, he would *almost* have deserved Milton's praise of him—

And sweetest Shakespear, Fancy's child,
Warbles his native wood-notes wild.

But as it is, he deserves rather more praise than this.

Excerpt from *A Study of Shakespeare* (1880)

Algernon Charles Swinburne

What was highest as poetry in the *Comedy of Errors* was mainly in rhyme; all indeed, we might say, between the prelude spoken by Ægeon and the appearance in the last scene of his wife: in *Love's Labour's Lost* what was highest was couched wholly in blank verse; in the *Two Gentlemen of Verona* rhyme has fallen seemingly into abeyance, and there are no passages of such elegiac beauty as in the former, of such exalted eloquence as in the latter of these plays; there is an even sweetness, a simple equality of grace in thought and language which keeps the whole poem in tune, written as it is in a subdued key of unambitious harmony. In perfect unity and keeping the composition of this beautiful sketch may perhaps be said to mark a stage of advance, a new point of work attained, a faint but sensible change of manner, signalised by increased firmness of hand and clearness of outline. Slight and swift in execution as it is, few and simple as are the chords here struck of character and emotion, every shade of drawing and every note of sound is at one with the whole scheme of form and music. Here too is the first dawn of that higher and more tender humour which was never given in such perfection to any man as ultimately to Shakespeare; one touch of the byplay of Launce and his immortal dog is worth all the bright fantastic interludes of Boyet and Adriano, Costard and Holofernes; worth even half the sallies of Mercutio, and half the dancing doggrel or broad-witted prose of either Dromio. . . .

Reprinted from *A Study of Shakespeare* [1880]. New York: AMS Press, 1965, pp. 48-49.

"The Female Page" from
Disguise Plots in Elizabethan
Drama (1915)

Victor Oscar Freeburg

> Dost thou think, though I am caparison'd like
> a man, I have a doublet and hose in my disposition?
>
> —As You Like It

I

Starting from medieval French romance, and threading her way through the novels or plays of Italy, the heroine in hose and doublet at last reached the England of Shakespeare, where she became the most graceful and charming figure on the stage.[1] Perhaps in real life, too, the female page sometimes wandered through merry England. Queen Elizabeth herself once listened to an ambassador who offered to convey her secretly to Scotland, dressed like a page, in order that she might under this disguise see Queen Mary. Elizabeth appeared to like the plan, but answered with a sigh, saying "Alas! If I might do it thus!"[2] At any rate we shall see that as a literary tradition, in the novels and on the stage, the disguised heroine was already established in England when Shakespeare wrote his *Two Gentlemen of Verona*.

By that time the female page had often appeared in nondramatic literature in English. Rich's *Apolonius and Silla*, the second novel in his *Farewell*, had used substantially the plot of *Twelfth Night* as early as 1581. The eighth novel, entitled *Phylotus and Emelia*, has the same female page plot as the anonymous comedy *Philotus*, which was printed in 1603, but which may be as early as Rich's novel.[3] Sidney's *Arcadia* in 1590 told of Zelmane-page following Pyrocles unrewarded. And in the same year Lodge's *Rosalynde* presented the disguised heroine whom Shakespeare adopted. The pro-

Reprinted from *Disguise Plots in Elizabethan Drama: A Study in Stage Tradition*. New York: Columbia University Press, 1915, pp. 61–71. Cross references in notes refer to reprinted sources.

totype of Julia could have been found a decade earlier than the *Two Gentle-men* in the manuscript of Yonge's translation of Montemayor's *Diana*. A dozen of the ballads published by Percy or Child sing the fortunes of the lady disguised in male attire. Some of these too must have antedated and influenced the drama of Shakespeare and his contemporaries.[4]

In order to show to what extent Shakespeare was influenced by stage traditions in choosing and elaborating the Julia disguise, we shall examine a number of female page plays produced in England before the *Two Gentle-men*. We shall see that Shakespeare profited by the weaknesses as well as by the merits of these plays. If he borrowed the potency of certain disguise situations, he invariably improved their dramatic efficiency.

As early as 1569–70 a Latin play, *Byrsa Basilica*,[5] had presented a girl in the apparel of a boy. The disguise is quite incidental, merely afford-ing the heroine a method of escape from an awkward predicament.[6]

George Whetstone's *Promos and Cassandra*, which was printed in 1578, but was never acted, contains perhaps the earliest female page situ-ation in the vernacular drama. Cassandra enters "apparelled like a page" (Part I,iii,7), soliloquizes a few lines and goes out to keep her appointment with Lord Promos. She never reappears, nobody sees her, and no compli-cation results from the disguise. It is worthy of note that this disguise is not in the novel on which Whetstone based his play.[7] He was thus the first of many Englishmen who added disguise to plots borrowed from other literatures.

Sir Clyomon and Sir Clamydes,[8] although not printed until 1599, may have been written as early as *Promos and Cassandra*. It contains the romantic elements of the disguised girl serving her lover as page incognito, and mis-takenly wooed by some other woman. It has in addition such motives as the sentimental farewell, the girl's giving a jewel as a love token, her apology for wearing boy's clothing, and her expression of weariness from travelling—dramatic effects that recur in Shakespeare's plays. In technic *Sir Clyomon* with its loose and rambling plot reminds us of a medieval romance. The author, whoever he was, had only partially realized the dramaturgic value of disguise.

What we have just remarked may be illustrated by a summary of the play. Clyomon bids farewell to Princess Neronis, receiving her jewel as a love token, and departs to fight a combat. After he has gone Neronis is kidnapped, but escapes by disguising herself as a page. She gets employment as a shepherd's boy, and the first complication comes when the country lasses fall in love with "him." One day while strolling along she finds a dead body, decorated with Clyomon's sword and shield. She concludes that her love is dead, and attempts suicide, but "Providence," who is apparently on the watch for this opportunity, puts out his hand and thwarts her fell purpose.[9] Investigation proves that the body is that of the villainous kidnapper. Some time after this experience, Neronis-page accidentally gets service with her lover Clyomon, whom she presently recognizes. She remains incognito, and is sent ahead as his messenger to Denmark. At the Danish court she is finally revealed to him as his lady love and quondam page.

The plot of such a play suffers when compared with the firmer weaving in Lyly's *Gallathea* (entered in 1585[10]). There the disguise, suggested by one of Ovid's *Metamorphoses*,[11] results in many mistaken wooings and cross purposes. The action is very compact, and the dialog is full of ironical subtlety. Gallathea and Phillida have been disguised as boys in order to escape Neptune's demand for the sacrifice of a virgin. Each falls in love with the other, whom she believes to be a boy. The two girl-pages next join Diana's train, where they are wooed by three nymphs. Each girl-page pretends in jest that the other is a girl and woos her. Each of the two girls presently suspects the other's sex. Meanwhile, Cupid, the disguised intrigant, has been captured by Diana, and Neptune promises to waive the sacrifice of a virgin if Cupid is released. Gallathea and Phillida are then revealed as girls, but, since they are by this time truly in love with each other, Venus promises to transform one into a boy—which one, she will not say until they reach the church door.[12]

A technical defect, to which we have alluded in Chapter II, is inherent in this intricate tangle of cross-purposes and mistaken wooing; the plot does not contain within itself the power of resolution. The knot cannot be untied. Revelation of disguise does not lessen the central difficulty, and the resolution can be brought about only by Venus, the *dea ex machina*, who guarantees the metamorphosis.

Lyly, who was always fond of stylistic subtlety, put much comic irony into the dialog of *Gallathea*. Note, for example, Phillida's remarks to Gallathea (both being in page costumes): "It is a pretty boy, and a fair, he might well have been a woman" (II,1); "It is pity you are not a woman" (III,2), and, "I have sworn never to love a woman."

Shakespeare later used similar involved dialog and seems to have been directly influenced by Lyly. In *Gallathea* (III,2) occurs the passage:

> *Phil.* Have you ever a sister?
> *Galla.*　　　I pray have you ever a one?
> *Phil.* My father had but one daughter, and therefore I could have
> 　　　no sister.

These lines are similar to Viola's reply to the Duke (II,4), "I am all the daughters of my father's house, And all the brothers too." In act IV, scene 4, Phillida says to Gallathea, "Seeing we are both boys and both lovers,—that our affection may have some show, and seem as it were love,—let me call thee mistress." We are reminded of these lines in *As You Like It* (III,2), when Rosalind-page tells Orlando of a fictitious youth who "was to imagine me his love, his mistress; and I set him every day to woo me." We shall presently give a number of examples of Shakespeare's subtle dialog. He had learned it from Lyly, but the felicity of the pupil surpasses that of the master.

Soliman and Perseda, mentioned in the Stationers' Register in 1592, but possibly written about 1588 (Boas, *Kyd*, lvii), has a female page situation which seems to be original. At least it is only remotely suggested in Wotton's *Courtlie Controuersie*, the probable source of the play. But the closing incident may have had some influence on Beaumont and Fletcher's *Maid's Tragedy*, and will be discussed in that connection.[13] Perseda's male apparel only brings her to death; but in another play of Oriental color, the *Wars of Cyrus*, the heroine cleverly utilizes a page's costume in order to escape her royal captor. This play was printed in 1594 and had probably been acted by the Children of Her Majesty's Chapel by 1590.[14]

Lælia, a Latin adaption of *Gl' Ingannati*, was performed at Cambridge in 1590, and revived in 1598. The problem of this play's relations to Shakespeare's *Twelfth Night* has not received a solution. Churchill says (*Jahrb.*, xxxiv, 286) that no evidence forces the conclusion that Shakespeare knew *Lælia*. Schelling, on the contrary, says (II,77) that *Lælia* was the "undoubted immediate source of Shakespeare's *Twelfth Night*." But it is interesting to note that this play, whether Shakespeare ever borrowed from it or not, had the most complicated female page plot in England before 1590.

Greene's *James IV*, printed in 1598, but written perhaps as early as 1590,[15] contains a number of similarities to other female page situations both earlier and later. The essential disguise elements in the story are the queen's fleeing "disguised like a squire," her adventures which bring her to the care of Lady Anderson, the latter's mistaken wooing of the "squire," and the "squire's" fainting when hearing bad news about the king.

Greene did not fully realize the dramatic and theatrical opportunities of his situation. By omitting the female squire motive from the dénouement he departed from his source, a novel by Cinthio[16] in which the heroine comes to her husband's camp and is called the Unknown Knight. In the novel the heroine is brought before her husband still disguised, and some dialog takes place before the revelation. Greene omitted this part of the action, thus losing a chance for a theatrical undisguising, and an opportunity for the piquant and equivocal language which was used so successfully by Lyly and Shakespeare.

These early plays, *Byrsa Basilica*, *Promos and Cassandra*, *Sir Clyomon and Sir Clamydes*, *Gallathea*, *Soliman and Perseda*, the *Wars of Cyrus*, *Lælia*, and *James IV*, are evidences that English theater audiences were familiar with the female page by 1590. Playgoers had seen the heroine apprehensive lest her male garb seem immodest; weary from travel through forests; patiently following her lover to serve him unknown, or leaving him to carry his messages to a rival lady; wooed by that lady who was misled by outward appearance; wittily alluding to her real identity in veiled language; swooning like a woman, or fighting in man's harness, and dying like a soldier. The same playgoers may have heard similar events recited in the ballads, or may have read of them in English novels.

Yet these plays, novels, and ballads were by no means the only contemporary plots containing female pages. Plays especially were perishable. The number of non-extant plays before 1592 is much greater than the number of extant. They must have done their part in popularizing disguise. We may surmise that the lost play *Felix and Philomena* (Philismena?), 1584, contained the female page story from Montemayor's *Diana*, and that it may have been the immediate source of Shakespeare's *Two Gentlemen*. The extant plays described above are less important for their individual contribution than for the proof they give that the female page was by 1592 a well-established personage on the stage, and already endowed with distinct characteristics and functions in the drama.

II

Although the traditional disguises in the *Two Gentlemen*, the *Merchant*, *As You Like It*, *Twelfth Night*, and *Cymbeline* are all borrowed, they are all bettered. Either by new combinations of old materials, by stricter dramatic economy, by focusing the attention on the female page as a character, by the heightening of theatrical values, or by infusing poetic subtlety into the dialog, Shakespeare made his female page plays superior to those of his predecessors or rival contemporaries.

Shakespeare's skill in building a play around a disguised heroine is clearly exhibited in the *Two Gentlemen of Verona*, produced perhaps at early as 1591. Montemayor's novel *La Diana* seems to be either directly or indirectly the source of the Proteus-Julia-page story. But in Montemayor the love episode ends by Felismena's telling Don Felix that she had served him as page two years before. That method is undramatic. The undisguising should take place before the audience and should be an organic element in the dénouement; Shakespeare made it so in the *Two Gentlemen*. There the revelation of disguise is precipitated by a swoon, and identity is verified by the rings, the swoon and the rings both having been suggested by earlier plays. Thus three different dramatic motives are combined in one dramatic moment.

Such combination of material is dramatic economy. Economy is further shown in the construction of the serenade scene (IV,2). In Montemayor the Host wakes Felismena to hear a serenade. She listens and recognizes the voice of Don Felix in praise of a rival mistress; but, although watching until dawn, Felismena is unable to distinguish her false lover in the group. Montemayor shows us only the Host and Felismena, while Shakespeare's staging presents the Host, Julia, Proteus, Silvia, and others simultaneously. Thus the scene is made compact and effects multiplied by introducing in disguise the person most vitally concerned in the action, an action which could not proceed if that person's identity were known. Even when the subject of discussion is Julia herself, she participates with subtle speech.

A good theatrical effect in the *Two Gentlemen* is the swooning of the disguised heroine. Shakespeare may have borrowed this from Greene's *James IV*, where Dorothea, upon being informed that the king is "dreading death" because of the reported death of the queen, feels a sudden qualm at the heart and is revived with "licor" (V,1). The business of swooning has more dramatic occasion and theatrical effectiveness in the *Two Gentlemen*. In the last scene Proteus threatens to assault the resisting Silvia. Valentine arrives just in time to rescue her, and Proteus becomes surprisingly penitent, whereupon Valentine immediately forgives him, and, to show that there is no ill will, offers to surrender his sweetheart into the bargain. Julia-page promptly swoons and her identity is revealed within a few moments.

The action in that scene is further enriched by the use of the rings. This motive, borrowed perhaps from *Sir Clyomon and Sir Clamydes*,[17] is an accompaniment of disguise in *Two Gentlemen*, the *Merchant*, and *Twelfth Night*. All possible dramatic use of the rings is made in the *Two Gentlemen*. When Proteus and Julia have their farewell scene they exchange rings. At court Proteus sends Julia's ring to his new love, the love messenger being the disguised Julia herself. Then Silvia refuses the token, which leaves Julia in possession of two rings—the one she received from Proteus at Verona, and the one she gave him in exchange. The last use of the rings effects the dénouement. In the excitement of hearing Valentine offer Silvia to Proteus, Julia swoons. She retains enough presence of mind, however, to present the wrong ring and begs forgiveness for not having delivered it to Silvia.

Shakespeare's method in this play varies significantly from the method of the Italian dramatists. We have seen how they produced great complexity of plot by a process of combination. But they intensified their action without concentrating the attention on any single character. Shakespeare differed from them by focusing the attention on a single character, making that the axis of the plot.[18] In the *Two Gentlemen* the disguise of Julia is not, for example, counterbalanced by the disguise of Proteus as a woman—that would have been the Italian way—but is enhanced by combination with subordinate motives, such as the rings, and is dwelt upon until full dramatic emphasis results.

NOTES

1. Some illuminating remarks on the disguised heroine as a character are made by Marie Gothein in *Die Frau im englischen Drama vor Shakespeare, Jahrb.*, xl., 35.

2. Melville, 106.

3. See Chapter V, page 113.

4. Züge 6, 71.

5. Churchill and Keller, 281. We cannot say where this play was acted.

6. A brief summary of the plot is given in Chapter V.

7. Giraldi Cinthio, *Heccatommithi*, VIII, 5.

8. The date and authorship of *Sir Clyomon and Sir Clamydes* cannot at present be determined. Suggestions as to date vary from 1570 to 1584. See Schelling, I, 199.

9. The attempted suicide of Neronis upon mistaking the dead body for that of her lover perhaps offered a suggestion for act IV, scene 2 in *Cymbeline*, a situation which editors usually attribute to Shakespeare's invention. See also Forsythe (M.L.N., April, 1912) who suggests that the Cloten situation may have been borrowed from the Alcario impersonation in *I Ieronimo*.

10. Feuillerat, 576.

11. Bk. IX. Iphis, a girl, had been presented to her father as a boy and thus reared by her mother. The father promises his supposed son in marriage to Ianthe. Iphis, in spite of herself, falls in love with Ianthe. In answer to the prayers of Iphis and the mother, Isis transforms Iphis to a boy.

Lee, in discussing the sources of the *Decameron* (page 292), tells of two cases of pretended metamorphosis where lovers disguised as women pretend that some deity changes them into men. In the curious play *Philotus* (see Chapter V, page 113) a lover disguised as a girl pretends that the heavenly powers change him into a man. *Tristan de Nanteuil* presents an interesting metamorphoses. See Chapter III, page 42.

12. An interesting inverted parallel to this situation is found in Fletcher's *Loyal Subject*. Olympia is very fond of the supposed girl "Alinda," and when "Alinda" proves to be a boy Olympia admits love for him and they go off to church.

13. See below, page 92.

14. Keller, *Wars of Cyrus*, 9.

15. According to Fleay (*Biog. Chron.*, I, 265) although Collins (II, 79) is not convinced.

16. *Heccatommithi*, III, 1. In *Arrenopia*, a play which Cinthio based on his own novel, the heroine appears on the battlefield dressed as a knight, calling herself "Agnoristo." See Klein, V, 348.

17. In *Sir Clyomon* the hero receives a jewel from Neronis when he bids her farewell; but no dramatic use is made of it. In *Soliman and Perseda*, Erastus gives his

lady a ring, and receives a carcanet in return. The familiar ring story in the *Merchant of Venice* may have been borrowed from Fiorentino's novel. Did Shakespeare know that story early enough to get a hint for the ring motive in the *Two Gentlemen*?

18. To a certain extent Greene has the same method in the delineation of Dorothea in *James IV*.

THE ENDING OF *THE TWO GENTLEMEN OF VERONA* (1933)

S. Asa Small

I

In an interesting article on the ending of Shakespeare's comedies, Alwin Thaler tries to refute the opinion of the majority of critics that the last scene in *The Two Gentlemen of Verona* is "blind or incomprehensible."[1] Granted that Shakespeare purposely subordinated everything to the highly convention theme of friendship, before final judgment can be passed on the general fitness of the ending of the *Two Gentlemen*, one ought to consider carefully the requirements of romantic love in the play. The friendship theme, though greatly emphasised, is, after all, only a strong framework to motivate the love story.[2] Furthermore, Professor Thorndike informs us:[3]

> The dénouement is badly hurried and Valentine so far forgets his part
> as to offer Silvia to the penitent Proteus. Perhaps this fine gesture
> might be in accord with the code of honour for sworn friends, but it
> could scarcely be justified on a stage devoted to romantic love.

It is not hard to find in the early Elizabethan drama examples to show that love between man and woman is just as strong in the English mind as love or friendship between men.[4] In Greene's *Friar Bacon and Friar Bungay*,[5] the love story, though motivated by the friendship theme, is properly completed at the end. The devoted friends, Prince Edward and Lacie are both in love with Margaret. In the fifth scene the conflict between love and friendship begins, but the outcome of this conflict is clearly predicted when Bacon observes: "But friends are men, and love can baffle lords"; (v,76). When Edward looks through Bacon's glass, he hears Lacie musing to himself:

Reprinted from *PMLA* 48 (1933): 767–76.

Recant thee, Lacie—thou art put in trust,
Edward, thy soveraignes sonne, hat chosen thee,
A secret friend, to court her for himself,
And darest thou wrong thy prince with trecherie?—
Lacie, love makes no exception of a friend,
Nor deemes it of a prince but as a man.
Honor bids thee controll him in his lust;
His wooing is not for to wed the girle,
But to intrap her and beguile the lasse. (vi,54–62)

To Lacie, who is a true friend, honor in love is greater than honor in friendship. The same thought is brought out later when Lacie says:

Love taught me that your honor did but jest,
That princes were in fancie but as men; (viii,19–20)

Prince Edward scoffs at Lacie's faithless words:

Injurious Lacie, did I love thee more
Than Alexander his Hephestion?
Did I unfould the passion of my love,
And lock them in the closset of thy thoughts?
Wert thou to Edward second to himselfe,
Sole friend, and partner of his secreat loves?
And could a glaunce of fading bewtie breake
Th'inchained fetters of such privat friends?
Base coward, false, and too effeminate
To be corivall with a prince in thoughts! (viii,24–33)

Margaret, taking the side of Lacie, tells Edward that Love is greater than Friendship:

Then worthy Edward, measure with thy minde
If womens favours will not force men fall,
If bewty, and if darts of persing love,
Are not of force to bury thoughts of friends. (viii,47–50)

The triumph of love over friendship in this play is compensated for by the reconciliation of the friends:

Loves conquest ends, my lord, in courtesie. (viii,86)
Once, Lacie, friends againe. (viii,145)

These quotations from Greene's *Friar Bacon and Friar Bungay* show a normal ending for a sixteenth-century play involving romantic love and friendship. The love story and the friendship story are both properly cared for at the end. We cannot say as much for Shakespeare's *Two Gentlemen*.

The conflict between romantic love and friendship at the end of *The Two Gentlemen* cannot be settled by a cold application of the doctrine of friendship. Of the two gentlemen, Proteus is, throughout the play, false in both love and friendship. He is the active element in the story until near the end. On the other hand, Valentine plays a negative part in the plot until we reach the last scene. His actions then are sudden and baffling. It is he who offends the romantic conception of love. After the incident in which Valentine bestows Silvia on Proteus in the name of friendship and Julia swoons, Proteus asks pardon of Julia for his indifference.[6] The overstraining of romantic generosity in Valentine's part, even though Shakespeare knew similar instances in the popular stories of his day, comes, not in the generous act itself, but in its relation to Valentine's neglect of Silvia afterwards. The emphasis placed on the negation of Silvia's personality[7]—the principal element in the love story—is increased by setting it in an atmosphere of Valentine's many friendly acts toward others. Shakespeare's usual practice in handling the endings of comedies shows that a chivalric matter (such as a man's respect for a lady) does not have to be sacrificed for another conventional idea (such as the friendship idea). Valentine's impulsive gesture in the name of friendship should have been compensated for in one of three ways: by his asking Silvia's pardon; by his expressing a repentant conscience; or, by letting a lapse of time adjust circumstances.

Shakespeare and all other Elizabethan dramatists are regular in using one of these three methods when it is necessary to satisfy the imagination of the audience in a matter that appears often in romantic love stories. A case in point will first be selected from Greene's *Scottish History of James IV*[8] in order to show a contemporary's treatment of the penitent lover.[9]

King James of Scotland has married Dorothea, daughter of the King of England. At the beginning of the play, the latter is departing for home, when, suddenly, King James falls in love with Ida, a young virtuous lady, daughter of the Countess of Arran. This starts complications which are aggravated by the king's intention to get rid of Dorothea and openly marry Ida. The king is a villain-hero from this point to the end of the play. Urged on by the parasite, Ateukin, he orders the queen to be slain. She, like the virtuous type of romantic heroine, does not waver a moment in her love for her husband, but tries to escape his anger by disguising herself as a squire. Virtue is soon rewarded. The King of England invades Scotland to avenge his daughter; Ida marries a young English gentleman; the parasite deserts when his plans fail; and King James is left to himself to regret and make amends. This brings us to the last scene of the play, where the king is filled with keen pangs of repentance. He turns against those who have misled him, saying:[10]

> Ah, flattering broode of sicophants, my foes
> First shall my dire revenge begin on you!

The English king comes in with his troops and faces King James and his men. The Queen, whom all supposed to be dead, now suddenly appears. King James, who has outrageously offended his wife, almost to the point of causing her death, is yet, in the sixteenth-century mind, capable of being forgiven. The virtuous Queen does forgive him, but not until he has earned his pardon by humbling himself abjectly before her:[11]

> *K. of S.* Durst I presume to looke upon those eies
> Which I have tired with a world of woes,
> Or did I thinke submission were ynough,
> Or sighes might make an entrance to my soule,
> You heavens, you know how willing I wold weep!
> You heavens can say how firmly I would sigh!
> *Dor.* Shame me not, prince, companion in thy bed.
> Youth hath misled; tut, but a little fault!
> Tis kingly to amend what is amisse.
> Might I with twise as many paines as these
> Unite our hearts, then should my wedded lord
> See how incessaunt labours I would take.

This general manner of reconciliation between a lady and the man who has offended her is common in Shakespeare. Of course, the dramatist may reduce it to only a few words or lines, as in the case of Angelo in *Measure for Measure*; or the hero may make a straight plea for pardon, as in the case of Bassanio in the *Merchant of Venice*; or, less commonly, an intervening circumstance may bring out the pardoning words, as in the case of Claudio in *Much Ado*. Shakespeare's endings[12] will now be considered. Their sources will be glanced at in every case as showing Shakespeare's intention to follow the fashion of the day. Later we shall come back to *The Two Gentlemen.*

Shakespeare based his comedies on novels that were cluttered up with long sentimental passages, which the euphuistic tendency of his day encouraged. In translating this romantic story-matter into popular drama, Shakespeare retained many of the motives and ideas of his source. Shakespeare's custom is frankly to express these in his dialogue. We shall note that in the case of the repentant or pardon-asking lover only a few words or lines are put into his mouth, much of the spirit of the source being left to the appropriate gesture of the players.

The unexpected disclosure of the love between Oliver and Celia at the end of *As You Like It* has been objected to on the grounds that Oliver's actions in the play make him unsuitable as the husband of Celia. In Shakespeare's source for the play, Lodge's *Rosalynde, Euphues' Golden Legacie*, there is much preparation for this love affair. Oliver's former villainy is forgiven through his love for Celia. After Saladyne (Oliver) goes to Ganimede (Rosalind) and reports the wounding of Rosader, his farewell of them is described in this manner:[13]

> He having his message, gave a courteous adieu to them both, especially to Aliena: and so playing loath to depart, went to his brother. But Aliena, she perplexed and yet joyfull, past away the day pleasantly, still praising the perfection of Saladyne, not ceasing to chat of her new love till evening drew on.

When Rosalind, Celia, and Oliver meet in the scene that corresponds to this passage in *As You Like It* (Act IV, Sc. iii, 76–183), no hint is given of this love affair. It is only revealed to Orlando in Act V, Sc. ii. Near the end of the play, Rosalind divulges a complete knowledge of the affair:[14]

> For your brother and my sister no sooner met but they looked; no sooner looked but they loved; no sooner loved but they sighed;

This speech carries out the spirit of the passage just quoted from the novel. In the stage representation of the play, the actors taking the parts of Oliver and Celia no doubt should show the audience by look and gesture that a love affair is brewing in Act IV, Sc. iii. This constitutes preparation enough for the later marriage of the two, and also mitigates Oliver's former acts of villainy.

In *Much Ado*, the unpleasant ending felt in the marriage of Hero and Claudio seems very unfair to Hero, unless we can find proper compensation for Claudio's cruelty. Claudio actually does express his grief at the thought of his evil inferences about Hero's character. A whole scene is devoted to his repentance in order to impress it upon the audience. The key to it is in a song:[15]

> Pardon goddess of the night,
> Those that slew thy virgin knight;
> For the which, with songs of woe,
> Round about her tomb they go.

The whole scene is taken from a passage in Bandello's "Timbreo di Cardona," in which Timbreo, who corresponds to Claudio in *Much Ado*, repents of his own accord. The following quotation is only a small part of this passage:

> Dette queste parole, ambidue amaramente piangendo, s'inginocchiarono innanzi alla sepoltura, e con le braccia in croce umilmente, l'uno della sceleraggine fatta, e l'altro della troppa credulita, a Fenicia e a Dio domandarono perdono.[16]

Thus, in *As You Like It* and *Much Ado* we are made to understand that Claudio and Oliver are forgiven for their past offenses. This properly motivates the characters for the marriage at the end of each play.

In *Twelfth Night* the expectancy throughout the play is strong enough to warrant the marriage of Viola to the Duke. It is interesting to note, however, that in "Apolonius and Silla" the author makes the Duke act true to form. At the end of the novel, which is the source of *Twelfth Night*, the Duke, when he perceives that the boy, as in the case of Viola, is really the lady, Silla, bursts out into a long speech of repentance, which is typical of the pardon-asking lover in sixteenth century fiction.[17]

> Oh the braunche of all vertue and the flowre of curtesie it self pardon me I beseeche you of all suche discourtesies, as I have ignorantlie committed towardes you: desiring you that without farther memorie of auncient greefes, you will accept of me, who is more ioyfull and better contented with your presence, then if the whole worlde were at my commaundement. Where hath there ever bin founde such liberalitie in a Lover, which havyng trained up and nourished emon-

gest the delicacies and banquettes of the Courte, accompanied with traines of many faire and noble laides living in pleasure, and in the middest of delightes, would so prodigallie adventure yourself, neither fearing mishapps, nor misliking to take such paines, as I knowe you have not been accustomed unto. O liberalitie never heard of before! O facte that can never bee sufficiently rewarded! O true Love moste pure and unfained.

Boccaccio's "Giletta of Narbona," the main source of *All's Well*, ends with the breaking of the Count's obstinacy against the lady that loves him. The hero, we are told:[18]

knowing the thynges she had spoken to be true (and perceiving her constaunt minde, and good witte, and the twoo fairer yonge boies: to kepe his promisse made, from that time forthe as his lawfull wife, and to honour her) abjected his obstinate rigour.

This passage plainly tells us that the Count (Bertram) realizes at the end the cruelty of his indifference toward his wife, and that he abjected or humbled his spirit before her as compensation for his former cruelty. In Shakespeare, the spirit of this passage is briefly and dramatically conveyed by Bertram's repentant exclamation: "Both, both, O, pardon."[19] If this remark is accompanied with suitable stage action, it sufficiently serves to represent the hero's repentant state of mind.

In the source material for *Measure for Measure*, the ending shows the same care on the part of the author to bring about a change of heart in the hero. In the story of Promos, included in Whetstone's *Heptameron of Civil Discourses*, we are told that Promos deserves pardon: "Whereupon (quoth he), regarded soveraigne, if lawe may (possibly) be satisfied, Promos true repentance meritteth pardon."[20] In Whetstone's *Promos and Cassandra*, a scene between the hero and heroine,[21] wherein the former is forgiven for his cruelty, properly prepares for the marriage at the end. Shakespeare's play ends differently. The past or Cassandra in her relations with Promos is taken by Mariana. Promos is given the name, Angelo. Shakespeare, as is his habit, gives only a few words to Angelo to indicate his penitent feelings:[22]

I am sorry that such sorrow I procure:
And so deep sticks it in my penitent heart
That I crave death more willingly than mercy;
'Tis my deserving, and I do entreat it.

Likewise, in the other comedies, the offenders utter their penitent feelings. Portia, in the *Merchant of Venice*, manages by the playful trick of the ring to draw from Bassanio the admission that he had really committed a fault:[23]

> Pardon this fault, and by my soul I swear
> I never more will break an oath with thee.

In *Cymbeline*, Posthumus utters his grief in the presence of Imogen, though she is a page unknown to him.[24] Leonatus, in the *Winter's Tale*, exclaims just before the statue-scene:[25]

> I am asham'd; does not the stone rebuke me
> For being more stone than it?

III

To come back to *The Two Gentlemen of Verona*, many scenes in the play follow closely the corresponding parts in *The Shepherdess Felismena*, its main source. The letter-scene between Julia and Lucetta, Proteus' going to court, Julia's following Proteus in disguise as a man, the serenade-scene, her employment as a page and messenger to Silvia, her sympathy with herself, her conversation when she pleads with Silvia, and Silvia's intuitive dislike of Proteus—all follow the original. The love affair between Felismena (Julia) and Felix (Proteus) is more minutely described in the novel than in the play. But Shakespeare introduces a new character, Valentine, into his play, and also the sentimental friendship between the two men. These two new features are the very things that cause the trouble at the end of the play.

Valentine and his friendship obsession no doubt were grafted on by the dramatist to form a framework for the romantic love story which forms the body of the play. It is not difficult to show that the kind of love which actuates Proteus is merely fanciful like that which runs through parts of the *Merchant of Venice*. Both men within the body of the play, especially Proteus, busy themselves with their affairs of love. Proteus is the active element in the story, and his first soliloquy outlines the love-theme of the play:[26]

> He after honor hunts, I after love.
> He leaves his friends to dignify them more;

I leave myself, my friends, and all, for love.

The main body of the play details Proteus' love experiences, which are characterized by Proteus himself in the words:[27]

> Inconstancy falls off ere it begins,
> What is in Silvia's face, but I may spy
> More fresh in Julia's with a constant eye?

This reminds us of the "Jewess' eye" in the *Merchant of Venice*, and the light form of love that the song, "Tell me where is fancy bred," warns Bassanio against. The structural plan of *Two Gentlemen*, therefore, brings out clearly, in a contrasting light, the two main ideas. The strong framework of friendship, supported by Valentine, encloses the fancy-bred love experiences of Proteus. This contrast displays Valentine's friendship on a spiritual plane far superior to Proteus' earthly love. But the more earthly the love story is, the more romantic and conventional it naturally becomes. Hence, from the structure of the play, we have reason to expect the proper courtesy toward Silvia at the end.

Unfortunately, the *Commedia dell' Arte* of the period, which is the Italian source for plays of the general type of *The Two Gentlemen*, throws no particular light on our problem. Shakespeare seems to have caught the spirit of his Italian prototype only through Greene. O.J. Campbell speaks only in general terms when he states that the dénouement of *Flavio Tradito*, which, taken as typical of the *Commedia dell' Arte*, "is like that in *The Two Gentlemen of Verona*."[28] The general way of ending both plays is the same. Those particular details, however, which involve our problem of the penitent lover, differ in each play. Here Shakespeare, as is usual with him, clarifies the motives of his characters. Certainly, Silvia, Proteus, and Valentine are simpler in nature and far easier understood than the corresponding figures of Isabella, Oratio, and Flavio in *Flavio Tradito*.

In describing the parts played by the latter trio, Campbell says:[29]

> Oratio in *Flavio Tradito*, renouncing the obligations of friendship, contrives to make Flavio believe that Silvia has been false to him with the result that he abandons her. Flavio learns of his friend's falseness through the craftiness of a servant, but bides his time for unmasking Oratio and exposing his treachery. His opportunity comes one day when the false friend is defeated in a duel and about to be slain. Flavio exhibits his unswerving friendship by rescuing him from this pressing danger. This generous act fills Oratio with so great remorse that

he forthwith gives up Isabella to Oratio and consoles himself immediately with the ever willing Flaminia. Friendship thus triumphs, as
it should in the soul of a Renaissance gentleman. However, Oratio,
by quick thinking and equally quick acting, enables the comedy to
close with the rigorously prescribed double marriage.

The triangular relations as described here do not require a pardon from
Flavio as his abandonment of Isabella is motivated by the deceptive actions
of Oratio. In *The Two Gentlemen*, the abandonment of Silvia by Valentine
is based on the simple idea of friendship, which has nothing to do with
Silvia's character. Her innocence in the whole matter should have had the
proper romantic atonement of a pardon at the end. Let us now go over in
detail the last scene in *The Two Gentlemen*.

We shall first deal with Proteus. He, together with Julia and Silvia,
comes on the stage just after he has rescued Silvia from the hands of the
outlaws. He expects the favor of Silvia and puts love above friendship. When
he is prevented from forcing Silvia to his will, he naturally comes to his senses
and begs forgiveness (lines 73–77). We see by his actions that he illustrates
the superiority of love over friendship. At the beginning of the play, his soliloquy at the end of Act II, sc. iv, argues for love. In this speech, which definitely portrays Proteus' character for us, he says:[30]

> Methinks my zeal to Valentine is cold,
> And that I love him not as I was wont.

In his attack on Silvia, he says:[31] "In love Who respects friend?" His pursuit of Silvia, then, is the climax of his character as illustrating the victory
of love over friendship. At the end of his conversation with Julia about the
ring, Julia upbraids him for his fickleness. Shakespeare, in accordance with
his custom as seen in the mature plays, makes him ask pardon of Julia for
his long indifference.[32] The dramatist was doing nothing more than following the regular convention which I have illustrated from the novels on which
he based his plays. In *The Shepherd Felismena*, Don Felix, who corresponds
to Proteus, asks his lady's pardon for his changeable disposition:

> What words are sufficient to excuse the faults, that I have commit-
> ted against thy faith, and firmest love, and loyaltie? Wretched and
> accursed for ever shall I be, if thy condition and clemencie be not
> enclined to my favour and pardon.[33]

By making Valentine the exponent of friendship, Shakespeare bound together the two features which are not in the novel from which he derived most of the plot. Valentine guides all the action at the end, and his many courtesies are done in the name of friendship. He denounces Proteus as a "friend of an ill fashion,"[34] and then lectures to him on friendship. When Proteus is shamed, he offers Silvia in the name of friendship. He aids in bringing Proteus and Julia together with the remark: "'T were pity two such friends should long be foes."[35] He protects Silvia from Thurio, and receives her only as a "gift" from the Duke. Immediately after this, he seeks the pardon of his robber friends. Finally, in the closing lines of the play, he pleasantly leads in the conversation with the Duke. That Valentine should have acted so thoughtfully about every character present, and yet not have acknowledged an affront to Silvia, cannot be explained by a cold application of the doctrine of friendship. The claims of romantic love, the expectancies that grow out of the body of the play, the fine sense of balance perfected by Greene in the composition of his plays, and the good taste found in the endings of Shakespeare's other comedies, are not fulfilled in the ending of the *Two Gentlemen*.[36] Hence, the ending is not executed artistically.

NOTES

1. "The Unhappy Happy Ending," *PMLA*, XLII, 744.—Cf. Sampson in the *Tudor* ed.

2. Even Valentine is "a faithful lover as well as a faithful friend." See R.W. Bond, *The Two Gentlemen of Verona*, in the Arden Shakespeare, (1906), p. xxviii.

3. *English Comedy* (1929), p. 99.

4. When O.J. Campbell speaks of the ending of the *Two Gentlemen* as a "complete victory of friendship in its mortal struggle with love," he is rightly interpreting it as Italian in spirit.—*Studies in Shakespeare, Milton, and Donne* (1925), p. 56.— That Shakespeare's audience accepted this kind of ending as good in sentiment, is highly improbable. The English conception of strong friendships like that between Prince Edward and Lacie in Greene's *Friar Bacon and Friar Bungay* never wholly sacrifices the claims of romantic love to those of friendship.

5. Written about 1590.

6. V,iv,110–115.

7. Not Silvia's silence, but Valentine's indifference to her.

8. Written about 1592.—W.W. Greg, *The Scottish History of James the Fourth*, in the Malone Reprints (1921), p. vi.

9. Shakespeare may have had Greene's play in mind when he was writing at this early period.—Thorndike, op. cit., 98; E.K. Chambers, *William Shakespeare*, I, 330.

10. V,vi,36–37 (ed. Manly).

11. V,vi,152–164 (ed. Manly).

12. *The Comedy of Errors, Love's Labor's Lost*, and *The Taming of the Shrew* are not dealt with in this paper, as no wrongdoing is done in these plays which would alienate the sympathy of the audience from the hero.

13. *Shakespeare's Library*, ed. Hazlitt (1875), II, 118.

14. V,ii,35–36.

15. *Much Ado*, V,iii,12–15.

16. *Shakespeare's Library*, III, 124.

17. Ibid., I, 410.

18. Ibid., III, 150–151.

19. *All's Well*, V,iii,309.

20. *Shakespeare's Library*, III, 166.

21. V,iv.

22. *Measure for Measure*, V,i,479–482.

23. V,i,247–248.

24. V,v,210–264.

25. V,iii,37–38.

26. I,i,63–65.

27. V,iv,113–115.

28. "The Two Gentlemen of Verona," *Studies in Shakespeare, Milton, and Donne*, (Michigan Studies, 1925), p. 55. Campbell is a little extravagant in another general statement. In describing what takes place in *The Two Gentlemen*, he says: "Then follows a generous passing back and forth of the ladies without any regard for their wishes," (p. 56). Only one lady is involved, and she (Silvia) is passed only twice, first by Valentine to Proteus, then by her father to Valentine. We might even omit the latter case as a "passing" on the ground of paternal right. This leaves only one case of "passing" in the play.

29. Ibid., p. 55.

30. II,iv,191–214.

31. V,iv,53–54.

32. V,iv,110–115.

33. *Shakespeare's Library*, I, 310.

34. V,iv,61.

35. V,iv,118.

36. Cp. E.K. Chambers: "There is some poor writing towards the end of the play." *William Shakespeare*, I, 329.

SIR THOMAS ELYOT AND THE INTEGRITY OF *THE TWO GENTLEMEN OF VERONA* (1950)

Ralph M. Sargent

Dr. Johnson said of *The Two Gentlemen of Verona*: "When I read this play I cannot but think that I discover both in the serious and ludicrous scenes, the language and sentiments of Shakespear." But this play has since fared ill with the critics. Ignored by Coleridge, it was passed off noncommitally by Hazlitt with a few quotations from Speed and Julia. The depreciation of the play for various kinds and degrees of ineptness and obtuseness by such observers as Dowden, Chambers, G.P. Baker, Quiller-Couch, Dover Wilson, Tannenbaum, Charlton, and Van Doren, has tended to obscure its true import. Even the well-intentioned defenses of W.W. Lawrence, Alvin Shaler, and S.A. Small[1] have not been able to reinstate *Two Gentlemen* into a position of genuine significance in Shakespeare's development.

Not content with pointing out that the major characters lack the depth and winning qualities associated with those in Shakespeare's mature plays, the critics have struck at the very psychology and codes of conduct of these early characters. The disparagers have particularly joined in condemning the jam-packed concluding scene. The points of attack there have been three: 1. The sudden conversion of Proteus is psychologically unconvincing; and Valentine's forgiveness even worse. 2. The (in)famous line in which Valentine offers to surrender Silvia to Proteus is both unbelievable and ungallant. 3. The silence of Silvia at this point is untrue to feminine nature, and a major dramatic lapse.

Nor have the critics stopped with mere unfavorable judgment on the play. Representative of the radical approach to *Two Gentlemen* are the editors of the Cambridge New Shakespeare. Since he cannot approve the actions in the final scene, Sir Arthur Quiller-Couch refuses to accept the central passage as Shakespeare's; he asserts it to be a "piece of theatre botchwork patched on the original. . . . Our hypothesis being . . . that Shakespeare had

---

Reprinted from *PMLA* 65 (December 1950): 1166–80.

another denouement which possibly proved ineffective on the stage, and that the one we have is a stage-adapter's substitute." J. Dover Wilson, as textual editor of the same volume, becomes more specific: "This scene (v,iv), 'a damned spot,' as it stands, upon Shakespeare's dramatic reputation, has long been suspected of serious corruption. . . . Distinct scenes in Shakespeare's original, we believe, went to the manufacture of this, the adapter's masterpiece."[2] Wilson then attempts to construct the adapter's very hand. Thus, starting from a preconceived notion of what is "Shakespeare," the Cambridge editors proceed to disintegrate and reconstruct the Shakespearean text.

It is often easy to misread Shakespeare, especially when the critic's own standards of conduct and ideas of psychology differ, without his realizing this fact, from Shakespeare's. Some attention to the literary background of *Two Gentlemen* makes it plain that Shakespeare is simply assuming, without explanation or question, standards and goals the exact nature and force of which may not be readily apparent to the modern reader. The present study, therefore, proposes: 1. To indicate certain standards of conduct and ideals of life with which Shakespeare is working in this play, and to suggest Shakespeare's literary sanction for them. 2. To point out the second of Shakespeare's two major literary sources for the action of the play itself. 3. To review a portion of the play in the light of these sanctions and actions; to note the problems posed and the terms in which Shakespeare achieves his solution. 4. To show that the final scene derives consistently from the play, is thoroughly Shakespearean, and provides a dramatic finish to the comedy; in short, that no omissions, no adapters' hands need be posited.

> There is no disposition on the part of the writer to claim *Two Gentlemen* as a masterpiece. But it is believed that such a study will reveal in this play at the start of Shakespeare's career major concerns, convictions, and aims which became fundamental to the peculiarly Shakespearean view of human life and relations.

I

The Two Gentlemen of Verona was long regarded as primarily a comedy of love, something of an early sketch, for example, of *As You Like It*. It is certain that romantic love is given its just due at the conclusion. But the play contains a disturbing factor, the theme of masculine friendship, involving an ideal which rivals the demands of romantic love. The title, indeed, calls attention to this second theme. Scholars anxious to defend the play have become so conscious of this second theme that they have ranked it above that of love between the sexes. Thus W.W. Lawrence (p. 24): "*The Two Gentle-*

men of Verona . . . has been very generally and wrongly taken to be mainly a love story, whereas it is really a tale glorifying friendship." It should be obvious, rather, that Shakespeare consciously introduces both themes (and ideals) on somewhat equal footing: romantic love and masculine friendship. Such a procedure is far from isolated. On the contrary it is a characteristic phenomenon of the Renaissance that in the field of personal relationships literature exalted two ideals: love and friendship. The resulting clash, with its infinite variations, provided comic writers with their opportunity. A commonplace in Italian literature,[3] this love-friendship conflict became in Elizabethan comedy from Peele and Lyly to Fletcher and Massinger almost as popular as did the revenge theme in tragedy. Shakespearean comedy formed a part of this Renaissance process.

Deeply committed to the idea and conventions of romantic love Shakespeare likewise recognized the claims of friendship. Obsessed, as Chambers puts it, with the theme of friendship in the *Sonnets*, Shakespeare introduced it not merely into *Two Gentlemen*, but into *Love's Labor's Lost, Romeo and Juliet, The Merchant of Venice, Much Ado About Nothing, Hamlet,* and *The Two Noble Kinsmen*, to mention only the most conspicuous instances. The changes he rang on the theme form a study in themselves. But in *Two Gentlemen* he presents the two ideals of love and friendship, and their contact, in what might be called the purest Renaissance form.

The story of the rise of these two ideals is long and impressive, forming a major strand in the development of occidental literature and society. To show the significance of the Shakespearean position, only a few facts need to be recalled. Of rare and late appearance in classical literature, the romanticizing of love between the sexes must be considered mainly a mediæval phenomenon. The all-justifying power of love, the beyond-earthly bonds, could scarcely be carried further than in the great mediæval cycles of romance. In the course of the mediæval period, the theme of romantic love accepted and absorbed the conventions of courtly love and chivalric code. By the time of Spenser and Shakespeare in the English Renaissance, romantic love, trailing its mediæval clouds of glory, was combined with a Christian ideal of marriage. The strong feminine element in this ideal should be noted: it gives woman, by her very sex, an essential role in ultimate human relations. To this day traces of the mediæval conventions remain, shards of the chivalric code of knights and ladies: in affairs of the heart, the lady must always be deferred to. It is the light of this part of the code, of course, that Quiller-Couch (p. xiv) condemns Valentine's offer in *Two Gentlemen* to renounce Silvia in favor of his friend, without consulting the lady herself.

Mediæval literature also exalted a kind of friendship. Among other elements, the mediæval conception included the sworn-brother idea. Two men, often of different rank, swear an oath of loyalty to the death in some undertaking.[4] This notion of friendship excludes consideration of general virtues in the friends, or even of the merit of the project on which the sworn-brothers may be engaged. Its aim is utility. A strong echo of this mediæval idea of friendship sounds in *Hamlet*, in which Horatio, of lower rank, is sworn in fealty-friendship to his Prince, without even knowing the true object of their league.

But it was classical literature, from Plato and Aristotle to Cicero and Plutarch, which really apotheosized friendship between men. Greek and Roman moralists regarded friendship as one of the amenities of life, an expression of the good life, an ultimate good in itself, in fact a supreme good. In the words of Cicero: "Est enim amicitia nihil aliud nisi omnium divinarum humanarumque rerum cum benevolentia et caritate consensio, qua quidem haud scio an excepta sapienta nil quicquam melius homini sit a dis immortalibus datum."[5] Such friendship was based on equality of status and congeniality of minds; above all, it required virtuous life of both parties. By implication, classic literature found friendship between men superior to love between man and woman. Hence it represented a masculine view of human relations.

It was precisely this classical ideal of friendship which the Renaissance recovered and injected into the literature of its own time. Obviously in the society of the Renaissance, with its recognition of the importance of women, there was bound to be some clash between ideals of love and friendship.

Immediately preceding or contemporary with *Two Gentlemen* appeared, for example, two plays, Lyly's *Endimion* (c. 1588) and Peele's *Old Wives' Tale* (c. 1591), as well as two prose fictions, Lyly's *Euphues* (1578) and Sidney's *Arcadia* (1590), which took up the challenge. Each of these exalts both friendship and love, brings them into conflict, and then provides a resolution. All make the same point: if the claims of friendship are first fully lived up to, then, and only then, is it possible also to achieve the rewards of true love. Loyalty in friendship and loyalty in love go, as it were, hand in hand. In *The Old Wives' Tale* the bonds of friendship between Eumenides and (the ghost of) Jack resemble those of the mediæval sworn-brothers; in *Euphues*, Philautus learns his lesson about friendship and love in a negative way: treacherously stealing his friend's mistress, he finds her likewise unfaithful to him; Sidney's *Arcadia* does not bear any useful parallel to the situations in *Two Gentlemen*; but *Endimion*, with its fantastic battery of renunciations at the conclusion, may well have furnished Shakespeare with some stimulus for his comedy.

Here, then, is the background against which *Two Gentlemen* must first be seen. It is the literary milieu out of which *Two Gentlemen* arose, a knowledge of which Shakespeare assumed in his audience: four works which presented the contact between love and friendship—and all came to the same conclusion as *Two Gentlemen*. A recent analyst of Shakespeare's moral ideas says of *Two Gentlemen*: "In this play, Shakespeare makes his first bold, characteristic, important moral assumption: that perhaps you can give away your cake and eat it too."[6] In the light of his own day the conclusion to *Two Gentlemen* can scarcely be called bold. That Shakespeare accepted, and tried in his own way to reconcile, the rival claims of love and friendship is, of course, important; but the conventionality of the actual conclusion suggests that Shakespeare's originality lies elsewhere. Shakespeare's contribution to the love-friendship theme in *Two Gentlemen* can be seen, rather, in his scrutiny of the ideals in terms of human beings; a study of what those ideals entail; the human difficulties which thwart them, the cost to men and women, and the conditions on which the goals may be achieved.

For his own treatment of the love-friendship theme, Shakespeare could have got suggestions from Lyly and Peele; for the nature and ideal of true friendship he could have gone to the classics, let us say to Cicero and Plutarch. But it is much more likely that he turned to the *locus classicus* for the exposition of friendship in the English Renaissance, namely to *The Boke of the Gouernour*, by Sir Thomas Elyot (1531). We know that Shakespeare found this a congenial work, drawing upon it for ideas on government and episodes in his plays of the middle period.[7] In Book II, Chapter xi, on *Friendship*, or *Amity*, Shakespeare would have found all necessary ideas on friendship for the Renaissance ideal. When a study of this chapter reveals that Shakespeare stresses exactly the elements in friendship which Elyot does, the probability that Shakespeare used the book for *Two Gentlemen* is greatly enhanced.

Elyot, who is consciously reviving the classic ideal of friendship, refers specifically to Aristotle and Cicero for his authority. He places friendship at the pinnacle of human esteem, without even Cicero's exception of wisdom as the one possible superior achievement: "For in god, and all thinge that commeth of god, nothing is of more greater estimation than loue, called in latin Amor, whereof, *Amicitia* commeth, named in englisshe frendshippe or amitie" (II,122).[8] Elyot points out that true friendship is only likely between equals, and that these men must be of similar minds, of virtuous conduct, and given to liberality and "swete countenaunce." But the one essential quality of friendship to which Elyot returns again and again is *constancy*. (He refers to it no less than four times in his short chapter on friendship.) It is worth noting that this is the key quality stressed in Shakespeare's *Two Gentlemen*. Elyot admits that the ideal of friendship is a rare achievement in this world. Nevertheless, trust in friendship forms a very foundation stone in the moral order of man's universe: "the whiche taken a way from the lyfe of man, no house shall abide standinge, no felde shall be in culture. And that is lightly parceiued, if a man do remember what commeth of dissention and discorde. Finally he semeth to take the sonne from the worlde, that taketh frendshippe from mannes life" (II,122–123). Here in Elyot, then, may be seen the nature and sanctions of friendship which lie behind *Two Gentlemen*. These are the ideals which Shakespeare proposed to illustrate in drama, and to integrate with the ideals of romantic love.

The first of Shakespeare's two major literary sources for *Two Gentlemen*, the story of Felix and Felismena contained in the *Diana Enamorada* of Montemayor, represents a typical love romance of the Renaissance. The story, told by the injured woman herself, with a thoroughly feminine point of view, relates her reactions and her stratagems in regaining her financé, who has fallen in love with a lady at Court. In Montemayor, Shakespeare found ample source material both for Julia's bold conduct and for the development of her inner responses as a heroine of romantic drama. In fact, it is possible that one of the factors which commended this tale to Shakespeare was its relatively rich portrayal of the psychological states of the heroine. The germ for Shakespeare's conception of Proteus' character, however, is of the slightest in Montemayor. And the issue of masculine friendship does not enter into this story at all.

A second major literary source for *Two Gentlemen*, presenting this friendship theme in action, has long been conjectured.[9] It is now suggested that we simply look at the chapter in *The Gouernour* following that on Friendship, namely Book II, Chapter xii, entitled: "The wonderfull history of Titus and Gisippus, and whereby is fully declared the figure of perfet amitie." There follows the tale of an ideal friendship between two aristocratic students in Athens, the one Greek, the other Roman. Gisippus, the Greek, becomes engaged; he makes the mistake of extolling his fiancée to his friend Titus, and then introducing her to him. Titus falls deeply in love with his friend's fiancée. Inner turmoil results for Titus. Finally, upon learning of the situation, and the struggle within Titus, Gisippus in a supreme gesture offers his fiancée to his friend. And the offer is made in almost the exact terms which Shakespeare's Valentine uses in making a similar gesture to Proteus.[10]

This story of Titus and Gisippus proved a ubiquitous favorite of the Renaissance. Widest currency had been given it by Boccaccio in the

Decameron, where it is put in the mouth of Fiametta as the Eighth Story of the Tenth Day. It had actually been used much earlier by Petrus Alfonsi, a converted Spanish Jew of the twelfth century, in his *Disciplina Clericalis,* as Exemplum II, *De integro amico.*[11] Here the story is set in Egypt, and clearly reveals its oriental origin. This version was incorporated in the *Gesta Romanorum* of the fourteenth century. An English translation of this collection was published by Wynkyn de Worde in the sixteenth century, a few years before the appearance of Elyot's version.[12] Although the latter is based on Boccaccio, it may well owe something to Petrus and the *Gesta Romanorum.* Boccaccio, of course, gave the story a classical background, thus obscuring its Eastern source. His story was also published in Latin translations, one by Philip Beroaldo in 1491, and another by Matteo Bandello in 1509; needless to say, these versions enhanced its classical appearance.

Two verse redactions of Titus and Gisippus in the English of the sixteenth century have survived, that of William Walter (*c.* 1530), apparently based on Beroaldo, and that of Edward Lewicke (1562), based on Elyot.[13] More important, the story was twice dramatized in England during this same century, in plays now lost. There was a Latin play for schoolboys, *De Titi et Gisippi firmissima amicitia,* produced by Ralph Radcliff at Hitchin in 1538; and also an English play, *The History of Titus and Gisippus,* performed 19 February 1588, at Whitehall, by the Children of Paul's.[14]

It has been shown that Lyly used elements of Elyot's story of Titus and Gisippus, in a sort of reverse way, in *Euphues.*[15] Finally, as late as 1639, John Fletcher in *Monsieur Thomas* picked up and developed neglected aspects of the story.[16] English poets of the Renaissance, including Spenser,[17] put the non-classical friends, Titus and Gisippus, alongside the classical pairs of Damon and Pithias, and Pylades and Orestes. What made the story of Titus and Gisippus so apt for the Renaissance was the fact that it introduced, as the classical stories of friendship did not, the twin ideals of love and friendship.

There can now be little doubt that it was exactly this story of Titus and Gisippus which Shakespeare used as the second of his major sources for the action of *Two Gentlemen.* It provides the theme of friendship, the two characters, the mental responses of the love-smitten friend, and the denouement of *Two Gentlemen.* And a perusal of all the extant versions reveals that at divergent passages Shakespeare follows the version of Sir Thomas Elyot.

II

With this summary review of the background, we may turn to a few crucial points in the play itself for a reassessment of its integrity and achievement. In *The Two Gentlemen of Verona* Shakespeare stresses two major characters: Julia, the girl who is left behind—and does something about it—and Proteus, the man who is fickle in both love and friendship. The rôle and character of Julia have been adequately appreciated and need not detain us here. It is the part of Proteus which needs attention. Doubtless the rôle of Proteus (Titus) in Elyot attracted Shakespeare's interest; he had a predilection for the fallible creature caught between impulse and ideal, who finds the ideal too much for him. It should be apparent that Proteus became a central figure for his play; most of the important soliloquies are his. His inner struggle and fall form the heart of the dramatic conflict; these lead to his overt perfidy, which is the mainspring of the dramatic action. Or, to put it the other way round, Shakespeare, taking the outward events produced by Proteus' conduct, traces them to their source in Proteus' inner breakdown.

The play opens with Proteus and Valentine united in Renaissance bonds of friendship. When, in Act II, Proteus follows Valentine to Court, he finds Valentine in love there with Silvia. Valentine makes the mistake of introducing Silvia to Proteus, and praising both his friend and his beloved in front of them both. Just how Shakespeare took over this incident from Elyot's story of friendship may be realized by glancing at the account in *The Gouernour*. There, Gisippus, having become secretly engaged to a maiden, Sophronia, is unable to keep his pleasure to himself:

> Nat withstandyng the feruent loue that he [Gisippus] had to his frende Titus, at the last surmounted shamefastnes. Wherfore he disclosed to him his secret iournayes, and what delectation he toke in beholdinge the excellent beautie of her whom he purposed to mary . . . And on a tyme he, hauynge with hym his frende Titus, went to his lady, of whom he was resceyued moste ioyously. [II,135–136]

Later, when forced by his friendship to confess his infatuation with Sophronia, Titus reminds Gisippus that it was Gisippus himself who had led him (Titus) into his predicament in the first place.

> "Alas, Gysippus," says Titus, "What enuious spirite meued you to bringe me with you to her whom ye haue chosen to be your wyfe, where I receyued this poison? I saye, Gysippus, where was then your wisedome, that ye remembred nat the fragilities of our commune nature? What neded you to call me for a witnesse of your priuate delites? . . . Gysippus, I saye your trust is the cause that I am intrapped; the rayes or beames issuinge from the eyen of her whom

ye haue chosen, with the remembraunce of her incomparable vertues, hath thrilled throughout the middes of my hart." [II,139]

This recognition of initial incaution by the first friend, Shakespeare picks up and enlarges upon, before the fall of Proteus. Shakespeare makes it as plain as he can that Valentine, unwittingly, but unwisely, leads Proteus directly into temptation. For Valentine (II,iv) not only presents Silvia to Proteus, but insists several times that Proteus admit Silvia's pre-eminence in beauty and character: ". . . and is she not a heavenly saint?" Valentine demands of Proteus. "No," replies Proteus, "but she is an earthly paragon." "Call her divine," Valentine insists. If Silvia is indeed such a superior creature, Valentine, for one, should not have been surprised at her effect on Proteus!

Now in Elyot, the fall of Titus is so swift as scarcely to be dramatic. And he is completely in the power of love for Sophronia before the moral dilemma strikes him.

> But Titus furthwith, as he behelde so heuenly a personage adourned with beautie inexplicable, in whose visage was moste amiable countenaunce, mixte with maydenly shamefastnesse, . . . was therat abasshed, and had the hart through perced with the firy darte of blinde Cupide. Of the whiche wounde the anguisshe was so excedinge and vehement, that neither the study of Philosophie, neyther the remembraunce of her dere frende Gysippus, who so moche loued and trusted hym, coulde any thinge withdrawe hym from that unkynde appetite, but that of force he must loue inordinately that lady, whom his said frende had determined to mary. All be it with incredible paynes he kepte his thoughtes secrete. [II,136]

Nevertheless, Titus remains perfectly aware of his own obliquity. In his later confession to his friend Gisippus, he complains of what this lapse from the ideal has done to his friendship:

> "And now nat withstandinge, only with the loke of a woman, those bondes of loue be dissolued, reason oppressed, frendship is excluded; there auaileth no wisedome, no doctrine, no fidelitie or truste; ye, your truste is the cause that I haue conspired agayne you this treason."
> [II,139]

This whole episode in Elyot was particular grist to Shakespeare. Both the uncontrollable course of such a love, and the consciousness of moral lapse which it brought, were of prime interest to him. Only, Shakespeare doubled the stakes, as it were: for Proteus to give himself up to love of Silvia meant being false to his former love (as in Montemayor) as well as to his friend (as in Elyot).

After Proteus has seen Silvia, and after Valentine has exalted her charms, Proteus comes forward alone. He reveals that he has been stricken by Silvia—and is himself disturbed by the event:

> "Is it mine eye, or Valentinus' praise,
> Her true perfection, or my false transgression,
> That makes me reasonless to reason thus?" [18]

But possibly Proteus has not yet wholly succumbed to this sudden love. He concludes the scene.

> "If I can check my erring love, I will;
> If not, to compass her I'll use my skill."

Thus Shakespeare at the end of this scene leaves a wisp of suspense about Proteus in the minds of the audience. Compared with Elyot's Titus, Shakespeare's Proteus puts up a slightly longer struggle. And he considers the consequences before his full commitment.

In II,vi, we are shown Proteus deciding the issue for himself in a long soliloquy. He clearly announces to himself—and his audience—the nature of the perfidy involved in his contemplated action:

> "To leave my Julia, shall I be forsworn;
> To love fair Silvia, shall I be forsworn;
> To wrong my friend, I shall be much forsworn."

(Note that treachery to friendship is regarded as the culminating fault.) He blames his predicament on the invincible power of Love: "Love bade me swear, and Love bids me forswear." In presenting the struggle and downfall of Proteus, therefore, Shakespeare is dramatizing the course of the man who knows in advance perfectly well what the ideal calls for, but when seized by the power of desire cannot summon up the moral will-power to hold to the ideal. He is laying bare the sense of helplessness felt by such a person:

> "All this the world well knows; yet none knows well
> To shun the heaven that leads men to this hell."

This interest in the psychology of the perfidious man, who knows what he should do, yet runs contrary to his own conscience—and in the process condemns himself—forms a major preoccupation of Shakespeare from the start of his career. A similar self-conscious struggle is revealed with much greater detail, for tragic purposes, in the mind of Tarquin in *The Rape of Lucrece* (lines 183–301). And a like process is shown again, for example, with Angelo in *Measure for Measure*. It is part of Macbeth's tragedy that he attempts to obscure this issue. Each man knows the code, the ideal, which he is breaking, yet succumbs to the power of desire or impulse.

Here, it is Proteus who condemns his own weakness (see, particularly IV,ii), just as Hamlet is later to do with himself. But Proteus must somehow justify himself to himself. And this is how he does it: "I to myself am dearer than a friend." As a defense, this position results from a state of mind which Shakespeare characterized in Sonnet 62: "Sin of self-love possesseth all my eye."

Proteus is presented, then, as a man who recognizes and admires fidelity in love and friendship. But he is also susceptible to the pressures of the moment. He is, for Shakespeare, the kind of man who is not yet morally lost; he still has the potentialities for reclamation when the pressures are altered, when the right appeals are put to him. But once having let himself succumb to Silvia, Proteus determines to pursue and win her, at all costs. The first act of perfidy leads to extended treachery to his friend. And here, of course, Shakespeare departs from Elyot. Titus, in the story, once having been smitten by his friend's fiancée, can do nothing but collapse; unable to solve his dilemma, he lies on his bed and bemoans his fate. Shakespeare's Proteus, a man of action, now follows the course of Montemayor's Felix, in his pursuit of his new love. But he carries with him the moral discrimination and conscience of Elyot's Titus.

The central drama of *Two Gentlemen* depends on the consequences of the decision made by Proteus. And the action reaches its culmination in the disputed final scene (V,iv). At this late point in the play, although he has broken all rules in the attempt, Proteus has failed to win Silvia; Julia has followed Proteus to Court, disguised as a page boy, and now at last, all— first Valentine, then Silvia, Proteus, and Julia—have taken to the woods. There, in "Another Part of the Forest," Shakespeare releases his rapid succession of shocks which bring the play to its speedy denouement.

Proteus overtakes Silvia (alone, he thinks) and attempts to force himself on her. In her defense, Silvia tries to appeal to Proteus' better nature. She proves a spirited and well-informed dialectician. First she insists she does not love Proteus; this appeal does not move him. Then she accuses him of faithlessness to his first love, Julia; and finally, bringing up her weightiest charge, she brands him perfidious in friendship to Valentine: "Thou counterfeit to thy true friend," she proclaims. Proteus, who has long since considered the nature of his own conduct, replies in cynical fashion: "In love, / Who respects friend?" The instant reply of Silvia is fully revealing of her attitude: "All men but Proteus." These are the last words but two (an exclamation when Proteus lays hands on her) by Silvia in the play. With them, Silvia indicates that she understands the code of masculine friendship.

Exactly at this juncture, Valentine, who has been watching these proceedings of his erstwhile friend with his fiancée, leaps forward and saves Silvia from Proteus. Valentine then turns to Proteus. Not a word to Silvia; Valentine trusts her, and she can now make her own decisions. But the attack on Pro- teus is bitter. On what grounds is it made? Valentine says nothing of Proteus' love for Silvia, nor of his faithlessness to Julia; it is only the lapse in friendship which Valentine berates in Proteus. This entire passage, culminating in Valentine's startling gesture, is treated wholly within the convention of the friendship ideal. Valentine, who has tried to live by the ideal, voices his disillusion:

> "Thou common friend, that's without faith or love—
> For such is a friend now! Treacherous man,
> Thou hast beguil'd my hopes! . . .
> Who should be trusted now, when one's own right hand
> Is perjur'd to the bosom? Proteus,
> I am sorry I must never trust thee more,
> But count the world a stranger for thy sake."

Now look at Proteus. However lightly and conventionally the audience and critics may take the sudden appearance of Valentine, it was an intervention to shock Proteus to his depths. He had been caught at the very nadir of his perfidy; and here is Valentine in the flesh, condemning him, by showing Proteus that his own conduct has shaken the foundations of both their worlds, which had been based on the rock-bottom of trust in friendship. Proteus' quick repentance, in such a situation, and upon such an appeal, is neither undramatic nor implausible:

> "My shame and guilt confounds me.
> Forgive me, Valentine . . .
>
> . . . I do as truly suffer
> As e'er I did commit."

Valentine's reply, if still consciously self-righteous, rises to the occasion:

> "Then I am paid;
> And once again I do receive thee honest.
> Who by repentance is not satisfied
> Is nor of heaven nor earth."

Both the act and the sentiments of Valentine occur so frequently in Shakespeare that they have come to be regarded as typically Shakespearean. They can be seen in the *Sonnets,* and right up to the end of his career in *The Tempest.* To question the genuineness of repentance and forgiveness in Shakespeare is to deny a fundamental tenet of his drama.

From the vantage of moral elevation, then, Valentine proceeds to his famous gesture of renunciation. Up to this point, be it remembered, it has been Proteus who has had to make all the hard decisions. Everything has worked out automatically to the advantage of Valentine. And Valentine has talked grandly about the claims of friendship. Now, for the first time, Valentine has the chance to make a decision which will prove *his* willingness to accept the code of friendship by really costing him something: "And," he says to Proteus, "that my love may appear plain and free, / All that was mine in Silvia I give thee." It is the ultimate acknowledgment of the claims of friendship. Not only is the offer conceived wholly within the convention of Elyot on "Amity"; actually, the very gesture is taken directly from Elyot's version of the Titus-Gisippus story. When Gisippus, in Elyot, learns that Titus is pining away for love of Sophronia, Gisippus declares: "Here I renounce to you clerely all my title and interest that I nowe haue or moughte haue in that faire mayden." The offer of fiancée to friend forms a high point, a supreme gesture, of Elyot's story illustrating the noble state of friendship. And as such Shakespeare doubtless took it over from Elyot. In terms of a code which he assumed his audience would recognize, Shakespeare has carefully led his characters up to this position. Yet Valentine's gesture comes as a shock. That was Shakespeare's aim as a dramatist.

But what of Silvia in all this business? exclaim the critics. She is not consulted, nor does she, as things stand, say a word. Here, either Shakespeare has faltered, in presenting human nature or in exemplifying human conduct; or else his original scene has been cut. Now there can be no doubt that Shakespeare did foresee and consider Silvia's position at this juncture. And he has turned a necessity (her silence at this point) into a virtue. Just before Valentine's gesture—as we have noted, a point overlooked by so many critics of Silvia's silence—Shakespeare had taken pains to reveal Silvia as recognizing the ideal of masculine friendship. When, therefore, Valentine reaches the ultimate in that code by his gesture of renunciation, Silvia can scarcely do less than hold her tongue. To add to, or detract from, Valentine's proposal would be equivalent to upsetting her delicate role of ideal feminine conduct at the moment. It is part of Silvia's character, as presented by Shakespeare, to be capable of such rigorous devotion to accepted codes. By her silence—golden in this light—she reaches her peak of propriety. No, there is no secret about Silvia's silence. Nor has anything been subtracted from Shakespeare's scene at this point; nor do we need to call in an "adapter."

In the Elyot story the offer is accepted, and thus devotion to friendship as an ideal is demonstrated. For Shakespeare, however, the gesture at one and the same time carries Valentine to the peak of loyalty in friendship, and opens the way to Proteus' regeneration and restoration to moral dignity. If Proteus is really repentant, if he has really been recalled to his better self, he must be given the chance to demonstrate that reconstruction by being allowed to choose for himself between Silvia and Julia. By the same token, if Julia is actually to be *chosen* by Proteus, not just forced on him because he cannot get Silvia, Proteus must be given a free hand for that choice.

Of course, in offering Proteus that choice, Valentine is taking some risk. It is taken in devotion to friendship, but it is also based on confidence that the friend will now live up to an equal standard. And Valentine is so confident of the outcome that he does not hesitate to let Silvia take the same risk. As presented by Shakespeare, however, does the offer actually involve much of a risk? Valentine has just seen, a few moments before, that Silvia has completely rebuffed Proteus; and Proteus has acknowledged the error of his way.

At this point, Valentine and Silvia have played their parts. Now again Proteus has a decision to make. But immediately Shakespeare brings in the warmth of the feminine touch. Julia, bold but pathetic, lacking the sterner stuff and rigid confidence of Valentine and Silvia, by nature or design, swoons at the offer of Silvia to Proteus. In the discovery which follows, Julia reveals her loyalty to Proteus. It is the final shock for Proteus. Thus confronted with the presence of Julia, and the evidence of the lengths to which she has gone for love of him, he completes his return to his former self and ways, and deliberately chooses Julia. Then, the regenerated Proteus, who has by now earned the right to them, speaks the tag lines of the play: "O heaven! were man / But constant, he were perfect."

In the postscript, Shakespeare finishes off all in proper fashion by having Valentine remove Thurio as a suitor (Valentine thus demonstrating once more his full virility), and then receive formally the hand of Silvia from her father the Duke. So friendship and love triumph together in the play.

Thus, by seeing the material and conventions with which Shakespeare has been working in *Two Gentlemen*, we can realize that he has shown his characters as human beings involved in the problems of loyalty to two ideals. When one character finds himself unable to live up to either, all is upset. But the willingness of the other three characters to live up to the highest demands of their ideals ultimately lifts that fourth character to their level. And at this level, the conflicting claims of friendship and love may be reconciled. In *The Two Gentlemen of Verona* Shakespeare is revealing his theme that human beings are fallible, but when presented with confidence in friendship and love, and allowed sound decisions by deepest convictions, then it may be possible for them to achieve durable human relationships—a fundamental value in his universe.

NOTES

1. *Shakespeare's Problem Comedies* (New York, 1931), p. 24; *Shakespere's Silences* (Cambridge, 1929), pp. 16–18; "The Ending of *The Two Gentlemen of Verona*," *PMLA*, XLVIII (1933), 767–776.

2. *Two Gentlemen*, New Shakespeare (Cambridge, 1921), pp. xviii, 102.

3. See O. J. Campbell, "*The Two Gentlemen of Verona* and Italian Comedy," *Studies in Shakespeare, Milton and Donne* (New York, 1925), pp. 54–55.

4. For a detailed study of the friendship theme in English literature of the late Middle Ages and Renaissance, see Laurens J. Mills, *One Soul in Bodies Twain: Friendship in Tudor Literature and Stuart Drama* (Bloomington, Ind., 1937).

5. *De Amicitia*, ed. W.A. Falconer, Loeb Library (New York, 1927), p. 130.

6. Donald Stauffer, *Shakespeare's World of Images* (New York, 1949), p. 38.

7. See D.T. Starnes, "Shakespeare and Elyot's *Governour*," *Univ. of Texas Studies in English*, No. 7 (Austin, 1927), pp. 112–132. Although Starnes indicates Shakespeare's probable indebtedness to *The Governour* in *2 Henry IV, Henry V, Troilus and Cressida*, and *Coriolanus*, he does not mention *Two Gentlemen*.

8. References are to *The Boke named The Gouernour*, ed. H.H.S. Croft (London, 1883).

9. See e.g., Campbell, op. cit.

10. Mills (p. 407) remarks on the similarity of this passage in Elyot to the gesture in *Two Gentlemen*, not realizing, evidently, that the whole story is closely related to *Two Gentlemen*. Lawrence, p. 24, suggests the Titus and Gisippus story in Boccaccio as an analogy to parts of *Two Gentlemen*. Had he scanned the Elyot version of the story with Shakespeare in mind, he could not have failed to see the much closer relationship.

11. A. Hilka and W. Söderhjelm, edd. (Heidelberg, 1911), p. 5.

12. See J.H. Herrtage, *The Early English Versions of the Gesta Romanorum*, EETS (London, 1879), pp. 196–205.

13. Both are printed in H.G. Wright, *Early English Versions of the Tales of Guiscardo and Ghismonda and Titus and Gisippus from the Decameron*, EETS (London, 1937). It is clear that neither Elyot nor Shakespeare owes anything to these "poetic" versions of the tale.

14. John Bale, *Index Britanniae Scriptorum*, ed. R.L. Poole (Oxford, 1902), pp. 332–333; and A. Feuillerat, *Documents relating to the Office of the Revels in the Time of Queen Elizabeth*, W. Bang, 21 (Louvain, 1908), pp. 270, 276. It is extremely unlikely that Shakespeare knew the Latin schoolboy play; but by date and subject

matter the English play may well have been of first-rate importance in the writing of *Two Gentlemen*. Lacking the play itself, we can say only that it suggests an intermediary source between Shakespeare and Elyot; but even so, considering Shakespeare's established knowledge of Elyot, it remains more than likely that he also went directly to Elyot for source material for *Two Gentlemen*.

15. C.T. Goode, "Sir Thomas Elyot's Titus and Gysippus," *MLN*, XXXVII (1922), 1–11.

16. See Mills, pp. 317–319.

17. *Faerie Queene*, IV,x,27.

18. *Two Gentlemen*, II,iv,197–199. The first words of 197 are corrupt; cf. New Cambridge ed., pp. 79–80.

19. This dramatic declaration occurs only in Elyot's version of the story. The similarity between Valentine's forgiveness and renunciation, and certain passages in the *Sonnets* (notably 40–42), has often been remarked, e.g., by A.C. Bradley, *Lectures in Poetry* (London, 1909), p. 335, and R.M. Alden, *The Sonnets of Shakespeare* (Boston, 1916), pp. 108–112; but both these critics fail to appreciate the *force* of the friendship ideal and conventions accepted in both instances. For an informed discussion of this point, see Mills, pp. 239–247, and notes on pp. 434–435.

20. In the original the fulfilment of the offer is achieved by means of the bed trick. When the lady, and subsequently her family, learn the truth about the substitution, they arouse the whole local population in protest. It is interesting to notice that Shakespeare, who does not use the bed trick in this play, introduces it into *Measure for Measure*, where it does not occur in his sources. Could his sense of thrift have caused him to carry this over from Elyot to *Measure for Measure*? In that case, the bed trick there, as in *All's Well*, could be attributed to Boccaccio.

21. How different is all this from Montemayor! There, Julia's prototype has to kill two of three men who are engaging her fickle lover in deadly combat, before he recognizes her devotion to him.

Proteus, Wry-Transformed Traveller (1954)

Thomas A. Perry

> *... A busy loving courtier, and a heartless threatening Thraso; a self-wise seeming schoolmaster; a wry-transformed traveller; these, if we saw walk in stage names, ... therein were delightful laughter, and teaching delightfulness.*
>
> *Sidney,* An Apologie for Poetrie

Students of Shakespeare too generally have ignored or minimized the travel motif in *The Two Gentlemen of Verona*. True, it is the story of faithfulness in friend and lover; yet that faithfulness is consequent to an inexperienced youth's traveling abroad and is part of his transformation into an Italianate courtier. To understand Proteus properly one must see him first of all as the wry-transformed traveller.

Hints for this Italianate character of Proteus exist in the principal source—the tale of Felis and Felismena in Montemayor's *Diana*. Felis, not yet out of his "mocedad," is sent to the far distant court lest he waste his youth at home, "donde no se podían aprender sino los vicios de que la ociosidad es maestra."[1] The reasoning is typically Renaissance-Humanist and is paraphrased in the opening lines of Shakespeare's play. In sharp contrast to this Felis is the later, sophisticated Felis among the courtiers of the Princess Augusta Cesarina. This Felis is revealed with striking suddenness when the reader, following Felismena, one night hears the unfaithful Felis serenading another lady—with an Italianate sonnet! Then, as Felismena arrives at the court, the reader sees Felis for the first time since his departure from Vandalia—a richly dressed, clothes-conscious Felis. In an unusually detailed passage Montemayor describes the clothes. In this changed Felis two traits stand out, traits commonly attributed to the Italianate: sonneteering and concern with fashionable dress. To these must be added a third, inconstancy.

Reprinted from *Shakespeare Quarterly* 5 (1954): 33–40.

This, basically, is also the story of Shakespeare's Proteus. In the first act he is yet to be "tried and tutor'd in the world" (I.iii.21). He is urged to "see the wonders of the world abroad" lest "living dully sluggardiz'd at home [he] / Wear out [his] youth with shapeless idleness" (I.i.6–7). Then, when he is sent to Milan and its new world of "wailful sonnets" and fashionable dress, and amorality, he changes as completely as did Felis. The new Proteus is not only inconstant, but he also becomes increasingly sophisticated and amoral, so that eventually even the Duke turns to him for worldly advice and for instruction in intrigue (III.ii.16–30).

This basic plot Shakespeare has reinforced with elements not in the *Diana* but contributing to the more complete picture which it suggests of a wry-transformed traveller. For instance, the conventional reason for travel—obviously transplanted from the *Diana*—appears in the opening speech of the play, but is developed further in the third scene, when Antonio and Panthino are discussing Proteus' education. Here Shakespeare obviously draws upon the great mass of didactic literature stressing the role of travel in such education. Proteus' uncle, of the ambitious lesser nobility, conventionally pronounces that it "would be great impeachment of [Proteus'] age, / In having known no travel in his youth." Since the traveller was expected to see and observe foreign courts,[2] Panthino suggests the Milanese court, which he naively idealizes as a place where a youth may "practise tilts and tournaments, / Hear sweet discourse, converse with noblemen, / And be in eye of every exercise / Worthy his youth and nobleness of birth." This is, of course, a piece of Shakespearian irony. Another original touch is the realism of the uncle's jibe about Proteus' spending "his youth at home, / While other men, of slender reputation" are providing the proper education for their sons (I.iii.4–34).

The twenty-day journey of Felis from Vandalia to the court (*Diana*, p. 105) becomes a sea voyage in Shakespeare's play so that Valentine and Proteus may be identified as young Englishmen "about to make the continental tour of Elizabethan days."[3] The questioning of Shakespeare's geography in this play has been irrelevant. Likewise unnecessary to an understanding of the play has been the careful evidence of the late Professor Ernesto Grillo that Shakespeare's geography is essentially accurate.[4] The truth of the matter is, as Professor Karl Young has pointed out, Shakespeare must have in mind "a departure by sea from London rather than pretending to accuracy in Italian geography and topography."[5]

Those who argue Shakespeare's careless disregard of geographical fact have overlooked his consistent and apparently deliberate placing of puns and water images to emphasize that the young Veronese leave aboard ship. At the same time he has carefully ordered his expository details to make this clear to his audience. For instance, from the very beginning of the play and throughout the first two acts, the primary interest is in the "shipping" of Valentine and Proteus, and later (II.iv.187) with the disembarkation of Proteus in Milan. Meanwhile, puns on *sheep* and *ship, tied* and *tide* (I.i.71–73; II.iii.36–57) are placed strategically at the exact moments of embarkation—as the servants rush to catch the ship. The play on the double meaning of *tide*—"The tide is now:—nay, not thy tide of tears; / That tide will stay me longer than I should"—as Proteus bids Julia farewell, likewise emphasizes the mode of travel (II.ii.14–15).

The skillful scattering of water images throughout the first half of the play—especially in the first two acts—suggests that Shakespeare was consciously reminding his audience of water travel at the critical moments of departure. For example, Proteus' figure of speech as he reacts to the news that he is being sent to Milan carries double meaning: "Thus have I shunn'd the fire for fear of burning, / And drench'd me in the sea, where I am drown'd." Again, Julia's comment as she decides to follow Proteus serves as an apt figure and also suggests the probable sea voyage: her love is like a current that "by many winding nooks he strays / With willing sport to the wild ocean." "Hinder not my course," she adds significantly, "I'll be as patient as a gentle stream" (II.vii.25–34 *et passim*). Valentine's allusion in the opening scene to young Leander, who "cross'd the Hellespont" may presage his crossing the sea to find Sylvia. It also comes as the conversation shifts from the first major topic, sea travel, to the other, love, and within itself contains elements of both topics.

While other water images refer less directly to the action and are apparently introduced for ornament's sake only, yet they too appear at the critical moments when the dramatist is creating an impression of sea travel. Subtly and indirectly they make their contribution, as though they were the natural figures for a people living close to the sea and for the moment intent upon traveling. One of these images appears when Lucetta and Julia are discussing Julia's following Proteus and Lucetta raises doubts as to whether Proteus will like it. In answer Julia quotes the evidence of his "thousand oaths" and his "ocean of tears" (II.vii.69). Again, immediately after the disembarkation of Proteus in Milan, Valentine praises Sylvia at some length to Proteus: "I as rich in having such a jewel / As twenty seas, if all their sand were pearl, / The water nectar, and the rocks pure gold." It is only a few lines later that Proteus interrupts: "Go on before; I shall inquire you forth. / I must unto the road, to disembark / Some necessaries that I needs must use" (II.iv.169–171, 186–188).

The last of these water images, which appear just as Valentine (III.i.224) and Sylvia (IV.iii.33) leave Milan, present a special problem, since they are supposedly traveling by land. The apparent inconsistency can be resolved, however, by looking closely at a third passage, also containing a reference to water travel: the play upon the words *mastership* and *master's ship* just after Valentine's departure from Milan. Here is the same pattern used earlier in the departures from Verona: after a sad farewell there is comic relief in which one of the servants plays upon a word having reference to sea travel. "What news with your mastership?" Speed asks just after Valentine and Proteus have left the stage. "With my master's ship?" answers Launce. "Why, it is at sea" (III.i.280–281). Does it not seem likely that in an early stage of composition or in some earlier version of the play Shakespeare conceived of Valentine's leaving as well as arriving in Milan by sea? If so, would not this banter between the servants refer directly to the action of the play, especially if Launce's words were originally assigned to Speed? Then, if Shakespeare, needing the conventional woodland setting for his outlaws, should have decided to abandon sea for land travel, he could have kept the pun—now irrelevant to the action— best by exchanging speakers. If there were such a revision, the original water images at this point might have been overlooked, or they might have been retained as nothing more than pleasing Petrarchan conceits. This hypothesis is strengthened by the fact that Shakespeare avoids the water image for the rest of the play.

Granted Shakespeare's emphasis on water travel, is it not possible, as Professor Grillo has suggested (pp. 142–144), that Shakespeare is only being careful to conform to the geographical fact that sixteenth-century Verona was an important port for large ships navigating the Adige? It is true that two of the water images are unmistakably river images, and that others could refer as well to river as to sea travel. Julia compares her love to a gentle stream, a current straying to the wild ocean. Launce, hurrying after the departing Proteus, exclaims: "Lose the tide, and the voyage, and the master, and the service, and the tied! Why, man, if the river were dry, I am able to fill it with my tears" (II.iii.56–58). On the other hand, most of the images suggest or unmistakably pertain to sea travel, not river travel. The difficulty is resolved when one remembers that London is on the Thames, and that the Thames, unlike the Adige, soon runs into the sea. Its ships are sea vessels. Down it Julia may follow Proteus "like a current . . . with willing sport to the ocean." From here Valentine may cross his Hellespont to find a Hero. Likewise, the several allusions to tides, more notably characteristic of the Thames, would suggest London to the English audience. Shakespeare may have chosen Verona for his play because it was a port on a navigable river, but the embarkations of Valentine, Proteus, and Julia are more like departures from London than Verona.

This new world into which Proteus comes, to undergo his metamorphosis into an Italianate courtier, like the court in the *Diana*, is fashion conscious. In choosing Milan as the setting, Shakespeare makes use of its popular reputation, not only as the traditional seat of the imperial court but also as an important fashion center and maker of fashionable clothing.[6] Here the Elizabethan would expect to see the "bravery," the "strange accoutrements," the "quaint array" of the Italianated youth.[7]

Shakespeare's periodic allusions to special styles of dress exploit this reputation and keep the audience aware of it. Lucetta, preparing Julia for her journey to Milan, asks, "What fashion, madam, shall I make your breeches?" Then she suggests a codpiece, recalling Nashe's Italianates with their "fewe moath-eaten cod-peece sutes" in *The Terrors of the Night* (1592/3).[8] Valentine's pun on *doublet* and *double* (II.iv.20–21) calls attention to the dress of Thurio and especially to an article of dress whose frequently changing style was an important feature of Renaissance fashion. Likewise, the rather lengthy business of the cloak under which the Duke is to hide a ladder (III.i.130–136) focuses attention on the dress of Valentine and again on a style which attracted considerable comment in the 1590's. The jests about farthingales (II.vii.51; IV.iv.42) direct similar attention to women's styles.[9]

Other fashions come in for comment, too. That "squirrel," Proteus' dog Jewel, is a tenth the size of Crab (IV.iv.51–63). Proteus' expert advice on the "wailful sonnet" and its conceits (III.ii.68–87) is, of course, of a piece with the discussion of fashions in love-making between the Duke and Valentine (III.i.86ff.). Finally, the periodic occurrence of the word *fashion* (II.vii.49–52; III.i.86–135; V.iv.61) carries through as a kind of refrain to this tale of Milan. In the light of all this evidence, might not Valentine's bitter exclamation to Proteus in the final scene carry double meaning: "Thou friend of an ill fashion!"

Like Euphues in Naples, Proteus in Milan eats "sugar with the courtiers of Italy" and addicts himself "wholy to the seruice of women . . . , [his] lands in maintenance of brauerie, [his] witte in the vanities of idle Sonnets."[10] He also begins to show other Italianate traits. He is a "complement-munger" and flatterer. "Thou subtle, perjur'd, false, disloyal man! / Think'st thou I am so shallow, so conceitless, / To be seduced by thy flatter," Sylvia angrily answers his smooth words of courtship. His hypocrisy stands without question, so that his advice to Thurio rings ironic: "Frame some feeling line / That may discover such integrity" (III.ii.75–76). He is a Machiavellian slanderer and plotter (III.ii.31ff.), so gifted in intrigue that he can make Thurio and even the Duke his dupes. Finally, he is the "leacher" in whom "love [obtaines] the name of lust,"[11] at the last guilty even of attempted rape. In this patterned description of an Italianated youth one naturally expects inconstancy and disloyalty.

In the background are the other Milanese, echoing these qualities in Proteus, though they are not so extreme nor so intolerable. Even Valentine, admirable as he is throughout most of the play, is not above advising the Duke in his intrigue for possession of the "lady of Verona" and suggesting the use of flattery. The Duke is a willing partner in Proteus' plot to slander Valentine. Thurio, the third partner, in his way proves as inconstant to Sylvia as Proteus to Julia. The shift from court to woods must have been intended as a welcome relief from the insincerity and immorality of the court. One could hardly expect Proteus' repentance in Milan.

Shakespeare's choice of name for Proteus is a happy one. In the mass of literature in the late sixteenth century attacking the Italianate, the classical Proteus loses his gray beard to become the graceful, showy, fickle, insincere courtier, "ape" of foreign manners, or, sometimes, the foreign courtier living in England. Marlowe, for instance, in *Edward II* (1592) describes Gaveston as wearing

> . . . a lords reuenewe on his back,
> And Midas-like he iets it in the court,
> With base outlandish cullions at his heeles,
> Whose proud fantasticke liueries make such show
> As if that Proteus, god of shapes, appearde. (lines 700–704)

Drayton, in his *Legend of Piers Gaveston* (1596) has Gaveston describe his fellow French courtiers with the same figure:

> Others that stem'd the Current of the Time,
> Whence I had falne, strove suddenly to clime.
> Like the Camelion, whilst Time turnes the hue,
> And with false Proteus puts on sundrie shapes.[12]

Nashe in *Pierce Pennilesse* (1592) describes the Italian as having "more shapes than Proteus" and shifting "himselfe, vppon occasion of revengement, into a mans dish, his drinke. . . ."[13] In *The Beggars Ape* (undated but from context obviously written during Elizabeth's reign), the "ape" takes delight "to play the *Parasite*, / To sooth, to cogge, to fawne, to lye, to sweare," "for neuer more did *Proteus* change his Shape."[14] The dancing courtier in Davies' *Orchestra* (1595) is likewise figured in Proteus:

> Wherefore was Proteus said himself to change
> Into a stream, a lion, a tree,
> And many other forms fantastic strange,
> As in his fickle thought he wished to be?
> But that he danced with such facility . . .

This figure had such connotation for the Elizabethans at least as early as 1584, when Thomas Hudson in the *History of Judith* compares the court flatterer to Proteus.[15] Greene uses it in much the same way in *Morando* (1587).[16] Shakespeare, then, had at hand a name that already suggested to the Elizabethan, not only fickleness, but also other attributes belonging to the conventional concept of the Italianate: youth, insincerity, showy dress.

Shakespeare's use of the motif of the "wry-transformed traveller" acquires additional importance when one sets *The Two Gentlemen of Verona* within the social framework of the 1590's. To assume that because this was a perennial topic for Renaissance writers it did not have particular pertinency around 1590 is to misunderstand the play. While Renaissance England came under the powerful influence of Italy on the one hand, and witnessed with dismay the moral decay of that same Italy and a disturbing revolution in her own youth; on the other hand, certain events around 1590 gave a special timeliness to the issue and put an edge on Elizabethan opinion of the Italianate.

Professor Edwin Greenlaw has called attention "to the hatred of French gallantry and intrigue especially characteristic of these years [circa 1590]."[17] His observation is substantiated by the appearance of works like Spenser's *Mother Hubbard's Tale* (1589?), Marlowe's *Edward II* (1592), Drayton's *Legend of Piers Gaveston* (1596), and the anti-Italianate tales and pamphlets of Nashe and Greene within a few years.

Despite a temporary wave of feeling against the Italianate Earl of Oxford in the 1570's, England had seen hundreds of translations of Italian books, a growing frequency in the visits of traveling Italian actors, a marked increase in the number of Italian grammars and dictionaries, and English books and plays with Italian settings. In this period the vogue of the sonnet and sonnet sequence, with their Petrarchan conceits, was strongest. This influence had reached its peak in the 1580's.[18] But by the time of *The Two Gentlemen of Verona* a reaction had set in, aggravated by the unrest following the execution of Mary Stuart and the defeat of the Armada. These two events, instead of quieting, intensified English fears. The next decade was a period of strong nationalist feeling, marked by hatred of everything foreign. Spaniard, Italian, and Papist were often synonymous, a fact that is not surprising since much of Italy was politically under the Spanish king and thousands of Italians served in the Spanish army.[19] Camden in his *Annals* for 1590 testifies that this feeling often extended to the French: "Some there were who advised . . . not to trust the *French*" because they were "false and treacherous."[20] The growing hatred is reflected in the all-inclusive attacks of Hall and Marston on Italian clothes, vice, poisoning, and English imitations of Italian verse.[21]

In such an atmosphere it is not surprising to find sentiment against foreign travel, and some attempts to restrict it. According to Camden (p. 457), in 1591 it was considered treason to travel in Spain. A letter from a traveller to Italy, preserved in the *Calendar of State Papers* and dated August 1591, answers a censure by Burleigh for spending so much time abroad and shows uncertainty as to the nature "of the restraint in this last traveling license," which seems to close the territories of Venice and Florence to him.[22] An act of the Privy Council in 1593, addressed to the County of Sussex, called for a census of all gentlemen having sons or kinsmen "beyond in the Seas obtaining Education." While this is obviously an anti-espionage measure, much of the language of the order resembles that of current anti-Italianate literature: ". . . the Queenes Majestie finding noe small inconvenience to growe unto the Realme by sending out of the same the Children of many gentlemen under coulour of learning the Languages, whereby they are for the most parte bredd . . . in the Popish religion and corruptness of manners, to the manifest prejudice of the State heere. . . ."[23]

At such a time Shakespeare wrote his tale of the wry-transformed traveller.

To dismiss *The Two Gentlemen of Verona* as only another tale of friendship and love is to misread it. It is primarily the timely story of the Italianated youth in whom false friendship and false love accompany the attempts of the youth to acquire sophistication. Unfortunately the idealized pattern envisioned for the traveling Proteus by Panthino was not realized. Rather, Proteus was to become the Machiavellian plotter, the inconstant. That travel does not always have such drastic effects is illustrated by Valentine, only slightly affected by the lesser vices of the court, who never is at home there so much as Proteus is.

Towards the early Proteus Shakespeare is sympathetic. Towards the repentant Proteus of the Mantuan forest he is forgiving. He is mildly satirical of sonnet fashions (as he is in his own sonnet sequence). He laughs at the fashionable tiny dogs and at foibles in dress. But he has no patience with treachery, intrigue, lust, or inconstancy, whether in Proteus or Thurio—until there is an honest self-appraisal and an honest change of heart. Therefore, one must read this play as comedy. Proteus is no villain in the accepted sense of the word; he is the inexperienced youth being tried and tutored in the world—the Italianate world. This particular youth is finally brought to his senses and is able to profit from his experiences. He is at last neither the untutored youth nor the Machiavel. Like the outlaws, he may be forgiven for "what [he has] committed here." They are all "reformed, civil, full of good, / And fit for great employment."

Here the common sense of Shakespeare speaks out again on a topic that too often was treated hysterically or unfairly. He can smile and he can frown at Proteus, but at the last, knowing that the Proteus of Milan is a passing phase, he accepts him—with his more sensible and less susceptible companion—just as he is later to accept the chastened Jaques of *As You Like It.*

NOTES

1. Jorge de Montemayor, *Los Siete Libros de la Diana,* ed. Francisco Lopez Estrada (Madrid, 1946), pp. 104–105.

2. Bacon in his essay "On Travel" may speak for the many Elizabethan writers on the subject.

3. Martin W. Sampson, ed., *The Two Gentlemen of Verona* (New York, 1923), p. 99.

4. Ernesto Grillo, *Shakespeare and Italy* (Glasgow, 1949), pp. 132–149.

5. In his notes in the Yale Shakespeare.

6. See Edward H. Sugden, *A Topographical Dictionary to the Works of Shakespeare and His Fellow Dramatists* (Manchester, 1925), under "Milan." See also the origin of "milliner" in the *N.E.D.*

7. "I addicted my selfe wholy to the seruice of women to spende my lyfe in the lappes of Ladyes, my lands in the maintenance of brauerie. . . ." John Lyly, in *The Complete Works,* ed. R. Warwick Bond (Oxford, 1902), I, 241.

See also Spenser's description of the Ape in *Mother Hubbard's Tale:* "He was clad in strange accoustrements, / Fashion'd with queint deuises neuer seene / In Court before, yet there all fashions beene" (lines 672–675); Gabriel Harvey's description of the Earl of Oxford as an Italianate, "delicate in speach, queynte in araye, conceited in all poyntes," in *Speculum Tuscanismi* (G. Gregory Smith, ed, *Elizabethan Critical Essays* (Oxford, 1904), I, 107); and Jaques' "strange suits" in *AYLI.*

8. Thomas Nashe, *Works,* ed. Ronald B. McKerrow (London, 1910), I, 361.

9. M. Channing Linthicum, *Costume in the Drama of Shakespeare and His Contemporaries* (Oxford, 1936), pp. 198, 193, 180–182. Iris Brooke, *Western European Costume, Thirteenth to Seventeenth Century, and Its Relation to the Theatre* (London, 1939), pp. 138, 133, 142.

10. See footnote 7.

11. Nashe, op. cit., 10, 220, 361.

"*Italy*, . . . how doth it forme our yong master? . . . It maketh a man an excellent Courtier, a curious carpet knight: which is, by interpretation, a fine close leacher, a glorious hipocrite." Nashe, *Vnfortunate Traveller* (1593) in *Works, cit,* II, 301.

"Such is the contemptuous condition of these Imitators: that there is not any vice particularly noted in any Country, but ye Englishman will be therein as exquisite . . . If it be in . . . *Italy* he can flatter . . . " William Rankin, *The English Ape* (1588). Printed at London by Robert Robinson (photostatic reproduction by the Huntington Library), A3b.A4.

12. Michael Drayton, *Works*, ed. William Hebel (Oxford, 1932), II, 437.

13. Nashe, *Works*, I, 186.

14. Richard Niccols, *The Beggars Ape*, Scholars' Facsimiles & Reprints (1936), B3.

15. Reproduced as Number 510 in Robert Allot, *England's Parnassus*, ed. Charles Crawford (Oxford, 1913).

16. Robert Greene, *Works*, ed. Alexander B. Grosart, Huth Library (1881–1886), III, 148.

17. Quoted in H.S.V. Jones, *A Spenser Handbook* (New York, 1930), p. 100.

18. Lewis Einstein, *The Italian Renaissance in England* (New York, 1913), Chapter IV ("The Italian Danger"). Louis B. Wright, *Middle-Class Culture in Elizabethan England* (Chapel Hill, 1935), p. 403. Mary A. Scott, *Elizabethan Translations from the Italian* (Boston, 1916), pp. xix–xxi, xxvii, xxxi.

19. *Calendar of State Papers, Domestic Series, 1591–94*, pages 110–111, 112–114, 162, 298, 302, 398; *Domestic Series, 1595–97*, pages 60, 103.

20. William Camden, *The History of . . . Princess Elizabeth*, Fourth Edition (London, 1688), p. 443.

21. Einstein, pp. 166–167.

22. *Calendar of State Papers, Domestic Series, 1591–94*, p. 95.

23. *Original Letters Illustrative of English History*, ed. Henry Ellis, Second Series (London, 1827), III, 171–174.

Excerpt from *Shakespeare's Comedies* (1960)

Bertrand Evans

Most immediately, this is the way of *The Two Gentlemen of Verona*. Whereas *The Comedy of Errors* afforded for exploitation only one discrepancy in awareness, all Ephesus being denied and ourselves provided with one all-important fact, *The Two Gentlemen of Verona* exploits multiple gaps that involve no fewer than six notable secrets. The first comedy used no deliberate 'practisers'; the second has almost as many as it has participants. In *The Comedy of Errors* a single, initial expository scene sufficed to establish the single, static situation, open the single gap between awarenesses, and sustain our single advantage over participants for all of five acts; in *The Two Gentlemen of Verona* the first two acts are used to create the principal situation and open the main gaps, and thereafter repeated expository passages, including asides and soliloquies, are added to keep the circle of our vision complete. Whereas in the earlier play the participants remained equally ignorant of the situation, here we share with one participant our advantage over others with respect to one part of the situation, and with another participant our advantage with respect to another part of it. In *The Comedy of Errors* the single exploitable gap lay between all the participants on the one side and ourselves on the other. But in *The Two Gentlemen* Shakespeare makes use of differences in awareness between participant and participant, besides those between participants and ourselves: the fact represents a great step from the earlier comedy toward the mature ones.

All the named persons of *The Two Gentlemen* except the clowns—who here as hereafter, like the heroines of comedy and the villains of tragedy, are commonly immune to the condition of unawareness—stand at one time or another ignorant of some relevant fact. On the other hand, each of these persons except Thurio sometime holds advantage over another par-

Reprinted from *Shakespeare's Comedies*. Oxford: Clarendon Press, 1960, pp. 9–19.

ticipant; each, that is to say, serves either as a secret-holder or as a perpetrator of practices on others. We are provided with advantage over some participant or other during nine of nineteen scenes—a much lower proportion than in *The Comedy of Errors*.

In summary, although alike in that both make large use of exploitable discrepancies in awareness, the two plays contrast markedly in the complexity which characterizes their paraphernalia of exploitation. The first is Roman in this respect, the second Elizabethan, elaborate. The *Two Gentlemen* is clearly on the high road to *Twelfth Night*.

Although Shakespeare does not begin until the third act to exploit the main discrepancies, two scenes in Act II deserve notice as the first in which we hold advantage over participants and also as prophetic of greater scenes in later plays. In II.i we share with Silvia and Speed an advantage over Valentine. "Last night," says Valentine to his servant, "she enjoin'd me to write some lines to one she loves." Since we have not yet seen Silvia or otherwise been prepared, we cannot know just yet that her request is in fact a way of hinting her interest in Valentine and of inviting him to woo her. Indeed, it is uncertain at what exact point in the ensuing dialogue the dramatist intends us to catch on:

> *Val.* As you enjoin'd me, I have writ your letter
>   Unto the secret nameless friend of yours;
>   Which I was much unwilling to proceed in
>   But for my duty to your ladyship.
> *Sil.* I thank you, gentle servant. 'Tis very clerkly done.
> *Val.* Now trust me, madam, it came hardly off;
>   For being ignorant to whom it goes
>   I writ at random, very doubtfully.
> *Sil.* Perchance you think too much of so much pains?
> *Val.* No, madam; so it stead you, I will write,
>   Please you command, a thousand times as much;
>   And yet—
> *Sil.* A pretty period! Well, I guess the sequel;
>   And yet I will not name it; and yet I care not;
>   And yet take this again; and yet I thank you,
>   Meaning henceforth to trouble you no more. (II.i.110–25)

By the time of Silvia's final speech, certainly, we have gained advantage over Valentine; even Speed, by this time, perceives the truth, for he remarks, aside, "And yet you will; and yet another 'yet.'" But Valentine—true prototype of heroes and secondary heroes of comedies to come, of Orlando, Orsino, Claudio, Bassanio, some better, some worse, but all essentially obtuse, less aware than heroines—does not glimpse it, either here or during the next eighty lines, though Speed exhausts himself with pointing out the truth:

> My master sues to her, and she hath taught her suitor,
> He being her pupil, to become her tutor.
> O excellent device! was there ever heard a better,
> That my master, being scribe, to himself should write the letter?
> (Ibid. 143–6)

With this device Silvia becomes the first practiser in the play, Valentine the first victim whose ignorance is exploited for comic effect.

The second scene in which we hold advantage ends Act II. Here the discrepancy in awareness is exploited not for loud laughter, as in the scene just noted and as throughout *The Comedy of Errors,* but for subtler effect of a kind Shakespeare would seek again and again by means of adroit manipulation of the awarenesses. It will be well, therefore, to examine in detail this first of a frequent kind.

This is a scene of ninety lines between Julia and her waiting woman, Lucetta. It is primarily expository, existing to inform us of Julia's intention to dress in weeds "As may beseem some well-reputed page" and seek out Proteus in Milan. As an expository scene announcing this purpose, it is forerunner of many: of Portia and Nerissa, leaving Belmont for the Venetian Court-room; of Rosalind and Celia, fleeing to the forest of Arden; of Viola and her sea captain, as she prepares to invade Orsino's court; of Helena, leaving the palace of the Countess to track down Bertram; of Imogen, with Pisanio, setting off for Milford-Haven to find Posthumus. Like some of these, it is a gay scene:

> *Luc.* What fashion, Madam, shall I make Your breeches?
> *Jul.* That fits as well as, 'Tell me, good my lord,
>   What compass will you wear your farthingale?'
>   Why even what fashion thou best likes, Lucetta.
> *Luc.* You must needs have them with a codpiece, madam.
> *Jul.* Out, out, Lucetta! (II.vii.49–54)

The vein is richer than mere jest, however; it is a fresh, lyrical scene, in which Julia's eager youth and beauty, and her love for Proteus, shine out:

Then let me go, and hinder not my course.
I'll be as patient as a gentle stream,
And make a pastime of each weary step,
Till the last step have brought me to my love;
And there I'll rest, as after much turmoil
A blessed soul doth in Elysium. (Ibid. 33–38)

Viewed only in its own light, with nothing before or after, it would be a sparkling scene, its qualities of love, youth, wit, and lyricism rendering it pleasing and dramatic. But it is not to be viewed only in its own light.

Shakespeare has equipped our minds with special knowledge just before he shows this scene. The scene just preceding it, set in Milan, is all composed of a sharply pointed soliloquy uttered by Proteus, in which he expresses determination to commit "three fold perjury," by leaving Julia, loving Silvia, and betraying Valentine. The lines of this soliloquy are emphatic, as though the dramatist meant their impression to be indelible:

I to myself am dearer than a friend,
For love is still most precious in itself;
And Silvia—witness Heaven, that made her fair!—
Shows Julia but a swarthy Ethiope.
I will forget that Julia is alive,
Rememb'ring that my love to her is dead
And Valentine—I'll hold an enemy,
Aiming at Silvia as a sweeter friend. (II.vi.23–30)

Immediately the scene shifts to Verona, where we hear Julia asking Lucetta to tell her "How, with my honour, I may undertake / A journey to my loving Proteus." Proteus's soliloquy inevitably casts a special light over what follows—a light which is surely as much a part of the total scene as the dialogue itself. Julia's expression of devotion to Proteus, the merriment as the girls plan her costume, Lucetta's doubts and Julia's certainties—our view of all this is conditioned by Proteus's soliloquy; seen by a double light, its own and that from Proteus's soliloquy, the whole takes on a richness which, though inferior to that of the great scenes of later comedies, is yet precious enough. It is not merely for the bold flashes of irony that starkly outline the gap between Julia's awareness and ours—

But truer stars did govern Proteus' birth;
His words are bonds, his oaths are oracles,

His love sincere, his thoughts immaculate,

His tears pure messengers sent from his heart,

His heart as far from fraud as heaven from earth. (II.vii.74–78)

—that the dramatic effect is notable; flashes of irony are the most spectacular but not always the richest effects produced by exploitation of discrepant awarenesses. In the fuller scenes of mature comedies it will be appropriate to distinguish the subtler, pervasive effects from the flashier surface manifestations. It may suffice to say here only that the Julia-Lucetta scene, exhibited under the special light of Proteus's soliloquy, anticipates these finer effects of later scenes.

In the scene just reviewed our advantage owes simply to the device of scene-placement, the dramatist having immediately preceded the particular action by a speech calculated to cast a transforming light on it. The deliberateness of this placement is itself noteworthy. The soliloquy spoken by Proteus could easily have been placed not to precede but to follow the Julia-Lucetta scene. It would then have occurred at the opening of Act III, and the action which at present opens Act III could then have gone straight ahead, with no interruption, directly after the soliloquy. Again, the soliloquy could readily have been incorporated in Proteus's earlier soliloquy which closes II.iv, where it would have joined on smoothly. Either of these placements would have been less awkward than that which in fact Shakespeare chose. But had he placed the soliloquy after rather than before the Julia-Lucetta scene, we should have lacked its special light as we watched that scene; coming afterward, it would of course have cast some light back upon the scene already played, and in retrospect we might have caught a little of the irony of Julia's lines. *But almost invariably Shakespeare preferred to project light forward upon a scene to be played rather than to cast it backward on action already past.* On the other hand, he regularly avoided setting his light-casting scene too far in advance of the action it should illuminate, lest intervening action blur the effect. In this instance, had the second Proteus soliloquy been incorporated in the first, which ends II.iv, the Speed-Launce dialogue of II.v would have intervened before the Julia-Lucetta scene. It is a mark of Shakespeare's method from the first that he took no risks with effects he intended: when he provided us with a special advantage over participants, he took care to make this advantage active in our awareness at the moment of its greatest usefulness. Since, thus, Julia was to say "tell me some good means / How, with my honour, I may undertake / A journey to my loving Proteus," Shakespeare's method required that we hear Proteus say—neither afterwards, nor several scenes before, but immediately before—"I will forget that Julia is alive."

Dramatically the most significant speech in the play, Proteus's light-casting second soliloquy is indispensable both to our view of the Julia-Lucetta scene and to our view of the three subsequent acts. It contributes greatly to the disposition of awarenesses with which Act III opens—the first truly complex disposition that Shakespeare had attempted in comedy. Excepting the clowns, all persons who take part in Act III are ignorant of one or another crucial fact of the situation. Moreover, the participants are stationed on different levels of awareness, some higher, some lower, rising from Thurio at the bottom to Proteus at the top. Excepting Thurio, every principal person attempts deception, with Proteus as the outtopping practiser. It is the Duke who stands on the lowest level when the act opens, as Proteus, feigning reluctance, exposes Valentine's elopement plan:

> Know, noble lord, they have devis'd a mean
> How he her chamber-window will ascend
> And with a corded ladder fetch her down. (III.i.38–40)

Proteus speaks truthfully in that Valentine does intend to carry off Silvia—but the Duke is nevertheless deceived because he knows nothing of the motives which Proteus exhibited to us in that same indispensable soliloquy which earlier gave us advantage over Julia. So the Duke thanks Proteus, and, himself unwitting, lays a trap for the unsuspecting Valentine, who, being practised on by one who is himself ignorant, accordingly replaces the Duke on the lowest level of awareness. Yet Valentine, entering immediately after Proteus has exposed the elopement plan, supposes himself to occupy a vantage point above the Duke's, and, knowing nothing of Proteus's practices, supposes that no point higher than his own exists. Hiding beneath his coat the corded ladder he expects to use, he is privileged, as he imagines, to relish his advantage. With Silvia's image in his mind and the ladder under his cloak, being asked how one may woo, win, and wed "a lady of Verona here" whom the Duke pretends to affect, he replies boldly, describing the details of reaching her chamber "aloft, far from the ground, / And built so shelving that one cannot climb it / Without apparent hazard of his life"—

> Why then, a ladder, quaintly made of cords,
> To cast up, with a pair of anchoring hooks,
> Would serve to scale another Hero's tower. (Ibid. 117–19)

Such a ladder, he brazenly suggests, might be hidden under just such a cloak as his own. The cat-and-mouse game here played between Proteus's two mice, each supposing himself the cat, extends through eighty-five lines, until the Duke snatches off Valentine's cloak and exposes the ladder and a sonnet to Silvia. With that act, of course, which equalizes the awarenesses of the two, the main exploitable discrepancy on which depend the effects of the scene vanishes, leaving only Proteus's unsuspected vantage-point above them, and above all others.

Or so Proteus supposes. Throughout Act III, like a minor Iago, he overpeers, deceives, and manipulates Valentine, the Duke, and Thurio. In the dialogue that follows the Duke's banishment of Valentine, Proteus consoles his friend, brings him the latest news, advises him, seems solicitous for his safety, offers to escort him to the city-gate, and, with Valentine gone, he turns his attention to stealing Silvia under the very auspices of the Duke and Thurio. As though reluctant, he promises to slander Valentine, and, as he "unwinds" Silvia's former love, promises "to bottom it" on Thurio. The Duke and Thurio urge him on in perfect confidence, for, as the Duke says,

> . . . we know, on Valentine's report,
> You are already Love's firm votary
> And cannot soon revolt and change your mind. (Ibid. 257–9)

Thus throughout Act III Proteus rides high over the others, exulting in his position, practising on them all. But even as the Julia-Lucetta scene which ends Act II is changed by Proteus's soliloquy which immediately precedes it, so the effect of Act III is transformed by the Julia-Lucetta scene. For while we watch Proteus's confident manipulation of Valentine, the Duke, and Thurio, we hold an advantage that makes his villainy laughable rather than dangerous: we know that as he is making his triply treacherous play for Silvia, Julia, habited like "some well-reputed page," is on the road to Milan. Though still ignorant of Proteus's duplicity, she must surely discover it before Proteus learns that all his passes are observed. *The heroines of Shakespeare's comedies either hold from the outset, or very shortly gain, the highest vantage-point in their worlds.* Julia is the first of these heroines, and Proteus, from our point of view, can appear only a somewhat taller mouse than his own dupes, Valentine, the Duke, and Thurio.

In Act IV, still working his imagined advantage, Proteus continues his successful practice on the dull Thurio, but fails miserably in his attempts to deceive the heroines. From any point of view, perhaps, but certainly from that of the management of awarenesses, the finest scene of this act is the serenade of Silvia, ostensibly for Thurio's but in reality for Proteus's own purposes. The song to Silvia, exquisite in itself, certainly unmatched by any ear-

lier lyric of Shakespeare's and possibly by any afterwards, is at the same time
transformed by its context, which exists, as the scene progresses, only in our
own minds. In our perspective, the song is itself a practice by Proteus directly upon Thurio, indirectly upon the Duke, Valentine, Julia, and Silvia
herself. Moreover, with great shrewdness, Shakespeare has made it virtually
impossible for us to lay aside our awareness of the total situation while we
hear the song, for he has opened the scene with a new soliloquy which prods
our recollection of Proteus's perfidy. We are thus prompted to hear the song
not in itself alone, but in its special meanings for the participants who hear
it, and particularly we are kept mindful of Valentine, who, though absent,
has with Julia the keenest interest in any wooing of Silvia by Proteus. To
Thurio, quite oblivious, nothing is apparent in the situation or the song itself except what is obvious and quite wrong: it seems to him that his own
suit to Silvia is being forwarded. To Proteus, gloating in his sense that he
alone comprehends all that is happening, the song is a device for betraying
everyone and winning Silvia for himself. To the Host, to whom the details
of the situation are quite irrelevant, it is only a lovely song in the night. To
Silvia, while the music plays, it is hardly more than a flattering serenade for
which she thanks the unknown musicians. But when she hears Proteus speak,
her quick wit catches the full import:

> Thou subtle, perjur'd, false, disloyal man!
> Think'st thou I am so shallow, so conceitless,
> To be seduced by thy flattery,
> That hast deceiv'd so many with thy vows? (IV.ii.95–98)

But what, now, is it to Julia? It is her presence, "unobserved, in boy's
clothes," that most transforms the scene. Like Silvia, she catches the significance of the song, which advises her of Proteus's treachery with jolting
abruptness. Entering with the Host just before the music began, she had had
no more doubts of Proteus than the intuitive ones that had inspired her journey to Milan. But when the song is done, she has caught on, and our real-
ization of the effect of the song upon Julia is, then, the key factor in its effect upon ourselves. The effect is complex in character, bearing the forces
of both pleasure and pain. The song is a thing of exquisite beauty; yet it
pierces the heart of Julia—but, again, Julia is resilient, capable of swift recovery, and, besides, her position is actually improved by this experience.
She had left Verona in ignorance, and now, having heard the serenade and
the conversation of Proteus and Silvia, she knows all. Her discovery raises
her abruptly to our level of awareness. Unobserved, she has observed

Proteus's passes, heard his lies, recognized Silvia's integrity, and at the end of the scene is quite ready—like her very capable heroinely successors—to use her advantage for victory: "Pray you, where lies Sir Proteus?" It is not she, but Proteus, suddenly the hunted rather than the hunter, who is now to be pitied. Fallen from top place in the scheme of awarenesses, he is lost and does not know it.

The inferiority of his position is conspicuous in IV.ii, when, oblivious, he dispatches his disguised and watchful mistress to woo Silvia for him—sending a ring that Julia had once given him. If Julia's situation is hardly a happy one, yet neither is it desperate. Her vision has full sweep; she is perfect mistress of her situation, and knows it. So absolute is her advantage that she can pity her prodigal lover, who, in confident obliviousness, has chosen an inappropriate love-emissary.

In his relation to Julia, then, Proteus the practiser has become the practisee, she the practiser: he is under her eye, his waywardness observed, his duplicity exposed. In relation to Silvia he is no better off. She has recognized and castigated his hypocrisy from the first. And now, immediately before the scene in which Proteus sends Julia to woo Silvia, Shakespeare has set a scene which lights the latter and displays a further depth in Proteus's unawareness. For in the preceding scene Silvia tells us that she will go to find Valentine in Mantua, "where I hear he makes abode." The true position of Proteus, then, is hardly enviable: supposing himself the master practiser with all strings in hand, he sends as love-envoy his own mistress, who can cross him at need; and she to whom the messenger is sent has already arranged to leave the city. The case of Proteus, hero bent on making a villain of himself, is typical: in the comedies, villainy can but peep at what it would, for it is circumscribed and rendered impotent, if not ridiculous, by the bright-eyed heroines who with their superior awareness control everything in this woman's world.

The gap between Proteus's awareness and ours continues as the principal exploitable condition during Act V. Here not only is Julia constantly at his elbow, her disguised presence reminding us of the true state of things, but, within this situation, Shakespeare contrives to set him at a further disadvantage in relation to both Silvia and Valentine. Act V.ii, when Proteus and Thurio discuss Silvia while Julia speaks "asides," is noteworthy as showing Shakespeare's first use of four simultaneous levels of awareness. At the top is our own awareness, packed with all the facts of the situation: that Silvia has fled the court (as the dramatist, taking no chances with our forgetfulness, has just reminded us in the preceding scene); that Proteus's page, "Sebastian," is in fact his betrothed Julia; that Proteus supposes himself to have deceived Julia, the Duke, Valentine, and Thurio in his wooing of Silvia and that he is now in the act of deceiving Thurio by reporting his progress with Thurio's love suit. On the level just below ours stands Julia, possessed of all our facts but one: that Silvia has fled the court. Below Julia is Proteus, who is ignorant that Silvia has gone, ignorant that Julia is beside him, and aware only that Thurio is deceived. And at the bottom is Thurio, who here as before and after is wrong about everything. The dialogue which exploits the gaps between these levels is itself not so remarkable as is this first appearance of the stair-stepped structure of awarenesses which becomes a fixture in the climactic scenes of subsequent comedies.

In the final scene of the play the disposition and uses of awareness again significantly mark the direction of Shakespeare's development. The preparation of our minds for this scene was begun far, far back—when Julia first took up her boy's masquerade. It continued through to Act IV, when Valentine became the outlaws' captain on his own terms:

> I take your offer and will live with you,
> Provided that you do no outrages
> On silly women or poor passengers. (IV.i.70–72)

When in IV.iii, therefore, fleeing the court to seek Valentine in Mantua, Silvia fears for her safety—"And, for the ways are dangerous to pass, / I do desire thy worthy company"—we have had reason enough to know that this forest is safe for her. Even so, in the third scene of Act V, when she is caught by outlaws, the dramatist—making doubly sure that we shall feel no alarm for Silvia's safety—again reminds us that no harm can befall her; for in the first line of the scene the First Outlaw, struggling with his captive, commands her, "Be patient; we must bring you to our captain"—who, of course, can be none but Valentine. When Proteus snatches Silvia from the outlaws, it is noteworthy that Shakespeare neither shows her in his company—more dangerous to her than the outlaws—nor even lets us know that he has taken her, until we have again been assured that all is well. The final scene opens with Valentine's brief soliloquy which ends abruptly at the approach of Proteus, Silvia, and Julia: "Withdraw thee, Valentine; who's this comes here?" And thereafter, lest the excitement of threatened violence to Silvia make us forget Valentine's comforting presence, Shakespeare has him speak an "aside" to remind us that he is at hand, hearing, observing, armed, and ready to act.

Once more, then, in this final moment, it is this comedy's eager but thwarted representative of villainy who stands in the inferior place, unwittingly circumscribed and impotent. Proteus is doubly, pitifully unaware: for not only is Valentine, Silvia's betrothed, hidden within a sword's length of him, but also, at his side, disguised, is his own betrothed. When, therefore, rebuffed, he turns savage and seizes Silvia with "I'll force thee yield to my desire," we perceive that any real peril in the situation is his, not hers. For Silvia, knowing no more than Proteus of the presence of Julia and Valentine and accordingly in mortal terror, the truth apparent to us is much better than she imagines; for Proteus it is far worse. Hemmed in, he can only expose himself to humiliation. Such is always the plight of the villain in the comedies: as Proteus in *The Two Gentlemen of Verona,* so also Shylock in *The Merchant of Venice,* Don John in *Much Ado about Nothing,* and Angelo in *Measure for Measure.* Not only cannot villainy harm innocence; it is even prevented from doing irreparable harm to itself.

Two Clowns in a Comedy (to say nothing of the Dog): Speed, Launce (and Crab) in *The Two Gentlemen of Verona* (1963)

Harold F. Brooks

Despite warm appreciation of Launce as a comic character, it has often been denied that he and Speed have an organic part in the structure of *The Two Gentlemen of Verona*. According to Professor H.B. Charlton, for instance, "Launce has no real right within the play except that gentlemen must have servants, and Elizabethan audiences must have clowns."[1] This is to see the dramatic structure too exclusively in terms of plot.[2] There does appear to be only a single place where the behaviour of one of the clowns contributes to the progress of events; the critical moment when Julia, disguised as "Sebastian," seeks service with her truant Proteus. Here, Proteus is influenced by Launce's recent misconduct: he is the readier to enlist the well-bred Sebastian because Launce has been missing for two days, and by the account he now gives of himself is proved too boorish to be entrusted with further missions to Silvia. Without question, dramatic unity is stronger when, as with Bottom or Dogberry, the clown impinges upon the romantic plot more obviously and decisively than this. There can be unity however, resulting from development of theme as well as from development of plot: when a play has a plot and themes, the *action* (which is what must have unity) may be regarded as comprising the development of both.[3] Side by side with the causal sequence that carries forward his romantic plot, Shakespeare, in the parts he has given to Speed and Launce, is developing his play by means of comic parallels that illustrate and extend its themes. The parallels, as well as the causal sequence, are part of the organic structure.

They have not gone altogether unrecognized. "*Two Gentlemen* is . . . more integrated and patterned than has often been supposed," writes Professor Danby in the *Critical Quarterly* (Winter, 1960); and although it is not his purpose to demonstrate the particular pattern I am concerned with, he remarks an item of it: "Even Launce and his dog going through the pan-

---

Reprinted from *Essays and Studies* 16 (1963): 91–100.

tomime of leave-taking translate the central seriousness into a comic mode."
The existence of the pattern, and half a dozen of its leading features, were
emphasized by R.W. Bond in the old Arden edition (1906); he was the editor of Lyly, and familiar with the same technique in him. Had Bond's observation been fully accepted, and his fifteen lines on the subject been followed
up, there might have been no occasion, by this time, to say more. But in the
New Cambridge Shakespeare edition (1921) Quiller-Couch took no notice
of them; and Professor T.W. Baldwin's reference, in *William Shakspere's Five-
Act Structure* (1947), is sceptical, perhaps because he is thinking more in
terms of characters than of themes: "Bond, indeed, has suggested," he writes,
"that several is a comic foil to and partial parody of his master, but this appears true to me only in its most general sense."

The themes in question are those of friendship and love, the first and
second subjects of *Two Gentlemen*, which, as in *The Knight's Tale* and some
of Shakespeare's own sonnets, are treated in relation to each other. The friendship is that which in Renaissance literature is constantly held up as an exemplar of noble life.[4] The love is courtly.[5] Julia, seeming at first full of "daunger,"
soon reveals her "pité,"[6] and later sets out as Love's pilgrim. Valentine, like
Troilus in Chaucer, begins as the Love-heretic, but quickly becomes the penitent votary. Proteus, from Love-idolator falls to Love-traitor, until reclaimed
and redeemed from his treachery both to love and friendship by the sacrificial fidelity of his lover and the sacrificial magnanimity of his friend. Thurio
is Love's Philistine, and the clowns, in this pattern, are Love's plebeians.

From Launce's first entry, each of his scenes refers, by burlesque parallels, to the themes of friendship on the one hand and of love on the other.
Speed's scenes earlier, so far as I can see, do not depend on this particular
sort of parallelism: Speed is not shown in burlesque roles as lover or friend,
except momentarily, when he explains a piece of negligence, comparable to
his love-lorn master's, by confessing he was in love with his bed. The scenes
for the clowns are mostly built up from comic turns. Together, they play at
cross-questions and crooked answers; Launce has his monologue of imper-
sonations with the aid of comic "props," and Speed on his first appearance
(I.i) has his mock-disputation (like Dromio of Syracuse) and his routine of
witty begging (like Feste).[7] The episode, all the same, is not irrelevant
clownage. It underlines at a single stroke both Proteus' friendship and his
love: the friendship with Valentine has allowed him to make Speed, his
friend's man not his own, carry his love-letter to Julia. So, at the onset, a
clown is linked with both themes. Speed reports Julia "hard as steel," thus
preparing for the next scene of her metamorphosis to the compassionate
lover. Proteus has exclaimed already:

the motif is implied in his name, and belongs especially to him: yet Julia and Valentine are each to know metamorphoses, too. In the mock-disputation and its sequel here, this motif (as elsewhere in Shakespeare) is accompanied by imagery of human beings as animals. Speed (or alternatively Valentine) is a "sheep," and he and Julia are "muttons." He is, moreover, a "lost mutton," and in literal fact is search of his master: he is in peril of failing to sail with him, a serious defection. The situation, then, and some of the backchat, are in keeping with a drama where defection, near-loss, and seeking are to be important: where Proteus' defection is almost to lose him his true self,[9] and cause him to be lost to Valentine and Julia; where Valentine is almost to lose Silvia, and the heroines must seek their lovers. Among the clown-scenes themselves, two others form a series with this one. Launce at his parting (II.iii) is likewise in danger of missing the ship, and is warned that he would thereby lose his master and his service. And his ultimate dismissal in favour of "Sebastian" (IV.iv) echoes not only that warning, but Proteus' final comment on Speed here, that he is too unprepossessing a love-messenger and another must be found.

Some of these correspondences an audience will never be consciously aware of, though it will be affected by them. In the next clown-episode, in II.i, everyone sees the relation between Speed's humour and Valentine's high-flown romance. Speed comments directly on his master's love-melancholy. In taking over Valentine's former part as critic of love's absurdities, he helps to mark the metamorphosis:[10] the critic of Proteus' love has become vulnerable to similar criticism himself. The parallels are brought out when Speed quotes him on Proteus and tells him he is blinder now than Proteus was. As critics of love, Speed and Valentine are not, of course, the same. With the eye of yet unconverted scepticism, Valentine had seen its irrationality and its exactions; with the plebeian eye, permanently limited though clear, Speed sees its absence of practical common sense. In one respect, his function is that of the Duck and the Goose in Chaucer's Council of Birds, assembled on St. Valentine's Day. Love in the courtly manner, partly because it is so stylized, is very liable, once we entertain an inadequate, everyday view of it, to arouse mere mockery and impatience. Aware of this, both Chaucer and Shakespeare embody the dangerous attitude within the poem or play itself, so as to control and place it; but they place it somewhat differently. In Chaucer, the plebeian view, whatever sympathy he may have with it outside the poem, is introduced chiefly to be rejected. But when Speed protests that while his master may dine on Silvia's favour, he himself needs meat, this is not "a parfit resoun of a goos": it commands sympathy within the ambit of the play, and partial assent: it is one contribution to the complex dramatic image of courtly love that Shakespeare is building up.

In contrast, there is the admired elegance of the device by which Silvia confesses her love for Valentine. The dullness which prevents his understanding it is a perfectly orthodox effect of love-melancholy;[11] besides, as her true "servant" he has too much humility to be expecting any such confession. That so ultracourtly a gambit has to be explained to him by the uncourtly Speed is humorous enough. And it is ironical that Speed should do him this office of a good friend in his love, when his courtly friend Proteus is soon to be his false rival. Diffidently blind here in love, Valentine is to be too rashly and confidingly blind in friendship. The theme of blindness and sight, especially lovesight, is one of the most central in the play. It is because Proteus' fancy is bred only in his eyes, which until the dénouement see no further than outward beauty, that he is altogether unstable.[12] The truest praise of Silvia is that

> Love doth to her eyes repair
> To help him of his blindness.[13]

The theme continually recurs; and in the present scene the greater part of Speed's cut-and-thrust with Valentine relates to it: "Love is blind," "if you love her you cannot see her," and the rest, from Valentine's question, on the marks of the lover, "Are all these things perceived in me?" to Speed's, on Silvia's "invisible" stratagem, "But did you perceive her earnest?"[14]

From Launce's entry, the relation between the clown episodes and the leading themes, of love and friendship, becomes simpler to describe; for it rests quite evidently throughout on the principle of comic parallelism. One has of course to bear in mind that in Elizabethan as in medieval work, burlesque need not mean belittlement of what is burlesqued.

The scene of Launce's parting (II.iii) is a counterpoise to the high courtly parting of friends, with which Valentine and Proteus open the play. More directly, it is the humorous sequel to the scene of pathos which it follows, the lovers' parting between Proteus and Julia (II.ii). One phrase, on Launce's sister, "as white as a lily and as small as a wand," is in the very idiom of love-romance. Proteus has punned emotionally on the tide or season of his departure, and Julia's "tide of tears;" Launce puns outrageously on the tide and "the tied," namely Crab. At the end of the lovers' scene, Julia, weeping, has made her escape in silence: "Alas!" cries Proteus in his exit-line, "this parting strikes poor lovers dumb." The clown enters in tears, but voluble, and in his monologue re-enacts the weeping of all his kin. Crab's silence is taken otherwise than Julia's; unaccompanied by tears, it is supposed to betoken hardness of heart, and gives his master great offence. Attempting to identify the *dramatis personae* of the reenactment with the "props" available, Launce confuses himself completely, and in this self-confusion about identities the comic mode of his monologue chimes with what Professor Baldwin[15] has called the inward self-travesty of Proteus and the outward self-travesty of Julia, soon to be seen, and indeed with the whole theme of true identity and its recognition. The final claim Launce makes for his tears and sighs is likewise in tune with what is to happen. If he did miss the tide, he declares, they would float him and waft him to overtake Proteus. To overtake Proteus is just what Julia's love-sorrow, of which they are the comic counterparts, will shortly impel her to do.

The reunion of Launce and Speed in Milan (II.v) immediately succeeds that of the friends, their masters; and their dialogue comments on the love-theme. It is certain, Launce tells his comrade, that it will be a match between Proteus and Julia. Proteus has just left the stage soliloquizing on his change of allegiance, and is about to return resolving to court Silvia as though Julia were dead. Yet in the end, Launce will prove right after all. Again, he furnishes a comic reminder of the discretion proper in communicating love-secrets even to the bosom-friend. His display of caution ("Thou shalt never get such a secret from me but by parable") contrasts with Valentine's indiscreet disclosure to Proteus of the plans for his elopement, a disclosure made in the previous scene (II.iv). In the next (II.vi) Proteus determines on betraying his friend's confidence to the Duke. His entry alone, meditating this treachery, is set against the amicable exit of Speed and Launce, going off "in Christian charity" to drink together.

The episode of Launce and his letter (which ends III.i) affords even more striking parallels with both the love and friendship themes. It evokes comparison with the two romantic letter-scenes earlier (I.ii,II.i): Julia receiving Proteus' love-letter, and Silvia giving Valentine the love-letter she has made him write on her behalf. In burlesque contrast with Julia's emotion and Silvia's graceful device, Launce's letter is a step towards a bargain in the marriage-market. It is a report from a go-between on the merits and demerits of his intended; and on the strength of it he makes up his mind to have her, because though toothless she is well-off. This love-transaction, which is not pursued in the courtly way, by courtship of the lady, and which is clinched by mercenary considerations, clean against the canon of true love, casts a light on the next scene (III.ii) and its sequel (IV.ii). Here, by the courtliest kind of courtship—a serenade—but no less against the canon of true love, the assault upon Silvia's loyalty to Valentine is planned on behalf of the foolish Thurio, whom her father prefers for his wealth, and is used by the faithless Proteus as cover for own pursuit of her. Beside the moral deformity of Proteus' conduct in love, the comic deformity of Launce's is as nothing.

When the letter-episode begins, we have just seen Valentine banished, in consequence of having enlisted Proteus' counsel about the elopement. Launce soliloquizes on Proteus' knavery, and his own secrecy: "I love . . . but what woman I will not tell myself"—burlesquing at once the code and Valentine's breach of it. Then, like Valentine, he enlists a confidant; and like Proteus, betrays his friend. He cajoles Speed into helping him read the letter, and rejoices that Speed will earn a beating by it. Though the roles are switched (since the confidant, not the confider, is betrayed), the parallel is clear.

Launce's last monologue, just before his dismissal by Proteus and from the play (IV.iv), is of course his tale of Crab's crimes at court, with his own quixotic devotion and fidelity to the ungrateful, ill-conditioned cur. It comes almost straight after Proteus' nocturnal courtship of Silvia, in triple treachery to Julia, Valentine, and Thurio; and between the arrival of Julia in her devotion and fidelity, only to witness this treachery of his (IV.ii), and her taking service with him (in IV.iv), ungrateful and ill-conducted as she has found him. "When a man's servant shall play the cur"—so Launce starts his complaint of Crab, and so Proteus might complain of Launce himself, "who still . . . turns [him] to shame." But we have heard this word "servant" repeated in the sense of "courtly lover": what when a lady's "servant" shall play the cur? Yet Julia does not refuse the quixotic task of bearing Proteus' love-plea to her unwilling rival.[16]

I am hinting a comparison of Proteus with Crab; and I do not think it extravagant, provided one is not too serious about it, to see reflected in Crab, comically and a little pathetically, the transgressor in Proteus. The want of sensibility to old ties and to his friend Launce's feelings which Crab is alleged to show at parting from home, is ominous as a parallel to Proteus' parting from Julia and impending reunion with Valentine. As a present for Silvia, Crab resembles the love the Proteus proffers her. He is a sorry changeling for the true love gift Proteus meant to bestow. He is unfit for Silvia (persecuting her with most objectionable attentions!), and offensive where true courtliness should rule. Like Proteus, he gets his friend into trouble. And as Crab is only saved by Launce's quixotic, self-sacrificial affection, so Proteus is only saved by the extremes to which Valentine is ready to carry his friendship and Julia her love. From them Proteus learns his lesson. As in *Love's*

Labour's Lost, an opening debate in which love and education were pitted against each other has led into a drama of education in and through love. The theme of education is touched occasionally in the earlier clown-scenes (Speed has been corrected for inordinate love—of his bed), but it appears more plainly when Launce reproaches Crab: "did I not bid thee still mark me, and do as I do?" Crab cannot learn; but Proteus learns the value of constancy from the example and reproaches of Julia, Valentine, and Silvia.[17] Whether Crab says ay or no, and whatever the antics of Proteus the transgressor,[18] it is a match between the regenerate Proteus and his Julia. Yet with all this, Crab is the clown's dog, not a symbol or a piece of allegory: I mean simply to suggest that the impression the dog makes on an audience has this various aptness to the main action and its themes.

The structural use of parallels between main and subsidiary actions, in conjunction with plot or otherwise, is not infrequent in our drama. In subsequent plays of Shakespeare's there are many examples. Hal's interview with his father is rehearsed beforehand in Eastcheap, and Malvolio, no less than Orsino and Olivia, cherishes an illusory ideal of love. The underplot of *The Changeling* owes its relevance to the same technique. But while Bond was right to discern it in *Two Gentlemen,* he was in error when he traced it solely to Lyly. It was not initiated, as he seems to have thought, by *Endimion:* it unites the comic and serious actions in the *Secunda Pastorum,* (*c.* mid-fifteenth century) and in *Fulgens and Lucres (c.* 1500). It is not confined to plays "in two tones"; the most famous instance of all is the double plot of *King Lear.* It is something to look for before assessing a dramatist's construction. Congreve's intrigue-plots are not among the finest features of his art, but he is a master of construction in parallel, witness the successive quarrel-scenes in the second Acts of *Love for Love* and *The Way of the World;* and the fourth Act of the latter, made up of contrasted wooings. In Shaw's *Major Barbara,* the organic contribution of the first episode is better appreciated when we recognize the parallelism of theme: the play is about different kinds of power, and the opening shows the sort of power Lady Britomart wields in her household. Similarly, to look at the use of parallels in *The Two Gentlemen of Verona* alters our estimate of its construction.

NOTES

    1. *Shakespearian Comedy,* 1938.

    2. I am confining "plot" to the causal sequence; not extending it, with Una Ellis-Fermor in her fine chapter "The Nature of Plot in Drama" (*Shakespeare the Dramatist,* 1961), to cover what she and Professor Wilson Knight call the "spatial" pattern of a play.

    3. By "action" I intend the total movement of the play, the enacted development of everything the play is vitally concerned with (story, situation, character, mood,

theme, whatever that concern may comprehend), which conducts to the conclusion. So developed, and so concluded (even if sometimes the conclusion is deliberately inconclusive), these concerns, in good drama, are formed into an artistic whole, a whole greater than the unit of plot alone. The test of dramatic relevance is the contribution made to this larger whole, and the contribution may well be, not to the causal sequence, but to some other element in the developing pattern. "Action" is perhaps the most variously used term in dramatic criticism. According to context, it can mean, for example: (1) "business"; physical action as opposed to speech; (2) that part of the story which is enacted on the stage, in contrast with that part which is "reported" or implied; (3) the events, especially the decisive events, of the drama, whether physical or mental, and whether occurring on stage or off; and perhaps (4) the designed sequence of those events, preferably, I think, called "plot".

4. Cp. J.W. Lever, *The Elizabethan Love Sonnet*, 1956, p. 164.

5. Cp. M.C. Bradbrook, *Shakespeare and Elizabethan Poetry*, 1951.

6. For "daunger" and "pité", see C.S. Lewis, *The Allegory of Love*, on the *Roman de la Rose*.

7. Cp. L. Borinski, "Shakespeare's Comic Prose," *Shakespeare Survey* 8, 1955; and (on Launce and Will Kempe's slippers) J. Isaacs, "Shakespeare as Man of the Theatre," *Shakespeare Criticism 1919–35*, ed. Anne Bradby, 1936.

8. Quotations and references are from *William Shakespeare: The Complete Works*, ed. Peter Alexander, 1951.

9. Well indicated by his sophistical argument to the contrary, II.vi.19–22.

10. "And now you are metamorphis'd with a mistress" (II.i,26).

11. Cp., e.g., the Dreamer in Chaucer's *Boke of the Duchesse*.

12. M.C. Bradbook, op. cit.; and J.R. Brown, *Shakespeare and his Comedies*, 1957, q.v. for the whole topic of the lover's ability or failure to see beyond appearance.

13. Richmond Noble overlooks this (in *Shakespeare's Use of Song*) when he finds the lyric comparatively lacking in dramatic relevance.

14. See the passages in full: II.i,29–71, 124–145.

15. Op. cit.

16. Though it must be admitted that, unlike Viola, she doesn't propose to put her heart into it.

17. Cp. Harold Jenkins, "Shakespeare's *Twelfth Night*," *The Rice Institute Pamphlet*, xlv. 4, Jan. 1959.

18. "If he say ay, it will; if he say no, it will; if he shake his tail and say nothing, it will." (II.v,31).

Laughing with the Audience: *The Two Gentlemen of Verona* and the Popular Tradition of Comedy (1969)

Robert Weimann

Laughter with the audience can be and has been approached from at least two quite different angles: on the one hand from that of the theatre and social custom and ritual, on the other from that of aesthetics and the theory of comedy. Dover Wilson was perhaps the first to remark, many years ago, that Shakespeare "gets his audience to laugh, quite as often *with* his characters as *at* them."[1] In more recent years, the social and dramatic background of the actor-audience relationship has been brilliantly explored by Anne Righter and C.L. Barber, and this has—in connexion with the reassessment of the Elizabethan platform stage by G.F. Reynolds, Richard Hosley, W.C. Hodges, Glynne Wickham, Bernard Beckerman and others—considerably modified our conceptions not only of the Elizabethan theatre but of the theatrical modes and possibilities of Shakespearian comedy and, of course, of laughter in this comedy.

Now such laughter on the comic stage has both a history and a theory, and from a comparative point of view it may perhaps be desirable to try and link up the historical (or theatrical), and the theoretical (or typological) aspects. Quite to integrate them must in the last resort involve both a historical view of theory and a theoretical view of history, and it would of course call for a vast amount of documentation.[2] It seems therefore more fruitful just to raise the problem (without necessarily suggesting all the answers) and to do so within the limited context of one Shakespearian play. I shall take as my text *The Two Gentlemen of Verona*, where laughing with the audience can be studied in its dramatic functioning and where it serves, perhaps for the first time in Shakespeare's work, as an essential means of organizing, controlling and evaluating experience through a larger comic vision. Here, then, it assumes something of a structural significance, in the light of which some problems as to the reading of this early and experimental, but seminal, comedy can perhaps be viewed from a fresh angle.

Reprinted from *Shakespeare Survey* 22 (1969): 35–42.

I

But before we come to the play itself, let us take a hasty glance towards a theoretical problem which has repeatedly come up in recent criticism of Shakespeare, particularly in the course of the 1968 Stratford Conference: the nature of comedy and the question of *types* or *kinds* of comedy. If the comedy of laughing with the audience were to be fitted into a typological scheme, or into a system of types, it would certainly not be classed among what has traditionally been called "New Comedy." In the largely neoclassical tradition of Menander, Jonson, Molière, Lessing, Ostrowski and Ibsen, the audience, if indeed it laughs at all, definitely laughs *at* but never *with* the comic figure. The comic figure so laughed at, usually is the comic *character* of dramatic illusion, but hardly ever the comic *actor*. The resulting laughter is inspired not by a more or less traditional feeling of social unity between audiences and *actors* but by a critical view of the contradictions between the norms of society and the unconventional standards of comic *characters*, be they the dupes or intriguers, the cheats or butts of society. The inform- ing comic vision is essentially critical (or satirical, ironical, etc.) because the resolutions it offers are so many ways of exposing the human inadequacy of the antisocial attitudes of hypocrisy, vanity, snobbery, bureaucracy, as well as all kinds of mechanical or inorganic ways of isolation from the given norms of living.

It is, at any rate, this kind of comedy, which the classic writers on the subject (such as Meredith) are discussing, and it is this kind of comic effect with the psychology of which Bergson, in *Le Rire*, is concerned. While some of the more important recent studies on the subject, such as Jurij Borew's long book *On the Comic,* follow this tradition and consider laugh- ter mainly as a "weapon," as directed "against any phenomenon which de- serves to be criticised and condemned,"[3] we have to go as far back as Hegel to find a more relevant, though still very general, theory of what I (for the sake of brevity) call laughing with the audience. Hegel in his *Aesthetics* draws attention to the fundamental distinction in comedy, "whether the acting char- acters are for themselves comic or whether they appear so only to the audi- ence."[4] While the latter appear—to Hegel—as merely ridiculous, the former are more truly comic in the sense that they enjoy the "blessed ease of a sub- jectivity which, as it is sure of itself, can bear the dissolution of its own ends and means" (*"die Seligkeit und Wohligkeit der Subjectivität, die, ihrer selbst gewiß, die Auflösung ihrer Zwecke und Realisationen ertragen kann"*). Hegel gives no examples, but is probably thinking of the security and ease of such comic characters in Aristophanes as Dikaiopolis in *The Acharnians* or Trygaios in *Peace*. Such a comic figure is truly comic, when "the seriousness of his will and purpose is not to himself serious," and when his own mode of existence is free from any *Entzweiung*, any disunion or disruption of self and society.[5] Now this theoretical or comparative approach to comedy, which my summary very much oversimplifies, suffers, in our present context, from several weaknesses which result from the highly speculative nature of these theories but especially from the fact that they completely ignore the practical and historical experience of the theatre as a social and technical institution. As recent research into Shakespeare's platform stage has made clearer than ever before, his theatre is, historically speaking, a highly complex and transitional institution in which there was room for (in Lyly's words) the most astonishing "mingle mangle," for a true "gallimaufray" of medieval and traditional as well as Renaissance and classical conventions, from which no single formula of comedy can be abstracted. Consequently, laughter in Shakespearian comedy cannot be reduced to any one comic pattern, or structure, or mood, and to realize this is to realize the limitations of any typological system, and the limited extent to which Shakespeare's comedy can be fitted into the categories of such a system.

II

If, then, we understand the various types of Shakespearian comedy and laughter against the historical background and the various social traditions of Shakespeare's theatre, we hardly have to remind ourselves that, in *The Two Gentlemen of Verona*, laughing with the audience is part of a larger whole: it is limited and defined by its context of speech, character and plot. To study the traditional popular mode in comedy, then, is first of all to be aware of this dramatic context which, in *The Two Gentlemen*, is largely built up by several conventions of speech and disguise, and various degrees and ways of audience awareness, such as are mainly associated with the characters of Speed, Launce and Julia.

To suggest the significance of this context, I can look at only two such conventions. First of all there is the series of *comic asides* by Speed in the first scene of the second act; Valentine, addressing Silvia in the style of courtly romance, greets her as "Madam and mistress" with "a thousand good morrows"—which Speed, turning aside, echoes as "a million of manners" (II,i,88ff.).[6] While Silvia and Valentine are exchanging their high-flown compliments and Silvia is wooing her Valentine, in Speed's words, "by a figure" (the figure of his self-written love-letter), the clown continues to comment aside. These comments are definitely not over-heard by Silvia and Valentine: they form no part of their dialogue, nor are they in the nature of any monologue or self-expression. Rather, they address the audience as from the angle of some kind of comic chorus; and it is through the comic chorus quality of Speed's comments that a dramatic interplay between the wit of the audience and the wittiness of the clown is achieved. The resulting laughter, both in the yard and on the scaffolds, shares the same perspective towards its object. The object (Silvia's and Valentine's high-flown addresses) is part of the play world, but the perspective of his comic asides links the clown with the real world of everyday experience. This involves some contact not simply between the audience and the character Speed, but between the audience and the actor of Speed's part who, as comic chorus with his asides, enjoys a perspective of awareness which is not strictly limited by the play world. The resulting unity of mirth, between the audience and the actor-character, cannot be dismissed as a clowning concession to the groundlings or as to so much genial atmosphere; for it turns out to be highly functional and quite relevant to any reading of the play as a whole. Its functional achievement can be measured by the degree to which it succeeds in the building up of a wider comic vision through which the main theme of friendship and courtly love (so underlined, in this scene, by words such as "mistress" and "servant")[7] is dramatically controlled and comically evaluated.

Another and different kind of context in which the audience laughs with, rather than at, a comic person, is marked by Launce's famous leave-taking speech (II,iii). Again, this is in the tradition of direct address, and, as it is spoken on Launce's first entrance, still harkens back to the extended self-introduction of the older comic figure in Tudor drama. But the way in which this speech achieves a comic concurrence of actor and audience is quite different from Speed's asides which, while they provoke laughter on the stage, direct this laughter at others. Launce, however, enters by himself, and while he and his family experience are the objects of his own mirth, he is also its free and willing subject—subject in the sense of *Subjekt* or ego, or self. His, indeed, is (in Hegel's words) the "blessed ease of a subjectivity which, as it is sure of itself, can bear the dissolution of its own ends." For the comic tension between the ridiculousness of the object and the hilarity of the subject (the *Subjekt*) of this speech is altogether remarkable, and it points to the dramatic quality of its comic achievement. This achievement, I suggest, can be measured by the degree to which the given tension between the fictitious object and the actual medium of this speech is solved in terms of the unity (and the contradiction) between the illusory character Launce and the real actor behind this character. For Launce to become the clowning object and the laughing subject of his own mirth and that of the audience, reveals an astonishing stability in his relations to the social whole. These relations connect the character and the actor, illusion and reality, so that the imaginative flexibility of his relation to the play world has much to do with the social security of his relation to the real world. And it is one of Shakespeare's supreme achievements in *The Two Gentlemen* to make these two relations not simply co-exist, but so interact that the resulting phenomenon attains a dramatic coherence and artistic integrity which, I think, is hardly surpassed in any of the mature comedies.

To suggest the comic effects of such laughing with the audience, one can say that Launce, much like Falstaff, is not merely witty in himself but the reason that others have and enjoy their own wit. The audience, or at least a certain section of it, is made to share the implicitly burlesque approach to the experience of leave-taking, but the actor, in performing this, shares the audience's hilarious experience over the scene so enacted. The clowning actor has, as it were, a public capacity for distancing the dramatic illusion and for undermining the social prestige of the main theme of courtly love and friendship; he is, at any rate, still very close to the social attitudes of a popular audience, but the audience in their turn, are no passive spectators, but share in the post-ritual community of theatrical mirth. The comic actor, in fact, does not merely play *to* the audience: to a certain degree he still plays *with* the audience, though already much less directly so than Richard Tarlton did, when he took up his cue from a so-called "theamer" among the onlookers, or when he reacted upon a thrown apple with a piercing couplet.[8]

But a traditional element of audience awareness survived the decline of the extemporal mode of clowning, and Shakespeare, who condemned the latter, revived the former on a newly literary basis, at a time when, in the nineties, the popular platform dramaturgy of the clowning convention was attacked with increased vigour, as in the words of Joseph Hall who took up Sidney's assault upon the "hotch-potch" tradition by his scornful but immensely suggestive comments on the clowning convention, especially the mode of entering of the clown, who, apparently, would emerge laughing, and grinning, and gasping, in the midst of the "applauding crowd" that greeted him with "gladsome noise." Says Hall:

> midst the silent rout,
> Comes leaping in a self-misformed lout,
> And laughs, and grins, and frames his mimic face,
> And justles straight into the prince's place:
> Then doth the theatre echo all aloud,
> With gladsome noise of that applauding crowd.
> A goodly hotch-potch! when vile russetings
> Are match'd with monarchs, and with mighty kings.

A goodly grace to sober Tragic Muse,
When each base clown his clumsy fist doth bruise,
And show his teeth in double rotten row,
For laughter at his self-resembled show.[9]

These lines seem to me to be the most telling contemporary account we have of laughing with the audience, and they provide us with a highly significant hint at its popular background and origins. Hall, I think, attacks not the Shakespearian clown, but the clowning figure in the popular drama of the eighties and early nineties, the immediate predecessor of Launce. The early Elizabethan clown, Hall says, shows "his teeth in double rotten row / For laughter at his self-resemble show." The clown, to be sure, is no mere object of laughter; he himself laughs and grins at his own performance, and the "self-misformed" nature of this performance is such that it does not so much create the illusion of a dramatic role, as incorporate the actor's own clowning pure and simple; it is, in short, "his self-resembled show."

The tradition of the "self-misformed lout" (about which Hall is so scornful) reaches, of course, much further back than Tarlton, and the actual background of this tradition is suggested by Shakespeare himself when, upon Launce's quibbling speech, he makes Speed reply: "Well, your old vice still: mistake the word . . ." (III,i,279). The allusion, which is itself in the form of a pun, is unmistakable.

Among Shakespeare's three explicit references to the Vice, the one in *The Two Gentlemen* is the earliest, and it is here that, after the Plautine servants in *The Comedy of Errors* and the dictionary humour of Costard, in *Love's Labour's Lost*, Shakespeare first harkens back, quite deliberately, to the most popular figure in the morality tradition. Launce has been called by Isaacs "the beginning of the true Shakespearean clown"; as such he is of course no vice, and—with Tarlton before him—not even his direct descendant, but the dramatic function of his laughter and audience awareness are very much indebted to the farcical-allegorical anti-hero of the morality plays. If the contemporaries viewed Will Kempe as "Jestmonger and Vice-regent general to the Ghost of Dick Tarlton,"[10] then this witty phrase itself was a quibbling reminder of the continued relevance of the Vice tradition which, as early as *Mankind*, can be shown to produce the comic concurrence of audience and actor.

When, for example, in this undoubtedly popular play the allegorical Virtue Mercy wards off the impertinent assault of vicious Myscheff ("Ye ben culpable / To interrupte thus my talkynge delectable"), the vicious reply reads: "I say, ser, I cumme hedyr to make you game." And when Mercy continues to persist—in heavily latinized terms—on his "clerycall manere" and his "doctryne," we have an even more telling reply from Now-a-days, another figure of Vice, who says to Mercy:

> Men haue lytyll deynte of yowur pley,
> Be-cause ye make no sporte. (260 ff.)[11]

Mercy, a most serious virtue, is here addressed not as an illusory figure of dramatic allegory but as an *actor* who provides no sport. The comic figure of Vice identifies himself with the point of view of the audience whose traditional right to indulge in "sporte" (line 78), in "game" (69), in "reuel" (82), in "mery chere" (81) he maintains. His frame of reference is not provided by a moral convention or an allegorical illusion but by an awareness of the actual conditions of, and the expectations roused by, a fifteenth-century travelling troupe's performance. The comic figure's reproach to Mercy, in fact, says not that "Men do not enjoy your *role*"; he says, rather, "Men haue lytyll deynte of yowur *pley*." The traditional criterion of the comic figure is not the impersonation of the *role* but the "self-resembled show" of the actor.

The comic concurrence of audience and actor is well-nigh complete; and, indeed, there is more than laughing with the audience; there is *singing* with the audience when, somewhat later, the figures of Vice strike up a bawdy "crystemes songe" (325ff.), in which all the onlookers are expected to join (*cantant omnes* is the original stage direction). The figures of Vice—in their reckless fashion—sing and play and laugh with the audience, and in their quibbling, riddling impertinency they can again and again "mistake the word" and thereby establish a traditional community of laughing, gasping and guessing. I call this community traditional, because the popular origins of this kind of wordplay are considerably older than *Mankind*, and can quite definitely be traced in the speech of the Wakefield Garcio (*Mactacio Abel*), the "Lechys man" Hawkyn (*Mary Magdalene*) and the cheeky boy Colle in the Croxton *Play of the Sacrament*. Parallel with these there is, of course, the topsy-turvy patter of Jack Finney in the mumming plays and, behind all these, finally, the more ancient topsy-turvydom of the late rituals of release inversion, such as have survived in the Middle Ages through the good luck of their semi-toleration.

III

Shakespeare, who used, and experimented with, the Vice and the Tarlton traditions, also absorbed the clown's "laughter at his self-resembled show," but he did so critically, on a newly limited and functional basis. For the comic acting of William Kempe, even though Kempe was acclaimed as Tarlton's "Vice-regent generall," was increasingly integrated into a socially much more heterogeneous division of theatrical labour. Accordingly, the clown Launce—if indeed acted by Kempe—no longer carries the comedy before him, but, more modestly and more effectively, assumes a functional role in a larger whole, thereby fulfilling—much as Speed does—the structural task of helping to organize and control the play's larger comic perspective. He becomes, as Speed does, an important element in the "implicit judgment" of the play.[12]

As has recently been shown by Harold F. Brooks,[13] this involves a series of comic parallels between the clowning and the romantic scenes—a burlesque kind of parallelism which is quite essential to any understanding of the peculiar poise of the play's meaning; including, I suggest, the vexed problem of the play's denouement through Valentine's outrageous generosity (which of course can be and has been variously understood in terms of textual corruption, or source study, or the history of ideas on friendship, etc.).[14] Whatever the explanation, the resulting comic vision on courtly love yields a highly complex image in which the joint actor-audience perspective of laughter helps to define and to control, though not necessarily to belittle, the main theme of love and friendship.

The point, then, is not that Shakespeare absorbed the clown's "self-resembled show," but the really interesting question is as to how and by which means this tradition was integrated into the much more self-contained structure and the larger meaning of Shakespearian comedy. To attempt an answer to this question, one might first of all suggest that, in *The Two Gentlemen*, the real performance of the comic actor's true clowning is achieved through the role of the fictitious character of Proteus's comic servant. The real performance of the actor and the imaginative role of the servant interact, and they achieve a new and very subtle kind of unity. Within this unity, the character's relations to the playworld begin to dominate, but the comic ease and flexibility of these relations are still enriched by some traditional connexion between the clowning actor and the laughing spectator—a connexion which has its ultimate origins in the rituals of a less divided society. The continuity and the flexibility of this position (which, in the last resort, involves some kind of freedom from shame and isolation) are remarkable.

To be sure, such freedom is a social and historical phenomenon, which has to do with, say, Elizabethan economic history, the contemporary division of labour, the extent of the enclosure of the commons, etc., but this freedom becomes so meaningful to the art of Shakespeare's comedy precisely because it finds an imaginative equivalent in the structure and the dramaturgy of the play itself. To illustrate the dramatic nature of this equivalent one can observe that the joint audience-actor perspective of the play world involves a mutual extension of awareness, if I may here use Bertrand Evans's fruitful term in a somewhat wider and perhaps slightly different sense. Such awareness, one would suggest, reflects and interconnects both the social security of *actor's* relation to the real world and the imaginative and spatial flexibility of the *character's* relation to the play world, his implicit insight into and criticism of, the action of the play.

This extension of mutual awareness, or what I have called the comic concurrence of actors and audiences, is of course not restricted to Speed's asides or Launce's direct address. A more exhaustive treatment of the subject would have to consider Julia and the problem of disguise—a vast problem, almost too huge to be mentioned here, although like the clowns, the disguised person (such as Julia) is the character who is usually laughed with, but rarely laughed at, by the audience. Julia's disguise, just like Speed's asides and Launce's direct address, form perhaps the most sustained context in which the comic character is comic for himself, that is to say, in which that character himself enjoys the comic situation that he is either watching (as Speed does) or creating by himself (as in the case of Launce).

In *The Two Gentlemen*, as in the mature comedies, this awareness is as characteristic of the disguised person as it is of the clown or fool. In our examples it is shared by Speed who alone can interpret the figure of the self-written love letter by which his master is wooed; but it is also, if more indirectly, shared by Launce whose privileged perspective is implicit in the burlesque quality of his parallel action so that, in a later scene, again in direct address, he can say, quite explicitly:

> I am but a fool, look you, and yet I have the wit to think my master is a kind of knave: but that's all one, if he be but one knave . . .
> (III,i,262ff.)

Here, Launce is utterly secure in the actor's awareness of his own comic function ("I am but a fool," he says, and in saying this he harkens back to the "self-misformed lout" who never was afraid of his self-resembled show). But at the same time he is and remains a character, and as a character he is equally secure in his awareness of other characters: he is aware—as Valentine is not—of the true significance of Proteus's doing.

To express this awareness, he (much as the old Vice does) uses two very revealing figures, a proverb together with a pun. The proverb, as the New Cambridge editor notes, says "Two false knaves need no broker," but Proteus, being but one knave, does need his broker, that is his go-between.

In using the proverb in this quibbling or perhaps riddling fashion, Launce renews and emphasizes his comic concurrence with the audience and he again appeals, from within the romantic comedy, to the Elizabethan world of everyday experience. But, by using the proverb incomplete, almost in the way of a riddle, he does more than simply express his privileged awareness: he uses this awareness so as to make the audience, as it were, participate in the playing of the game or the solution of the riddle. Basically, this invites the same kind of participation that the gravediggers in *Hamlet* provoke by their quibbling riddling question as to who was the first gentleman, or that the porter in *Macbeth* so ostensibly challenges ("and drink, sir, is a great provoker of three things," II,iii,24ff.). Through these riddling jests, of which of course Tarlton was the supreme master, the audience in their turn, being still very keen on sports and mirth, are imaginatively invited to join in the building-up of the comic perspective of the play. It is on the basis of the popular tradition that the clown achieves his comic concurrence with the audience. It is a concurrence which, in Shakespeare's comedy, does not merely relate the play world to the real world but which makes the representatives of the real world, through the associations of proverb, pun and riddle, and disguise, form an implicit element in the dramaturgy, the judgement, and hence the larger comic vision of the play.

NOTES

1. John Dover Wilson, *Shakespeare's Happy Comedies* (1962), pp. 23ff.
2. For a more comprehensive documentation see the present writer's *Shakespeare und die Tradition des Volkstheaters: Soziologie Dramaturgie, Gestaltung* (Berlin, 1967).
3. Jurij Borew, *Über das Komische* (Berlin, 1960), pp. 19, 22, 166.
4. J.W.F. Hegel, *Ästhetik*, ed. Friedrich Bassenge (Berlin, 1955), p. 1091.
5. Ibid.; cf. p. 1075.
6. Quotations from William Shakespeare, *The Complete Works*, ed. Peter Alexander (London/Glasgow, 1951).
7. Cf. II,i,87; 90; 97; 123. This seems unique in Shakespeare. The play's debt to the romance tradition is fully brought out by John Vyvyan, *Shakespeare and the Rose of Love* (1960). See also H.B. Charlton, *Shakespearian Comedy* (1952), pp. 27ff.
8. Cf. *Tarlton's Jests and News out of Purgatory*, ed. J.O. Halliwell (1844), pp. 14, 22f., 27, 44.
9. *Virgidemiarum Libri Sex*, Book I, Satire III; in *The Works of Joseph Hall* (Oxford, 1839), XII, 162.
10. *An Almond for a Parrat*, in *The Works of Thomas Nashe*, ed. R.B. McKerrow (1905), III, 341.
11. Quotations from *The Macro Plays*, ed. F.J. Furnivall and A.W. Pollard, E.E.T.S., E.S. XCI (1904).
12. See J.R. Brown, *Shakespeare and his Comedies* (1957), pp. IIff.
13. H.F. Brooks, "Two Clowns in a Comedy (to say nothing of the Dog): Speed, Launce (and Crab) in *The Two Gentlemen of Verona*," *Essays and Studies 1963* (1963), pp. 91–100.

14. See, for example, R.M. Sargent, "Sir Thomas Elyot and the Integrity of *The Two Gentlemen of Verona*," *PMLA*, LXV (1950), 1166–82; also the introduction to the New Cambridge Shakespeare; pp. xiiiff.; Vyvyan, op. cit. pp. 130ff.; E. Th. Sehrt, *Wandlungen der Shakespeareschen Kömodie* (Göttingen, 1961), p. 14; etc.

"Were man but constant, he were perfect": Constancy and Consistency in *The Two Gentlemen of Verona* (1972)

Inga-Stina Ewbank

I

In the early spring of 1855 George Eliot (still Marian Evans) read *The Two Gentlemen of Verona* and found that the play

> disgusted me more than ever in the final scene where Valentine, on Proteus's mere begging pardon when he has no longer any hope of gaining his ends, says: "All that was mine in Silvia I give thee"!—Silvia standing by.[1]

In itself there is nothing unusual about George Eliot's reaction. Most critics of the play have felt that in this, his first, dramatization of romance narrative Shakespeare was tied and partly defeated by the conventions he was attempting to use. Such "disgust" as has been expressed has often focused on the last scene as typifying the play's problems: in the unbelievable magnanimity of Valentine (at two girls' expense), thematic considerations appear to override any thought of character development or psychological motivation. As an affirmation of male constancy it may have satisfied an Elizabethan audience; for, insofar as they believed with Geron, in Lyly's *Endimion*, that friendship is "the image of eternitie in which there is nothing moveable, nothing mischeevous" and that there is as much difference between love and friendship as between "Beautie and Vertue, bodies and shadowes, colours and life," they would have seen Valentine's lines as a noble and universally valid climax to the action of the play.[2] But this moment in the play has troubled audiences and readers ever since.

Reprinted from *Shakespearean Comedy* (Stratford-upon-Avon Studies 14). Ed. Malcolm Bradbury and David Palmer. New York: Crane, Russak, 1972, pp. 31–57.

It may have been particularly troubling to George Eliot, who, like Julia, had defied the notions of "modesty" held by her society, and who may have given special assent to Julia's couplet against a double standard:

> It is the lesser blot, modesty finds,
> Women to change their shapes than men their minds. (V.iv.108–9)

If so, her objection would again have been part of a more general one, for Valentine's grand gesture is all the more inconsistent in that, up to the final scene where Sylvia is mutely handed around from one man to another and Julia's chief contribution is a swoon, the women in the play have been the active ones, going forth to seek their lovers, making decisions on a basis of profound love *and* commonsense, while the men talk or write letters and poems about their love. Like Shakespeare's more mature comedies but unlike the traditional friendship story, where the woman tends to be merely an object or a touchstone in the testing of friends,[3] the play has shown us some of the most important parts of the action from a woman's viewpoint. Though it is in Valentine's idealistic words that Proteus' betrayal is forgiven, it is through Julia's eyes and mind that we have seen what that betrayal really means. Valentine's attitude resolves a theme, but it is Julia's heartbreak which, if anything, has proved the human content of that theme on our pulses. Valentine's constancy appears to be built on a dramatic inconsistency; and one wonders how far Proteus' reply to Julia,

> Than men their minds! 'tis true. O heaven, were man
> But constant, he were perfect! (V.iv.110–11)

is, wittingly or unwittingly, a self-reproach on the part of the dramatist.

But there is also a background to George Eliot's reaction to *The Two Gentlemen of Verona* which makes it more remarkable and more interesting as a departure point for an exploration of the play's inconsistencies—which indeed makes those inconsistencies more worth exploring—than other similar reactions.[4] She was reading, or rather re-reading, the play during some lonely weeks at Dover, while George Henry Lewes was in London arranging his affairs and hers, as well as those of his legal wife and children. The two of them had just returned to England, after eight months in voluntary exile, to face the music of outraged Victorian morality and to try to build a life together. She trusted the man in whom she had "garner'd up her heart," but she must also have known how precarious their liaison looked to outsiders, and how even her best friends were praying "against hope" that the protean Lewes would prove constant. So when, in the evenings, she turned from translating Spinoza's *Ethics* to reading *The Two Gentlemen of Verona*—and it may speak more of her emotional state than of a scholarly desire to be chronologically thorough that she was also reading *Venus and Adonis, The Passionate Pilgrim* and some of the sonnets—it was with a peculiar personal involvement. Between the lines of her journal entry we may sense that the play, in provoking disgust, had activated a deep fear at the centre of her life. "Could men really bandy a noble woman's love about like that?" is how her biographer puts into words what she dared not express, even to herself.[5] Out of the allegedly "romantic and dehumanized atmosphere" of this play, something must have spoken to her about what it feels like to be alive and loving—and therefore vulnerable.

Now, *The Two Gentlemen of Verona* is not a play usually discussed in those terms. Shakespeare seems not yet to have developed the uncanny way he later has of engaging with our own lives so that our own experiences modify our reactions to his lines, and *vice versa*: so that we read *King Lear* differently once we have an aged parent in the household, or reject Lady Macbeth each time we nurse our babies, or even feel able to "identify" with the anguish and confusion of the puppet-like movements of the lovers in *A Midsummer Night's Dream*. The sphere of human experience in *The Two Gentlemen of Verona* is not only narrow—excluding alike birth, copulation and death—but it is so restricted by remote codes and patterned by an artificial language that we tend to feel it represents a world to which Shakespeare was not much committed. Perhaps we feel that, if our feelings go out to anyone in the play, it is to Launce with his dog Crab. A great deal has recently been written on the dramatic technique of the play, and in particular on the way in which Shakespeare has managed to make the parodic scenes of Speed and Launce (and Crab) into organic parts of the structure;[6] but no one has felt like saying, borrowing T.S. Eliot's words about Tennyson, that the poet's technical accomplishments were intimate with his depths. Most discussions conclude either that Shakespeare was preoccupied with form at the expense of truth to human feeling, or that he was laughing at the feelings embodied in courtly convention, or both—that is, that he criticized the convention most of the time but, with an inconsistency worthy of Proteus, found it dramatically expedient to embrace it at the end. Either way—whether we nod an Elizabethan assent to the friendship code or laugh at "Shakespeare wringing the last drop of silliness out of Valentine's conventions"[7]—we have an explanation for Valentine's gesture and words which does not involve us, or Shakespeare, very deeply. But George Eliot's reaction, from a disturbed and divided consciousness, prompts one to consider the possibility that Shakespeare is here at least trying, if with very partial success, to be as truthful to troubled, complex human relationships as he was in the sonnet celebrating an apparently similar plot situation, "Take all my loves" (40). Possibly he is saying about the moment of Valentine's magnanimity *not* "this is what life should ideally be," nor "this is not life," but "this is, and is not, life."

II

Clearly it will not do to pretend that *The Two Gentlemen of Verona* is really a *Troilus and Cressida*. Clearly this very early play[8] is in many ways a piece of apprenticeship (so that one natural reason for anyone's "disgust" with it is that it is not as good as the rest of Shakespeare) and a seed-bed for themes, characters and situations which are to be developed in later plays. But it can be unhelpful to pre-judge the play according to notions of development: to assume that the reason why *The Two Gentlemen of Verona* troubles us is that Julia is not as "rounded" as Viola, that the Proteus-Valentine relationship is not as fully realized as the friendship of Bassanio and Antonio, or that the outlaw scenes do not have the thematic importance of their counterparts in *As You Like It*. What is more helpful, if we want to see what impulses produce the particular inconsistencies of *The Two Gentlemen of Verona*, is to relate the play to the sonnets. Whatever the exact chronology of either play or sonnets, a kinship between them has long been a recognized fact. It consists both of verbal echoes—similar, often Petrarchan, topics and conceits being developed through similar vocabulary—and of a kind of plot similarity.[9] Whatever the true story behind either play or sonnets, in both cases Shakespeare is creating a fiction to explore the joys and agonies, the betrayals and fulfilments, of interconnecting love relationships. Proteus, the betrayer of both love and friendship, is most like the Youth of the sonnets, with an element of the Dark Lady; Valentine and the two girls all share features of the sonnets' "I": adoration of the beloved, faithfulness, constancy; and Valentine in the end takes up the all-forgiving and renouncing position of, for example, Sonnet 40. Obviously I am not concerned here with "plot" similarities as indicating any autobiographical truths behind these works: the "truth" of the sonnets lies in Shakespeare's dramatic ability—unique among Elizabethan sonneteers[10]—to create a sense of "what it feels like" in a given human situation. Paradoxically, the dramatic ability is less evident in the combinations and permutations of love and friendship (with, it should be noted, the friendship theme being given much less scope than the love theme) which make up the pattern of the play. Nor am I suggesting that a single sonnet, like 40, *justifies* the final scene of the play, but that it may help to illuminate its dramatic inconsistencies.

For, in the end, the really important relationship between *The Two Gentlemen of Verona* and the sonnets seems to me to have to do with Shakespeare's attitude to his own poetry and to the traditions of love poetry in which he finds himself writing. More important than any local similarities is the fact that the sonnets, like the play, show us Shakespeare working within a well-established convention, both using it and criticizing it—writing, as it were, through and around it. Apart from a handful of simply conventional Petrarchan exercises, his aim (explicit and implicit) in the sonnets is to subordinate his style to his subject matter, to use the convention only insofar as it helps him to render the true image of the person he is writing to and of.[11] Thus, to take an extreme example, what he wants to say about the Dark Lady in Sonnet 130 only makes sense through an evaluation of the Petrarchan convention; yet the real point of the poem remains the "rareness" of the Lady, not the dig at the convention. Related to this feature of the sonnets is Shakespeare's attitude to language: an apparently paradoxical combination of a tremendous belief in the powers of his own poetry (again both implicit in the writing itself and explicitly stated) with an equally insistent sense that language is inadequate to express the beloved's identity—the quintessential statement being "that you alone are you" (84). It is in the sonnets that Shakespeare most clearly faces the problem which, of course, he shares with any love poet: that he needs language to define the uniqueness of the beloved and his feelings about him or her, but that, at the same time, language itself is conventional and conventionalizes experience.

When love poetry is transferred to the stage, when the inner drama of a sonnet's "I" and "thou" has to be translated into the flesh-and-blood interaction of two lovers and probably also their conflicts with several other "I"s and "thou"s, then the problem is further confounded. In *Romeo and Juliet* Shakespeare partly solved it by contrasting the empty attitudinizing of Romeo's love for Rosaline with the beauty of the formality which surrounds and expresses his love for Juliet, from their first meeting on a shared sonnet.[12] Present-day playwrights, handling a tired and cliché-ridden language, have to face the problem in one extreme form—as Arnold Wesker discovered when he wanted a lover to tell his lady that she had "autumn soft skin" and found that this would put audiences in mind of TV advertisements for Camay soap[13]—and generally find it easier to let their characters make love in the flesh than in words. The playwrights of the 1590s were not afraid of verbal cliché in the same way; and the lovers in *The Two Gentlemen of Verona* can liken each other to the sun, or the moon, or the stars, can be blinded by love or weep floods of tears, or generally draw on the stock-in-trade of Petrarchan love poetry. But, as in the sonnets, Shakespeare in this play also shows an awareness that conventionalized language, like conventionalized behaviour, may be false. In this self-consciousness about conventional language and situations lie many of the play's inconsistencies, but also much of its sense of life.

We do not have to read or listen to *The Two Gentlemen of Verona* for very long before we discover a tendency in its main characters to be self-conscious about the language they use, to veer between exuberance and deflation, indulgence in Lyly-like wit games and sudden dismissals of them. In I.i Valentine deflates Proteus' love rhetoric even before he has had time to utter any of it; in II.iv the positions are reversed, as Valentine takes up exactly the role he ascribed to Proteus in the first scene and, in his turn, has his hyperboles punctured:

> *Pro.* Why, Valentine, what braggardism is this?
> *Val.* Pardon me, Proteus; all I can is nothing
>   To her, whose worth makes other worthies nothing;
>   She is alone.
> *Pro.*   Then let her alone. (II.iv.160–63)

Proteus shifts the sense of Valentine's "alone"—reminiscent of the sonnets' "that you alone are you"—with a brusqueness which anticipates Timon's dismissal of the Poet:

> *Poet.*   I am rapt, and cannot cover
>   The monstrous bulk of this ingratitude
>   With any size of words.
> *Tim.* Let it go naked: men may see't the better. (*Timon of Athens*,
>   V.i.62–5)

This effect of contrast and deflation does not seem to be tied to character as much as to the needs of the situation or scene. In II.iv Silvia initially has something of the same function of commonsense critic as, at other times, is given to Speed or Launce. She undercuts the sparring between Valentine and Thurio, and she exposes the absurdity of Valentine's conceits to the cold light of reason:

> *Val.* This is the gentleman I told your ladyship
>   Had come along with me but that his mistress
>   Did hold his eyes lock'd in her crystal looks. . . .
> *Sil.* Nay, then, he should be blind; and, being blind,
>   How could he see his way to seek out you? (II.iv.82–9)

Not that this stops Valentine's flow of images; on the contrary, Silvia has supplied him with the perfect cue for a further conceit,

Why, lady, Love hath twenty pair of eyes,

and this gives Thurio, too, a chance to have a go after his feeble fashion, so that we have one of the rare occasions in the play where the dialogue, in an anticipation of *Much Ado About Nothing*, arrives at a kind of differentiated group wit. But only a few lines later, as Proteus has arrived and entered upon a courtesy duologue with Silvia, the function of commentator has also passed from her to Valentine:

Leave off discourse of disability. (II.iv.105)

Related to this tendency in the play, and also tied to scene rather than to character, is a reminder, which tends to crop up at key moments, of the impotency of words. Proteus' motivation of the brevity of the parting scene between him and Julia—"For truth hath better deeds than words to grace it" (II.ii.18)—may in itself be merely conventional, but Julia on her next appearance makes an ironically genuine-sounding statement of the reality of love being beyond the power of words. "Didst thou but know," she says to Lucetta, "the inly touch of love,"

Thou wouldst as soon go kindle fire with snow
As seek to quench the fire of love with words. (II.vii.18–20)

The irony is double here, for not only does Julia's paean to her and Proteus' love come just after we have witnessed his decision to abandon her, but the very questioning of the power of words is put in such an exuberant form as to question the question. Ironically, too, Julia's argument is inverted and perverted by Proteus as he threatens to rape Silvia:

Nay, if the gentle spirit of moving words
Can no way change you to a milder form,
I'll woo you like a soldier, at arms' end,
And love you 'gainst the nature of love—force ye. (V.iv.55–8)

And significantly it is, at this point, visual and not verbal evidence that brings about Valentine's recognition: "nought but mine eye / Could have persuaded me" (V.iv.64–5). The questioning of language does not loom as large, nor occupy as thematically central a place, in *The Two Gentlemen of Verona* as it does in *Love's Labour's Lost*, but it is in some ways still more disturbing. In *Love's Labour's Lost* reliance on fine words and clever patterns indicates an empty idealism, an ivory tower knowledge of life, which collapses before real experience—be it of love or death. The collapse can be funny, but it can also be poignant, as when the Princess holds up the irrelevancy of the King's diction in the final scene: "I understand you not; my griefs are double" (V.ii.740). Berowne—for it takes the wittiest mind to see the limits of wit— is the one to take the point: "Honest plain words best pierce the ear of grief" (l.741). And so we are prepared for the play's final resting point, on good deeds versus words. In *The Two Gentlemen of Verona*, "honest plain words" play little part, and the alternatives to wit are, on the one hand, silence and, on the other, force and brutality.

III

It would be tempting to suggest that in Valentine's passage of *peripeteia* and *anagnorisis* Shakespeare anticipated those moments in his later plays where the reliance on eyes rather than ears is an essential part of his technique as a theatre poet. But it is probably closer to the truth to say that it is one of the moments in a play heavily dependent on its language where we are yet reminded that experience may outrun language. For the technique of this play is almost entirely verbal. Ingenious producers have to add to *The Two Gentlemen of Verona* those scenes of "pure theatre" which are so important in the structure of other Shakespearian comedies. The social ritual, with the exception of Proteus' serenade, consists (even for the clowns) exclusively of talk; the text provides for no banquet, no masked ball, no concluding dance but just a verbal promise of social harmony—

> One feast, one house, one mutual happiness—

and, though the Duke promises to "include all jars / With triumphs, mirth, and rare solemnity," we are allowed to see none of this take place. The outlaws do not slay deer or sing; the romance wanderings include no shipwrecks nor anything more spectacular than an attempted rape, and that a pretty verbal one, too. The spectrum of lovers, if we include the chaste Sir Eglamour and the "foolish rival" Thurio, do not add to the physical life of the play in the fashion of Sir Andrew Aguecheek or Malvolio, or even the spectacularly unlucky suitors in *The Merchant of Venice*. So love as courtship, and love and friendship as social forces, are handled through language alone—to the point where we feel that characters are used as an excuse for speeches and the plot as a device to bring about situations where characters can make speeches or engage in duologues. In this respect the play is still close to the descriptive-contemplative mode of non-dramatic poetry. Shakespeare's technique is still limited almost exclusively to three devices: soliloquy, duologue and the asides as comment.[14] Clearly the debate structure of Lyly's plays underlies the pattern. And yet, as I have already suggested, there is also an action *in* the language itself which makes it uniquely Shakespearian (and relates it to the sonnets)—a sort of dialectic between a sense that "much is the force of heaven-bred poesy" (III.ii.71), on the one hand, and a doubt and undercutting of that force (even as that *credo* by the Duke is undercut by the ironical situation in which it is uttered). Delight in wit, in verbal conceits and Petrarchan diction, co-exists not only with the conventional regret that love, in Berowne's words, "sings heaven's praise with such an earthly tongue," but also with a critical awareness that words may substitute for or falsify experience.

Because of this dialectic there is more to the real form—by which I mean that which relates the parts of the play to each other—of *The Two Gentlemen of Verona* than a "structure-ridden" narrative,[15] opening on a parting in which the themes of love and friendship are introduced and closing on a double reunion and an exaltation of love-through-friendship. That structure is obviously there, but it is questioned and explored so that only rarely may we take it at its face value. Longitudinally, the exploration seems to move through three stages. In the first of these—I.i through to the beginnings of Proteus' defection at II.iv.188—a perspective is established for us in which the play's world of witty artifice, in action as in language, is both celebrated and criticized. The opening scene between Valentine and Proteus moves rapidly through a duologue which, in Lyly's manner, sets up two antithetical attitudes, leaving Proteus alone on stage to clinch the antithesis in a soliloquy:

> He after honour hunts, I after love;
> He leaves his friends to dignify them more;
> I leave myself, my friends, and all for love. (I.i.63–5)

At this stage there is no reason to doubt that these lines are a straight-forward enunciation of theme, but subsequent action and speeches will question all the key-words: "honour," "love," "friends"—even "self." Indeed the last line ominously looks forward to having its meaning revalued when Proteus, in II.vi, discovers that "I to myself am dearer than a friend" and so leaves his true self for the selfish gratification of pursuing a new love. The Speed-Proteus duologue which completes I.i casts the light of burlesque on courtly wit, but, with its puns on ship/sheep/shepherd/mutton, it also keeps us in a dramatic world where life is dealt with as a kind of linguistic game. In the next scene this perspective is delightfully maintained by Julia's coquetry over Proteus' letter, both in the duologue with Lucetta and in her one-woman show with the letter as the only prop. In a scene like this we obviously do not regard language and action from Launce's unsophisticated point of view: "to be slow in words is a woman's only virtue"; but, on the other hand, a sense is developing that sophistication may be mere padding. As one of my students recently said, when Julia rips up her letter from Proteus and then changes her mind and from the torn pieces picks out simple phrases like "kind Julia," or "passionate Proteus," or just "Proteus," then we feel that she probably has the essence of the letter and has not lost much by losing the conventional decorations. It is notable— and in the context not just an inherited plot-trick—that so much of the intercourse between characters in this play is carried out by way of letters, a medium even further conventionalized than formal speech. Typically Proteus comes on reading a letter from Julia:

> Sweet love! sweet lines! sweet life!
> Here is her hand, the agent of her heart; (I.iii.45–6)

And this, apart from their brief parting scene, is the only dramatic statement of their mutual love—just as later Launce's lady-love exists only through her "conditions" set down in writing. "Lines" are made the vehicle, indeed the essence, of "love" and "life" in this world, even as the "hand" that writes is the chief agent and evidence of the "heart" that feels.

The first scene between Valentine and Silvia (and the only one in which they have any kind of privacy, though even here Speed is present) develops this perspective further: in their relationship at this instance, love is the stuff for words; and the words are delightful and wittily patterned, but at the same time curiously depersonalized. It is absurdly apt that Valentine should have been asked to, *and* been able to, write a letter on behalf of somebody else to an unknown recipient. The separation of word and feeling could not go much further than this, and, unlike the love-blinded Valentine, we do not really need Speed to see how deliberate the absurdity is:

> "Herself hath taught her love himself to write unto her lover."
> All this I speak in print, for in print I found it. (II.i.156–7)

The deliberateness goes outside even Speed's superior awareness (it is significant that the letter-carriers are basically so much wittier than the letter-writers and receivers in the play), to a comment from the dramatist on how in this kind of courtship one situation is interchangeable for another, how relationships are as formalized and as dependent on verbal elaboration as conceits. Indeed, in this part of the play Shakespeare delights in constructing scenes which are, as it were, verbal conceits (and often standard Petrarchan conceits) turned into stage-tableaux—such as Julia's game with names in I.ii and the two parting scenes in II.ii-iii.

The clown scenes are obviously used to puncture by parody this tendency to formalization—without, therefore, demolishing the inherent truth in a conceit. Launce's one-man show with Crab has, by now, probably received more critical attention than all the other scenes of the play put together, and deservedly so. It draws together several other scenes: in technique it echoes Julia's speaking tableau in I.ii; in his delicious confusion over which prop represents which member of his grieving family, Launce recalls the gay confusion over the identities of letter-writers and receivers in II.i but also anticipates the serious confounding of identities involved in Proteus' betrayal; in theme, of course, the scene parodies the excessive emotion of the parting between Proteus and Julia which has just taken place. But it is interesting that, in his rebuking of the silent Crab (hard-hearted as Proteus is soon going to be), Launce is so much wordier than the lovers themselves, and also that, within the comic frame of the scene, the diction and patterning of courtly love poetry came so easily to Launce. He uses them both seriously and facetiously and in a mixture of both. His sister is "as white as a lily, and as small as a wand." The "tide," which echoes Proteus' conceit—

> The tide is now—nay, not thy tide of tears:
> That tide will stay me longer than I should—(II.ii.14–15)

is wilfully confused with the "tied" Crab. And there is a mixture of genuine feeling and mockery in his elaboration on Proteus' image:

> Why, man, if the river were dry, I am able to fill it with my tears; if the
> wind were down, I could drive the boat with my sighs. (II.iii.47–9)

So Launce makes comically explicit a critical perspective on the absorption in the conventional attitudes and language of love—a perspective which the "serious" scenes have implicitly demonstrated—without in any way denying, as might happen in a satire, the holiness of the heart's affections or the need to put them into words.

IV

In the second stage of its dialectic—from the end of II.iv through the rest of Act II and the whole of Acts III and IV—the play seems to take us in two new directions, on the one hand putting the patterned and apparently conventional language to serious uses and, on the other, establishing scenes which are, as it were, counter-conceits and in which the language and attitudes of courtly convention are found altogether invalid.

Under the pressure of the serious complications in the plot, those involving tension of mind and suffering and heartbreak, verbal ingenuity itself becomes a vehicle for a sense of life. The first sign of this is Proteus' soliloquy in II.vi:

> To leave my Julia, shall I be forsworn;
> To love fair Silvia, shall I be forsworn;
> To wrong my friend, I shall be much forsworn.
> And ev'n that power which gave me first my oath
> Provokes me to this threefold perjury:
> Love bade me swear, and Love bids me forswear . . .
> I cannot leave to love, and yet I do;
> But there I leave to love where I should love.
> Julia I lose, and Valentine I lose;
> If I keep them, I needs must lose myself;
> If I lose them, thus find I by their loss:
> For Valentine, myself; for Julia, Silvia.
> I to myself am dearer than a friend;
> For love is still most precious in itself. (1–24)

In this speech many of the stylistic features of the play are concentrated: the end-stopped lines; the antitheses or paradoxes pivoted on the caesura or brought out by the perfect symmetry of two consecutive lines; the patterning of repetitions towards a climax; the argument through conceits (mainly in such lines as the following pair: "At first I did adore a twinkling star, / But now I worship a celestial sun"). But here, instead of drawing attention to itself as it would have done earlier in the play, and unlike the careful patterning in the apparently similar weighing of love against friendship in *Endimion*,[16] the verbal scheme truly suggests the staccato movements, the to-and-froing, the see-saw of impulses within a mind which, while it believes itself divided, is already set on its course. Compared to Euphues in a similar conflict situation,[17] Proteus is much less self-conscious or concerned with looking before and after, much less aware of the appearance of the situation from every viewpoint; indeed the most impressive feature of this speech is its enactment of gradual self-absorption, until Proteus gives us the first hint of the Iago figure whose limited self—"'tis in ourselves that we are thus and thus"—is the centre of any argument. The casuistical argument against vows (common, as Clifford Leech points out, in early Shakespeare) is not merely, or mainly, an exhibition of clever wit; it produces a dizzy sense of the precariousness of language. When Lyly's debaters weigh up "love," in a much more intellectualized fashion than Proteus, the word remains an entity with a permanent reference; here it means what Proteus' heedless emotion wants it to mean: "I cannot leave to love, and yet I do." In the mouth of the unscrupulous, language changes its meaning, and—like Iago—Proteus can pretend to change actuality through words:

> I will forget that Julia is alive,
> Rememb'ring that my love to her is dead. (II.vi.27–8)

On the other hand, of course, a metamorphosed actuality can give a new human content and poignancy to an old game of words, as when Julia speaks of her heavy task of wooing Silvia on Proteus' behalf:

> I am my master's true confirmed love,
> But cannot be true servant to my master,
> Unless I prove false traitor to myself. (IV.iv.99–101)

The same is true for Valentine's banishment speech which, one might almost say, bears the same relation to the partial sonnet which the Duke discovers on him as Romeo's love for Rosaline does to that for Juliet. Valentine's discovery that he has so "garner'd up his heart" in another person that his own identity can only be defined through her,

> To die is to be banish'd from myself,
> And Silvia is myself; banish'd from her
> Is self from self, a deadly banishment.
> What light is light, if Silvia be not seen?
> What joy is joy, if Silvia be not by? (III.i.171–5)

passes beyond conventional attitudinizing to an attitude in which verbal patterning is functional and central. It is the sort of recognition which even in naturalistic drama calls for patterned speech:

George who is good to me, and whom I revile; who understands me, and whom I push off; . . . who can make me happy, and I do not wish to be happy, and yes I do wish to be happy. George and Martha: sad, sad, sad.[18]

There is a genuine ring of agony as the metaphors in Valentine's speech stop being conceits and become live reality—as we can feel if we compare the opening and key line of his poem to Silvia,

My thoughts do harbour with my Silvia nightly,

with his outcry in the banishment speech,

> Except I be by Silvia in the night
> There is no music in the nightingale;
> Unless I look on Silvia in the day,
> There is no day for me to look upon.
> She is my essence . . . (III.i.140 and 178–82)

The echoes here of themes and images from several sonnets may help us to see that, as in the sonnets, Shakespeare is working *through* the convention. At least one of the finest moments in the play is arrived at—much like Sonnet 130, "My mistress' eyes are nothing like the sun"—through a kind of anti-sonnet technique. When Silvia questions the supposed Sebastian about Julia, "Is she not passing fair?," and Julia replies by fictionalizing herself,

> She hath been fairer, madam, than she is.
> When she did think my master lov'd her well,
> She, in my judgment, was as fair as you;
> But since she did neglect her looking-glass,
> And threw her sun-expelling mask away,
> The air hath starv'd the roses in her cheeks,
> And pinch'd the lily-tincture of her face,
> That now she is become as black as I, (IV.iv.147–54)

then her nouns—the looking-glass, the sun, the roses, the lily-tincture—are those of the Petrarchan convention; but her verbs—neglect, throw away, starve, pinch—enact the reality behind the convention, the vulnerability of the roses and the lilies. We are, at one and the same time, reminded that "brightness falls from the air" and made to sense "what it feels like" in the particular dramatic situation. As fiction and reality in Julia's narrative meet in "That now she is become as black as I," language has become truly dramatic, indeed hardly more than a stage-direction.[19]

V

If Shakespeare's handling of convention and language at this stage of the play suggests a new seriousness and critical alertness, then we might in this context re-view two scenes which are often criticized for the wrong reasons and which, it seems to me, are in fact carefully controlled counter-conceits. The first is the one where Valentine with unbelievable stupidity gives away to the Duke his love for Silvia and his plan for elopement with her. The Duke's ruse of asking Valentine to "tutor" him in how to court "a lady in Verona here / Whom I affect" provides the scaffold for a duologue (especially III.i.89–105) which is a take-off on conventions of courtship in the rest of the play. The main comic point lies not just in Valentine's stupidity but in the freewheeling, or in terms of Valentine's consciousness almost mesmeric, effect which the convention has once the duologue is under way, so that the right key-word planted by the Duke will provoke the right (in terms of convention *and* of the Duke's intentions) response from Valentine:

> *Duke.* That no man hath access by day to her.
> *Val.* Why, then I would resort to her by night.
> *Duke.* Ay, but the doors be lock'd and keys kept safe,
>   That no man hath recourse to her by night . . .
> *Val.* Why then a ladder quaintly made of cords, (III.i.109ff.)

and so on. Shakespeare is, by the structure of the dialogue and by a slight quaintness of syntax, exaggerating the mechanical effect of patterned speech; for the Duke is putting to use the question-response technique which Kyd employed to dramatize Balthazar's love-worries:

> Yet might she love me for my valiancy:
> Ay, but that's slander'd by captivity.
> Yet might she love me to content her sire:
> Ay, but her reason masters his desire.
> Yet might she love me . . .
> Ay, but . . . [etc.] (*The Spanish Tragedy,* II.i.19ff.)

In the Shakespearian situation, love behaviour and language is seen to have become a mechanized gesture, the lover a puppet who can be manipulated at will by a detached outsider. Valentine is not just stupid[20] but a comic character in the Bergsonian sense. Not only is the love convention, in attitudes and speech, tested and found absurd but, in a microcosm of the whole play's pattern, it is seen to explode in violence. The image with which the Duke starts his dismissal of Valentine may, in its magnitude, seem to ameliorate the situation by exalting it:

> Why, Phaethon—for thou art Merops' son—
> Wilt thou aspire to guide the heavenly car,
> And with thy daring folly burn the world?
> Wilt thou reach stars because they shine on thee?

But that, too, explodes in ugly, unvarnished brutality:

> Go, base intruder, over-weening slave,
> Bestow thy fawning smiles on equal mates. (III.i.153–8)

If this situation is artificial, there is yet a sense of life in its implicit comment on artificiality and its effects.

The second scene to be set in this context is that in which Proteus, the most wickedly clever character in the play, in response to Silvia's reproaches can only produce two identical, and identically feeble, excuses:

> I grant, sweet love, that I did love a lady;
> But she is dead. . . .
> I likewise hear that Valentine is dead. (IV.ii.101–9)

To see this as "so feeble that it reflects from the incompetence of Proteus to that of the dramatist"[21] is to disregard the criticism built into this scene and its relation to the rest of the play. Much like Valentine in the scene just discussed, Proteus is moving as a puppet of the courtly love code, which for a situation like this prescribes, in Valentine's words to the Duke:

> If she do chide, 'tis not to have you gone,
> For why the fools are mad if left alone.
> Take no repulse, whatever she doth say;
> For "Get you gone" she doth not mean "Away!" (III.i.98–101)

The trouble is that Silvia does not go by the courtesy book but by genuine human reactions. Proteus, who was so voluble a letter-writer to Julia and so articulate in sacrificing an old love to a new, is inventive enough as long as he can play with conceits in the wooing-the-reluctant-mistress game:

> *Sil.* Who is that that spake?
> *Pro.* One, lady, if you knew his pure heart's truth,
> You would quickly learn to know him by his voice. . . .
> *Sil.* What's your will?
> *Pro.* That I may compass yours. (IV.ii.83–8)

But he cannot cope with a woman who persists in taking a severely practical view of his wit (ll.89–90) and in being ruthlessly literal about the conceit of his "pure heart's truth" (ll.91–5). So, as she gives him the wrong cues (as against the all-too-right ones in the case of the Duke vis-à-vis Valentine), he has no language to reply with but a cry of "dead." Once, indeed, he thinks he has picked up a cue, as Silvia assures him that in Valentine's grave (if he is dead) "my love is buried":

> Sweet lady, let me rake it from the earth.

But Silvia quickly disabuses him of the idea that he has found an idiom through which he can advance his interests:

> Go to thy lady's grave, and call hers thence;
> Or, at the least, in hers sepulchre thine. (IV.ii.111–3)

From this deadlock—"he heard not that," the listening Julia significantly comments—the only way forward is via a totally new conceit, that of Silvia's picture, which leads to a sonnet game on "shadow" and "substance" (ll.120–27). The presence of Julia and the sleeping Host throughout this scene enables Shakespeare not only to puncture Proteus' conceits and inanities with Julia's sharp asides but also to construct a situation which consists of several layers of non-communication. And the scene closes on Julia's words, as directly in contact with human reality as Desdemona's "Faith, half asleep":

> it hath been the longest night
> That e'er I watch'd, and the most heaviest. (135–6)

So, in exploring its world of romantic courtship, *The Two Gentlemen of Verona* repeatedly and in various ways reminds us that there is a world elsewhere. We are made to delight in the beauty and wit of the romance world, but we are also made to sense that it is fragile and vulnerable, ready to topple over into absurdity on the one side and brutality on the other. The sense of life that informs the play is something like a tightrope walk, and the scene which I have just discussed in an epitome of the tightrope pattern.

But IV.ii (which is generally regarded as the best scene in the play) is also an indication of where the play's radical dramatic weakness lies: in the tendency for each scene to form, much as each Shakespearian sonnet does, a kind of "still" from a play,[22] a virtually self-contained picture of human relationships. Shakespeare has obviously had difficulties in translating the "I" and the "thou" (and occasionally "she") of the sonnets into the multiple voices and interactions of a dramatic structure. The lovers hardly ever meet: apart from the last scene, each twosome comes together in two scenes,[23] but even then their contacts are often perfunctory. There is nothing like Romeo's and Juliet's minds meshing in a sonnet, nor like the formalized intimacy of the couples and cross-pairings in *Love's Labour's Lost* and *A Midsummer Night's Dream*. Lovers appear apart, talking about their love; and paradoxically Valentine and Silvia "meet" more in his banishment speech than in any actual co-presence on stage. The same is true for the two friends: their relationship is most alive and meaningful in Proteus' soliloquy in II.vi. All this means that the fulfillments in Act V—which forms what I have here called the third stage in the structure of the play—operate in something of a vacuum. When Valentine, faced with Proteus' perfidy, speaks of his friend as physically and morally part of himself—"one's own right hand / Is perjured to the bosom"—and voices an almost Cleopatra-like sense that the whole world has turned a stranger, then these words do not have tentacles which reach back into the play.

VI

The real inconsistency, then, of this play, and the one which becomes most apparent when he tries to dramatize constancy, is that Shakespeare is trying to use as his raw material what characters say (attitudes) rather than what they are (people). Plot is forever crystallizing into attitudes, and the structural pattern is one of scenes, each demonstrating one or more attitudes to love (or friendship). Some scenes are entirely contained in a single emblematic stance, like the two versions of parting with dear ones in II.ii and II.iii; some, like II.iv, move through a whole gamut of attitudes—more by adding one tableau to another than by casually linking each other with the other. The longest scene of all—III.i (374 lines)—is the longest not because more happens (the final scene in which so much happens is less than half as long) but because we move through a particularly wide range of stances: through moments deeply moving, moments which implicitly reveal their own absurdity, and moments which explicitly deflate the love code (Launce's and Speed's duologue on Launce's mistress). And what applies within the longer scenes also holds true for the relationship between scenes in the play as a whole. Their interconnection is determined not by growing and changing personalities but by their evaluation of the word and concept of "love." In other words, Shakespeare is trying to handle dramatic structure as if it were the verbal structure of a sonnet. To show what I mean, I should like at this point to return to Sonnet 40, which not only is very close in idea to Valentine's renunciation but also helps us to see why in *The Two Gentlemen of Verona* Shakespeare produced a work which is ultimately less dramatic than many of his sonnets.

It is necessary to quote the sonnet in full:

1   Take all my loves, my love, yea, take them all;
     What hast thou then more than thou hadst before?
     No love, my love, that thou mayst true love call;
     All mine was thine before thou hadst this more.
5   Then if for my love thou my love receivest,
     I cannot blame thee, for my love thou usest;
     But yet be blam'd, if thou thyself deceivest
     By wilful taste of what thyself refusest.
     I do forgive thy robb'ry, gentle thief,
10   Although thou steal thee all my poverty;
     And yet love knows it is a greater grief
     To bear love's wrong than hate's known injury.
          Lascivious grace, in whom all ill well shows,
          Kill me with spites; yet we must not be foes.

Without pressing the analogy, one might suggest that the handling of the word "love" in the sonnet forms something of a paradigm of the way individual scenes have been structured and related to each other in *The Two Gentlemen of Verona*. The syntax of sonnet line 3 produces a clash between the three different uses of "love," so that each comments upon and modifies our attitude to the other—much like what happens in the sequence of scenes iv, v and vi in Act II of the play. The shock-effect and cross-evaluation brought about by the apparent paradox of line 5 is similar to the operation of II.vi and vii: Julia's affirmation of her faith in Proteus' love following immediately upon his betrayal. The structure of relationships in the multidimensional scene IV.ii, where Julia suffers more from her unrequited love than Proteus from his, is based on much the same combination of paradox and antithesis as lines 11 and 12 in the sonnet. And similarly one can see a parallel mode of composition in the second quatrain of the sonnet and the Launce/Crab-Julia/Proteus-Julia/Silvia scene of IV.iv. Pivoted on the paradoxical self-sacrifices of Launce on behalf of his dog and Julia on behalf of her lover, as the quatrain is on the lines "Then if for my love thou my loving receivest, / I cannot blame thee for my love thou usest," the scene shows a similar structure of attitudes: overall wit and intercriticism of parts, overall lightness around a real heartbreak.

But when we come to look at the total achievement of the pattern in the sonnet and the play, respectively, its limitations in the play become apparent. In the sonnet, through the verbal action of devices like pun, paradox, antithesis and oxymoron, the pattern becomes an enactment of the poet's feelings for his friend; and the meaning of this "love" grows both more specific and more evocative, until it is defined—or, rather, held in suspension—in the contrary pulls of the couplet. Verbal ingenuity is entirely in the service of the dramatic evocation of "what it feels like." This is, of course, exactly what happens to the word-patterns and images in Shakespeare's mature plays; to a keyword like "see" in *King Lear*, which changes and grows in human meaning, from Lear's first to his last "see" and right through to Edgar's closing "never see so much." The sonnet is dramatic, too, in its dynamic form: what may look like a static attitude in the opening line develops through the fourteen lines into a live and complex relationship. The final "yet we must not be foes" is both a desperate appeal and an affirmation—a far more troubled statement than the apparent nonchalance of the first line. It reveals the quality which perhaps most definitely bespeaks the dramatist in the sonnet: the dual voice (or viewpoint), which asserts and yet also questions, affirms an utter self-effacement in devotion and is yet also aware of the absurdity of such an attitude—the ability, in other words, to be both inside and outside an experience.

The play is less dramatic on all these counts. The character interaction and development which *should* translate the verbal action of the sonnet is lacking, and so the sense of "what it feels like" is fitful and there is no overall dynamism. In the structural climax marked by Valentine's couplet,

And, that my love may appear plain and free,
All that was mine in Silvia I give thee,

"my love" *should* be a more meaningful dramatic reality than the "love" bandied about in the opening debate of the play. (The dénouement of *Twelfth Night*, for example, shows how the word "love" has been through just this dynamic process.) But in fact it is not. Nor is the ending sustained by that complex viewpoint which we find in the sonnet (and again in the final scene of *Twelfth Night*). Involvement and detachment have alternated during the first four Acts, sometimes (as in IV.ii) coalescing; but in the last scene, and particularly in Valentine's lines, the drama seems to fall between the two.

If, with due care, we continue the sonnet analogy, it would appear that Shakespeare conceived this last scene in much the same way as in several of his sonnets he used a surprise couplet—one which, after twelve lines of argument in one direction, leaps to a sudden reversal with an antithetical "Yet" or "But" or "Ah, but."[24] In the sonnets where this happens, the break in the logic and the frequent introduction of a new simplicity (not to be mistaken for facility) suggests that the couplet records more of a desperate wish-fulfilment than a real conclusion, a willed belief rather than a state of emotional conviction. The same seems to me to be true for the last scene of *The Two Gentlemen of Verona*. The trouble (the ultimate inconsistency) is that there is a theoretical pressure on the scene which is not practically realized. The connections, both thematic and verbal, between Valentine's situation and other instances of inconstancy and betrayed trust in Shakespeare—not least, of course, in the sonnets—indicate that pressure.[25] The sonnets which contain a reversal in the couplet are all in one way or another concerned with what Derek Traversi has called "the necessary flaw at the heart of passion"[26]— the fear that one's love and trust may be betrayed—and this fear, it seems to me, is what Shakespeare tries and fails to instil as an undertone in the scene. The central episode is dealt with in an extraordinary shorthand fashion.[27] There are 24 lines between Proteus' attempted rape and Julia's swoon, and in these we are bounced from one extreme attitude to another: disillusionment and reproach, penitence, forgiveness and demonstration of magnanimity. The shock to Valentine's consciousness is hauntingly expressed:

> Proteus,
> I am sorry I must never trust thee more,
> But count the world a stranger for thy sake. (68–70)

But thereafter the experience does not seem to pass through either character's mind. We are asked to accept it through general truths and universal statements, like Valentine's motivation of his forgiveness:

> Who by repentance is not satisfied,
> Is nor of heaven, nor earth; for these are pleas'd
> By Penitence th'Eternal's wrath's appeas'd. (79–81)

In a sonnet like "Why didst thou promise such a beauteous day" (34), which also turns from reproach to sudden forgiveness, the reversal in the couplet is organically part of the whole, for it embodies the very point of the poem: the irrationality, recognized as such and yet treasured, of a deep commitment. Nor is the couplet a simple reversal, for there is a strong undertone of irony in the way its imagery relates to the rest of the sonnet and contradicts the assurance it is supposed to state:

> Ah! but those tears are pearl which thy love sheds,
> And they are rich, and ransom all ill deeds.

How can the artificiality of pearl be commensurate with, still less compensate for, the unnatural hurts which the friend has inflicted?[28] The irrationality of Valentine's argument is not placed in a saving perspective—Speed and Launce have disappeared at this stage of the play, and the women are mute. Nor is there any room for irony in the interchange between sinner and forgiver: Proteus' plea that "hearty sorrow / Be a sufficient ransom for offence" is taken with the simplest "Then I am paid" from Valentine. Nor do Valentine's lines have any of the interpenetration of grief and the desire to forgive which dominates Sonnet 34.

It is easy enough to say that Shakespeare has here tried to do what he did not yet have the dramatic language or sense of structure to do. But before we condemn his failure, we should spare a thought for the magnitude of what he was trying to do. Perhaps his shorthand technique here is a first approach to the insight that one person's complete forgiveness of another, who has sinned vastly towards him or her, is a miracle beyond articulation in words—as the wordlessness of the reunion between Hermione and Leontes and the near inarticulacy of Cordelia's "no cause, no cause" would suggest. In the dénouements of the other comedies there are either no sins to forgive, only mistakes to rectify, or else the serious repentance and forgiveness take place off stage (*As You Like It*) or are structurally played down *(Much Ado About Nothing)*. We have to go to the qualified forgiveness of Isabella's plea for Angelo, or even as far forward in Shakespeare's career as Prospero's surprisingly bitter speech of forgiveness (*The Tempest,* V.i.130–34), before we find a dramatic language and situation which, like Sonnet 34, tells us that short of a miracle, forgiveness does not obliterate the offence.

The reason why I have paid so much attention to what is *not* there in *The Two Gentlemen of Verona* is that it is the combination of what *is* there with what is not that makes it a disturbing play. Certain aspects of its structure and language, as I hope to have shown, enable us to be in two minds at once: to accept and criticize the life presented to us. We are aware of the beauty *and* precariousness of the romance world. But individual characters' speeches cannot reach to the kind of *felt* uncertainty which is there in Helena's inability to settle for complete trust—"And I have found Demetrius like a jewel, / Mine own, and not mine own" (*A Midsummer Night's Dream*, IV.i.188–9)—and which rankles in many of the sonnets:

> Thee have I not lock'd up in any chest,
> Save where thou art not, though I feel thou art,
> Within the gentle closure of my breast. (48)

It is that uncertainty within the closest relationships ("where thou art not, though I feel thou art") which I think Shakespeare has wanted to render in *The Two Gentlemen of Verona*, and which gives a peculiar poignancy to Proteus' outcry: "O heaven, were man / But constant, he were perfect." If the ending is an example of ineptitude in early Shakespeare, then the very ineptitude suggests the troubled vision of a man who cares immensely about love and friendship, what they do to people and make people do to each other. Perhaps in the end the surface of this play is intimate with the depths; but perhaps, also, that intimacy will emerge more readily in the study, in the company of the Folio and the Sonnets, than in the theatre. Perhaps *The Two Gentlemen of Verona* must ultimately be seen as that rare phenomenon in Shakespeare's corpus: a play where the sense of life is greater in reading than in seeing it. If so, there will never be a fitter audience for it than George Eliot at Dover, stirred, perturbed—and disgusted.

NOTES

1. Gordon S. Haight, *George Eliot: A Biography* (Oxford, 1968), p. 178.
2. *Endimion*, III.iv.124–7. Cf. M.C. Bradbrook, *Shakespeare and Elizabethan Poetry* (London, 1951), p. 150.
3. As for example in the Titus and Gisippus story in Sir Thomas Elyot's *The Governour*, Book II, Chapter XII, which Geoffrey Bullough prints as a "possible source" of *The Two Gentlemen* (*Narrative and Dramatic Sources of Shakespeare*, vol. I (London, 1957), pp. 212–17).
4. I am not concerned here with the obvious but superficial inconsistencies of geography, timing, etc., which Clifford Leech discusses in the introduction to the new Arden edition (London, 1969), pp. xv–xxi.
5. Haight, loc. cit.
6. In particular, G.K. Hunter, *John Lyly* (London, 1962), chapter VI; Stanley Wells, "The Failure of *The Two Gentlemen of Verona*," *Shakespeare Jahrbuch* 99 (1963), pp. 161–73; Harold F. Brooks, "Two Clowns in a Comedy (To Say Nothing of the Dog)," *Essays and Studies*, 1963, pp. 91–100.
7. Hereward T. Price, "Shakespeare as a Critic," *Philological Quarterly* XX (1941), p. 398.

8. In the absence of external evidence, scholars have varied in their opinions as to where, exactly, to place *The Two Gentlemen* among the early comedies. It could have been Shakespeare's first comedy of all.

9. Cf. Leech, op. cit., pp. lxix–lxx, and Bullough, op. cit., pp. 210–11.

10. Cf. G.K. Hunter, "The Dramatic Technique of Shakespeare's Sonnets," *Essays in Criticism* 3 (1953), pp. 152–64.

11. See the helpful discussion of this point in Joan Grundy, "Shakespeare's Sonnets and the Elizabethan Sonneteers," *Shakespeare Survey* 15 (1962), pp. 41–9.

12. Cf. the chapter on *Romeo and Juliet* in Nicholas Brooke, *Shakespeare's Early Tragedies* (London, 1968).

13. See the Epilogue to *The Four Seasons (Penguin New English Dramatists* 9, p. 189).

14. See Wells, op. cit., p. 163.

15. T.W. Baldwin, *William Shakespeare's Five-Act Structure* (Urbana, 1947), p. 719.

16. Eumenides speaking; *Endimion*, III.iv.105–20.

17. Euphues, *The Anatomy of Wit:* see Bullough's reprint of the relevant passage in *Narrative and Dramatic Sources of Shakespeare*, vol. I (London, 1957), p. 222.

18. Edward Albee, *Who's Afraid of Virginia Woolf?* Act III (Penguin edition), p. 113.

19. In the passage from the *Diana Enamorada* which is the source of this scene, Felismena (Julia) tells Celia (Silvia) about the former love of Felix (Proteus) and the effect of the betrayal upon the scorned lady; but the conversation turns into an abstract discourse on the relationship between "content of minde" and "perfect beautie" (see Bullough, op. cit., pp. 243–4), whereas Shakespeare's passage is concretely and dramatically emotive.

20. Nor do I think that the scene can be summed up as "situation at variance with character" (Wells, op. cit., p. 167).

21. Leech's note at IV.ii.109. The corresponding passage in *Diana Enamorada* supplies Felix (Proteus) with an eloquent argument (see Bullough, pp. 241–2), which further suggests that Proteus' "incompetence" is deliberate on Shakespeare's part.

22. Cf. G.K. Hunter, "The Dramatic Technique of Shakespeare's Sonnets," loc. cit., p. 154.

23. Proteus and Julia meet to part in II.ii, and with Julia disguised as "Sebastian" in IV.iv; Valentine and Silvia meet in the letter-game in II.i, and in the sparring of II.iv; Proteus and Silvia have a brief encounter of civilities in II.iv, and then meet in the abuse scene of IV.ii.

24. Thirteen sonnets use the couplet in this way: 19, 30, 34, 42, 60, 84, 86, 91, 92, 131, 133, 139, 141. For a somewhat negative critique of their technique, see Edward Hubler, *The Sense of Shakespeare's Sonnets* (Princeton, N.J., 1952), pp. 26–7.

25. R. Warwick Bond, in the "old" Arden edition of the play, draws attention to similarities between Valentine's language and that of Henry V to the traitor Scroop (*Henry V*, II.ii.138ff.); and also to Imogen in *Cymbeline*, III.iv.62. Other betrayals, in the plays and sonnets, though with no reference to *The Two Gentlemen*, are discussed in the fascinating article by M.M. Mahood, "Love's Confined Doom," *Shakespeare Survey* 15 (1962), pp. 50–61.

26. *Approach to Shakespeare* (London, 1946), p. 46.

27. It is of course possible that this is due to textual cuts between early performances and the first appearance of the play in print, in the Folio. But even if the interchange between Valentine and Proteus was originally longer, and was abbreviated for an age no longer interested in a love-friendship debate, this makes only a quantitative difference to my argument.

28. Professor Mahood suggests that the last line "may well be spoken with deep irony to the man who thinks his patronage can pay for his unkindness" (*Shakespeare Survey* 15, p. 53).

THE TWO GENTLEMEN OF VERONA AND THE COURTESY BOOK TRADITION (1983)

Camille Wells Slights

> *hee being understood*
> *May make good Courtiers, but Who Courtiers good?*
> *John Donne, "Satyre V," ll. 3–4*

I

Although commentary on Shakespeare's comedies contains little enthusiasm for *The Two Gentlemen of Verona*, in recent years critics have found a great deal to admire in the comic byplay provided by Speed and Launce, in the character of Julia—the first of the spirited heroines to don male clothing and take to the road in pursuit of love—and in the delicate beauty of some of the poetry. While some critics stress the satiric elements and others the celebratory, on the whole they agree that by combining mockery of artificial conventions with lyric evocation of romantic love, *The Two Gentlemen of Verona* prepared the way for the great romantic comedies to follow. Only the climactic final scene has presented an interpretative crux and provoked almost universal condemnation.

In the last scene, immediately after saving his beloved Silvia from being raped by his treacherous friend Sir Proteus, Valentine accepts without question Proteus' protestations of remorse and offers to withdraw his own suit in favour of Proteus, saying:

> And that my love may appear plain and free,
> All that was mine in Silvia I give thee. (*V.iv. 82–83*)[1]

Critics who see the play primarily as a celebration of romantic love are understandably perplexed when the romantic hero suddenly offers the heroine to his rival. From this point of view, Shakespeare has violently contra-

Reprinted from *Shakespeare Studies* 16 (1983): 13–31.

dicted the premises of his own romantic comedy, transforming his young lover into an insensitive brute. Another standard approach places the play in the Renaissance tradition that exalts friendship over love. From this perspective, the scene, far from undermining the basic conventions of its own fictional world, is "the germ or core of the play" and Valentine's offer to give up Silvia to Proteus is not boorish but generous, the magnanimous sacrifice of love to friendship.[2]

From either point of view, the exchange between Proteus and Valentine is an artistic failure. If *The Two Gentlemen of Verona* is a celebration of the experience of falling in love—the absurdities and joys of youthful passion—the hero's cheerful offer of his mistress to the man who has just tried to rape her is certainly a blunder. On the other hand, if Valentine is intended as a model of selfless generosity according to Renaissance conceptions of ideal friendship, he is a remarkably weak exemplar of the tradition. In Sir Thomas Elyot's story of Titus and Gisippus, which apparently served as a source for the Valentine-Silvia-Proteus triangle, Gisippus relinquishes his betrothed to Titus, who marries her. Years later, when Gisippus is threatened with execution for murder, Titus confesses to the crime in an effort to die in his friend's place.[3] But in Shakespeare's play, neither Valentine nor Proteus actually sacrifices anything for friendship. After all, Valentine runs little risk that the repentant Proteus will take him up on his offer and even less that Silvia would accept him if he did.[4]

Without denying weaknesses and confusions in the early comedies, I think we should be suspicious of any critical position that convicts Shakespeare of inept bungling. It is not unthinking bardolatry to assume that even as an apprentice playwright Shakespeare would not construct a dramatic climax that signally fails to resolve and clarify any of the emotional or intellectual issues at stake. If the resolution of *The Two Gentlemen of Verona* does not illuminate the relationship of love to friendship, it is probable that interpretations emphasizing the triumph of one or the other are slightly askew. Indeed, in the play itself only Proteus refers to a conflict between the claims of love and those of friendship, and he uses this formulation to justify betraying Julia's love as well as Valentine's friendship.

Although critics have been misled by Proteus' pat generalization ("In love, / Who respects friend?" [V.iv.53–54]), they have also responded to the ideas and values that recur throughout the play. For example, Sir Arthur Quiller-Couch denounces Valentine's offer of Silvia to Sir Proteus in these terms: "there are, by this time, *no* gentlemen in Verona."[5] And M.C. Bradbrook defends the same action as "displaying in transcendent form the courtly virtue of Magnanimity, the first and greatest virtue of a gentleman."[6] While Quiller-Couch and Bradbrook obviously disagree over how a gentleman should act in Valentine's awkward situation, they both assume that the play directs us to evaluate Valentine's action in terms of the conduct appropriate to a gentleman. Valentine's gesture, like Arveragus' offer of his wife to her suitor in Chaucer's *The Franklin's Tale*, expresses a particular conception of "gentilesse" that has provoked variously admiration and censure.[7] *The Two Gentlemen of Verona* is less an evocation of what it feels like to fall in love or an analysis of the relative significance of love and friendship than a comic exploration of the nature and function of a gentleman.

Quiller-Couch's outraged denunciation of fictional characters of whom he disapproves as "*no* gentlemen" may strike us today as a quaint expression of his own Edwardian values, but we should remember that the scanty biographical knowledge we have suggests that the status of a gentlemen was a subject Shakespeare personally took seriously enough. In the sixteenth century, moreover, the education, qualities, and functions of the gentleman were issues of considerable political and cultural importance.[8] Works as popular and significant as Castiglione's *The Courtier*, Sir Thomas Elyot's *The Governor*, and Edmund Spenser's *The Faerie Queen* demonstrate the lasting interest and significance of Renaissance discussions of how to fashion a gentleman. In *The Two Gentlemen of Verona*, Shakespeare draws on and contributes to this tradition of courtesy books.

II

The opening scene introduces us to the play's unifying theme—the question of the proper behavior for a young gentleman—and to its dominant verbal mode—the indirections of polite discourse. Valentine, excited by his imminent departure "To see the wonders of the world abroad" (I.i.6), and Proteus, "over boots in love" (l. 25) with Julia, are engaged in conventional activities for two young gentlemen of Verona, or of London. They debate the merits of their respective choices—foreign travel and love—with the verbal wit of the young gallant. For example, Valentine's taunting of Proteus with the follies of love leads to the following exchange:

> *Pro.* Yet writers say: as in the sweetest bud
> The eating canker dwells, so eating Love
> Inhabits in the finest wits of all.
> *Val.* And writers say: as the most forward bud
> Is eaten by the canker ere it blow,
> Even so by Love the young and tender wit

Is turn'd to folly, blasting in the bud,
Losing his verdure, even in the prime,
And all the fair effects of future hopes. *(11. 42–50)*

Valentine might have been reading in Castiglione's *The Courtier* of the "merry conceites and jestes" that may appropriately grace the conversation of the perfect courtier:

> . . . among other merry sayings, they have a verie good grace, that arise when a man at the nipping talke of his fellow, taketh the verie same words in the selfe same sense, and returneth them backe againe, pricking him with his owne weapon. . . . Also merry sayinges are much to the purpose to nippe a man, . . . so the metaphors be well applyed, and especially if they be answered, and he that maketh answere continue in the selfe same metaphor spoken by the other.[9]

Although the form of their speech, nipping and pricking at each other, implies opposition, Valentine and Proteus are actually in total agreement. For all his scorn at love's folly, Valentine does not seriously attempt to dissuade Proteus from loving; he wishes his friend well in love, acknowledging that in time he too expects to fall in love:

> But since thou lov'st, love still, and thrive therein,
> Even as I would, when I to love begin. *(ll. 9–10)*

And Proteus expects a friend's feelings of vicarious pleasure and protective concern from Valentine's travels:

> Wish me partaker in thy happiness,
> When thou dost meet good hap; and in thy danger
> (If ever danger do environ thee)
> Commend thy grievance to my holy prayers. *(ll. 14–17)*

Privately he concedes Valentine's point: love has made his "wit with musing weak" (l. 69). Ostensibly denoting rivalry, their wit actually expresses affectionate concord.

The word-play that signals the young men's pretensions to courtly elegance also indicates their youth and inexperience. Valentine and Proteus, like Romeo and Mercutio or Beatrice and Benedick, use puns and ripostes and ironies to impress others with their mental and verbal agility and to give themselves a sense of control over their world as well as to express their high-spirited exuberance and to exercise their developing powers for sheer enjoyment. Their linguistic ingenuity is not the effortless command of language that expresses unselfconscious ease and assurance in a social situation but rather the ostentatious display of wit that indicates vulnerability and insecurity. When Valentine and Proteus are together, like-minded friends who understand and respect each other, mocking repartee is subsumed within the context of frank and open talk, and their conversation has some claim to grace as well as to vitality. In other situations, they are less able to balance the indirections of rhetoric with straightforward communication and consequently appear noticeably more awkward.

In the dialogue between Proteus and Speed that follows Valentine's exit, for example, repeated quibbles on "ship," "sheep," and "mutton" grow tiresome. Since Proteus fails to get a clear report of the delivery of his message to Julia, while Speed does succeed in exacting his tip, Proteus emerges as loser in this contest of wits with his friend's servant. In his next appearance Proteus' language is even more completely at variance from literal truth, and his ingenuity is used to more disastrous—and comic—effect. In scene three, Proteus is exulting in a letter from Julia—"her oath for love" (I.iii.47)—when his father interrupts to ask what he is reading. Proteus replies that his letter is from Valentine:

> he writes
> How happily he lives, how well-belov'd,
> How daily graced by the Emperor;
> Wishing me with him, partner of his fortune. *(11. 56–59)*

Ironically, the lie designed to hide and protect his relationship with Julia precipitates his separation from her by reinforcing his father's decision that Proteus should join Valentine to complete his education. The adolescent's instinctive impulse to hide his love letter from his all-too-solicitous parent should not be interpreted as evidence of a basically duplicitous character, but the spectacle of Proteus blundering into a trap he has set for himself certainly provokes amusement at his expense.

The same type of youthful gaucherie is the source of humor in both in the preceding and following scenes. In the preceding scene Julia indignantly scolds her maid Lucetta first for delivering Proteus' letter and then for interpreting her angry words literally instead of understanding them as conventional expressions of maidenly modesty:

> What fool is she, that knows I am a maid,
> And would not force the letter to my view!
> Since maids, in modesty, say "no" to that
> Which they would have the profferer construe "ay." *(I.ii.53–56)*

After another round of verbal sparring with Lucetta, Julia histrionically tears the letter in pieces and finally is reduced to searching the ground for the precious fragments to piece together. Although subsequently Proteus' fickleness contrasts with Julia's constancy, in Act I it is their similarity that is most striking. Both feel the need to protect the privacy of their new, tender emotions, and both are comically inept in their attempts at dissimulation.[10]

Valentine too finds himself out of his depth in the emotional subtleties and linguistic indirections of polite society. While Proteus and Julia betray their naiveté in their bungling attempts at dissimulation, Valentine displays his through his literal-minded incomprehension. When the scene shifts to Milan we discover that Valentine, the scoffer at love, has fallen in love with Silvia, the Duke's daughter, and is suffering all the paradoxical pain and ecstasy, exaltation and humiliation of the conventional courtly lover. He has even complied with Silvia's request that he write a letter for her to "one she loves" (II.i.83). Silvia then feigns anger at Valentine's reluctance to send her love to another and tells him to keep the lines of love he has written for himself:

> I will none of them: they are for you.
> I would have had them writ more movingly. *(ll. 120–21)*

And, to Valentine's offer to repeat his effort:

> And when it's writ, for my sake read it over,
> And if it please you, so; if not, why, so. *(ll. 123–24)*

Although Silvia's jest, as Speed says, is as "unseen, inscrutable, invisible, / As a nose on a man's face" (ll. 128–29), Valentine fails to understand that she is teaching him to court her in earnest.

Silvia, in fact, is instructing Valentine in just the kind of courtly wit and elegant discourse the young gentlemen from Verona have come to Milan to learn. When Proteus' father and uncle worry that he is wasting his time at home, they canvas the alternatives open to a well-born young man:

Some to the wars, to try their fortunes there;
Some, to discover islands far away;
Some, to the studious universities. *(I.iii.8–10)*

Apparently on the basis of the paramount importance of acquiring the social graces, they decide to send Proteus to court where he will be able to

practise tilts and tournaments,
Hear sweet discourse, converse with noblemen,
And be in eye of every exercise
Worthy his youth and nobleness of birth. *(ll. 30–33)*

Several critics have condemned this courtly behavior as trivial or even
corrupt, an unworthy goal that Valentine and Proteus must discard before
real eduation can take place.[11] J.A. Mazzeo's defense of Castiglione's *The
Courtier* from similar criticism illuminates, I think, the attitude to courtly
sophistication in Shakespeare's play. Mazzeo acknowledges that "the attention Castiglione gives to gesture, manner, games, jokes, and anecdotes might
seem to some of his readers an extraordinary trivialization of the ideals of
true education." But, he argues, by neglecting these "non-verbal modes of
communication and expression, or the non-referential uses of language,"
modern education often produces narrow specialists:

. . . "experts" with extraordinary capacities in certain well-defined
areas and no grasp of the meaning of human actions, activities, gestures, or of the varieties of emotional expression. Such are those who
cannot distinguish between what men say and do and what they mean
by what they say and do, who cannot truly understand speech because speech is much more than the words it uses. What the modern
reader may see as trivia in Castiglione's program of education are after
all the vehicles of those subtle and feeling interchanges between people
which do as much as anything to give them the sense that they are
really alive.[12]

Castiglione's emphasis on style and gesture, on jokes and games, is essential
to his subject, "the creation of the self as a work of art through education,"
and to his concept of individual perfection as a balance and harmony of all
important human capacities without excessive development or suppression of
any. This attempt to delineate human perfection in an ideal courtier links *The
Courtier* to the important cultural impulse in the Renaissance that produced

so much utopian literature and so many books outlining ideal social forms of various kinds.[13] In addition, the popularity of *The Courtier* and other courtesy books reflects concern with social cohesion as well as with individual development. The courtesy books all agree that public service is the gentleman's primary function and that the end of his education in the ways of society is his ability to advise his ruler effectively.[14] The qualities of behavior that characterize the gentleman are those that bind people together in social harmony. Thus, according to Edmund Spenser, the courtly virtue of courtesy is the source of all "goodly manners" and "ciuill conversation" *(The Faerie Queene,* VI.i.l).[15] It includes not only personal appearance and manner—"all gracious gifts . . . / Which decke the body or adorne the mynde"—but also "friendly offices that bynde" and correct social behavior:

> how to each degree and kynde
> We should our selues demeane, to low, to hie;
> To friends, to foes, which skill men call Ciuility. (F.Q., *VI.x.23)*

In this context, we can see that when Antonio worries that his son Proteus "cannot be a perfect man" (I.iii.20) without more experience in the world, he is not identifying himself as a Neoplatonic philosopher striving toward perfection, but neither is he betraying hopelessly superficial values. He endorses an educational program similar to Castiglione's when he chooses life at court as most suitable to his son's "youth and nobleness of birth." The play's early scenes have demonstrated clearly that young gentlemen need social tact, verbal dexterity, even some adeptness at polite dissimulation in order to get along harmoniously with servants, fathers, and women. In the first court scene, Silvia uses the letter as an "excellent device" (II.i.132) to express her own desires and to help Valentine overcome his timidity without violating social decorum. By calling on the "clerkly" skills of her "gentle servant" (l. 101) she utilizes Valentine's gentlemanly accomplishments of the most artificial and conventional kind—courtly love conventions and literary skills—in order to liberate real feeling.[16] The grace and wit with which she employs the artifices of sophisticated society in order to circumvent the obstacles erected by conventions of rank and sex role are no mean accomplishments.

III

While *The Two Gentlemen of Verona* presents courtly elegance as a positive value, it also shows how fragile and easily corrupted this ideal is. Superficially trivial manners are the necessary texture of a humane society that encourages people to develop their full human potential and that fosters a variety of subtle feelings and relationships among people, yet these same manners may degenerate into hypocrisy or cynical intrigue. The courtly ideal is a precarious balance of self-enhancement and social responsibility. The aristocratic code blends strict devotion to truth (so that proverbially a gentleman's word is his bond) with an elegant grace of manner that involves artifice and pretense, the art of concealing art.[17] Sir Calidore, Spenser's knight of courtesy, for example, "loved simple truth and stedfast honesty" *(F.Q., VI.i.3)*, but the "friendly offices" he performed sometimes required deception.[18] *Sprezzatura,* the graceful nonchalance that Castiglione recommends for the ideal courtier, may degenerate into the disdain and contempt that, according to Mazzeo, are "vaguely present" in the concept.[19] Gentlemanly dignity may degenerate into cold arrogance or ostentatious self-display, and playful wit into either irresponsible frivolity or malicious deceit.[20]

The plot of *The Two Gentlemen of Verona* unfolds out of Valentine's and Proteus' acquisition of courtly values and style. Not surprisingly, superficial manners prove to be more easily learned than the ability to use them to develop well-rounded individuality and social harmony. Valentine, who initially cannot distinguish between what Silvia says and what she means, readily picks up the art of courtly circuitousness and dissimulation. The next time he appears he courts Silvia indirectly by bandying insults with another suitor. His language in this scene demonstrates both the social utility and the danger of courtly linguistic conventions. By rejecting Speed's advice that his hated rival Sir Thurio should be "knocked" (II.iv.7) and instead expressing his hostility in what Silvia commends as "A fine volley of words" (l. 30), Valentine acts out sexual rivalry with wit and gaiety rather than brutality. But when he adopts the langue of courtly love without Silvia's ironic detachment from it, his perceptions are blunted rather than refined by the conventions. By acknowledging that "Love's a mighty lord" (l. 131) and by confessing the sorrow and joy of love's service, Valentine joins in civilized humanity's transformation of sexual appetite into love. But lie betrays self-deceit and insensitivity when he insists that Proteus acknowledge Silvia as "divine," not earthly, and when he refers to Julia, Proteus' beloved, with gratuitous contempt:

> She shall be dignified with this high honour,
> To bear my lady's train. *(ll. 153–54)*

The contradictory tensions inherent in the sixteenth-century idea of gentlemanly behavior become even more evident in Valentine's scheme to elope with Silvia. By planning to release Silvia from the tower where her father locks her and from marriage to the wealthy but doltish Sir Thurio, Valentine is rescuing a damsel in distress in the best chivalric tradition and insisting on the dignity and delicacy of love and marriage. Yet he is also violating the Duke's parental right and abusing his hospitality. When Valentine first confides his plan to Proteus, considerations of the first sort combine with the conventional comic endorsement of youth and love against age and law to direct audience sympathy toward the lovers. The irresponsibility of the plot comes more forcibly to mind later when the Duke, under the guise of seeking love-advice himself, tricks Valentine into revealing his plan. In this scene, Valentine hypocritically praises Thurio as a match for Silvia, cynically explains that women reject men's advances only in order to egg them on and that any woman can be won with gifts and flattery, and proposes a rope ladder to gain access to a woman whose friends have promised her to someone else. The Duke's reply,

> Now, as thou art a gentleman of blood,
> Advise me where I may have such a ladder, *(III.i.121–22)*

reminds us that Valentine is fulfilling his gentleman's duty to advise and serve his ruler in a particularly tawdry way. In this context, we watch with amusement rather than anxiety as the Duke outwits Valentine, discovering the ladder and the incriminating letter to Silvia hidden under his cloak.

In Valentine, then, we can discern the danger of aristocratic self-assurance becoming pride and of delicacy and subtlety becoming duplicity. Proteus perverts the gentlemanly ideal even more radically. As we have seen, his family encourages him to strive to perfect himself. Valentine, who gracefully apologizes for his own failure to achieve "angel-like perfection" (II.iv.61), praises his friend as a model gentleman:

> He is complete in feature and in mind,
> With all good grace to grace a gentleman. *(ll. 68–69)*

When Proteus joins Valentine at the court of Milan, this exemplar of the art of self-cultivation becomes the apologist for sheer selfishness. No sooner does he learn of Valentine's love than he determines to win Silvia himself, consoling himself for the loss of Valentine's friendship with the thought, "I to myself am dearer than a friend" (II.vi.23), and justifying the plot he immediately formulates to betray Valentine to the Duke and subsequently to slander him to Silvia:

> I cannot now prove constant to myself,
> Without some treachery us'd to Valentine. *(ll. 31–32)*

While Valentine becomes guilty of disdain and deceit, it remains for Proteus to stoop to the even more contemptible practice of detraction and slander.[21] His attempts at self-justification are so absurdly sophistical, however, and his machinations to win Silvia so obviously self-defeating that the audience is again not so much morally outraged by his perfidy as amused by the mess he is getting himself into.

In a sense, aristocratic values seem to contain the seeds of their own destruction. In the process of developing the qualities of a gentlemen both Valentine and Proteus lose their status as gentlemen: the Duke denounces Valentine for aspiring to his daughter as a "base intruder, overweening slave" (III.i.157) and Proteus, even as he undertakes to destroy Silvia's love for Valentine by accusing him of "falsehood, cowardice, and poor descent" (III.ii.32) admits that slandering his friend is "an ill office for a gentleman" (l. 40). This breakdown of civilized manners extends even to Launce's dog Crab, who "thrusts . . . himself into the company of three or four gentlemen-like dogs, under the Duke's table" and there disgraces himself (IV.iv.16–18).

The elegant, courtly society that draws all the young people to it through the first two acts begins, in Act III, to self-destruct, literally and physically as well as figuratively and spiritually. Valentine's introduction to courtly love and dissimulation culminates in his banishment from court. His exile precipitates Silvia's flight, which in turn causes the Duke, Proteus, and Thurio to pursue her, while Julia, disguised as a page boy, follows Proteus. By the end of Act IV, all the major characters have abandoned the court of Milan with its dangers and frustrations and have fled to the lawless and dangerous forest.

This contrary motion toward and away from the court suggests that the very qualities that bind people together in civilized society also threaten to fragment and dissolve those bonds. The aristocratic insistence on excellence as a standard and on perfection as a goal encourages individual fulfillment in a complex and humane society, but it is also inherently competitive. This paradox underlies the pattern of imitative desire producing increasing violence that René Girard discerns in Shakespeare's portrayal of love. Girard demonstrates that the confusions and conflicts of *A Midsummer Night's Dream* arise out of the young lovers' aspirations for sexual dominance deriving from an erotic ideal.

> . . . they all worship the same erotic absolute, the same ideal image of seduction which each girl and boy in turn appears to embody in the eyes of the others. This absolute has nothing to do with concrete qualities; it is properly metaphysical. Even though obsessed with the

flesh, desire is divorced from it; it is not instinctive and spontaneous; it never seems to know directly and immediately where its object lies; in order to locate that object, it cannot rely on such things as the pleasure of the eyes and the other senses. In its perpetual *nocheoscura,* metaphysical desire must therefore trust in another and supposedly more enlightened desire on which it patterns itself.[22]

Thus, Helena, Hermia, Lysander, and Demetrius all "choose love by another's eyes" (I.i.140). According to Girard, the "crucial point" about this mimetic desire is

> . . . the necessarily jealous and conflictual nature of mimetic convergence on a single object: If we keep borrowing each other's desires, if we allow our respective desires to agree on the same object, we, as individuals, are bound to disagree. . . .
>
> Metaphysical desire is mimetic, and mimetic desire cannot be let loose without breeding a midsummer night of jealousy and strife. *(pp. 191–92)*

As Girard suggests, not only in *A Midsummer Night's Dream* but throughout the canon Shakespeare dramatizes the conflicts arising from this kind of romantic passion that is not a spontaneous response to a desirable and desired other but primarily an imitation of a model. So, in *The Two Gentlemen of Verona* when Valentine insists that Silvia is the ideal woman "whose worth makes other worthies nothing" (II.iv.161), he teaches Proteus to forsake Julia and make Silvia the object of his desire. Even Proteus admits that "Valentinus' praise" has as much to do with his passion as his own perception of Silvia's perfections (II.iv.192–94). And we realize that for him Silvia *"excels each mortal thing"* (IV.ii.50) primarily *because "all our swains commend her"* (l. 39). Proteus' sudden desire for Silvia destroys the social group through betrayal and banishment and also undermines his sense of his own identity. As Girard explains, a metaphysical, mimetic passion is necessarily self-destructive: it is "destructive not only because of its sterile rivalries but because it dissolves reality: it tends to the abstract, the merely representational" (p. 193). It feeds on rejection and failure: "The impossible is always preferred to the possible, the unreal to the real, the hostile and unwilling to the willing and available" (p. 195). Although the aspiration to an erotic ideal is basically self-elevating, the worship of an unattainable idol results in the lover's self-abasement expressed in animal images: "Far from raising himself to the state of the superman, a god, as he seeks to do, the subject of mimetic desire sinks to the level of animality. The animal images are the price the self has to pay for its idolatrous worship of otherness" (p. 197).

Thus Proteus complains that

> spaniel-like, the more she spurns my love,
> The more it grows, and fawneth on her still. *(IV.ii.14–15)*

He begs for a picture of Silvia, announcing that since he cannot possess "the substance of [her] perfect self,"

> I am but a shadow;
> And to your shadow will I make true love. *(IV.ii.120–22)*

And Silvia agrees that it is entirely appropriate for false Proteus "To worship shadows, and adore false shapes" (l. 127).

IV

Sending Valentine and Proteus to court to learn to act like perfect gentlemen by observing the best models ironically results in loss of self-respect and destruction of social cohesion, but the play also makes clear that refusal to emulate models of decorum can have equally disastrous consequences, as Launce complains to Crab:

> I remember the trick you served me, when I took my leave of Madam Silvia: did not I bid thee still mark me, and do as I do? When didst thou see me heave up my leg, and make water against a gentlewoman's farthingale? Didst thou ever see me do such a trick? *(IV.iv.34–39)*

The genteel lovers experience the disadvantages of life without the restraints of civilization when they flee from court to the lawless wilderness. By escaping from the capricious dangers of courtly hypocrisy and ducal tyranny, they become vulnerable to physical brutality, threatened with robbery, murder, and rape. In the woods outside Milan they learn the worth and the limitations of their conception of gentility.

In this first example in Shakespearean comedy of a rural retreat where courtly lovers overcome their difficulties and adjust their values before returning to civilization, the sylvan setting is far from being a pastoral world of innocence and peace. The woods are inhibited by society's outcasts, outlaws banished for murder and "such like petty crimes" (IV.i.52), who live by terrorizing and robbing hapless travelers. In this setting, Proteus' frustrations erupt in violence. When Silvia continues to reject him and to condemn him after he rescues her from the outlaws, he tries to rape her.

But if the woods are a setting for violence and uncontrolled passion, they do not represent a state of nature free from social distinctions and hierarchy. The outlaws are absurdly proud that some of them are gentlemen by birth and feel acutely the need for a leader to command them. Rather than the possibility of an egalitarian society they embody an alternate and older idea of the gentleman, that is, the aristocrat as armed warrior. Fiercely loyal to their own band, sensitive to slights on their honor, they recognize no authority or social obligation beyond the immediate group. Their recognition of Valentine as their natural leader on the basis of his general deportment and linguistic ability is Shakespeare's comic rendition of actual historical process. The chivalric armed warrior, though romantically appealing, must inevitably make way for the educated, accomplished courtier.[23] Given the choice of joining the outlaws as their leader or of being killed for insulting them with his refusal, Valentine accepts an offer he cannot very well refuse, but he soon understands the undesirability of living with men who "make their wills their law" (V.iv.14). He finds the "unfrequented woods" a better place to lament his loss of Silvia than "flourishing peopled towns" (ll. 2–3), but he knows that total isolation is not possible. He must perforce relate to other people in some kind of social structure, if not as a lawful subject in a civilized community, then as a member of a faction of outlaws whose "uncivil outrages" (l. 17) he can restrain only with difficulty.

In this situation, when Valentine witnesses Proteus' solicitation and attack on Silvia, his response reflects his developed understanding of the individual's relation to society as well as his personal hurt:

> Ruffian! Let go that rude uncivil touch,
> Thou friend of an ill fashion.
> . . . . .
> Thou common friend, that's without faith or love,
> For such is a friend now. (V.iv.60–63)

Proteus' treachery epitomizes the point at which the selfishness and shallow hypocrisy of courtly fashion is indistinguishable from uncivilized savagery, a paradox expressed in the ambiguous epithet "common": by adopting the debased manners of the fashionable world, Proteus forfeits his claim to being a true gentleman. Betrayal by his most trusted friend forces Valentine to see feelingly that total disillusionment both with the manners of society and with their rejection, instead of allowing him a superior position of intellectual detachment, leads to the terrifying isolation of complete alienation:

> Who should be trusted now, when one's right hand
> Is perjured to the bosom? Proteus,
> I am sorry I must never trust thee more,
> But count the world a stranger for thy sake. *(ll. 67–70)*

Shocked into realizing what he has become, Proteus repents. Valentine accepts his apology both because forgiveness is at once naturally human and imitative of divinity and because for him the alternative to trusting Proteus is to trust no one. Valentine and Proteus have glimpsed a world of sheer brutality and total cynicism, and together they draw back from the abyss. Their reconciliation fills personal emotional needs and indicates their renewed acceptance of their place in civilized society where men are bound together by mutual trust as well as by civil authority. Valentine's speech accepting Proteus' repentance marks his return to a world where a gentleman's word is his bond but where gentlemen characteristically communicate through indirection. It modulates from the plain statement of the terms of their relationship:

> Then I am paid;
> And once again I do receive thee honest, *(ll. 77–78)*

to the elegant indirection of offering to give up Silvia. Because he accepts Proteus as honestly repentant, he has faith that his friend will not renew his pursuit of Silvia. His offer is a courteous gesture that will give Proteus a chance to be his best self.

At this point Shakespeare averts the threatened bathos of repeated, elaborate gestures of repentance and forgiveness and reestablishes the prevailing comic tone by having Valentine's attempt at sophisticated indirection miscarry once again. Although his gesture demonstrates love and trust in Proteus with considerable tact and subtlety, he has no way of considering its effect on the disguised Julia. For her it is the last straw: she faints, revives, and immediately reveals her identity and her claim to Proteus' love and fidelity. Indeed, the happy ending is possible not only because Valentine and Proteus have gained a more complex understanding of themselves and their relation to other people, but because Julia and Sylvia have always had a more balanced view. Both women defy convention and abandon society's protection in pursuit of love, but they struggle to preserve whatever decorum is possible. They do not choose love by others' eyes. Silvia is impervious to slander against Valentine and to praise of Proteus and Thurio. Julia justly resents Proteus' eulogizing of Silvia without learning to despise herself. Because they are confident of their own worth and their own judgment of the men they love, without claiming perfection for either, they can meet the situation that pushes them toward rivalry and conflict with mutual sympathy.

The reestablishment of the bonds of civilization begun with the reconciliation of the friends and lovers is completed by the entry of the Duke and by Valentine's deference to him. The Duke confirms the "new state" (1. 142) of things, announcing, "Sir Valentine, / Thou art a gentleman, and well deriv'd" (1. 144) and blessing his union with Silvia.[24]

The play has not, however, merely come full circle back to a celebration of courtliness and conventionality. If the outlaws and Proteus have discredited the image of the noble brigand, the gentleman simply as courtier and courtly lover has also proved inadequate. Silvia has trusted to the protection of Sir Eglamour on the grounds that he is a gentleman (IV.iii.11–13) and suffered for her folly when he is unable to save her from the outlaws. Thurio, the Duke's choice for son-in-law, proves to be a coward. Valentine no longer relies on indirection and subterfuge to win Silvia but directly warns off Thurio with violent threats. He wins the Duke's favor and reappraisal of his social rank, not by his obedience, but by his high spirit. And for the first time Valentine explicitly mentions serving the state as the gentleman's natural vocation, urging the Duke to pardon the outlaws for they are "fit for great employment" (V.iv.155). Indeed, perhaps the secret of Valentine's success is his flexibility—witty and courtly with Silvia, respectful to the Duke, stern but helpful to the outlaws, fierce and violent with Thurio, contemptuous and then trustful of Proteus.[25]

The Two Gentlemen of Verona ridicules the inadequacies of the elegant courtly lover, reckless adventurer, and sycophantic courtier, but the ideas of the gentleman current in the sixteenth century—as polished courtier, scholar, soldier, and statesman—all contribute to the unattainable ideal it suggests. By the end of the play, we feel that Valentine has proved himself a gentleman through an elusive combination of courtliness, high-spirited courage, social responsibility, and faithful love and friendship. If the play hints darkly that pursuit of an external standard of perfection and lawless self-will both destroy social cohesion and civilized life, it also celebrates the communal happiness possible when people combine idealism with realistic understanding of human imperfection and join self-cultivation and self-assertion with respect for other people. Proteus may be right that "were man / But constant, he were perfect" (V.iv.109–10), but in a world of imperfect men the play prescribes a virtue closer to what Spenser calls courtesy:

> how to each degree and kynde
> We should our selues demeane, to low, to hie;
> To friends, to foes, which skill men call Ciuility. (F.Q., VI.x.23)

NOTES

1. *The Two Gentlemen of Verona*, ed. Clifford Leech (London: Methuen, 1969). I quote from this edition throughout.

2. M.C. Bradbrook, *Shakespeare and Elizabethan Poetry* (London: Chatto & Windus, 1951), p. 151.

3. *The Book Named The Governor*, ed. S.E. Lehmberg (London: Dent, 1962), pp. 136–51.

4. Ralph M. Sargent makes this point in "Sir Thomas Elyot and the Integrity of *The Two Gentlemen of Verona*," *PMLA*, 65 (1950), 1166–80.

5. "Introduction," *The Two Gentlemen of Verona* (Cambridge, U.K.: Cambridge Univ. Press, 1921), p. xiv.

6. Bradbrook, p. 151.

7. A.C. Hamilton suggests a parallel with *The Franklin's Tale* in *The Early Shakespeare* (San Marino, Calif.: Huntington Library, 1967), p. 126.

8. See J.H. Hexter, "The Education of the Aristocracy in the Renaissance" in *Reappraisals in History* (London: Longmans, 1961), pp. 45–70; Ruth Kelso, *The Doctrine of the English Gentleman in the Sixteenth Century* (Urbana: University of Illinois Press, 1929); Lawrence Stone, *The Crisis of the Aristocracy 1558–1641* (Oxford: Clarendon Press, 1965).

9. *The Book of the Courtier*, trans. Sir Thomas Hoby, in *Three Renaissance Classics*, ed. Burton A. Milligan (New York: Charles Scribner's Sons, 1953), pp. 388, 408, 413.

10. Proteus' subsequent behavior suggests that the particular lie he fabricates may well express a subconscious desire for just what happens—avoidance of the emotional responsibility of his new relationship with Julia and a chance to join in his friend's adventures. If so, it does not mean that his feelings for Julia are feigned but that he finds the confusing intensity of a new kind of emotional experience difficult to deal with and intuitively recognizes that he is not ready to make that relationship public.

11. For example, Peter Lindenbaum, in one of the best recent discussions of the play, points out that in Act I "the 'perfect man' envisioned by Proteus' guardians, and presumably by those of Valentine as well, is merely a gentleman adept in the social arts" (p. 232). The significant dramatic action, he argues, is the education of the characters to redefine the "perfect man" in religious rather than social terms. "Education in *The Two Gentlemen of Verona*," *Studies in English Literature*, 15 (1975), 229–44.

12. "Castiglione's *Courtier*: The Self as a Work of Art" in *Renaissance and Revolution* (New York: Pantheon, 1965), p. 147.

13. Mazzeo, pp. 149, 135, 134.

14. See Castiglione, *The Courtier*, p. 542; Elyot, *The Governor*, passim.

15. I quote from *The Poetical Works of Edmund Spenser*, ed. J.C. Smith and E. De Selincourt (London: Oxford Univ. Press, 1912).

16. *The Courtier* explains the courtly lover's duty to serve his mistress. English courtesy books place less emphasis on love, but they insist "that all gentlemen

worthy of the name must be clerks" (Hexter, p. 49). On the distrust of love in English courtesy books, see Kelso, p. 85.

17. See Kelso, p. 78; Elyot, p. 172. According to Daniel Javitch, *Poetry and Courtliness in Renaissance England* (Princeton: Princeton Univ. Press, 1978), "Courtly grace, to the extent that it can be prescribed, is shown to rely on tactics of dissimulation. . . . For instance, *sprezzatura,* one of the chief sources of such grace, always employs deliberate subterfuge" (p. 36).

18. He equivocates, for example, to protect Priscilla's reputation (*F.Q.,* VI.iii.16,18). On this and other instances of innocent duplicity in *F.Q.,* VI, see William Nelson, *The Poetry of Edmund Spenser* (New York: Columbia Univ. Press, 1963), p. 283.

19. "The root of the word is from the verb *sprezzare,* 'to disdain' or 'to hold in contempt,' and this sense is vaguely present in Castiglione's concept, although without pejorative connotations" (Mazzeo, p. 145).

20. In Spenser's "Legend of Courtesy," Despetto, Decetoo, and Defetto (disdain, deceit, and detraction) appear as villains both because they are negators of courtesy and because they are the dangers courtesy or civility is most susceptible to.

21. Again, Shakespeare is dramatizing problems of behavior strikingly similar to those Spenser treats in the nearly contemporary Book VI of *The Faerie Queene*: Proteus' willingness to slander Valentine demonstrates the absoluteness of his betrayal of his friend and the completeness of his degradation; the quest of Sir Calidore, the knight of courtesy, is to subdue the Blatant Beast, a monster embodying slander and calumny.

22. "Myth and Ritual in Shakespeare: *A Midsummer Night's Dream,*" in *Textual Strategies: Perspectives in Post-Structuralist Criticism,* ed. Josué V. Harari (Ithaca, N.Y.: Cornell University Press, 1979), p. 191.

23. On the gradual disappearance of this figure, see Stone, esp. pp. 199–270.

24. A.C. Hamilton agrues that until this point Proteus is the only gentleman of Verona, Valentine being lowly born and becoming a gentleman by merit (pp. 120–21). The Duke's reasoning—Valentine has merit and is therefore well derived—may well parody the Elizabethans' penchant for constructing genealogies appropriate to their sense of their own dignity. Hexter, for example, mentions William Cecil's attempt "to provide his grandfather . . . with a fancier set of ancestors" ("The Myth of the Middle Class in Tudor England" in *Reappraisals,* p. 102), and Stone comments on the virtuosity of "those imaginative creative writers, the Tudor heralds" who could provide family trees beginning with the Trojans or Old Testament figures such as Noah (pp. 23–24). I think, however, that Valentine's lineage is not as significant a factor as Helena's in *All's Well That Ends Well.* Although the play is vague about Valentine's antecedents, it does not make a point of any social disparity between Valentine and Proteus. In *The Two Gentlemen of Verona,* Shakespeare is not interested in how the governing class is recruited but in the qualities desirable in its members.

25. Valentine's sensitive flexibility is the benign counterpart of Proteus' inconstancy; together they demonstrate contrasting possibilities inherent in human adaptability and potential for shaping individual identity. For the importance of these ideas in Renaissance culture, see Thomas Greene, "The Flexibility of the Self in Renaissance Literature," pp. 241–64, and A. Bartlett Giametti, "Proteus Unbound: Some Versions of the Sea God in the Renaissance," pp. 437–75, in *The Disciplines of Criticism: Essays in Literary Theory, Interpretation, and History,* ed. Peter Demetz, Thomas Greene, and Lowry Nelson, Jr. (New Haven: Yale University Press, 1968). Also see Stephen J. Greenblatt's *Sir Walter Ralegh: The Renaissance Man and His Roles* (New Haven: Yale University Press, 1973), esp. pp. 31–41, and his *Renaissance Self-Fashioning* (Chicago: University of Chicago Press, 1980).

Love Letters in *The Two Gentlemen of Verona* (1986)

Frederick Kiefer

The Two Gentlemen of Verona are what their youth and courtly upbring-
ing predispose them to be—bookish. Appropriately, the word *book* appears
in their opening conversation when Proteus, contemplating the dangers his
friend may encounter on a journey, pledges, "I will be thy beadsman," and
Valentine replies, "And on a love-book pray for my success?" (I.i.18–19).[1]
The expression *love-book* anticipates the conjunction of love with reading
and writing that characterizes the entire play. This conjunction is apparent
in the first scene when, the conversation having turned to love, both Proteus and Valentine solemnly cite what "writers say." It is also apparent when
the two gentlemen, each having fallen in love, become writers themselves.
Their writing takes the form of letters to their ladies, and those letters in
turn beget additional letters as the initial talk about what writers say gives
way to a blizzard of paper. No other Shakespearean comedy contains so
many letters; no other devotes so many scenes to the composition, delivery,
and reception of love letters.

The very number of these letters suggests the dramaturgical importance they have in *Two Gentlemen,* where they fulfill a variety of functions.
They advance the plot, reveal character, generate laughter, and evoke emotions in the audience ranging from shock to pathos. Whatever their particular
purpose in particular scenes, though, the letters have this in common: even
if their inspiration is to be found ultimately in prose romance, the letters are
eminently theatrical. As hand properties, they command attention: in full
view of the audience, the characters give and receive, hide and destroy, write
and read those letters.

The letters, moreover, have a significance that transcends the obviously theatrical. For Shakespeare uses them to explore a paradox: that people
seek to express the most intense emotion by the most conventional of liter-

Reprinted from *Shakespeare Studies* 18 (1986): 65–85.

ary modes, the epistolary. Because the act of writing involves some delib-
eration, there is no necessary congruence between written expression and
heartfelt sentiment. In fact, the stylistic patterns of love letters are at variance with the turbulent nature of lovers' passions. Therefore, although reading and writing may have the most profound significance for lovers, the letters that pass between them may lead to misunderstanding and even permit
deception. In the world of the play characters learn to distrust amatory dec-
larations, no matter how artful or affecting.

Because Shakespeare wrote *Two Gentlemen* early in his career and
because he would employ such devices as love letters again in later plays,
Two Gentlemen has come to be thought of chiefly as an apprentice piece. It
is, however, a better comedy than is implied by its status as precursor to other
comedies. By examining Shakespeare's handling of the letters, we shall see
that *Two Gentlemen* is at once a more theatrically adroit and a more
thoughtful play than is usually supposed.

Letter-writing begins early in *Two Gentlemen.* In fact, when the play
opens, Proteus has already written of his love to Julia, and he has entrusted
his letter to the servant Speed.[2] Concerned that she may deem the messenger unsuitable, Proteus frets, "I fear my Julia would not deign my lines, /
Receiving them from such a worthless post" (I.i.152–53). But he has at least
put his feelings into words, and his words into writing. And that, in *Two
Gentlemen,* is the first step in encouraging love. For Proteus, as for Valentine later, the written word is an essential ingredient of wooing.

Proteus' letter becomes the focus of the following scene, where, from
the moment the letter appears onstage, it claims the attention of its recipient—
and of the audience. In assigning the letter so much importance, Shakespeare
purposefully departs from what he found in his chief source, the Spanish romance *Diana Enamorada* by the Portuguese author Jorge de Montemayor. For
the playwright, with an eye to the stage, adds to and subtracts from *Diana.*[3]
In comparing the first episode involving a letter in the play with the corresponding episode in the romance, we can appreciate Shakespeare's capacity
for exploiting the theatrical possibilities he found in the prose narrative.

The letter writers in *Diana* are Felismena and Don Felix. Having fallen
in love with her, Don Felix seeks to convince Felismena of his affection,
though to little effect at first. One day he decides to express his feelings in a
letter, which he gives to Rosina, Felismena's maid. The letter will prove the
turning point in their relationship, though its importance is difficult to gauge
by Felismena's frosty demeanor when Rosina produces the letter. Instead of
accepting it graciously, Felismena strikes a haughty, even reproachful, pose.
Taken aback by her mistress's vehemence, Rosina apologizes, saying defen-

sively and a little disingenuously, "I gave it you, bicause you might laugh at it, and not to moove your pacience with it in this sort."[4] The maid then leaves the room, taking the letter with her. Felismena, despite her cool exterior, is interested in Don Felix's attentions but does not wish to appear improperly eager. That night when Rosina returns to help her mistress to bed, Felismena hopes that Rosina will offer the letter again, but the maid, having been rebuffed earlier, says no more about the matter. Then in frustration Felismena broaches the subject, again feigning indignation in order to conceal her true feelings: "And is it so *Rosina*, that *Don Felix* without any regard to mine honour dares write unto me?" The ploy fails. Rosina says only that "These are things Mistresse . . . that are commonly incident to love, wherfore I beseech you pardon me." She leaves the room without presenting the letter, and so a disconsolate Felismena spends a sleepless night. The next morning, however, when Rosina reappears, "she let the letter closely fall." Felismena demands to see it, and the maid explains that it is the same letter proffered the day before. Pretending skepticism, Felisimena denies Rosina's claim: "Nay that it is not . . . wherefore shew it me, that I may see if you lie or no." At last Rosina puts the letter into her mistress's hands.

When the corresponding characters in *Two Gentlemen* make their first appearance, Julia asks her maid Lucetta,

> Of all the fair resort of gentlemen
> That every day with parle encounter me,
> In thy opinion which is worthiest love? *(I.ii.4–6)*

The two women discuss the merits of various suitors, and when Lucetta praises Proteus, Julia says wistfully, "I would I knew his mind" (l. 33). Seizing this auspicious moment, Lucetta produces his letter: "Peruse this paper, madam" (l. 34). The letter, a hand property for Shakespeare, enables the playwright to dramatize the internal conflict between propriety and passion, as well as the tension between mistress and confidante.[5]

Like Felismena, Julia professes irritation so as to conceal a depth of feeling that others might regard as unseemly: "Dare you presume to harbor wanton lines? / To whisper and conspire against my youth?" (I.ii.42–43). She peremptorily orders her maid, "There! take the paper; see it be return'd." Like Montemayor's heroine, however, Julia is less hostile in her heart (or less affected) than she appears. In fact, no sooner does Lucetta exit than Julia reflects, "And yet I would I had o'erlook'd the letter" (l. 50). With more boldness than Felismena, Julia immediately calls back her maid, who proceeds just as quickly to drop the letter deliberately and then pick it up. Her attention caught by this byplay, Julia makes a trumped-up, if not wholly serious, charge: "Some love of yours hath writ to you in rhyme" (l. 76). After some witty badinage Julia says, "Let's see your song" (l. 85), and takes the letter. Then, with exaggerated scorn she tears it to pieces, unread.[6]

Shakespeare has deftly dramatized the incident in Montemayor, displaying in this early comedy a gift for converting a slowly moving narrative into a lively entertainment suited for the stage. He makes a number of changes, each of which enhances the physicality of the situation. For example, he creates stage action when Julia accepts the letter, then hands it back; when she seizes the letter, then tears it to pieces; and when, after Lucetta exits, Julia scurries about the stage, frantically gathering together the scraps of paper, and reads aloud parts of what Proteus has written. By introducing the destruction and then reconstruction of the letter (neither of which occurs in Montemayor), Shakespeare not only satisfies the audience's desire to see some engaging incident but also makes that incident comically surprising. By telescoping time, moreover, Shakespeare accelerates the pace of the action. Between Lucetta's dismissal and return, there is no intervening night, only a soliloquy in which Julia reflects, "What 'fool is she, that knows I am a maid, / And would not force the letter to my view!" (I.ii.53–54). And although, in *Diana*, Rosina waits until the next day to produce the letter again, Lucetta drops it at once upon her immediate return. By giving Julia something to do as well as to say, and by quickening the sequence of events, Shakespeare effectively engages the interest of the audience.

Proteus' letter provides the basis not only for the dialogue between Julia and Lucetta but also for the soliloquies spoken by Julia in this scene. In composing those two speeches, Shakespeare is mindful of both the resources and the limitations of his stage. He knows that a dramatist cannot present the contents of Proteus' letter to the audience as easily as Montemayor presents Don Felix's letter to the reader of *Diana*. What Shakespeare can effectively convey is Julia's state of mind, as the audience eavesdrops on her thoughts. Consequently, he shifts the focus of the episode from the words of the letter itself (furnished by Montemayor) to the psyche of the letter's recipient. We hear of Julia's frustration and anger in her first soliloquy: "How angerly I taught my brow to frown, / When inward joy enforc'd my heart to smile!" (I.ii.62–63). In the second soliloquy, after she has torn up the letter, we hear of her affection for Proteus and her self-reproach: "O hateful hands, to tear such loving words!" (l. 102); "I'll kiss each several paper for amends. / Look, here is writ 'kind Julia.' Unkind Julia . . ." (ll. 105–06). Exuberant at discovering Proteus' profession of love, she even hints at her sexuality. Suggestively handling the pieces of paper, she says:

> Lo, here in one line is his name twice writ,
> "Poor forlorn Proteus, passionate Proteus:
> To the sweet Julia"—that I'll tear away—
> And yet I will not, sith so prettily
> He couples it to his complaining names.
> Thus will I fold them one upon another;
> Now kiss, embrace, contend, do what you will. *(I.ii.120–26)*

As she speaks these lines, Julia presses together the pieces of paper, folds them, and perhaps holds them close to her heart. Through this action and the soliloquies, Shakespeare dramatizes the vitality of the character. What he may have sacrificed of Proteus' words, he more than compensates for in the presentation of Julia's feelings as she responds to the letter.

In the scene following Julia's receipt of the letter, Shakespeare again embellishes what he found in Montemayor. Shaping his material for the theater, the playwright employs another letter, this one without precedent in *Diana*. It is as though, having discovered how useful a letter could be, Shakespeare decided to construct a second scene around the same prop. In Montemayor's romance he had read of parental intrusion when Don Felix's father, learning of his son's love for Felismena, sends him away to court. Shakespeare exploits the theatrical possibilities by creating between father and son a confrontation triggered by the father spotting a letter in Proteus' hands.

The young man comes onstage with Julia's letter, saying, "Sweet love, sweet lines, sweet life! / Here is her hand, the agent of her heart" (I.iii.45–46). The mood changes abruptly when Antonio enters, sees the paper, and inquires, "what letter are you reading there?" (l. 51). Unwilling to disclose his love for Julia (just as she in the preceding scene was unwilling, albeit with a difference, to disclose to Lucetta her love for him), Proteus dissembles. He pretends to be reading a letter from Valentine. When Antonio asks to see it, his son demurs, saying only that Valentine wishes Proteus would join him in Milan. Seizing on this news, Antonio, as he has already determined to do, instructs his son to leave Verona: "I am resolv'd that thou shalt spend sometime / With Valentinus in the Emperor's court" (ll. 66–67). Like many another parent in the world of comedy, Antonio, even if unwittingly, by his stubbornness frustrates his son's love affair: "Muse not that I thus suddenly proceed; / For what I will, I will, and there an end" (ll. 64–65). A despondent Proteus is left to ruminate on the role Julia's letter has played (or so he thinks) in their imminent separation:

I fear'd to show my father Julia's letter,
Lest he should take exceptions to my love,
And with the vantage of mine own excuse
Hath he excepted most against my love. *(ll. 80–83)*

The image of the forlorn Proteus, the letter in his hands, contrasts vividly with our fresh memory of the buoyant Julia, the letter from Proteus in hers. In each of these juxtaposed scenes, a letter moves the plot swiftly forward, first drawing Proteus and Julia together, then apart.

Not only does Shakespeare invent letters that have no counterpart in *Diana,* he also extends the reading and writing to characters who themselves have no source in Montemayor's romance. Hence the letter-writing of Valentine, whose origin apparently lies in a Continental story of friendship told by Boccaccio in the *Decameron* (10.8) and by Sir Thomas Elyot in *The Boke named the Governour* (2.12).[7] Elyot's version tells of two friends, one of whom (Gisippus) generously offers his bride to his friend (Titus), much as Valentine offers Silvia to Proteus in the play's final scene. There is no letter-writing on the part of the friends in Elyot, whereas Shakespeare creates a scene in which Valentine (the counterpart of Gisippus) writes a letter at the behest of his beloved.

If earlier letters in the play advance the plot, Valentine's letter-writing is primarily to amuse the audience while the plot stands still. Silvia, in Milan, asks him for a letter, telling Valentine that she means to send it to a suitor of hers, as though she herself were its author. Valentine diligently applies himself to the work, for he tells her, "As you enjoin'd me, I have writ your letter / Unto the secret, nameless friend of yours" (11.i.104–05). Alas, the result fails to please Silvia, who remarks, "'tis very clerkly done" (l. 108). Sensing her disapproval, Valentine begins to make excuses: "I writ at random, very doubtfully" (l. 111). Seemingly unmoved, Silvia claims to detect a lack of enthusiasm in Valentine's words, and so, while conceding that "the lines are very quaintly writ," she adds, "(since unwillingly) take them again" (ll. 122–23). When an anguished Valentine protests, she says, "I would have had them writ more movingly" (l. 128).

Valentine is the very embodiment of naiveté. Silvia's true purpose, he fails to realize that the letter requested is really intended for his benefit—she has no other suitor to whom she means to write. The playwright, however, is not here concerned to explore Valentine's character, for that is manifest from the outset. Shakespeare's purpose in this scene is rather to create a comic effect: he generates laughter by the absurdity of Valentine's situation. In an aside Speed points the way for the audience's response: "O excellent device, was there ever heard a better, / That my master being scribe, to himself should write the letter?" (II.i.139–40). Servant must laboriously explain to master the significance of what has happened:

> *Speed*. Why, do you not perceive the jest?
> *Valentine*. No, believe me.
> *Speed*. No believing you indeed, sir: but did you
>   perceive her earnest?
> *Valentine*. She gave me none, except an angry word.
> *Speed*. Why, she hath given you a letter.
> *Valentine*. That's the letter I writ to her friend.
> *Speed*. And that letter hath she deliver'd, and there an end.
>
> *(ll.153–62)*

In their conversation Speed invites us to relish the contrast between the compliant Valentine's grave demeanor and the ridiculousness of his plight, a contrast heightened by the physical presence of the letter.

If a letter can form the basis of a comic scene, one in which nothing very important happens, a letter can also provide the focus of a theatrically big scene, in which the plot moves rapidly forward in a tragicomic direction. The letter that accomplishes this is written by Valentine on the brink of his elopement with the Duke's daughter, Silvia. It comes to light after Proteus, having joined his friend in Milan and having fallen in love with Silvia himself, betrays Valentine's plans to the Duke. The angry Duke finds Valentine in a great hurry: the young man explains, "there is a messenger / That stays to bear my letters to my friends, / And I am going to deliver them" (III.i.52–54). Sensing a lie, the Duke seeks to delay Valentine. On the pretext of seeking advice, the Duke claims to have fallen in love and says he needs to know how best to reach and woo his lady. Valentine, perhaps unconsciously, proceeds to counsel the very methods he means to employ with Silvia. Interpreting this as confirmation of what Proteus had told him, the Duke throws open Valentine's cloak to find the incriminating evidence—a rope ladder and a love letter addressed to Silvia.

This letter of Valentine's (actually a fusion of letter and poem) has a distinction denied other letters in the play: it receives a word-for-word recitation. Until now, we have not been given the text of anyone's letter—neither Proteus' letter to Julia (except for snippets), nor Julia's to Proteus, nor Valentine's for Silvia. In each instance Shakespeare prefers the revelation of the reader's character to the recitation of the writer's words. The playwright treats the words themselves as theatrically unimportant: the dramatic context and the response of the reader within the play suggest the gist of the letters. By omitting the actual text, Shakespeare demonstrates his instinct for what works onstage. Realizing that there is nothing particularly stageworthy about reading a letter, either silently or aloud, he dispenses with the contents altogether.

The Duke's reading of Valentine's letter, one without precedent in *Diana Enamorada* or in Elyot's *Governour*, manages to be at once complete and dramatically effective:

> "My thoughts do harbor with my Silvia nightly,
> And slaves they are to me that send them flying:
> O, could their master come and go as lightly,
> Himself would lodge where, senseless, they are lying!
> My herald thoughts in thy pure bosom rest them,
> While I, their king, that thither them importune,
> Do curse the grace that with such grace hath blest them,
> Because myself do want my servants' fortune.
>> I curse myself, for they are sent by me,
>> That they should harbor where their lord should be."
>>> *(III.i.140–49)*

It is easy to see why it would have been theatrically inappropriate for either Valentine or Silvia to have recited these lines. They are conventional thoughts expressed conventionally.[8] The opposition of "slave" and "king," of "curse" and "blest"—this is the familiar stuff of Elizabethan love poetry. And the rhymes—"nightly" and "lightly," "flying" and "lying"—are comically grotesque. Spoken by one of the lovers, the poem might well seem treacly or tiresome. Spoken by the Duke, however, the words create dramatic tension: the Duke's public reading is utterly out of keeping with Valentine's sentiments. Spluttering with rage, the Duke (if the actor does his work properly) invests the public reading—and thus the scene—with an energy and impact that it never would have had otherwise.

If a letter can help to raise the energy level of a scene, a letter can also contribute to the denouement, relaxing through laughter the tension created by the Duke's outburst. Thus Shakespeare employs, later in the same scene, a second "letter." Actually, this is not so much a proper letter as it is a compilation of the virtues and vices that make a certain woman a suitable, or unsuitable, match for Launce.[9] He shows the paper to Speed, who proceeds to read it aloud, beginning, *"Inprimis,* She can milk" (III.i.301). After the recitation of each item, Launce provides a commentary. For example:

Speed. "Item, She is slow in words."

Launce. O villain, that set this down among her vices! To be slow
in words is a woman's only virtue. I pray thee out with't,
and place it for her chief virtue. *(III.i.332–36)*

Although what the servant reads is, strictly speaking, scarcely more than an
inventory, Speed treats it as though it were a letter. In fact, when he discovers that he is late in meeting his master, he tells Launce, "Pox of your
loveletters!" (ll. 380–81). Of course, this letter (in prose) is nothing like
Valentine's paean to Silvia (in verse). The one is romantic and fanciful, the
other literalminded and pragmatic. In mood and style there is a complete
contrast, one that Shakespeare uses to spoof the conventions which Valentine and, presumably, Proteus observe in their writing. The send-up of epistolary conventions allows us to catch our breath after the Duke's tirade, and
it prevents the play from veering too closely toward tragicomedy.

The use of two letters in a single scene may appear to some playgoers excessive. M. C. Bradbrook contends that "whenever Shakespeare can
think of nothing else to do, he puts in a misdirected letter, of which there
are a record number in this play."[10] A "record number" there may be, but
it does not necessarily bespeak a flagging imagination. The plenitude of letters may just as well be interpreted as an expression of Shakespeare's ingenuity. Indeed, there is an exuberance about their use that betokens creative
energy. In tracing the handling of the love letters, we appreciate how many
variations Shakespeare could work on a motif: a letter torn to shreds; a letter read with delight; a letter rebuffed; a letter read aloud by the hostile parent
of its intended recipient; a letter read aloud by an amused and condescending friend. No other comic dramatist devised so many theatrical applications
for love letters or used them to better effect.

Despite their quantity in *Two Gentlemen,* love letters paradoxically
frustrate love as well as foster it. Julia's letter to Proteus becomes the agent
of their separation when he fears to reveal its contents to his father. Similarly, Valentine's letter to Silvia, falling into the hands of the Duke, helps
to precipitate his banishment. If letters as physical instruments can foil lovers, letters call present problems of another and more subtle kind, too. For
such letters are not always what they appear to be. Although they may contain pledges of enduring love, those oaths may not stand the test of time. It
is Proteus who brings this matter to issue.

When he joins Valentine in Milan, sees his friend's beloved, and
promptly falls in love with her himself, Proteus demonstrates the fragility
of words as guarantors of emotional commitment. Thinking back on all

that he had vowed to Julia, he sets about rationalizing his change of affections:

> Unheedful vows may heedfully be broken,
> And he wants wit that wants resolved will
> To learn his wit t' exchange the bad for better.
> Fie, fie, unreverend tongue, to call her bad,
> Whose sovereignty so oft thou hast preferr'd
> With twenty thousand soul-confirming oaths. (II.vi.11–16)

True to his name, Proteus changes abruptly, in this instance altering allegiance from one woman to another.

Unfortunately, Julia, not knowing of the transformation, continues to think of him as he was only a short while ago. In fact, she remains so much in love that she determines to follow him to Milan. Before setting out she affirms the congruence of Proteus' words and feelings:

> His words are bonds, his oaths are oracles,
> His love sincere, his thoughts immaculate,
> His tears pure messengers sent from his heart,
> His heart as far from fraud as heaven from earth. (II.vii.75–78)

Syntactically, the language of the first line ("words" and "oaths") is paired with that of the second ("love" and "thoughts"). Julia has complete confidence in this equivalence. But by the time she speaks these lines Proteus has already violated his oaths to her. His words, so lovingly recollected, are worthless. As Julia is shortly to discover, oaths need not signify permanence, and they may be broken with little or no remorse.

Full of self-righteousness, Proteus sets out to displace Valentine in Silvia's affections: first he will engineer his friend's banishment, then dislodge Thurio, whom the Duke intends as a husband for Silvia. Feigning solicitude, Proteus tells the Duke of Valentine's plan to elope with Silvia, and the Duke nabs Valentine.

Proteus succeeds in large measure because of hypocrisy: he manages to conceal his selfishness beneath the guise of good will. He tells the Duke that his motive for revealing Valentine's plan is noble: "For love of you, not hate unto my friend, / Hath made me publisher of this pretense" (III.i.46–47). Similarly, Proteus convinces Valentine of his solicitude, even after the betrayal. And the reprobate actually offers to act as intermediary between his absent friend and Silvia:

Thy letters may be here, though thou art hence,
Which, being writ to me, shall be deliver'd
Even in the milk white bosom of thy love. *(III.i.250–52)*

The prospect of aid is, of course, delusory, a sham designed to hasten the removal of a rival in love. But Valentine never guesses how improbable it is that Proteus should forward to Silvia any letters sent from exile.

Proteus' ability to convince others of his benevolence owes a great deal to his verbal fluency, apparent near the beginning of the play when Julia reads his first letter. It is apparent too when he betrays Valentine to the Duke and then suggests how Silvia may be made to forget her love: "The best way is to slander Valentine" (III.ii.31). Pointing out that his daughter may be skeptical of anything said against Valentine, the Duke thinks to have Proteus perpetrate the slander; a friend's knowledge of the accused man's character will presumably lend credence to the charges. It is not only the betrayal itself that is disturbing but also the connection between the ability to praise (so useful and appropriate in a speech or letter of love) and the ability to damn (so useful to the Duke and Proteus in besmirching Valentine's character). Thurio makes explicit the connection between the two actions when he asks that Proteus help him "by praising me as much / As you in worth dispraise Sir Valentine" (11. 54–55). Even though Thurio is something of a buffoon, his request raises a troubling question. For if verbal fluency may be perverted, if a man's word is not his bond, and if there is no necessary connection between eloquence of expression and nobility of feeling, then what significance can a profession of love have? It may be artful and clever, affecting and even compelling—without being true.

As if to underscore the untrustworthiness of words, Shakespeare portrays the schemers exulting in their skill with language. To woo Silvia, Proteus tells Thurio,

You must lay lime to tangle her desires
By wailful sonnets, whose composed rhymes
Should be full-fraught with serviceable vows. *(III.ii.68–70)*

Listening closely, the Duke endorses the advice: "Ay, much is the force of heaven-bred poesy" (l. 71). But as the audience recognizes, there is nothing "heaven-bred" either in Thurio's suit or in the notion of "tangling" one's beloved in lime. Indeed, Proteus' image of entrapment conveys a sinister suggestion. But, indifferent to such implications, Proteus becomes increasingly carried away with the prospect of what the written word can accomplish.

He tells Thurio:

> Write till your ink be dry, and with your tears
> Moist it again, and frame some feeling line
> That may discover such integrity. *(ll. 74–76)*

We might regard Proteus' injunction with more equanimity if we felt that Thurio were a suitable match for Silvia or if Proteus' affection for her were likely to be more lasting than that for Julia. But Thurio is bumbling and Proteus callow. So all the talk of "dire-lamenting elegies" and "sweet-complaining grievance" is offensive as advice proffered by a slanderer to a fool.

Of that advice the Duke says approvingly, "This discipline shows thou hast been in love" (III.ii.87). But the audience, at least, has grown skeptical of equating depth of feeling with force of expression. Although the Duke's notion may have seemed valid earlier in the play, it seems so no longer, for we cannot forget that Proteus has violated his oaths to Julia and betrayed his friend. We shudder at the thought of what Thurio may write and at what Proteus may accomplish. From this point on, we view with suspicion both praise and dispraise. Words have come to seem, at best, like coins that have lost their value. At worst, they are no better than counterfeits, employed by the unscrupulous for nefarious ends.

Paradoxically, Proteus' very glibness hastens the erosion of his credibility. Silvia instinctively distrusts his slander against Valentine, and she upbraids him for wooing her when he is supposed to be aiding the hapless Thurio. When she learns of Proteus' former love for another woman, he loses the last of whatever stature remains to him. He reflects,

> When I protest true loyalty to her,
> She twits me with my falsehood to my friend;
> When to her beauty I commend my vows,
> She bids me think how I have been forsworn
> In breaking faith with Julia whom I lov'd. *(IV.ii.7–11)*

With some relief we listen as Silvia sees through his designs and dismisses his eloquence:

> Thou subtile, perjur'd, false, disloyal man,
> Think'st thou I am so shallow, so conceitless,
> To be seduced by thy flattery,
> That hast deceiv'd so many with thy vows? *(ll. 95–98)*

She recognizes that the power to praise may also be the power to feign; the power to vow may be the power to lie. Armed with this knowledge, Silvia brushes aside Proteus' entreaties.

Even in the face of her rejection, Proteus doggedly persists. Maintaining faith in what words can achieve, he turns from speech to writing, and he has a servant deliver his letters to Silvia. In dramatizing the courtship, Shakespeare draws closely on Montemayor's *Diana*. Just as Felismena disguises herself as a page to follow Don Felix, so does Julia disguise herself in order to follow Proteus to Milan. Just as Felismena overhears Don Felix serenading Celia one evening, so does Julia overhear Proteus serenading Silvia. And just as Felismena in disguise enters Don Felix's service as a page (named Valerius), so too Julia enters Proteus' service as a page (named Sebastian). In his employ she functions, like Felismena, as an intermediary, carrying his letters to Silvia and her rebuffs back to him. Shakespeare's indebtedness to Montemayor here is strong and clear. He departs from *Diana* in a small but significant detail, however, and in so doing dramatizes the debasement that language has suffered during the dramatic action.

When Julia delivers Proteus' letter to Silvia, she finds that she has made a mistake, quickly takes back the letter, then replaces it with another:

> Madam, please you peruse this letter—
> Pardon me, madam, I have unadvis'd
> Deliver'd you a paper that I should not:
> This is the letter to your ladyship. *(IV.iv.121–24)*

Almost certainly the first letter is one that Proteus had written earlier to Julia, perhaps even the letter destroyed and then reconstructed in the play's second scene.[11] Seeing this letter together with the letter to Silvia, we cannot help reflecting on what they contain: equally ardent professions of love written by the same man to different women. Even though Julia obviously still treasures her original letter, we know that Proteus' words are no longer to be taken at face value. They lack the intrinsic worth which they seemed to possess in the opening scenes of the play. Thus we feel that Silvia's treatment of her letter is justified. She tells the page,

> I will not look upon your master's lines;
> I know they are stuff'd with protestations,
> And full of new-found oaths, which he will break
> As easily as I do tear his paper. *(ll. 128–31)*

Then, as the last line indicates, Silvia does something without precedent in *Diana*. Whereas her counterpart, Celia, accepts the letter of Don Felix and peruses it carefully, Silvia tears her letter to pieces. The dramatic action recalls Julia's similar tearing of Proteus' letter early in the play, and the repetition creates an obvious parallel—but with a difference. Proteus' letter to Julia (in I.ii) conveyed sincere feeling; and there was presumably nothing ignoble then about either the man or his letter. Therefore, when Julia destroyed that letter, we felt the disjunction between the contents and the letter's fate. The letter to Silvia (in IV.iv) is another matter altogether, for it is the creation of a slanderer and philanderer. And although Proteus' feelings may seem outwardly sincere, his profession of love for Silvia will soon be revealed as sham by his behavior in the forest. The second letter, then, deserves to be torn up; Proteus' words are now as valueless as the scraps of paper that fall to the stage.

If words seem diminished in Silvia's view, they no longer enjoy the same importance in Proteus' view either. Although he may continue to revel in what he imagines that language, written or spoken, can accomplish, Silvia correctly perceives that his attitude is essentially manipulative. He employs words not out of any respect for them, but out of selfishness. Words are useful to him only so long as they seem likely to win over Silvia. When importuning proves ineffectual, he abandons words, substituting brute force. He follows Silvia into the forest and, claiming that "the gentle spirit of moving words" has failed him, attempts to rape her. This demonstrates as nothing else could the essential falsity of his devotion to her. And with his perfidy revealed for all to see, Julia at last drops her disguise and rails at him:

> Behold her that gave aim to all thy oaths,
> And entertain'd 'em deeply in her heart.
> How oft hast thou with perjury cleft the root? *(V.iv.101–03)*

Here outrage vies with pain as Julia excoriates a history of betrayed oaths.

Ironically, she herself has participated in the misuse of language. As Sebastian she has had to diverge from the truth. "And now am I (unhappy messenger)," Julia said earlier, "To praise his faith which I would have disprais'd" (IV.iv.99, 102). And so in her conversation with Silvia she fell into equivocation not altogether different in kind from that of Proteus when he concealed the truth about Julia. Awkward in her role as go-between, she affected a certain detachment in manner: "Yet will I woo for him, but yet so coldly / As, heaven it knows, I would not have him speed" (ll. 106–07). This strategy, however, does not entirely absolve Julia of responsibility for manipulating language so as to obscure her own feelings and purpose. Only our knowledge of her suffering at Proteus' hands and of Silvia's determination to resist Proteus' blandishments tempers our judgment of what Julia does.

Even Valentine, who expresses shock at the disjunction between Proteus' past words and present deeds in the forest, has himself participated in the devaluation of language. Earlier, advising the Duke on how to win his lady, Valentine espoused an attitude that sounded uncomfortably like Proteus':

> Flatter and praise, commend, extol their graces;
> Though ne'er so black, say they have angels' faces.
> That man that hath a tongue, I say is no man,
> If with his tongue he cannot win a woman. *(III.i.102–05)*

Even if we posit a distracted state of mind on Valentine's part—this is the day of his planned elopement—there remains something distinctly unpleasant about these lines. In their calculation they are not so very different from Proteus' advice to the Duke and Thurio in the next scene (III.ii).[12]

That even Valentine should have become a little cynical is perhaps the inevitable corollary of a society that attaches inordinate importance to convention. The courtly world of Verona and Milan is one in which the "right" speech, writing, and behavior are expected. There may be nothing intrinsically unreasonable in deferring to social norms. But the more that language is used to serve the expectations of society, the less reliably does it express all individual's feelings. The fine line between observing and manipulating convention can easily be crossed by the unscrupulous or even the careless. A profession of love, then, may leave the recipient wondering where convention leaves off and genuine feeling begins.

Love letters become a repository of conventions for a variety of reasons: they allow a writer to express an otherwise ineffable state of mind; they give attractive form to passions that are by nature unruly and turbulent; and by their durability they obscure the fact that passion may subside as quickly as it surges. Of course, lovers would deny such inconstancy. They want— perhaps need—to believe that the beloved will remain steadfast; and they themselves want to be perceived in the same way. Whether consciously or unconsciously, they seek the illusion of permanence. To this end epistolary conventions prove useful: in a world of shifting emotion, conventions by virtue of their stability provide psychological reassurance.

In *Two Gentlemen*, the impermanence of passion, however intense, is most acutely revealed in Proteus, the most indefatigable letter-writer in the play. His language captures the vicissitudes of his nature. In a speech describing, successively, Silvia, Julia, and himself, he says:

> She is fair; and so is Julia that I love
> (That I did love, for now my love is thaw'd,
> Which like a waxen image 'gainst a fire
> Bears no impression of the thing it was).
> Methinks my zeal to Valentine is cold,
> And that I love him not as I was wont. *(II.iv.199–204)*

The imagery of warmth and cold conveys his notion that love is a fleeting disposition, destined to perish just as surely as a "waxen image."[13] This attitude issues in his concern with the conventions governing the expression of love. He imparts his concern to Thurio, who proves an enthusiastic pupil: "I have a sonnet that will serve the turn / To give the onset to thy good advice" (III.ii.92–93). Sonnets of this kind, apparently already prepared and awaiting a suitable occasion for deployment, are meant to lend dignity to an emotional state which the sonneteer knows is evanescent.

The Duke applauds Proteus' advice to Thurio and sends the two men forth to pursue Silvia: "About it, gentlemen!" This approval arises out of a concept of love virtually identical to Proteus'. Indeed, when he assures Thurio that Silvia will forget Valentine, the Duke uses terminology similar to Proteus':

> This weak impress of love is as a figure
> Trenched in ice, which with an hour's heat
> Dissolves to water, and doth lose his form.
> A little time will melt her frozen thoughts,
> And worthless Valentine shall be forgot. *(III.ii.6–10)*

Although Proteus' speech cited above concerns his own volatile temperament, and the Duke here is speaking of his daughter, both men share the notion that "love" is mercurial and its effect on personality slight. They even use the same term: the Duke speaks of love as a "weak impress"; Proteus speaks of an "impression" that no longer exists.

Proteus and the Duke may find encouragement in one another's views, but this does not prevent them from misunderstanding the nature of love. Hence they misconstrue Silvia's relationship to Valentine. If her father and her relentless wooer confuse love with infatuation, Silvia experiences love as an altogether stronger and more enduring force. When Proteus tells her,

"I . . . hear that Valentine is dead," she replies, "And so suppose am I; for in his grave / Assure thyself my love is buried" (IV.ii.112–14). Just as their attitude toward love is reflected in their attitude toward love letters, so is hers. She judges the letter that Valentine writes for her to be "very clerkly" and tells him that it is "very quaintly writ" (II.i.108, 122). Her criticism suggests that it is a tissue of conventional figures. What she finds missing, evidently, is language that by its vitality conveys the depth of love that she feels, for of Valentine's lines she says, "I would have had them writ more movingly" (l. 128). If writing comes easily to Proteus and Thurio, it does not to Silvia. Or at least she chooses not to entrust her thoughts to paper. Alone among the lovers in the play, she fails to write a single letter. Nor does the audience see her accept any proffered letter. Her reticence is the antithesis of Proteus' easy eloquence.

This does not mean that true love is necessarily antithetical to written expression: the one can and does accompany the other—witness Julia's letter to Proteus. But writing that reflects genuine love (as opposed to a fit of passion) is more than a matter of words on paper. Love involves a compelling interaction of one's words and one's innermost being. Julia alludes to this in her speech to Lucetta before embarking on the journey to Milan. Deeply in love with Proteus, Julia seeks her maid's advice:

> Counsel, Lucetta; gentle girl, assist me;
> And ev'n in kind love I do conjure thee,
> Who art the table wherein all my thoughts
> Are visibly character'd and engrav'd. . . . *(II.vii.1–4)*

Asking her confidante to articulate the impression that she (Julia) has created, mistress imagines that maid is a writing tablet or notebook on which her thoughts take visible shape in the form of words. Julia's speech concerns the relationship of two women, but her words "kind love" suggest that the imagery may have a wider application, that other relationships, including those between men and women, may be similarly imagined.

Much the same image that Julia uses in *Two Gentlemen* is employed in *Diana Enamorada* to express romantic love. There, literal and figurative writing coalesce when Felismena, the counterpart of Julia, ponders the effect of Don Felix's first letter:

> When I had now seene my *Don Felix* his letter, whether it was for reading it at such a time, when by the same he shewed, that he loved me more then himselfe, or whether he had disposition and regiment

over part of this wearied soule, to imprint that love in it, whereof he wrote unto me, I began to love him too well. . . . *(p. 85)*

The word "imprint" need not refer to the activities of a printing house, but the context here points to the importance of actual reading and writing for Felismena. It is not until she reads the letter that she is brought to a recognition of her love for Don Felix; his words are inextricably connected with her experience of love. For her, the act of reading seems to release an emotion already present within. Of course, this is not simply a matter of epistolary conventions having their desired effect. She responds to the genuineness of Don Felix's sentiments, and they, rather than the conventions *per se*, "imprint" his love. In short, the literal writing is but the means to a more important "writing." The most profound imprinting, after all, is not that which occurs on paper but in Felismena's "soule."

In *Two Gentlemen*, as in *Diana*, love is virtually inseparable from the written word. This, at least, is suggested by Silvia's reproof of Proteus in the play's final scene:

> Read over Julia's heart (thy first best love),
> For whose dear sake thou didst then rend thy faith
> Into a thousand oaths; and all those oaths
> Descended into perjury, to love me. *(V.iv.46–49)*

The word "read" has a variety of possible meanings, including look over, see, discern, study, and apprehend. But it can also, of course, specifically mean "comprehend the written word." If it has that meaning here, then it underscores the importance of reading and writing that transcend ink and paper. Silvia implies that Proteus' original words are registered in Julia's heart where they remain as vivid as on the day first formulated. They remain there because Julia's love is undiminished. Since the words remain unaltered, they represent a potential source of stability, a steady point in a world of emotional flux, for if Proteus recollects the words he wrote to Julia, and if he recollects the effect of his words upon her, then perhaps her love for him will evoke the memory of his love for her. His present feelings may become congruent with his past words.

By its presence in the play's final scene, Silvia's injunction to read Julia's heart prevents *Two Gentlemen* from concluding with a repudiation of words. Her speech affirms the value of language, especially the language of love. Despite Proteus' broken oaths, Julia's equivocation as go-between, Valentine's cynicism when he advises the Duke on wooing, and Thurio's literary contrivance, words have not lost their significance entirely. They retain the capacity not only to express a writer's love but also to shape the amorphous feelings of a reader. This does not mean that, in *Two Gentlemen*, words actually create love; if they could, love letters would be even more numerous than they are. But love and letters can have the most profound relationship.

NOTES

    1. *The Riverside Shakespeare*, ed. G. Blakemore Evans et al. (Boston: Houghton Mifflin, 1974).
    2. Proteus' employment of Valentine's servant to deliver the letter is one of numerous anomalies listed by Clifford Leech in the new Arden *Two Gentlemen of Verona* (London: Methuen, 1969), pp. xviii–xxi.
    3. Although it is generally accepted that *Diana* is Shakespeare's chief source, it remains unclear exactly how he came to know the romance. An English translation by Bartholomew Yong was published in 1598, but *Two Gentlemen* was probably written some years earlier. Shakespeare may have seen Yong's translation in manuscript; according to the translator, the work was completed sixteen years before publication. Shakespeare may have known *Diana* in a French translation by Nicholas Collin (1578 and 1587). It is also possible that Shakespeare was indebted to a lost play entitled *The History of Felix and Philiomena*, performed at court in 1585. Geoffrey Bullough, in *Narrative and Dramatic Sources of Shakespeare*, I (New York: Columbia Univ. Press, 1957), suggests that the lost play "was probably a pastoral based on Montemayor" (p. 206).
    4. *A Critical Edition of Yong's Translation of George of Montemayor's Diana and Gil Polo's Enamoured Diana*, ed. Judith M. Kennedy (Oxford: Clarendon Press, 1968), p. 84.
    5. The relationship of this scene to the incident in *Diana* is the subject of much commentary. See T.P. Harrison, Jr., "Shakespeare and Montemayor's *Diana*," *University of Texas Studies in English*, 6 (1926), 76–78; John A. Guinn, "The Letter Device in the First Act of *The Two Gentlemen of Verona*," *University of Texas Studies in English*, 20 (1940), 72–81; Bertrand Evans, Introduction to the Signet Classic *Two Gentlemen of Verona* (New York: New American Library, 1964), pp. xxvii–xxviii; Judith M. Kennedy, ed., *A Critical Edition of Yong's Translation*, pp. xliv–xlv.
    6. John A. Guinn, in "The Letter Device," suggests that Julia's tearing of Proteus' letter is indebted to *De Duobus Amantibus* by Aeneas Sylvius Piccolomini. However, William Leigh Godshalk, in *Patterning in Shakespearean Drama: Essays in Criticism* (The Hague: Mouton, 1973), finds Guinn's argument "inconclusive" (p. 45, note 6). Julia's tearing of the letter may be related to an incident in a German play, published in Germany in 1620, entitled *Julio und Hyppolita*. Clifford Leech, in the New Arden *Two Gentlemen*, observes, "we cannot determine the priority between this play and Shakespeare's, but that a connection exists seems likely" (p. xxxix). Geoffrey Bullough, who describes the German play as an analogue, notes that the letter torn by Hyppolita (Julia's counterpart) is forged (I, 208–09).
    7. Ralph M. Sargent, in "Sir Thomas Elyot and the Integrity of *The Two Gentlemen of Verona*," *PMLA*, 65 (1950), 1166–80, contends, "There can now be little doubt that it was exactly this story of Titus and Gisippus which Shakespeare used as the second of his major sources for the action of *Two Gentlemen*" (p. 1173). Elyot's narrative may have influenced Shakespeare not only directly but also indirectly through John Lyly, who, according to Sargent, "used elements of Elyot's story of Titus and Gisippus, in a sort of reverse way, in *Euphues*" (p. 1173). The extent of Lyly's influence on *Two Gentlemen* remains unclear. G.K. Hunter, in *John Lyly: The Humanist*

as Courtier (London: Routledge and Kegan Paul, 1962), enumerates certain resemblances between *Euphues* and the play, concluding, "one may justly suspect that *Euphues* has helped to shape Shakespeare's handling of his story" (p. 326). R. Warwick Bond, himself an editor of Lyly's works, in the Old Arden edition of *Two Gentlemen* (London: Methuen, 1906), suggests specifically that the letter writing of the play may have an inspiration in Lyly: "The six (or seven) letters that figure in the play remind us of Lyly's novel" (p. xxx). But Geoffrey Bullough, in *Narrative and Dramatic Sources*, sees a greater influence exerted by Lyly's plays than by his novel: "Shakespeare's debt to Lyly was probably more one of technique than of matter, and he worked out any suggestions got from *Euphues* in accordance with the symmetrical balance of character found more in Lyly's plays than in his moral romance" (I, 204).

8. R. Warwick Bond, in the Old Arden edition, observes Valentine's verse letter: "The lines form a regular Shakespearean sonnet lacking the first quatrain, like the ten lines spoken by Orlando, *As You Like It*, III.ii., and the ten spoken by Beatrice, *Much Ado*, III.i.107–116" (p. 55). Inga-Stina Ewbank, in "'Were man but constant, he were perfect': Constancy and Consistency in 'The Two Gentlemen of Verona,'" *Shakespearian Comedy* (London: Edward Arnold, 1972), pp. 31–57, points to a connection between this play and Shakespeare's sonnets: "the really important relationship between *The Two Gentlemen of Verona* and the sonnets seems to me to have to do with Shakespeare's attitude to his own poetry and to the traditions of love poetry in which he finds himself writing" (p. 35).

9. R. Warwick Bond notes: "This catalogue, read by one page with comments by the other, is adapted from the very similar scene in Lyly's *Midas* (printed 1592), I.ii.20–87, where the page Licio rehearses, to his fellow Petulus' comment, the properties of Caelia, his mistress (in domestic service)" (p. 64).

10. M. C. Bradbrook, *Shakespeare and Elizabethan Poetry* (London: Chatto & Windus, 1951), p. 153. It is worth noting that Shakespeare did not employ all the letters he found in *Diana*. For instance, Montemayor provides the song and the sonnet of Don Felix to Celia; in *Two Gentlemen* we hear a song but no sonnet to Silvia (IV.ii). In *Diana* Don Felix reads the text of Celia's letter to the disguised Felismena; Proteus recites no letter from Silvia because she has not written to him. And although Don Felix's letter to Celia is given in full, there is no corresponding text from Proteus to Silvia provided in the play.

11. In Kristoffer Tabori's production of *Two Gentlemen* at the Grove Shakespeare Festival (Garden Grove, California) in 1983, the first letter Julia presented to Silvia was lavender, and when she took it back she held it close to her heart, suggesting that it was a love letter received from Proteus.

12. Geoffrey Bullough, in *Narrative and Dramatic Sources*, notes that Valentine's advice to the Duke on wooing (III.i) recalls a scene in Lyly's *Sapho and Phao* (II.iv), where one character says to another: "Chuse such words as may (as many may) melt her mind . . . Write, and persist in writing; they reade more than is written to them, and write lesse than they thinke" (I, 204–05). Proteus' advice to Thurio in III.ii may have had the same inspiration.

13. Clifford Leech, in the New Arden edition, cites the explanation of George Steevens: "Alluding to the figures made by witches, as representatives of those whom they designed to torment or destroy" (p. 44).

"METAMORPHISING" PROTEUS: REVERSAL STRATEGIES IN *THE TWO GENTLEMEN OF VERONA* (1996)

Charles A. Hallett

Stanley Wells assessed Shakespeare's skills as a craftsman in *Two Gentlemen of Verona*. Among its most serious flaws, Wells named certain "organic deficiencies," chiefly those resulting from "Shakespeare's failure to devise a plot which would enable characters conceived within the conventions of romantic love to behave in a manner compatible with these conventions." Too often he says, "the situation is at variance with the character" (166–67). A valuable observation, and in this essay I would like to take it a step further, by attempting to discern the *causes* of this dramaturgical "fault." What are the young dramatist's goals in constructing a plot episode or "situation"? What is Shakespeare doing or not doing that creates a shattering disjunction between the situation and the characters involved in it?

These questions are best answered by a considered inspection of the process by which a playwright transforms his narrative into drama, and such a study requires, first of all, an awareness of the motivational units from which the play is made. Why motivational units? Because what distinguishes narrative from drama, in the sense that the narrative and dramatic aspects of the plot will be differentiated in this essay, is the element of motivation. What is mere story becomes dramatic to the extent that the motives driving the plot come, and come in a credible manner, directly from the characters. If a character acts in such and such a way for no perceivable reason or for an arbitrary one, the audience senses that disjunction between the character and the plot that Wells calls attention to—and remains unmoved. To the extent that the will of the character is fixed intently upon a perceivable objective and his desires are engaged, the emotions of the audience too will be engaged. Suspense comes into play and, hence, a dramatic question: *will the character attain that objective*? And as soon as there is a dramatic question, there is *action*, the structure that lifts a dialogue out of the realm of narrative and renders it dramatic. So much depends, then, upon motivation.

While credible and compelling motivation toward an objective in the propelling character, coupled with sufficient, well-motivated resistance in the responding one, energizes the narrative and brings the resulting tensions into sharp focus, there is another, equally significant structural element in any developing action—its climax. Each time the current objective is achieved (or thwarted), the accumulating tensions peak and are dispersed. Narrative, even in dialogue form, can conceivably go on forever at the same level of intensity. Drama, as a form, is composed of peaks and troughs, and any well-made play contains a continuous series of climaxes—of varying intensities, of course, those at major turning points in the action being more powerful than others.

Characteristic of Shakespeare's dramatic climaxes is the 180-degree reversal, where one or the other of the characters involved in the developing conflict is radically changed in some way, sometimes undergoing a change in fortune, sometimes a change of mood, sometimes a change of desire and thus of direction. Whatever the alteration, it moves the character from his initial position to another that embodies the polar-opposite position. In crafting the climaxes of a play's action, on all levels—whether short- or long-term—the more-experienced Shakespeare relies heavily on the reversal structure, using it to create a strong foundation for his action.

When creating the plot situations for *Two Gentlemen of Verona*, Shakespeare was experimenting with these techniques but had not yet mastered them. Motivation, in *Two Gentlemen*, is both minimal and unfocused; characters do what they do because Shakespeare requires them to it. Whereas those characters that we think of as characteristically Shakespearean seem self-motivated and themselves generate the actions that move the plot forward, Julia and Silvia, Valentine and Proteus remain the playwright's puppets. What they do is a function of the needs of the story and only occasionally—in an inspired moment—a function of a living, willing psyche. Thus, when, on different occasions, Shakespeare subjects one or another of these characters to some recognizable reversal, it seldom appears as an organic and inevitable outgrowth of the character's motives. Yet though Shakespeare's inability—or failure—to structure the narrative dramatically marks *Two Gentlemen* as an inferior play, it at the same time bestows upon that work a certain importance, insofar as this text gives us a unique opportunity to document a fascinating and valuable stage in Shakespeare's career as a playwright—that stage in which the young playwright, though he cannot adequately motivate a dramatic reversal, is already fascinated with the concept.

The notion of change, or reversal, is embodied in the very name of the play's most active character—*Proteus* means *the changing*—as well as in his dramatic life. In plotting the story of Proteus, Shakespeare develops two major structural and potentially dramatic reversals. The first occurs rather early in the plot. Proteus loves Julia and wins her; then, in a major reversal of direction, he shifts his allegiance and begins pursuing Silvia: Julia is dead to him, Silvia magnificently alive! Where he has up to this point been Valentine's warmest friend, now his "zeal to Valentine is cold." Beginning his dramatic life as a noble young man, Proteus turns traitor to all that he had loved. The second major reversal at the plot level involves the repentance of Proteus: Shakespeare ends the play with a recognition scene in which Proteus, so advanced in his passion for Silvia that he determines to use brute force to possess her, undergoes a sudden transformation and regrets his ignoble behavior:

> If hearty sorrow
> Be a sufficient ransom for offense,
> I tender't here. (5.4.74–76)[1]

The first of these reversals takes place in 2.4 in what many call the best scene in the play. The second reversal occurs in the play's last scene, which is almost universally condemned as the play's worst, partly because Proteus's final change is too sudden and partly because Valentine responds to it with his incredibly generous offer to give the repentant Proteus "all that was mine in Silvia." In creating the two more prominent reversals that the inconstant Proteus undergoes, Shakespeare achieved different degrees of success.

In the proper place, I intend to look more closely at the methods Shakespeare used to effect these primary reversals at the plot level. Before doing so, however, I want to demonstrate what Shakespeare is doing with the smaller-scale reversals, those that exist within the scenes and that form the structural bases of the actual *situations* from which the overall plot is built, for the reversal is as significant a feature of the play's parts as it is of the whole. In looking at individual motivational units, we will discover that at this level too Shakespeare was already captivated by the reversal structure, will study the methods he used to shape reversals, and will consider the degree of success or failure he achieved in making these early reversals dramatic.

Because there is a serious distinction between the formal *sequence* and the looser *dialogue unit*,[2] I think it imperative, before analyzing the units of *Two Gentlemen*, to present Shakespeare at his best. How does the mature Shakespeare organize narrative information into a structured action?—for action is above all a structure! A glance at the finely constructed sequence between Juliet and her Nurse will be helpful here.

The sequence I have in mind occurs in *Romeo and Juliet* 2.5, the narrative line of which is extremely simple: the Nurse, who has been conferring with Romeo and has received instructions for Juliet, must pass on to the girl what Romeo said:

> Bid her devise
> Some means to come to shrift this afternoon,
> And there she shall at Friar Lawrence' cell
> Be shriv'd and married. (2.4.179–82)

To appreciate what Shakespeare does in transforming the story into drama, one should bear in mind two factors. First, there is nothing inherently dramatic in the activity suggested by the narrative, reporting a conversation. In a less imaginative rendering of the same situation, the work assigned to the Nurse could have been assigned to either of those featureless figures so common to plays of the era, Messenger or First Servant. Second, the situation, in itself, contains no element of suspense, for the audience has already heard Romeo's plan. How, then, does Shakespeare make this seemingly unexciting situation dramatic? Motivation plays a key role in the process.

Notice, first, how Shakespeare defines each character by an objective that motivates her actions throughout the sequence. Juliet's goal is established in her opening soliloquy: she is driven by the desire to hear Romeo's words. The Nurse has been gone for three hours: Juliet feels the time as though it had been three years. "Love's heralds" should not be so "lame," so "unwieldy," so "slow" and "heavy" but should move "ten times faster . . . than the sun's beams." When the Nurse finally appears, Juliet's eagerness is displayed again: "O God, she comes! O honey, what news?" To Juliet, a moment's delay is agony. "Come," she begs, "I pray thee speak, good, good nurse, speak." The Nurse, on the other hand, pretends fatigue, and worse, indifference. If her ultimate objective is to report, she will get to that point by a roundabout route. Shakespeare has made the Nurse a resisting force; she opposes Juliet all along the line. Thus, in the development section of the sequence, the two characters are at odds, and the more insistent Juliet becomes, the more evasive is the Nurse.

However opposed the character's attitudes might be, there would be no drama if the one did not impinge on the other. Notice that Shakespeare so structures the relationship that the Nurse's attitude has a direct effect upon Juliet, first increasing her impatience and in time angering her, and Juliet's anger evokes an annoyance, or mock-annoyance, in the Nurse, who retaliates by marking Juliet's ingratitude:

O God's lady dear!
Are you so hot? Marry, come up, I trow;
Is this the poultice for my aching bones?
Henceforward do your messages yourself. (2.561–64)

The conflicting desires build the tensions to this point of seeming impasse and then precipitate a change. Having tantalizingly withheld the happy news from Juliet, the Nurse now blurts it out:

Hie you hence to Friar Lawrence' cell,
There stays a husband to make you a wife. (2.5.68–69)

The form contains a contagious reversal, initially in the Nurse who at first maintains secrecy and then provides the revelation, and subsequently in the feelings of Juliet, who moves from anxiety to relief, from fear to joy.

Analysis of the motivating forces in the unit 2.5.1–78 reveals the structure through which Shakespeare converted the narrative into a dynamic action. What was formerly a story has been transformed into a dramatic question, *Will the Nurse reveal her secret to Juliet?* Analysis of these structuring forces also allows one to appreciate the benefits gained from grounding the narrative in sound motives. The existence of these motives gives movement and direction to the action. The comic opposition of the motives allows for *tension*, the necessary ingredient for any development, or "build," and for *change*, another essential element of drama and the basis of the reversal. When the climax is precipitated by the motives (as here, where Juliet's anger causes the Nurse to relent and satisfy Juliet's desires), the structure conveys a satisfying sense that there is, first, a true-to-life relationship between the characters and, second, an inevitability to the outcome of their dialogue. These are valuable benefits indeed, which in turn bestow two further assets upon the episode, unity and credibility. Appropriateness of the motivation to both the characters and the situation goes far toward making both believable. In this sequence from *Romeo and Juliet*, all of these elements are present and operating. In the dialogue units from *Two Gentlemen of Verona*, various elements are often missing or, if present, only loosely integrated.

With this concrete model from *Romeo and Juliet* in place, we can proceed to examine the way Shakespeare motivates his characters—and their reversals—in *Two Gentlemen of Verona*.

The second episode of *Two Gentlemen* (1.1.70–153) provides an interesting starting point, for the situation Shakespeare has created between Proteus and Speed is much the same as that found in the sequence between Juliet and her Nurse. As Juliet longed to know "What said Romeo?" so Proteus keenly desires to hear "What said Julia?" while Speed, the messenger, has the desired information but, like the Nurse, refuses to divulge it.

The introductory passages of the episode from *Two Gentlemen* are more primitively engineered, less integrated to the whole, than in its counterpart. This encounter between master and servant is not pre-arranged but occurs by chance: Speed, while rushing to join Valentine to "embark for Milan," runs across Proteus, and in the opening lines the two engage in a bout of wordplay following from Speed's comment that he has "play'd the sheep" in losing his master. It turns out, however, that Speed's tardiness is not the primary subject of the episode. Shakespeare shifts the conversation rather abruptly and, with jarring suddenness, Proteus is inquiring whether Speed "gav'st . . . my letter to Julia." To determine Julia's response to his love letter turns out to be Proteus' main objective in this episode.

What does Speed want? Speed's reluctance to speak on the crucial subject derives in part from his desire to be funny, or Shakespeare's desire to make him so—Speed shares the Elizabethan passion for punning and lets no opportunity to score at wordplay escape him. Still, Speed is not without a more deliberately contrived motive for his stubbornness. Once the episode gets going, most of Speed's responses will arise from his desire to be rewarded for his efforts as a go-between.

Proteus has far less success in effecting a change in his servant than had Juliet, primarily because Shakespeare uses Proteus as a straight man for his comedian. The dialogue is so arranged that Proteus expends more energy in the verbal duel with Speed than in pressing for the information that would characterize him as an ardent lover:

> *Proteus.* But dost thou hear? gav'st thou my letter to Julia?
> *Speed.* Ay, sir; I (a lost mutton) gave your letter to her (a lac'd mutton), and she (a lac'd mutton) gave me (a lost mutton) nothing for my labor.
> *Proteus.* Here's too small a pasture for such store of muttons.
> *Speed.* If the ground be overcharg'd, you were best stick her.
> *Proteus.* Nay, in that you are astray; 'twere best pound you.
> *Speed.* Nay, sir, less than a pound shall serve me for carrying your letter.
> *Proteus.* You mistake; I mean the pound—a pinfold.
> *Speed.* From a pound to a pin? fold it over and over, 'Tis threefold too little for carrying a letter to your lover. (1.1.94–104)

Proteus tries again: "What said she?" Apparently, the lady nodded, and from this nod Shakespeare reaps sixteen more lines of wordplay. Proteus continues to press his point. "Come, come," he urges again, "open the matter in brief: what said she?" but he cannot shake Speed from his self-appointed purpose. Only when Proteus opens his purse will "the money and the matter be once delivered."

Whatever dramatic tensions exit in the scene originate from two sources—from the comic aspect, *will Proteus pay Speed?* and from the narrative line, *will Speed reveal what Julia said?* Ideally, the resolution of the first of these would lead to the revelation required by the second. Having received his testern, or sixpence, Speed would satisfy us all by providing a description of Julia. His conversation from resistance to compliance would give the episode a more distinct point of climax, and the report would better prepare us for the entrance of Julia, which follows, in the present version, somewhat too abruptly. Further, the submission of Speed to Proteus would make the latter appear more effective.

But no such shift is made. Will Proteus pay Speed? Shakespeare restrains Proteus from bestowing a generous tip, thus making the lover appear inexplicably cheap. Will Speed reveal what Julia said? Speed does undergo a perfunctory reversal, in that at the "climatic" moment he does at last reveal something about his interview with Julia. But Speed's "report" merely accuses Julia of being as cheap as Proteus:

> *Speed.* Truly, sir, I think you'll hardly win her.
> *Proteus.* Why, couldst thou perceive so much from her?
> *Speed.* Sir, I could perceive nothing at all from her; no, not so much
>   as a ducat for delivering your letter: and being so hard to me
>   that brought your mind, I fear she'll prove as hard to you in
>   telling your mind. Give her no token but stones, for she's as
>   hard as steel.
> *Proteus.* What said she? nothing?
> *Speed.* No, not so much as "Take this for thy pains." To testify
>   your bounty, I thank you, you have testern'd me; in requital
>   whereof, henceforth carry your letters yourself: and so, sir,
>   I'll commend you to by master. (1.1.133–47)

Though in structuring this situation Shakespeare has embodied within it the potential for a reversal, much as he will later do in the sequence between Juliet and her Nurse, one senses that he is not thinking in quite the same terms here. Where in the *Romeo and Juliet* action he was concerned with the relationship between the two characters and used the Nurse to elicit from Juliet the responses of a young girl eager to hear from her lover, in *Two Gentlemen* he is after a different effect. Throughout the play we see Shakespeare giving free rein to the comic servants, and what happens in this episode between Proteus and Speed is a good example. The climax Shakespeare envisions for the episode 1.1.70–153 has more to do with Speed's reward than Proteus's. Speed reports that he "could perceive nothing at all from [Julia], not so much as a ducat." Indeed, there is much ado on the stage about ducats. The obvious observation is, of course, that Shakespeare's interest is more in the mockery than in the motives, but what this predilection costs in terms of dramatic balance needs to be specified: its effect is to neutralize the impact of the reversal as well as our interest in the lovers. Notice that an audience will be far more aware of Speed's wit than of Proteus's purpose and, further, that the less important character, Speed, seems to dominate to the point of obscuring the love plot. It is a fault Shakespeare will himself rail against in later years: when "some necessary question of the play be then to be consider'd," warns Hamlet, the clown must be kept in check. The Proteus/Speed duologue has none of the dramatic perfection that we find in the action between Juliet and her Nurse. The conflict of motives, rather than supporting the dialogue, collapses beneath the weight of Speed's virtuosity.

Motivation is again employed in the service of humor in 1.2 when Julia and her maid Lucetta take over the stage from Proteus and Speed. Julia asks the question that will get the episode going, "But say, Lucetta, now we are alone, / Wouldst thou then counsel me to fall in love?" "Ay, madam," answers Lucetta, "so you stumble not unheedfully." From the ensuing dialogue, we gather that Julia is visited every day by a "fair resort of gentlemen," that Proteus is not among the suitors, and that she wishes he were. Lucetta seems to be of Julia's mind; she agrees that Julia should fall in love, and for her too the "heedful" choice is Proteus. In this episode, Shakespeare reveals (not too effectively) that Speed had delivered Proteus's love letter to the maid rather than to the mistress, and it turns up in Lucetta's pocket. Here again, Shakespeare develops the narrative through the medium of language rather than action. His method for establishing opposition, in this scene as in the previous one, is to have the characters dispute the meanings of words, and the conflicts take the form of lively banter. But here, too, it is instructive to look beneath the banter at the dramatic structure that should hold it together.

There is a sense in which this scene breaks down into two parts, one in which Lucetta manages to deliver the letter to Julia, who refuses it (1.2.1–65), and another in which Julia assays to recover and read the letter (1.2.66–

137). Moreover, in each part, one finds latent in the text motivation that could, with the right emphasis in performance, be made to look like the 180-degree reversal that will become a hallmark of Shakespeare's style. But if the reversal in the episode just studied goes unmarked because the humor detracts attention from it, here, on the contrary, where Julia and Lucetta spar, the reversal that takes place in Julia will be the *object* of the humor. The units are organized deliberately to thrust Julia comically from a positive emotion to a negative one and vice versa.

In 1.2.1–65, at the beginning of the duologue, the two ladies are in accord. But Shakespeare embues Lucetta with a desire to advance the cause of Proteus, which she does by presenting his letter to Julia, and this in turn motivates Julia to initiate a quarrel:

> Now, by my modesty, a goodly broker!
> Dare you presume to harbor wanton lines?
> To whisper and conspire against my youth?
> Now trust me, 'tis an office of great worth,
> And you an officer fit for the place.
> There! take the paper; see it be return'd,
> Or else return no more into my sight. (1.2.41–47)

Shakespeare has, somewhat baldly and mechanically, turned joy to anger, accord to discord.

Instantly, of course, Julia regrets her haste and wishes "I had o'erlook'd the letter." With this desire, Shakespeare motivates the second portion of 1.2, in which Lucetta functions as the obstacle to the achievement of that desire. Again, there appears to be a rudimentary reversal structure: Julia moves from anger to remorse. Despite her intention to "call Lucetta back / And ask remission for my folly past" (1.2.64–65), her attitude toward Lucetta when the maid returns remains saucy. Striving to appear indifferent, she becomes disdainful. Shakespeare makes Lucetta wise enough to recognize the testiness of her mistress and bold enough to point it out—more than once. Julia, on the other hand, finds the angry posture a useful cover for her interest in the letter and puts on more of it, until, finally, she feigns a passion, tears the letter up, and chases the maid out. Then comes the reversal—Julia's disdain turns to remorse. Not, though, for her conduct to Lucetta but for the injury she has inflicted upon Proteus's letter.

> O hateful hands, to tear such loving words!
> Injurious wasps, to feed on such sweet honey,

And kill the bees that yield it with your stings!
I'll kiss each several paper for amends. (1.2.102–05)

For the second time, this time more credibly, Shakespeare has turned Julia around a full 180 degrees.

In spite of the existence of a conflict, these experiments with the reversal in the Julia/Lucetta duets remain tentative at most. The reversals accomplish none of the things that reversals ought to accomplish. In the latter acts of the play, Julia is portrayed as long-suffering and sensible. At this point striving principally for the comic effect, Shakespeare gives the witty maid the best lines and makes Julia seem a flighty Lydia Languish whose moods change too abruptly and too often. The relationship Shakespeare develops between Julia and Lucetta remains stereotyped and leads nowhere, for Lucetta shortly disappears from the play. And even though a dramatic question is established once Lucetta produces the letter, *Will Julia read that letter?* the fact that Julia longs to read it seems secondary to the stage business. Everything depends on a prop from which comic situations are produced, and much of the comedy derives from the opportunities the fortunes of the letter give the playwright to play with language—evidence almost any line of the soliloquy Julia speaks as she gathers "each several paper":

Be calm, good wind, blow not a word away
Till I have found each letter in the letter . . . (1.2.115–16)

What Shakespeare gives us, then, is far more a scenario than a sequence, where the situation adequately fulfills the narrative function, establishing that Julia loves Proteus, but in terms of dramatic action remain only partially realized. One need only set this brief sketch beside the more developed version of the same idea in *The Merchant of Venice*, where Portia describes her suitors to Nerissa (1.2.1–134), to see how limited is this passage from *Two Gentlemen*.

Two other examples of Shakespeare's instinct to use the reversal structure in motivational units within the scene can be studied in the episodes in which Proteus receives confirmation that Julia loves him but is immediately torn away from her. This part of the exposition takes place in two stages: in the first, Panthino attempts to change Antonio (1.3.1–43); in the second, Antonio works a change upon Proteus (1.3.44–91).

The two old men are brought on for the sole purpose of causing the separation between Proteus and Julia that will make the rest of the plot possible. Shakespeare's concern in 1.3.1–43 is to be sure the audience recognizes Antonio's position. The concerned father's objective must be made clear, and Shakespeare accomplishes this by having Antonio reveal that objective to Panthino: Antonio wishes his son to "be a perfect man," a status that is acquired by "being tried and tutor'd in the world," and therefore determines to dispatch him after Valentine.

What is Panthino's goal? Though in truth Panthino appears in the scene only as an ear into which Antonio can report his thoughts and in that sense "hears" for the audience, we find in this episode an obvious attempt to structure the dialogue as more than simple reporting. As Bernard Beckerman notes, Shakespeare already has the dramatic intuition to use persuading as a motivational basis for the episode (11) and has employed that motive to activate Panthino. Panthino too has been given an objective, "to importune" Antonio to educate his son.

In form, then, the conversation becomes a duologue between the persuader and the persuaded:

> *Antonio:* Tell me, Panthino, what sad talk was that
> Wherewith my brother held you in the cloister?
> *Panthino:* 'Twas of his nephew Proteus, your son.
> *Antonio:* Why, what of him?
> *Panthino:* He wond'red that your lordship
> Would suffer him to spend his youth at home,
> While other men, of slender reputation,
> Put forth their sons to seek preferment out:
> Some to the wars, to try their fortune there;
> Some to discover islands far away;
> Some to the studious universities.
> For any or for all these exercises.
> He said that Proteus, your son, was meet;
> And did request me to importune you
> To let him spend his time no more at home,
> Which would be great impeachment to his age,
> In having known no travel in his youth.
> *Antonio:* Nor need'st thou much importune me to that
> Whereupon this month I have been hammering . . .
> Then tell me, wither were I best to send him?
>
> (1.3.1–18, 24)

It goes without saying that Antonio is persuaded; he not only accepts the position that Panthino would have him take but even begs for further direction. As a piece of dramatic craftsmanship, however, the reversal is fraught with problems. The missing ingredient here is resistance. Antonio's lack of resistance is so obvious, even to the playwright, that Antonio is made to apologize for "changing" so quickly. A reversal is hardly dramatic if the character to be reversed already holds the opinion he is to be moved to, as Antonio admits he does. The fact is that Antonio *cannot* offer resistance, because the whole point of bringing him into the play at all is to have him "desire" to send Proteus away. To attempt a reversal under these circumstances is to use the right technique in the wrong place.

Albeit inadequately, Shakespeare achieves with this "reversal" the end he is aiming for, which is to establish Antonio's intention:

> I like thy counsel; well hast thou advis'd;
> And that thou mayst perceive how well I like it,
> The execution of it shall make known:
> Even with the speediest expedition
> I will dispatch him to the Emperor's court. (1.3.34–38)

And by establishing Antonio's objective, he has (though not too compellingly) established the dramatic question, *Will Antonio send Proteus away from Julia?* Shakespeare can now bring Proteus on stage.

At this point, look where the poor wretch comes reading—reading the "sweet lines" of "heavenly Julia." As the unit 1.3.44–91 opens, we again discover Shakespeare striving to place a character firmly in the position from which he will be reversed. Proteus's reading of the letter from Julia shows us Proteus in ecstasy, secure at last in the knowledge that Julia loves him. As the episode develops, that letter becomes the means through which Proteus will be separated from Julia. Antonio inquires about the letter and the son hides its contents from his father, the outcome being that the letter becomes the instrument which causes Proteus's banishment from Verona.

The reversal, like all of those we have been examining in this play, takes place with amazing speed. Because Shakespeare has so clearly established in advance the intentions of Antonio, he wastes no stage time putting them into effect. In the fact that the father's will is so utterly contrary to the son's lie the seeds of conflict that could have made the narrative extremely dramatic. The conflict begins at the moment of meeting: Antonio, discovering Proteus with a letter, demands to see it; Proteus withholds it. Rather than declare his love for Julia, he claims that the letter is from Valentine who "wishes me with him." This statement (as Shakespeare uses it) puts an end to any potential conflict—the unlucky falsehood only opens the way for Antonio to inform Proteus that he is being shipped off to Milan to join Valentine. Proteus's protest, that "he cannot be so soon provided" and needs a day or two to prepare for the proposed journey, is feeble and so instantly dismissed that Antonio and Panthino have left the stage almost before hearing Proteus out. Far from experiencing an emotional conflict in this exchange between father and son, the audience feels the playwright's haste to get Proteus on his way. The speech Shakespeare has written for Antonio reads like an apology to viewers who sense that things happen a mite too rapidly:

> Muse not that I thus suddenly proceed;
> For what I will, I will, and there an end . . .
> Tomorrow be in readiness to go—
> Excuse it not, for I am peremptory. (1.3.64, 70–71)

That Shakespeare means us to experience the reversal from happiness to sorrow in Proteus's mood is clear from the lament with which the episode concludes. Love, says Proteus, is as changeable as an April day, "Which now shows all the beauty of the sun, / And by and by a cloud takes all away." But here, as elsewhere in the play, one understands why Hazlitt viewed the play as "the first outlines of a comedy loosely sketched in." We don't feel the change of mood so much as a straining for that effect.

In the expository episode of the Valentine/Silvia romance one can detect a rudimentary attempt at moving Valentine from ignorance to knowledge. This is the unit in which Silvia makes her love known to Valentine. The structuring motivation underlying the action is extremely bald, and of the sort that provoked Wells to remark that "the exigencies of the plot require this intelligent young man to behave" in an "unrealistic" and even "downright stupid" manner (167). Valentine wants to give Silvia the letter she has asked him to write to her lover—in other words, he wishes to please her (Shakespeare wastes no time making Valentine at all jealous or even curious about the identity of the unknown lover), while Silvia wants Valentine to take the letter—*she* means, though Shakespeare keeps Valentine ignorant of her purpose, to reveal to him her love. Silvia's objective requires, obviously, that Valentine discover her secret, that his ignorance change to understanding and, ideally, the playwright would find some way of making his romantic hero cleverly detect his lady's ruse. Alas, Shakespeare's attention gets deflected by Speed—the episode fails because Speed catches on before Valentine, and Valentine's "reversal" occurs not because Silvia but because Speed makes him aware of what is going on. Wells sees the grave error of this: Shakespeare has made Valentine "a vehicle for a type of comedy that deprives him of his whole basis for existence" (167). Though the reversal is clearly designed to move Valentine from ignorance to knowledge, the feeling Shakespeare conveys to the viewer is that Valentine remains ignorant.

Let's pause for a moment, before going on, to take stock of what Shakespeare has accomplished during the course of the expository section of *Two Gentlemen*. Shakespeare has not only introduced the lovers to his audience but has moved them to the point of having declared themselves to one another, all while working toward significant changes in each of the two heroes. Valentine, who in the play's opening segment had defined love as "shapeless idleness" and folly, "where scorn is bought with groans; / Coy looks with heart-sore sighs; one fading moment's mirth / With twenty watchful, weary, tedious nights" (1.1.28–30), has under Silvia's influence learned "to wreathe your arms, like a malecontent; to relish a love-song, like a robin-redbreast; to walk alone, like one that had the pestilence; to sigh, like a schoolboy" and so on (2.1.19–22). Shakespeare, through Speed, makes a point of the reversal:

> You were wont, when you laugh'd, to crow like a cock; when you walk'd, to walk like one of the lions; when you fasted, it was presently after dinner; when you look'd sadly, it was for want of money: and now you are metamorphis'd with a mistress, that when I look on you, I can hardly think you my master. (2.1.26–32)

Proteus too has undergone a change. In the introductory episode, he had chosen to spend his youth at home in Verona, defying Valentine's attempts to "entreat thy company, / To see the wonders of the world abroad" (1.1.5–6) and preferring to be near Julia. But fortune will not have it thus; Proteus is sent away. As the expository section closes, we find him sailing away from Verona and Julia.

Even on this larger scale, Shakespeare is working with reversals. And in this regard, it is interesting to look briefly at the transitional scene called 2.2, where Proteus takes leave of Julia. On the one hand, this 20-line passage provides a conclusion to the expository frames, when, fulfilling the promises of the scenes we have been examining, Shakespeare brings Julia and Proteus together. It is here that they exchange rings and seal with a kiss their vows of perpetual love. This passage neatly closes off and defines the expository section. On the other hand, the passage provides a foundation upon which a subsequent reversal can be built. There is hidden irony in Proteus's profession of faith to Julia:

Here is my hand for my true constancy;
And when that hour o'erslips me in the day
Wherein I sigh not, Julia, for thy sake,
The next ensuing hour some foul mischance
Torment me for my love's forgetfulness! (2.2.8–12)

Here is the same ironic foreshadowing of a reversal that will reappear in Othello's "When I love thee not, chaos is come again." Anyone familiar with the mature Shakespeare's handling of reversals will perceive that in this brief passage Shakespeare has Proteus state a position that he is going to be moved away from. Nor is the reversal long in coming; we will see it occur in 2.4.

Will Proteus be true to Julia? This is perhaps the most important of the structuring dramatic questions of the play, and it goes far in linking Shakespeare's plot to his theme. *Will Proteus be constant?* In 2.4, Shakespeare subjects Proteus to a temptation that will turn his constancy into betrayal. We noted at the beginning of this essay that Proteus's decision to abandon Julia in favor of Silvia marks one of the major reversals of Shakespeare's plot. In examining how Shakespeare engineers that reversal, I want to stress an important point—that the large-scale reversals, those major turning points in the plot, are invariably effected within the boundaries of a single episode. The reversal of Proteus from constant to inconstant lover occurs not so much in 2.4 as a whole but in a specific episode within it—the unit 2.4.122–214.

Narratively speaking, what has to be accomplished in 2.4? The audience needs to know first that Proteus meets Silvia and second that he falls in love with her, this complication to be conveyed within a framework that establishes Proteus in Milan and acquaints him with the current situation between Valentine and Silvia. Proteus's introduction to Silvia is handled in an earlier unit of the scene (2.4.49–121), where Silvia's father announces the arrival of Proteus and the newcomer is welcomed by both Valentine and Silvia. The two gentlemen are then left alone to "confer of home affairs." Shakespeare still has the task, then, of dramatizing the narrative fact that Proteus has fallen in love with Valentine's Silvia. What motivational structures does he adopt to achieve this end? And how successful is the result?

In 2.4.122–214, both gentlemen have fairly conventional objectives: Valentine strives to extol his lady, for "love delights in praises." He has, of course, much to tell Proteus; he has "done penance for contemning Love," and his wish throughout the unit is to explain his love. Essentially, however, Shakespeare casts Valentine as a persuader, with the ultimate aim of convincing Proteus that Silvia is "such a jewel / As twenty seas—if all their sand were pearl, / The water nectar, and the rocks pure gold." As the opposing character, Proteus's task here is to resist, which he does in varying ways— by refusing to flatter Silvia, by offering to minister "bitter pills" to Valentine to counteract the lovesickness, by preferring his own mistress Julia.

Now the persuasion Valentine mounts is rudimentary and conventional, a device, actually, that allows Valentine to praise Silvia. As the dialogue proceeds, no one except Valentine really expects Proteus to admit that Silvia is more divine than Julia; that Proteus perceives the hyperbole in Valentine's "braggadism" is to his credit. What is extraordinary here though is that Shakespeare is not trying for the expected reversal but aims at something more daring. Proteus isn't changed in the simple way Valentine intended him to change, by verbally admitting that Silvia is "a principality, / Sovereign to all the creatures on the earth," Julia included. Rather, Proteus is absolutely and totally transformed in the most unexpected way possible. He contracts a passion for Silvia:

> Even as one heat another heat expels,
> Or as one nail by strength drives out another,
> So the remembrance of my former love
> Is by a newer object quite forgotten.
> Is it mine eye, or Valentines' praise,
> Her true perfection, or my false transgression,
> That makes me reasonless, to reason thus?
> She is fair; and so is Julia that I love
> (That I did love, for now my love is thaw'd,
> Which, like a waxen image 'gainst a fire
> Bears no impression of the thing it was) . . .
> O, but I love his lady too too much. (2.4.192–202, 205)

The reversal astonishes even Proteus himself. But Shakespeare takes it yet farther in the meditation with which he concludes act two, where the language and the structure of the speech written for the young lover reflect the change that is taking place within him (2.6.1–43). Proteus shares Shakespeare's delight in playing with words: "I cannot leave to love, and yet I do; / But there I leave to love where I *should* love." Phrases are paired off, pro against con: "Love bade me swear, and Love bids me forswear." Proteus thinks in rhetorical oppositions: "Julia I lose, and Valentine I lose: / If I keep them, I needs must lose myself; / If I lose them, thus find I by their loss—/ for Valentine, myself; for Julia, Silvia." Even in the conclusion toward which all of this reasoning leads, he is toying with language:

I will forget that Julia is alive,
Remem'bring that my love to her is dead;
And Valentine I'll hold an enemy,
Aiming at Silvia as a sweeter friend. (2.6.27–30)

Yet already Shakespeare's imagination is captured by the spectacle of a psyche engaged in excusing what it clearly sees as transgressions and by the struggle between conscience and desire for control of the will. Proteus's thought processes are traced in minute detail, from his initial question to himself, "Shall I be forsworn?" through his decision that to pursue Silvia is the greater good, and—what is intensely interesting and especially pertinent to see—the entire speech is composed of couplets and triplets built out of the juxtaposition of opposites: each choice Proteus presents to himself involves polar opposites. He has sworn and will not be forsworn. He gave an oath and will now commit perjury. He is exchanging the bad for better, and in calling Julia bad and Silvia good Proteus makes polar opposites also of the two ladies. During the course of the speech, Julia becomes associated with death and Silvia with life, an image that remains active throughout the play. Valentine is cast as an enemy, Silvia as friend. As Proteus himself is reversed, so, in a sense, is his world; this new love turns everything in Proteus's world into its opposite. The symphony of 180-degree reversals in this soliloquy serves, appropriately, as the speech that confirms that Proteus has been altered from a true lover to an inconstant one.

Despite that daring aspects of this reversal, 2.4 is not without serious dramaturgical flaws. Why, for example, is Proteus, who has all along been Love's advocate, suddenly made into love's detractor? One is tempted to believe that having sensed the potential for a reversal that existed within the narrative, Shakespeare wanted to pull Proteus back to the opposite pole before depicting his transformation. But the fact that Proteus, who has all along been the prototype of the lover, stands during the major part of this episode as Love's detractor is disconcerting. As Inga-Stina Ewbank remarks, Proteus's deflating tactics "do not seem to be tied to character as much as to the needs of the situation or scene" (37).

A further problem exists because Shakespeare has not adequately prepared for the surprise ending. René Girard attempts to explain this sudden change in Proteus's feelings in terms of present-day psychological theory, arguing that Proteus is subliminally affected by his friend's enthusiasm and desires Silvia "not because their brief encounter made a decisive impression on him but because he is predisposed in favor of whatever Valentine desires." Shakespeare, says Girard, illustrates what we now call "*mimetic* or *mediated* desire" (232–33). To my own way of thinking, Shakespeare seems less concerned with the cause of this love than with the *error* of it. In writing the dialogue, he is obviously depending upon his audience's familiarity with the age-old convention that love strikes unpredictably and inexplicably and at this stage of his career feels no further explanation is necessary. These things happen. Dramaturgically speaking, of course, the transition is so sudden that a radical gap exists between the initial dialogue between the two friends and the revelatory soliloquy that follows it. A more nearly perfected version of this kind of reversal will come in *Measure for Measure* with the unexpected reversal of Angelo, where the presence and charm of the lady, not a description of her, turns a grave puritan into a cunning seducer (2.2.1–186).

Alerted to Shakespeare's tendency to think in terms of reversals, the reader will easily recognize the reversal format Shakespeare is working with in act three, where the second pair of lovers, all but united, are cruelly parted. Separation is the fate of all lovers, and the convention conveniently provides a catalyst for the reversal: the irate father. Just as Antonio had separated Proteus from Julia, so the Duke will separate Valentine from Silvia.

In the unit 3.1.51–187, Valentine is to be exposed and exiled, sent away from both Milan and Silvia, his happy heart overcome with anguish. To banish Valentine has been the Duke's purpose from the moment Proteus revealed to him Valentine's designs on Silvia, and that command bursts from him at the end of the episode in a stern and revelatory speech that astonishes the unprepared Valentine:

Go, base intruder, overweening slave,
Bestow thy fawning smiles on equal mates . . .
Be gone, I will not hear thy vain excuse,
But as thou lov'st thy life, make speed from hence. (3.1.157–58,
168–69)

One might speculate that the opening segments of this reversal structure were determined by the end toward which Shakespeare was working. Certainly in 2.4, the episode just studied where Valentine sings the praises of Silvia, Shakespeare has already begun to set the scene for Valentine's unexpected change of fortune. Here Valentine's joy is established and beyond that his sense of security. Valentine assures Proteus that "she is mine own," "we are betrothed"—nay more:

our marriage hour,
With all the cunning manner of our flight

Determin'd of—how I must climb her window,
The ladder made of cords, and all the means
Plotted and 'greed on for my happiness. (2.4.179–83)

"My happiness" is full—this same note is rung when Valentine enters in 3.1. Shakespeare introduces a Valentine who declares his "health and happy being" at the Duke's court (2.1.57). When 3.1.51–187 opens, Valentine is in bliss. This beginning allows for the widest possible swing in Valentine's emotions.

There is no question that the structuring form of this episode, 3.1.51–187, is that of the reversal; however, questions do arise about the way Shakespeare bridges the distance between these polar opposite points of bliss and woe. Let's look at the motives through which the playwright manipulates his characters. First, the Duke's, since the Duke is the propelling character here, and his objective brings about the catastrophe. The Duke receives his motive in the previous episode (3.1.1–50) from Proteus, who reveals to him that "Sir Valentine, my friend, / This night intends to steal away your daughter . . . / they have devis'd a mean / How he her chamber-window will ascend, / And with a corded ladder fetch her down." The Duke's objective is to intercept Valentine and prevent the elopement. The mode through which he pursues this end is to pretend to ask Valentine's advice: the Duke has "resolv'd to take a wife" and "would have thee to my tutor."

What is required to transform the given narrative into drama (a more mature Shakespeare will know this) is the natural resistance that the lover would experience in such a situation. On his way to elope with Silvia, Valentine would show concern when he runs smack into her father, along with fear that his plans might be discovered. Valentine's burning desire to escape, set against the Duke's supposed need for his help and consequent insistence on detaining him, would create more sharply focused tensions. Valentine's desire to assist needs to be as feigned as the Duke's desire for aid, so that there is resistance to the Duke's attempts to trap him.

The young Shakespeare, however, assigns Valentine the objective of aiding the Duke, with far more eagerness than anxiety. Valentine goes overboard in the role. Moreover, the assistance he so generously offers—to counsel the Duke on how to woo and win a scornful lady—requires Valentine to speak, with authority, as an experienced lover. This self-assurance as a lover is hardly consistent with what we have seen of Valentine elsewhere, Valentine in 2.1 having been so inept a lover that Silvia had to do the wooing. Unwarranted and unconvincing, his experience exists, alas, but for a momentary effect. Worse yet, his spaniel-like willingness to oblige the Duke, to the point of lending Silvia's father the very rope ladder he himself needs to climb to Silvia's balcony, provided that the old man will get it back to him in an hour's time, seems the essence of stupidity. The motivation Shakespeare has given to his hero in this case is the kind of motive one would foist upon the silliest of gulls in a low-comedy subplot.

The desires through which these two characters are motivated do get the dramaturgical job done. Once the ladder becomes an object of discussion, the Duke need do little more than seize Valentine's cloak, to find not only the ladder hidden beneath it but also a love letter to Silvia that reveals how the ladder is to be used—and from thence the reversal in Valentine's fortunes is assured. But the end hardly justifies the means!

Clearly, the reversal here detracts from rather than enhances character, for the narrative (rather than desires appropriate to the situation) is what drives Valentine to disaster: what occurs occurs because the plot demands it. Because the motives have no relationship to the characters, the reversal remains only a theatrical trick.

At the end of the episode, we witness once more two characteristics of early Shakespearean dramaturgy, Shakespeare's predilection for pointing to the reversal in a concluding soliloquy and his tendency to make the concluding soliloquy the locus in which he renders the character's emotion. The lover has, he tells us, been moved from joy to agony, from day to night, from light to darkness. Though the process of the reversal lacked credibility, Shakespeare's Valentine feels its effects deeply:

> To die is to be banish'd from myself,
> And Silvia is myself: banish'd from her
> Is self from self, a deadly banishment . . .
> She is my essence, and I leave to be. (3.1.171–73, 182)

Metaphorically speaking, Valentine has been moved two poles that are as opposed as two poles can be—from life to death. In his meditation on his "deadly banishment," there is touching sentiment.

I suggested at the beginning of this essay that Proteus was the play's controlling character, in the sense that his desires give direction to the plot. With Valentine's exile, Proteus's objectives come to the fore: he now has free access to the lady Valentine has left behind and, for most of act four, we will watch Proteus wooing Silvia. He has little success, for Silvia, like Valentine, stands among the constant characters in the play, and the wooing scenes in themselves are perfunctory, but—what seems to interest Shakespeare most in this section of the play—Julia is made a party to the wooing, and as we near the point at which Shakespeare will effect the reversal that all of the previous "action" is building toward—the exposure of Proteus—it will benefit us to look briefly at Julia's role in Milan.

Julia, of course, undergoes a reversal too. The starting position is set up in the dialogue between Julia and Lucetta when Julia is planning to follow Proteus to Italy. Here Shakespeare has Julia declare her expectations; she expects to find a faithful Proteus at the end of her journey:

> *Lucetta.* If Proteus like your journey when you come,
>   No matter who's displeas'd when you are gone:
>   I fear me he will scarce be pleas'd withal.
> *Julia.* That is the least Lucetta, of my fear:
>   A thousand oaths, an ocean of his tears,
>   And instances of infinite of love,
>   Warrant me welcome to my Proteus . . .
>   Truer stars did govern Proteus' birth
>   His words are bonds, his oaths are oracles,
>   His love sincere, his thoughts immaculate,
>   His tears pure messengers sent from his heart,
>   His heart as far from fraud as heaven from earth.
> *Lucetta.* Pray heav'n he prove so when you come to him!
>   (2.7.65–71, 74–78)

When in her disguise Julia arrives in Milan and is brought by the Host "to see the gentlemen that you ask'd for," she feels that to hear him speak "will be music." But Julia arrives when Proteus is singing his song to Silvia, and the music she hears is not to her taste. Julia finds that Proteus "plays false" (4.2.59).

The setup is strongly sketched in, and so is the disappointment, but the reversals here are more in conception than in form. Julia's disappointment is spread out over several episodes during which she is a witness to Proteus's courting. Nevertheless, all of this—her belief in Proteus's constancy and her discovery that he has played her false, has an important role in preparing us for the moment at which Julia confronts Proteus with the fact of his inconstancy and brings about a final reversal in him, the play's climactic and concluding reversal.

Having been concerned, as we have just seen, with the disloyalty, the inconstancy, the treachery exhibited by Proteus in the name of love, Shakespeare wishes to bring about his regeneration through a confrontation with the characters he has wronged. Consequently, everything in the second half of the play leads up to the meeting of all of the lovers in the forest, where

Proteus attempts to rape Silvia (the unit runs from 5.4.1 to 5.4.120). Shakespeare makes Valentine a hidden witness to the encounter, so that "false, perjur'd Proteus" is caught at his worst moment and exposed as being "without faith or love." He again makes an about-face.

> My shame and guilt confounds me.
> Forgive me, Valentine; if hearty sorrow
> Be a sufficient ransom for offense,
> I tender't here: I do as truly suffer
> As e'er I did commit. (5.4.73–77)

The reversal in Proteus is neatly effected.

Had the sequence concluded at this moment, it would not have aroused the critical storm that has resulted from its continuation, wherein Valentine awards Silvia to Proteus. E.M.W. Tillyard reports general agreement "that this scene is morally and dramatically monstrous: that a proposal to hand over a girl to the man who has just proposed to rape her revolts our moral sense and the perfunctory speed with which these staggering events are recounted can only provoke our laughter" (112). Ewbank concludes that "in the unbelievable magnanimity of Valentine (at two girls' expense), thematic considerations appear to override any thought of character development or psychological motivation" (31). And many commentators point out that Silvia's feelings about the matter are not consulted at all.

While agreeing wholeheartedly with these judgments, I think that what we have learned in this study of Shakespeare's handling of the reversal allows us to look at the dramaturgical factors that might have been in the novice playwright's mind as he planned his comic dénouement. I would like to propose that Shakespeare could not end the play here because of his desire—and his obligation—to make Proteus face Julia, who has also in her disguise as Sebastian witnessed the attempted rape. Shakespeare apparently felt strongly that Proteus should have this double come-uppance—confrontations with both Valentine and Julia—and the latter seems the more important for him; it is in fact this confrontation, not the other, that effects the comedy's dénouement. It seems safe then to suggest that Valentine's mysterious offer to give Proteus "all that was mine in Silvia" stems from a dilemma Shakespeare found himself in—how to give Julia the opportunity to reveal herself.

If one examines the action from the vantage point of dramatic structure, one realizes that the main thing Valentine's offer accomplishes is to cause Julia to faint. Julia's swoon quickly shifts attention away from Valentine's offer (Proteus need not accept it, Silvia need not respond)—and toward Julia, the deus ex machina who will resolve all by producing the two rings that reveal, simultaneously, her identity and her knowledge of Proteus's "erring love," thus bringing about the deeper reversal in Proteus, his final change from inconstant to constant lover.

It is in this reversal, not in that reflected in Valentine's theatrical gesture, that both the dramatic and thematic core of the play lie. As the affection toward Julia shown by so many commentators testifies, Julia has our sympathy. She also interests her creator, who throughout his career will continue to use the breeches part to explore the emotions of women in Julia's situation. So it is fitting here at the end to speak of the reversal structures Shakespeare developed for the dénouement of the play. There are two, both showing signs of being written in haste.

The one that concerns us most, since this essay traces especially the metamorphosis of Proteus, occurs in the episode 5.4.1–120, where Valentine (hidden) and Julia (disguised) watch Proteus wooing Silvia. What is the dramatic structure here, what the motives? Beckerman would describe the scene as a duet with observers. Shakespeare makes Proteus the controlling figure in this duet, Silvia the resisting one. Proteus begs a reward, Silvia's favor, concertized in his plea for "one fair look." And he would do much for it: "What dangerous action, stood it next to death, / Would I not undergo for one calm look?" Silvia's resistance is as strong here as it has been throughout Proteus's suit: Silvia wants only Valentine. But Shakespeare lets her resistance take an interesting form, so that the action here, despite its primitive quality, simultaneously reveals the thematic material that underlies it. In repulsing Proteus, Silvia measures him against Valentine, setting the man she adores beside the man she detests, and what she particularly detests about Proteus is the quality that he most needs to see in himself for the peripeteia to occur: Silvia continually portrays her opponent as "false perjur'd Proteus." In Silvia's lines, we find a statement of what Proteus's choice in 2.6 and his commitment to "three-fold perjury" have brought him to:

> Read over Julia's heart (thy first best love),
> For whose dear sake thou didst then rend thy faith
> Into a thousand oaths; and all those oaths
> Descended into perjury, to love me.
> Though hast no faith left now . . . (5.4.46–50)

Valentine is true, Silvia is true, while Proteus, "thrice perjur'd Proteus," is but a "counterfeit." The rebuke presents to Proteus the opportunity to see himself as he is but provokes him instead to intensify his suit, the next step being the brutal one, "I'll . . . love you 'gainst the nature of love" and "force thee yield to my desire."

At this climactic point, Shakespeare brings the observers out of hiding to pass judgment on what they have seen. Valentine hits Proteus with another, this time more comic, view of the contemptible person he has become, a friend "that's without faith or love," "treacherous" and "perjur'd to the bosom." Where Proteus's passion allowed him to ignore Silvia's warnings, the exposure of his actions and the rebuke of Valentine pierce that passion so that Proteus's boldness turns to shame and guilt. And this repentance effects the reunion between the friends that Shakespeare's plot requires.

But Proteus, remember, is "thrice-perjur'd," and his exposure is not yet complete. He will receive a third, and this time more subtle rebuke, for it comes from a source even dearer to him than his friend. Shakespeare has shown Proteus hiring a series of servants to advance his cause in love—first Speed, then Launce, and, finally, in 4.4 Julia— in her disguise as Sebastian, whom Shakespeare presents as "my master's *true* confirmed love" and "*true* servant to my master." The rebuke of this emblem of truth is the final one Proteus will have to endure:

> Behold her that gave aim to all thy oaths,
> And entertain'd 'em deeply in her heart.
> How oft hast thou with perjury cleft the root?
> O Proteus, let this habit make thee blush! (5.4.101–04)

The throwing off of Julia's disguise coincides with the falling away of error from Proteus's mind, so that he sees Julia once again "with a constant eye."

It remains, now, only for Shakespeare to reunite Valentine and Silvia. Valentine was but now filled with "distresses" and "woes" because separated from Silvia; Silvia "miserable" and "unhappy" at being plagued by Proteus. The reversal for this pair, realized in unit 5.4.121–73, occurs when the Duke applauds the spirit of Valentine and deems him "worthy of an empress' love," with which happy event "all jars" fittingly become "triumphs, mirth, and rare solemnity."

Again and again, in what must be one of Shakespeare's earliest plays, we see Shakespeare organizing his plot around major reversals, one occurring in the middle of the play, the other at the moment of the play's resolution, these reversals in the direction of the plot being the result of a whole series of smaller reversals through which Shakespeare attempts to transform the narrative into drama. And again and again we see the reversals strained and unconvincing, often inadequately motivated, and usually undercutting the assumed nobility of the characters. But, for all that, *Two Gentlemen* remains a valuable document, providing us with some of the earliest evidence available of Shakespeare's fascination with the reversal and his youthful struggles to make it work for him.

NOTES

1. Citations are to *The Riverside Shakespeare*.

2. The terms *motivational unit, dialogue unit*, or *plot episode* have been used throughout this essay rather than the term *sequence*. The sequence, in the sense that that term is defined and studied in *Analyzing Shakespeare's Action: Scene Versus Sequence*, is a fully developed action. The units Shakespeare gave us in *Two Gentlemen* cannot accurately be defined as *sequences*, for these are little more than dialogue units or episodes. One must be wary of applying technical terms like *sequence* or *action* in a play as dramatically inefficient as is *Two Gentlemen of Verona*.

WORKS CITED

Beckerman, Bernard. "Shakespeare's Dramaturgy and Binary Form." *Theatre Journal* 33.1 (March 1981): 5–17.

Ewbank, Inga-Stina. "'Were man but constant, he were perfect': Constancy and Consistency in *The Two Gentlemen of Verona*." *Shakespearean Comedy*. Ed. Malcolm Bradbury and David J. Palmer. Stratford-Upon-Avon Studies 4. London: Edward Arnold, 1972. 31–57.

Hallett, Charles A. and Elaine S. Hallett. *Analyzing Shakespeare's Action: Scene Versus Sequence*. Cambridge: Cambridge University Press, 1991.

Shakespeare, William. *The Riverside Shakespeare*. Ed. G. Blakemore Evans et al. Boston: Houghton Mifflin, 1974.

Tillyard, E.M.W. *Shakespeare's Early Comedies*. New York: Barnes & Noble, 1965.

Wells, Stanley. "The Failure of *The Two Gentlemen of Verona*." *Shakespeare Jahrbuch* 99 (1963): 161–73.

Shakespeare's Actors as Collaborators: Will Kempe and *The Two Gentlemen of Verona* (1996)

Kathleen Campbell

Shakespeare's theatrical work was almost certainly shaped by members of his theatre company, those actors who spoke the lines he wrote and may have impressed upon them their own particular rhythms, mannerisms, and theatrical styles. Their impact, however, is difficult to trace. We have the names of the members of the acting company, some miscellaneous facts about their lives, occasional details about their physical appearance, but little about their actual performances. Certainly some physical characteristics of characters derive from the actors who played them, but the influence may run much deeper.

Unfortunately, we know little or nothing about the give and take, the sharing of ideas, the use of improvisation, the contributions of specific actors, yet it is likely that all these elements contributed to the development of Shakespeare's scripts. Shakespeare's clowns provide a good starting part for examining the way in which an actor shapes a role. We know something about the two most famous clowns, Will Kempe and Robert Armin, with whom Shakespeare worked, and we can see the role of the clown in the plays change to fit the different styles of the two actors. In this essay, I will examine an early role—Launce in *The Two Gentlemen of Verona*—which I believe to be heavily influenced by Kempe, if not largely his own creation; I will also mention some other roles in which we can see the traces of an actor's influence that might be examined more closely.

Two Gentlemen is hardly a problem play, but it is a play with many problems—not so much the big, perplexing kind but the little annoying kind. In his introduction to the Arden edition, Clifford Leech points out no less than twenty-one "oddities" in the play, ranging from minor irregularities to disturbing, if not major, contradictions in character or action (xviii–xxii). The locale of the action, for example, is unstable: it appears to begin in Verona and then move to Milan, but the Duke refers to the lady he is supposedly wooing as being "in Verona here," and Speed in another scene welcomes Launce to Padua. Julia seems to have a father and then not, while Silvia's father may be a duke or an emperor. Proteus falls in love with Silvia at first sight, but she later indicates he has often told her about his love for Julia—strange behavior for a love-sick swain. And the name Sir Eglamour is used for what seem to be two entirely different people.

Less a problem, but still somewhat of an anomaly in the script, is the character of Launce. Launce exists almost independently of the plot of the play. Only briefly, at the end of 3.1 and in 4.4, does Launce's story intersect the main action. In the first of these scenes, he accompanies Proteus, looking for the banished Valentine. He tosses off a few jokes but is extraneous to the action. In the second scene, Proteus berates him for losing his dog and drives him away. The dog episode perhaps forces Proteus to engage Julia as his messenger, but he seems already to have decided on this course of action, the meeting with Launce at the most prompting him to complete the intended transaction immediately. Each of Launce's most important scenes—the incomparable monologue with Crab, his dog (2.3); his duet with Speed on the virtues and vices of his potential bride (3.1); and his account of Crab's behavior in the Duke's dining-chamber (4.4)—constitutes a set piece designed to entertain the audience and showcase the talents of a comic performer.

Although the Launce scenes seem to be grafted onto the plot, these are some of the most skillfully written sections of the script. Launce's role is written entirely in prose, unusual for this play, in which even the outlaws speak verse.[1] His language has an idiosyncratic ring that separates him from the other characters who, by and large, speak with one voice, the language of the play varying little from character to character. Again, Launce's scenes have a sureness of rhythm and comic timing that is not matched by the rest of the play. It is almost as if Launce and his dog have wandered in from another world.

Leech accounts for the independence of Launce's scenes (and for the general unevenness of the work as a whole) by suggesting that *Two Gentlemen* was composed in stages over a period of time (xxx). His scenario is plausible. Shakespeare first contrived the basic elements of the love and friendship plots, he argues. To these he made various adjustments and added other components, culminating with the addition of Launce. Leech's theory results in a comparatively late date for the play; while it may have been begun earlier, it would have been completed in late 1593. The Oxford editors, in contrast, believe it may be Shakespeare's first play and assign it to 1591.[2]

Leech does not discuss, however, what I think may be the strongest argument for dating the final version of *Two Gentlemen* around 1593, or even a bit later: the addition of Will Kempe to the newly reorganized Lord Chamberlain's company at about that time. Kempe previously had played with Strange's Men, with whom he performed in *A Knack to Know a Knave* in June 1592: that play was published two years later as including "Kempe's applauded merriments of the 'Men of Gotham,' etc." Prior to his association with Strange's Men, Kempe performed principally as an independent entertainer; he was better known at the time for his jigs and "merriments" than his performances as an actor. The episode of the men of Gotham is a short and independent comic routine with no bearing on the plot of the play, but Kempe's playing of it was well enough known to make it a selling point for the script. I suggest that Launce owes his distinctive voice and comic genius to Kempe, or at least to a fortuitous collaboration between Kempe and Shakespeare, who may have simply had the good sense to incorporate Kempe's comic improvisations into the script with little alteration.

There is little argument that Launce would have been Kempe's role. David Wiles, in *Shakespeare's Clown*, describes the features of those roles generally assigned to Kempe (73–82, 99–115). He includes among these Peter in *Romeo and Juliet* and Dogberry in *Much Ado About Nothing*, both of which plays mention Kempe in stage directions, and Bottom in *A Midsummer Night's Dream*, Launcelot Gobbo in *The Merchant of Venice*, and Costard in *Love's Labor's Lost* among Shakespeare plays. Roles in works by other playwrights include Cob in Jonson's *Every Man in his Humor*, Hodge in *Thomas Lord Cromwell*, Cock in *The Royal King and the Loyal Subject* by Heywood, Pipkin in *How a Man May Choose a Good Wife from Bad*, and the Clown in *Sir Thomas Wyatt*.

Kempe's characters are only loosely attached to the plots of their plays and are regularly missing from the final scenes, presumably to allow the actor time to prepare for the jig that would follow the performance. Kempe was a large man and his characters are often physically solid and slow-moving. Costard, for example, in *Love's Labor's Lost*, takes his name from a large apple, and he plays Pompey the Great in "The Nine Worthies" because of his "great limb" (5.1.125).[3] Dogberry is larger than Verges, and Pipkin (in *How a Man May Choose a Good Wife from a Bad*) describes himself as the greatest scholar in the school because of his size. Launce compares himself to the "prodigious" son (2.3.3), a mis-speaking of prodigal but also a reference to his size, and a number of his exits suggest his slowness. "Wilt thou go?" asks Panthino (2.3.57), and Proteus complains: "stayest thou to vex me here" (4.4.60). In several scripts, his character is an apprentice, and part of the comedy comes from the difference in age and size between character and actor. Launce functions in part in this way, for the character is paired and contrasted with Valentine's younger (and evidently faster) servant Speed.

The Kempe persona is always a lower class figure; he relies heavily on direct address and typically derives much of his humor from puns, mistakes in word usage, and similar confusions of language. Dogberry, for example, is famous for his misuse of vocabulary, and Peter refers provocatively to his dagger: "I saw no man use you at his pleasure, if I had, my weapon should have quickly have been out: I warrant you, I dare draw as soon as another man, if I see occasion in a good quarrell, and the law on my side" (*Romeo* 2.4.54–57).[4] Launce's prose marks him as a rustic, especially in contrast, again, to Speed, who not only speaks verse in his scenes with Valentine and Proteus but also shares their style of courtly wordplay. Much of Launce's humor, remarked upon several times by other characters, comes from his confusion, usually deliberate, of similar words. He has received his portion, as I mentioned earlier, "like the prodigious son." He converts tide to tied, mastership to master's ship, and interchanges understands and stands under. Launce characteristically uses the second person. "I'll show you the manner of it" (2.3.13–14), he says, and sometimes addresses his comments to a specific member of the audience: "Now, sir, this staff is my sister; for look you, she is as white as a lily, and as small as a wand" (2.3.19–20). The clown addresses the audience as a gathering of his peers and implies an intimacy with his sharing of his stories with them: "You shall judge," he offers as he recounts how he saved Crab from certain punishment (4.4.16).

Also found in other Kempe roles is a long string of loosely associated phrases and clauses such as at the beginning of Launce's first speech: "My mother weeping; my father wailing; my sister crying; our maid howling; our cat wringing her hands; and all our house in a great perplexity; yet did not this cruel-hearted cur shed one tear" (2.3.5–9). Note the structural similarity to this speech of Peter's: "Madam the guests are come, supper serv'd up, you called, my young lady asked for, the Nurse curst in the pantry, and every thing in extremity: I must hence to wait, I beseech you follow straight" (*Romeo* 1.3.101–04). Launce clearly fits the basic Kempe stage persona. And if Launce were created for (and perhaps in part by) Kempe, it is unlikely that the play reached its present form before Kempe joined the Lord Chamberlain's Company in 1593.

Then there is the matter of the dog. No one, as far as I know, has considered the existence of the dog Crab as a clue to the dating of *Two Gentlemen*, but its presence seems to me to be significant. I suspect the dog is ignored because, despite Launce's references to him in his monologues, he is not really present for a reader of the script. For players and audience, however, the dog is the center of the scene.[5] Crab is the reason for those scenes in which he appears, not just an incidental part of them. Shakespeare uses a live animal on stage only three times in his career: after *Two Gentlemen* and *Dream*, there is nothing until the bear appears in the third act of *The Winter's Tale*. That bear may well have been the same white bear that appeared in a performance of *Mucedorus* in December of 1610[6]—another example of reshaping a play to fit a performer. The scarcity of other animals in the plays combined with the apparent availability of a trained bear suggests that Shakespeare wrote the scene because the required animal was available. The same reasoning might well apply to the dog who appears in the two early comedies; given the difficulties of finding and working with live animals and the lack of any necessity for the dog in either play, I doubt that Shakespeare would have invented Crab had an animal not been at hand. Its appearance in two plays suggests a close temporal relationship between those scripts. After *Dream*, either Crab was no longer available or Shakespeare, having learned from experience the truth of the adage about dogs and children on the stage, chose not to use him again. (Interestingly, he never gives up using children, of whom he may have had a steadier supply.) Crab's influence, then, would seem to place the date of the completed play close to the 1594–95 dates usually proposed for *Dream* and *Romeo and Juliet*, both plays with roles for Kempe.

To argue this late date for the final version of *Two Gentlemen* does not necessarily mean that earlier versions of the script were ever performed. Since the theatres were closed because of plague for the latter half of 1592 and much of 1593, it is plausible that Shakespeare continued work on the script during this period, finally (and perhaps quickly) polishing it off for performance when the theatres reopened.

I would propose, then, a scenario something like this: Shakespeare begins work on a romantic comedy—quite possibly his first attempt at the genre. As Leech suggests, he first lays out the basic plot, derived from the story of Don Felix and Felismena in Montemayor's *Diana* and various examples of friendship stories common during the period. Subsequent alterations expand the plot but result in some inconsistencies: changes in locale are not clearly adjusted throughout the script, for example. Shakespeare has no reason to rush, because the closing of the theatres reduces the demand for new scripts, so he may be dabbling with possibilities rather than developing the play for immediate use. Near the end of 1593, however, with the reopening of the theatres, Shakespeare needs new material for the company that he himself has only recently joined, and he needs to find a place for

Kempe, who comes to the group as a well-known and popular entertainer whose presence in a cast should boost attendance. Either in response to his knowledge of Kempe's style and persona or, more likely, I believe, working directly with the comedian, Shakespeare fashions the role of Launce, connecting him only marginally to the already existing play. This version, a collaboration between Shakespeare and Kempe, is perhaps then rushed into production with a large number of inconsistencies still present, though nothing likely to bother an audience (or for that matter, an actor not immersed in modern psychologically-based acting methods).

The contributions of the two collaborators are not difficult to detect. Shakespeare provides a basic character and situation—a comic servant for one of the protagonists—and the experienced Kempe fleshes out the detail, inserting his stage persona and quite possibly improvising his dialogue around an agreed-upon theme. Shakespeare's hand can be seen in the parallels and contrasts between Launce's situation and that of his master. Launce's account of his farewell to his family, at which Crab does not shed a tear, follows the tearful farewell between Julia and Proteus, which ends with Julia's silent departure. Launce's comment on his master's duplicity precedes his own account of his impending betrayal of Crab for a milk-maid: "She hath more qualities than a water spaniel" (3.1.269–79). The resulting scenes, though, are shaped by Kempe's already conceived persona and his knowledge of comic timing. Other elements of the play suggest that Shakespeare at this point has little sense of how to write character—that is, of how to build a character through language and action. Thurio, Valentine's rival, is described as foolish and is clearly intended to be comical, but there is little in the role as written for an actor to play. Launce's character and humor, in contrast, are built into the scenes, which are much more surely written than the surrounding material. It is difficult to tell who actually wrote the lines, but if they are Shakespeare's he must have been strongly influenced by an experienced comedian.

I wish that I could support this scenario with a further connection between Kempe and the dog. Unfortunately, I have found no indication that Kempe worked with a dog on any other occasion. And the dog, in fact, does not seem to be associated exclusively with Kempe: in *Dream*, in which Kempe would have played Bottom, the dog appears only in "Pyramus and Thisbe," in which he accompanies Starveling in his character of Moonshine: "All that I have to say is to tell you that the lantern is the moon; I, the man in the moon; this thorn bush, my thorn bush; and this dog, my dog" (5.1.53–55). The availability of the dog, then, seems to have been a fortuitous coincidence of which Kempe and Shakespeare took advantage. (The two appearances of the dog, by the way, suggest that the animal had his own shtick: he was trained to do nothing.)

It is relatively easy to trace the influence of Kempe on the roles created for him, for they maintain a consistent underlying persona and use of language. In fact, it may have been Kempe's inability or unwillingness to vary his basic style and character that led to his departure from the Lord Chamberlain's Company by 1599. The separation does seem somewhat abrupt: he signed the lease for a share in the Globe in February but had left the company by the following autumn. While Kempe continued to perform his popular jigs and played a few other roles in London, he did not maintain a consistent connection with an acting company, perhaps preferring the career of an independent and often solo entertainer.

By mid-August 1600, Kempe's place as company clown was taken by Robert Armin, and many critics have noted how the clown roles change to take advantage of Armin's specific talents. While Kempe was large and slow and built his character on his rusticity, Armin was small, even dwarfish, and physically unattractive. Unlike Kempe, he played a variety of characters, often making use of his considerable skill as a musician. The ability to make quick shifts in character through vocal or physical changes shapes many of his roles, which often involve disguises or multiple characters: Feste playing Sir Topas in *Twelfth Night* or Autolycus's various disguises in *The Winter's Tale*, for example. Armin maintained a stricter separation from the audience than did Kempe; when he addresses the audience, he is more likely to leave them in the third person, like the Porter in *Macbeth*, whose speech seems an extension of Armin's practice of improvising comic bits in response to audience questions.[7]

Because of the distinctiveness of their roles, the company clowns are the easiest actors to look to when trying to determine the influence of the performers on Shakespeare's scripts. But there are many other tantalizing suggestions of a close relation between role and actor in Shakespeare's creation of character. Speed, for example, in *Two Gentlemen*, is a sort of prototype of Puck in *Dream*—running errands, teasing his master, and when caught claiming, like Puck, that he mistook. The role requires the same kind of actor—small and very fast: Speed's name indicates his movement style, and Puck brags of putting "a girdle round the earth in sixty minutes." The parts are created for a particular actor, in the case of Speed, probably for an apprentice, possibly Kempe's: Speed is clearly a boy and plays straight man to Kempe's Launce whenever they are on stage together.

Occasionally, an actor's influence on a role emerges in more subtle ways. Burbage, who played Hamlet, was also a painter, a fact largely unrelated to his career as leading actor in the Lord Chamberlain's Company. But then we find Hamlet holding Ophelia at arm's length, "And with his other hand thus o'er his brow, / He falls to such perusal of my face, / As he would draw it" (2.1.86–88). It is the gesture of a painter. And the gesture, while only described by Ophelia, quite likely is manifested throughout the play with the portraits of the elder Hamlet and Claudius, with Yorick's skull—it is, indeed, a gesture which helps define the character as a man who holds things at a distance in order to contemplate them. Is it not possible, even probable, that the gesture comes as much from Burbage as it does from Shakespeare?

Or, remaining with *Hamlet* for a moment, consider Osric. How and why would such a character come into being? All that is needed here is someone to bring Hamlet word of the proposed duel. Instead, we get Osric, a fully realized and completely unnecessary character. Certainly, he provides comic relief, and the conversation allows us to see how Hamlet has changed. Here, readers will say, we can see Shakespeare's mastery at work. And I do not disagree. But what I also see here is Shakespeare providing an opportunity for an actor. What actor? It is a showy role, one which draws attention to itself, the sort that might be written as compensation for an actor who has otherwise had little to do in the play. But *Hamlet* requires a large cast, and if doubling is used, most of the company will be kept busy most of the performance. The role is written for a young man (the Folio stage direction reads "Enter young Osricke"), perhaps not one quite experienced enough for a longer part (such as Polonius, for example, whom Osric functionally replaces). An older apprentice, ready to "graduate," might be given such a small but noticeable role as an opportunity to display his skills. Whoever he is, Shakespeare takes the performer, with his specific characteristics and skills, and builds a role around him. As with Launce, he makes use of the role for other purposes, but he tailors it to fit the actor who will play it.

Each of these instances suggests the nature of Shakespeare's collaborative relationship with his actors. The playwright establishes the function of the role that, in turn, will usually determine certain basic characteristics such as sex, class, action. He then develops the details of the character— language, gesture, business—with the actor in mind. In some cases, as with the clowns, the actor's stage persona and/or skills strongly shape the development of the role. In the case of Launce, for example, Kempe's persona almost runs counter to the character's function as Proteus's servant/messenger. With actors who play a variety of roles, however, the influence is slighter and less noticeable, surfacing mostly in recognizable physical details and similarities of character. Each play, however, is influenced by the actors who will play it. Throughout his career, Shakespeare weds his own impulses and inspirations and ideas with the raw material provided by the company. It is perhaps too much to say that without Kempe and Armin we would not have had Launce or Lear's Fool (although in the first case it may not be). But it is not, I think, too much to suggest that these characters owe their particular form as much to the actors for which the roles were created as to the imagination of the playwright.

NOTES

1. The Host also speaks prose, but his language has no distinctive sound or vocabulary to differentiate it from that of others.

2. A.E.J. Honigman proposes an even earlier date as part of his "early start" theory in *Shakespeare's Influence on his Contemporaries*.

3. Unless noted otherwise, quotations from Shakespeare's works are from the Hinman facsimile of the First Folio texts.

4. In Q1, the passage is more blatantly obscene: "I see nobody use you at his pleasure, if I had, I would soone have drawn; you know my tool is as soon out as others, if I see time and place."

5. I am presuming that Crab was played by a live animal. We know, of course, that stuffed or artificial animals, both natural and mythological, were employed on the stage, e.g., from Philip Henslowe's 1598 inventory of properties for the Rose, which includes "i. black dogge" (Foakes and Ricker 321), but the comic effects of Crab's presence in *Two Gentlemen* seem to depend on the dog's being a living presence.

6. The earliest mention of *The Winter's Tale* is May 1611 and the play is usually dated between January and May of that year.

7. Armin's *Quips vpon Questions* shows how Armin might respond to ideas or themes suggested by the audience. It is also possible that he answered his own questions, put to himself in a different voice, a practice echoed in the Porter's speech.

WORKS CITED

Armin, Robert. *Quips vpon Questions, or, A Clownes conceite on occasion offered.* London, 1600. In *The Collected Works of Robert Armin.* Ed. J.P. Feather. Vol. 1. New York: Johnson Reprint, 1972.

Foakes, R.A. and R.T. Rickert, eds. *Henslowe's Diary.* Cambridge: Cambridge University Press, 1961.

Honigman, A.E.J. *Shakespeare's Influence on his Contemporaries.* Totowa, NJ: Barnes & Noble, 1982.

Leech, Clifford, ed. Introduction to *The Two Gentlemen of Verona.* New Arden Shakespeare. London: Methuen, 1969.

Shakespeare, William. *The First Folio of Shakespeare.* Norton Facsimile. Ed. Charlton Hinman. New York: Norton, 1968.

Wiles, David. *Shakespeare's Clown.* Cambridge: Cambridge University Press, 1987.

"I AM BUT A FOOLE, LOOKE YOU": LAUNCE AND THE SOCIAL FUNCTIONS OF HUMOR (1996)

John Timpane

Humor performs a wide range of social functions, some of which contribute to the way in which social institutions reorganize. Humor keeps ideas in circulation; it can also generate new ideas, float hypothetical consensus, and clarify problems. Because it can do all these things, humor can be involved in the way people change their minds.

A test case is Launce of *Two Gentlemen of Verona*. Although one of the earliest, if not the very first, of Shakespeare's comic efforts, Launce nevertheless seems an assured performance within the kindred traditions of clown and fool.[1] Launce is an excellent example of how humor acts as a communal testing and teaching tool with the potential to contribute to social change.

Shakespeare's humorous characters are well known for corroborating themes and issues local to their plays. As many readers have felt, Launce teaches as much about love, pity, and human relations as any character in *Two Gentlemen*.[2] In his total (and totally unrequited) love for an uncaring dog, he is a very funny parallel to Valentine and his love for Sylvia. He is also a comic corrective to the inconstant Proteus. But Launce does much more. He also prompts thinking about male behavior, social organization, obedience, and language. These issues transcend any single play, and Launce's work with them amounts to social work. My argument is that Launce's social work contributed to the way Elizabethan society was changing in the 1590s. He fits into a set of practices—which today we call "humor"—that perpetually questions received ideas.

To explore the possible social functions Launce could have performed, let me conceive of humor in Shakespeare's theatre as a form of material exchange. Shakespeare and company are putting forth a product for which the audience pays money. What were they paying for? Nostalgia, for one thing, and all the ambivalence nostalgia suggests; silliness, for another, a particular way of seeing and subverting standards for human behavior; ambiguity, which calls on the mind to think for itself; and improvisation, an explosive challenge to normative ideas. These four elements characterize the Renaissance laugh. Shakespeare and company knew and exploited the audience's desire for them, in which project he was abetted by the original material conditions of performance. When Launce says, "I am but a foole, looke you" (3.1.263), he downplays his importance, but a closer look reveals how much there can be to laughing at something that is "only" a fool.

I. NOSTALGIA

Shakespeare never abandoned fools and clowns. He worked more with fools, and much more with court fools, than his contemporaries did.[3] From *Two Gentlemen of Verona* to *The Tempest*, from Launce to Thersites to Autolycus, Shakespeare stayed with clowns and fools even when they had become a subject of ridicule by other writers and dramatists.[4] Such idiosyncratic loyalty to clowns suggests a strong nostalgia for a simple, unified village communitarianism as opposed to a complex, disparate, urban commercialism.[5]

At first glance, nostalgia—from Greek words meaning "a longing to return home"—would seem to be the gentlest and most politically innocent of passions. If we consider nostalgia closely, however, especially in a comic figure such as Launce of *Two Gentlemen of Verona*, we may discover that its commercial exploitation actually helps promulgate potentially subversive alternatives to accepted ideas. Consider the material conditions surrounding Launce. A theatre is built as part of a nascent industry dedicated to the exploration of communal fantasies. Already there is a great deal of danger in that arrangement, as Philip Stubbes, the Council of London, the puritan theorists, and the players and writers themselves knew well. Onto the stage of that theatre staggers Launce, who incorporates many evocations of minstrelsy and foolery of an earlier age. Whoever may have played him—William Kempe, let us say, with Richard Cowley as Speed—was a master of just this sort of humor, time-tested, as popular in the city as in the provinces. Nostalgia is being bought and sold. Writer seeks to prosper from, and audience agrees to pay for, the evocation of a nostalgic catharsis.

Launce is a product of Shakespeare's anticipation of the audience's nostalgia for such figures. (He either knew or guessed that many in his audience felt displaced.) Kempe, a great clown, presents the audience with his personal version of Shakespeare's idea of what the audience wants: a funny, nostalgic fool, complete with the explosive, surprised humor that attends improvisation. (Kempe was far better-known than Shakespeare when and if he played this role; his own extensive and respected personal experience of minstrels, fools, rogues, and vagabonds is also for sale.) Actor, player, and audience are playing with group and personal experience.

In his first speech, Launce announces that "I have receiv'd my proportion, like the prodigious Sonne" (2.3.3–4). Malapropisms appeal to the audience not only for ridicule but also for happy identification with the malaprop, who portrays himself as the prodigal son out to make his way in the city (here, the Duke's court). Most beholders probably had read or heard stories and plays about country lads who came to London to be ruined, a popular moral cliché visible at least as early as the interlude *Youth* (1510), which the younger Shakespeare periodically echoes. Shakespeare here rings a change on this favorite theme. Plays like *Youth* and *Hick Scorner* concerned the power of Hatred, which has "made a vowe for ever to dwell in Englonde" (*Hick Scorner* 381). The city moralities embodied a conservative horror at the immoral tumult of urban life, the "Falshode, Favell, and Sotylte, / Ye, theves and hores . . . Lyers, bacbyters, and flaterers . . . Braulers, lyers, getters, and chyders, / Walkers by nyght, and grete murderers . . . Oppressers of people" (369–79).

In Launce, however, Shakespeare exorcises the freight of social conflict in the prodigal son motif. It's obvious that Launce won't be ruined: being a fool, he is impervious to ruin. In 3.1, Launce announces that he is in love with a "Milke-maid." Despite his urban setting, the prodigious son falls for a symbol of the pastoral. A sweet moment, happily sweet, and rapidly punctured as the picture of this rich, toothless harridan fills out. All these are appeals to the audience to feel nostalgia for old, familiar types. Such catharsis is potentially subversive because, nostalgia being a longing for return home, its expression and exploitation suggest that writer and audience feel *not* at home in some important way. People make commerce out of saying they are displaced. They create, admire, and presumably identify with comic throwbacks. Such behaviors undermine their allegiance to the present order, in which each man is to stay in one place, do one thing, and be content. Nostalgia on this scale, packaged, locatable, repeatable, commodified, is a communal wish that things were otherwise. Nostalgia thus illustrates the doubleness of humor: it can aid in complacency and containment while probing and questioning normally invisible ideologies. A character that audiences find sympathetic, sweet, comfortable—like Launce—can elicit attitudes and behaviors that challenge what the audience members think they think.

2. Silly Humor

"Blessed," "childish," "vulnerable," "innocent," "trivial"—in any sense, Launce is silly. Launce's devotion to Crab, his volunteering to be whipped and stocked in Crab's place, is very silly. When Proteus entrusts him with taking a dog as a present to Sylvia, he manages to have said dog "stolne from me by the Hangman boyes in the market place, and then I offer'd her mine owne, who is a dog as big as ten of yours, & therefore the guift the greater" (4.4.55–58), all of which is extremely silly, as well as embarrassing to the very serious Proteus.

Silliness feminizes,[6] as is clear from the entire history of Western laughter, from the Commissioner of *Lysistrata* and Gelasimus of *Stichus* on up through Keaton, Chaplin, the Marx Brothers, and Monty Python's Flying Circus. Where men are generally expected to be centered, controlled, unpassionate, and strong, Launce, along with many silly clowns before and since, is centrifugal, disorganized, weepy, clumsy, and weak. Launce fits within what amounts to the great western mockery of the male, in which thousands of male clowns—think of Tony Curtis and Jack Lemmon in *Some Like It Hot*—don dresses, speak in high voices, swivel hips, fret, complain, and are reduced to tears. Not to deny the deep-seated antifeminism in this tradition; only to acknowledge the reverse reciprocal, that silly humor solicits and interrogates what it is to be male.

Many Elizabethans tacitly supported the ideal of men as reserved, centered, and controlled. Such an ideal existed long before books such as Castiglione's *Courtier* codified it. Lewis, Count of Canosse, prescribes a "meane" for the courtier to follow, "betweene this excellent grace, and that fond foolishnes" (271).[7] Men should be "lowly, sober, and circumspect" (275) and not act "as those lustie lads doe, that open their mouth and thrust out wordes at a venture they care not how" (276). Emphasis on restraint and control reaches a climax as the Count approaches his definition of "grace." The respectable male

> governeth him selfe with that good judgement that will not suffer him to enter into any folly: but let him laugh, dally, jest, and daunce, yet in such wise that he may alwaies declare him selfe to be wittie and discreete, and every thing that he doth or speaketh, let him doe it with a grace (282)

Polonius may be a busy old fool, but his "precepts" to Laertes would not have been unfamiliar to the audience. Nor are they now:

> Give thy thoughts no tongue,
> Nor any unproportion'd thought his act,
> Be thou familiar, but by no meanes vulgar . . .

Give every man thine eare, but fewe thy voyce,
Take each mans censure, but reserve thy judgement (1.3.59–61,
68–69)

Launce proposes alternatives. Whereas the Count and Polonius advise men
to avoid situations that can render them emotionally exposed or vulnerable,
Launce volunteers his feelings and lays himself open to punishment. His first
line is "Nay, 'twill be this howre ere I have done weeping: all the kinde of
the Launces, have this very fault" (2.3.1–3). Protestations of weeping bracket
his opening monologue. Later, he announces that "He lives not now that
knowes me to be in love, yet I am in love" (3.1.265–67). All the kind of the
Launces—clowns, that is—do have the fault of being openly and violently
emotional, from the complaining Dromios of *Comedy of Errors*, often weeping, often bested, pleading doglike for affection, to the now-jubilant, now-
fearful Autolycus. Think of Harpo Marx, continually miming tears, laughter, and infatuation. Launce's protestations of excessive sorrow—"why man,
if the River were drie, I am able to fill it with my teares: if the winde were
downe, I could drive the boate with my sighes" (2.3.51–54)—would be
clichés except that the cause is a dog rather than a person. Men with a sur-
plus of labile, causeless emotion are comic.

As for vulnerability, Launce seeks it. His most heroic and silliest act
is to be whipped instead of the farting Crab, "to take upon me a fault that
he did" (4.1.14), which even he is aware is to be "one that takes upon him
to be a dog indeede" (4.1.11–12). I hope the reader finds this funny, because, wonderful to say, it still is. For love of Crab, Launce will do things
he knows are pointless, and he will share his feelings about them with anyone who will listen (no one on the stage, but everyone beholding the action). It has become a truism that the judgment in humor moves down-
ward on the social scale,[8] but, in fact, audience response to clowns is more
complex than that. As discussed below, clowns judge themselves before the
audience judges, thus rendering judgment redundant and freeing the audience to turn judgment in any social direction (toward peers, masters,
powerful men and women). "Judgment" is a front for the testing of con-
cepts central to the maintenance of culture. No audience would have
laughed at Launce only out of scorn. Robert Weimann has shown that
characters such as Launce call on the audience to laugh with as well as at
them. In *Two Gentlemen*, he argues, laughing with the audience "serves,
perhaps for the first time in Shakespeare's work, as an essential means of
organizing, controlling and evaluating experience through a larger comic
vision" (35).[9] If Launce's appeals for delighted sympathy are successful,

the audience will evaluate and reevaluate comic alternatives to the masculine codes of restraint.

That is, virtue lies in flying off the handle; sincere helplessness is superior to the facade of control. Such an alternative is crucial in a play exploring how men in love should act. Launce thus plays foil to at least two unfeeling males, the first being Crab: "now the dogge all this while sheds not a teare: nor speaks a word: but see how I lay the dust with my teares" (2.3.30–32). The second is Proteus, who, as Silvia tells him, "cannot love where he's belov'd" (5.4.44). Silvia and Valentine persuade Proteus to be true, not only to his most authentic feelings (his love for Julia), but also to the male standard of constancy: "It is the lesser blot modesty findes, / Women to change their shapes, then men their minds" (5.4.108–09). True, Launce adheres to a similar standard, since he is always true to Crab—but he flings it down and dances upon it where his master is concerned, and, in his constant laments about his authentic feelings, he explores (and invites the audience to explore, though laughter) some ways out of the emotional straitjacket prescribed for men.

Compare Launce with Pinky and Chiccolini (Harpo and Chico Marx) in *Duck Soup* during the scene with Edgar Kennedy as the tough-guy lemonade vendor.[10] They trade hats with him, mimic him, and work that marvelous trick in which he ends up holding their legs. With his manhood under intimate attack, the vendor is reduced to a hilarious, frustrated horror. He's rougher and tougher, but the Marxes are more mobile, more aware, more open—as if in relinquishing masculinity they gain in humaneness and freedom.

Launce is definitely humane. Feminine qualities imposed on a male template allow him a scope that a non-humorous male can't have, which forces us to recognize something not much discussed. Although ideals of male strength and restraint dominate western social institutions, these ideals have long coexisted with uneasiness about the consequences of such restraint: the coldness, humorlessness, and lack of sympathy called for in masculine standards.

3. ESPIÈGLERIE

Ambiguity can produce changed relations. A particular kind of ambiguous jesting, which I would like to call *espièglerie*, reached a peak in the sixteenth century. Espièglerie is polyvalent jesting in which ridicule is ambiguously distributed. An excellent example is jest 53 in *Tales and Quicke Answeres* (1535?), "Of hym that sayd he was nat worthy to open the gate to the kynge"[11]:

As a kynge of Englande hunted on a tyme in the countie of Kent, he hapt to come rydynge to a great gate: wherby stode a husbande man of the countrey, to whom the kynge sayde: Good felowe putte open the gate. The man perceyvynge it was the kynge, sayde: No and please your grace, I am nat worthy: but I will go fetche mayster Couper that dwelleth nat past ii. myles hense, and he shal open to you the gate. (sig. F.)

The compiler of *Tales and Quicke Answeres* usually appends some moral or summation to the jests, but none appears here. That's why it is one of the funniest printed jokes in the sixteenth century. This husbandman is either unbelievably stupid or unusually crafty. If the former, the joke is aimed at the husbandman and all stupid peasants. If the latter, the joke is aimed at the king and titled classes.

But in a practice seen throughout the century, *the joke is constructed so that we cannot tell*, revealing what Pierre Bourdieu has called "the *double reality* of intrinsically *equivocal, ambiguous* conduct."[12] Bourdieu coins this phrase to describe how empowered classes disguise exploitation; I point the term in the other direction, to describe how the less powerful classes disguise resistance. For resistance, without a doubt, is in this jest. Whether the peasant is stupid or crafty, the king is left sitting alone on his horse, and the gate is still closed. Either he waits for a long time, or he gets down and opens the gate himself. Either way, his order has not been followed; either way, he must get down from his horse.

One wonders how this clever joke would have struck a Londoner reading it in 1535, the year after Henry VIII became head of the Church of England. It is both similar to and different from other jestbook entries of the period. Barbara Bowen notes that in the Renaissance jest

We are in a firmly hierarchical, conservative universe, in which most kings are wise and magnanimous, most peasants are stupid, and most women shrewish, obstinate, and sexually insatiable. . . . But if we look at the question of who verbally outsmarts whom, we see that there are many exceptions to the stereotypes.[13]

If there are many exceptions, then the exceptions are not exceptions. Espièglerie was an intrinsic part of Renaissance humor.

To quote Louis Cazamian: "How greatly does doubt serve the ends of humor, when humor lies in the oscillation of thought between two alternatives and in the impossibility of turning the probable, that relative value, into that absolute, certainty!"[14] In jest 53, ridicule attaches both to the King of England and to the husbandman. In the same way, Falstaff's joke at Shrewsbury—"Rebellion lay in his way, and he found it" (5.1.28)—may be aimed either at Worcester (who claims he has not "sought" the rebellion) or the King (who asks rhetorically, "How comes it then?"); its ambiguity invites beholders to consider both men as abusers of language and power, proposing a position from which neither king nor rebel can claim legitimacy. This sort of jesting, which had long existed, simply explodes in the sixteenth century—as a direct result of social conflict. Religious and political change had turned the world inside-out the year before *Tales and Quicke Answeres* was published; food riots and sporadic unrest marked the London of 1597– 1598, when Falstaff was in process. Thus the heavy taste of resistance. Since the effect of espièglerie is to arouse radical humorous ambivalence, it makes sense that the most frequent occasion for ambivalence would be the class system; this effect marks espièglerie as a form of carnival.

Espièglerie is an appropriate name, deriving from *Eulenspiegel*, name of the ultimate in ambiguous jest-figures, who subjected both himself and his targets to ridicule. (Even the name is ambiguous, meaning "Owl-Mir-ror" in High German but "Wipe-Ass" in the lower German dialect of Braunschweig, his home district.)[15] Such humor, rightly understood, is truly ambivalent humor, a kind we have surely lost. As is well known, Eulenspiegel triumphs out of defeat; no one can determine with certainty whether the fool is a genius or an idiot. Minds are kept oscillating between the probable and the certain, to follow Cazamian's formula—which is healthy for the behold-ers as thinkers but which also reveals new possibilities and proposes new relations as that oscillation continues.

Now, it's hard to "best" someone who announces he's a fool—and that is why most stage fools announce their own foolishness loudly ("I am but a foole, looke you"), anticipating and thus blunting the opponent's main charge. Although Proteus calls Launce "yond foolish Lowt" (4.4.65), his epithet lacks power, partly because of Proteus's own situation, mostly be-cause Launce has already anticipated and confirmed his status as lout. It is also difficult to "best" someone with such tenuous control of words and deeds that certainty about intentions is impossible. From his first entrance, Launce makes nothing clearer than his lack of control over his emotions, his words, his dog, his staff, his shoes. This advertisement immediately moves Launce, with Eulenspiegel, beyond normative standards.

If fools were only foolish, they would not be dangerous. But fool fig-ures in the Eulenspiegel line combine idiocy with shrewd insight, as does Launce: "I am but a foole, looke you, and yet I have the wit to thinke my

Master is a kinde of a knave" (3.1.263–64). This truly startling statement forces beholders not to take Launce only humorously. In the same way, anglicized as Howleglas, Eulenspiegel convinces everyone in the town of Maybrough [Magdeburg] that he is about to fly off the top of the town hall. He flaps his arms, and the entire town rushes to see him. When they have gathered, he jeers at them ("a hole town ful" of fools)[16] for having believed him in the first place. The townspeople grant him his point: "And than departed the folke from thence som blaming him & som laughing saying he is a shrewed fole for he telleth us the truthe" (sig. B. iiii).

A second comic hallmark of Eulenspiegel is the technique of taking a turn of phrase, a command, or a word absolutely literally. Again, because his opponents can never tell whether he is shrewd or merely thick, the fool retains a certain authority over the near-mystical disaster that ensues as he takes words at face value. (Speed recognizes this penchant in Launce: "Well, your old vice still: mistake the word," 3.1.284). In one excellent tale, Howleglas comes to an inn where he is informed that the visitors "eate for mony."[17] Howleglas seats himself with the richest men at the table and stuffs himself until covered with sweat. When the hostess demands to be paid, *Howleglas* demands money from *her*, saying that she told him he could *"eate for mony"*: "Thynkest thou that I wyll eate so much and laboure my selfe so sore as I dyd, not to be payd for mi laboure?" In a single tale, Howleglas manages to upend both social structure and the entire relationship between labor and sustenance.

When it comes to words, Launce's lack of control is what gives him control. The ambiguity of his foolishness gives him a certain authority over the mayhem he causes. Where Speed exists within the action of the play, Launce exists to prevent action, and no one can be sure (although any may suspect) that he intends such obstructionism. Consider what he does to Speed. In 2.5, Speed welcomes Launce to town. So far, Speed has proven the quickest wit on stage, having bested Valentine in 2.1. But Launce explodes all of Speed's words into misunderstanding and bawdry. When Speed asks how it goes with "your Mastership," Launce takes it as his "master's ship." When Speed asks "how stands the matter" with Proteus and Julia, Launce replies "Marry thus, when it stands well with him, it stands well with her" (2.5.20–23). Is he stupid, crafty, hard of hearing? Launce could be, to adapt Susan Purdie's happy phrase, a master of discourse,[18] or he may be the abject slave of words. By the end of the scene Speed is crying out, "Why, thou Whorson Asse, thou mistak'st me" (2.5.47) before giving up and accompanying Launce to the alehouse. If humor is a form of exchange, with Launce it's hard to know what one is exchanging for what; since Launce both takes and gives language inappropriately, neither Speed nor the audience can gauge Launce's game, if there is a game, rightly. (Speed seems to have his suspicions—why else call Launce's verbal mistakings "your old vice"?) Launce's seeming lack of control with language gives directors and actors wonderful latitude in interpreting the part, allowing wide scope for some fruitful improvisation.

Whether intended or not, his victory over Speed is complete as of 3.1, the lengthy and ludicrous review of the "Cate-Log" of Launce's beloved milkmaid, after which Launce informs Speed that Valentine is waiting for him. As Speed runs off, Launce remarks, "Now will he be swing'd for reading my Letter" (5.1.382–83). Even here, the intention to communicate intention is ambiguous: Speed may be swinged, but it will be for keeping his master waiting, not for reading the catalogue.

As of the end of his part, Launce has gotten Speed into trouble, has delayed Valentine, and has humiliated Proteus. None of his victims can be sure he meant to victimize them. Still, as of 4.1, Launce's rounds are a little too complete. No one can dismiss the suspicion that Launce may have been looking for a way to play the cur all round.

Once again, resistance. As with jest 53 of *Tales and Quicke Answeres*, as with Falstaff's jest at Shrewsbury, ambiguity produces new positions, new possibilities—it gets the beholders to think thoughts they might not otherwise have thought. They may consider Speed, Proteus, and the absent Valentine as gullible. They may be led to sympathize with one who values his personal ties (Crab) above those to his supposed superiors (Proteus). Dog is king, servant is still servant, and master becomes—irrelevant.

4. IMPROVISATION

We have forgotten the sort of laughter that the minstrel's audience prized most: the explosive, delighted surprise as a "merryman" put together jests, quick answers, improvised plays, poems, and dances seemingly on the spot. This was the kind of laughter that Tarlton reportedly was a genius in eliciting—and Kempe of all Elizabethan clowns was most often mentioned by contemporaries as Tarlton's heir.[19] Granted, the craft of the improviser, one to which the audience readily assented, was to prepare for any and all humorous situations. Improvisers had the benefit of centuries of minstrel traditions—conventions of rhyming, jesting, dancing, and singing—into which they could fit almost any topic. If minstrels were any good at the craft, no situation should ever force them to improvise totally without preparation. So much was well understood by the audience as the jester's work; these rules were invoked consciously as part of the artificial structure of the performance. In *The Merchant of Venice*, Lorenzo praises Launcelot, who has just run rings around him in an impromptu wordgame:

> O deare discretion, how his words are suted,
> The foole hath planted in his memorie
> An Armie of good words, and I doe know
> A many fooles that stand in better place,
> Garnisht like him, that for a tricksie word
> Defie the matter. (3.5.65–70)

For improvisation to "work," professional improvisers had to invoke these performance-structures, then induce the audience to forget they knew them.

Launce is funny because improvisation is funny. Improvisation involves a show of the performer's talents, wit, and mastery of body and language. Beholders can weigh the speed of his associations, the justness of his quips, his power over his material. But the improviser holds the balance of power over his audience, in that they can't be certain what's coming next. (No more may he, but he does know that, whatever it is, he will be the source.) When Shakespeare incorporated improvisational space into Launce, it was this power over the audience, or at least the illusion of it, that he wanted.

Improvisation is potentially subversive because it suggests that social relations are provisional, subject at any time to revision. When actors improvise a dramatic situation, they immediately create, and have the power to rearrange, symbolic status relations. Inevitably, the improviser brings status to the surface, challenges the audience's perception of the underlying causes of human behavior. That means, as Keith Johnstone notes, that improvisation can change the way people see social reality: "Once you understand that every sound and posture implies a status, then you perceive the world quite differently, and the change is probably permanent."[20] Improvisation can awaken the audience's unease, make visible what they take for granted.

I once saw the musician Richard Thompson introduce himself to an audience this way: "Hello, I'm Richard Thompson, and you are the audience. This may change at any moment." Thompson's delightful words emphasize the unpredictable nature of the audience-performer relationship. With patterned yet seemingly anarchic abandon, the improviser can constantly shift the positions and relations of performer, beholders, and subject/butt. That paradoxical impression—control next to irrepressible, anarchic wit—is what makes improvisation funny, and what makes it potentially destabilizing.

Launce enters *Two Gentlemen of Verona* leading his dog Crab and weeping. The sheer length of his first monologue suggests that Launce is to be played by the "master merryman," the most experienced clown in the troupe. I invite the reader to read the following long section and try to *keep* from imagining improvisational space in it:

> Nay, 'twill bee this howre ere I have done weeping: all the kinde of the *Launces*, have this very faulte: I have receiv'd my proportion, like the prodigious Sonne, and am going with Sir *Protheus* to the Imperialls Court: I thinke *Crab* my dog, be the sowrest natured dogge that lives: My Mother weeping: my Father wayling: my Sister crying: our Maid howling: our Catte wringing her handes, and all our house in a great perplexitie, yet did not this cruell-hearted Curre shedde one teare: he is a stone, a very pibble stone, and has no more pity in him then a dogge: a Jew would have wept to have seene our parting: why my Grandam having no eyes, looke you, wept her selfe blinde at my parting: nay, Ile shew you the manner of it. This shooe is my father: no, no, this left shooe is my mother: nay, that cannot bee so neyther: yes, it is so, it is so: it hath the worser sole: this shooe with the hole in it, is my mother: and this my father: a veng'ance on't, there 'tis: Now sir, this staffe is my sister: for, looke you, she is as white as a lilly, and as small as a wand: this hat is *Nan* our maid: I am the dogge: no, the dogge is himselfe, and I am the dogge: oh, the dogge is me, and I am my selfe: I; so, so: now come I to my Father; Father, your blessing: now should not the shooe speake a word for weeping: now should I kisse my Father; well, hee weepes on: Now come I to my Mother: Oh that she could speake now, like a mov'd woman: well, I kisse her: why there 'tis; heere's my mothers breath up and downe: Now come I to my sister; marke the moane she makes: now the dogge all this while sheds not a teare: nor speakes a word: but see how I lay the dust with my teares.

Whether Shakespeare's or Ralph Crane's, the colons indicate improvisational space. So do the colons in Launce's monologue in 4.4:

> When a man servant shall play the Curre with him (looke you) it goes hard: one that I brought up of a puppy: one that I sav'd from drowning, when three or foure of his blinde brothers went to it: I have taught him (even as one would say precisely, thus I would teach a dog)

These colons, most of comparable length, establish a rhythm of statement and pause, statement and pause. A good comic actor (as Kempe) will use that rhythm and those pauses to improvise bits of humorous action. Recall that in 4.4, Launce has recently suffered a beating. Perhaps Kempe and company want Launce to be weepy throughout the production. In both 2.1 and 4.4, then, the actor could wring his hands or mop his eyes or do some comic business with staff, hat, and dog before continuing. If one bit gets a laugh (let's say that Launce mops his eyes with his hat at the first pause, with Crab at the second, realizes his error, and wipes his eyes with his hat), the actor can build on it for more laughs (putting the staff down to wipe his eyes with the dog, then wipe the dog's eyes with the hat, then wipe his eyes with the hat). Here are the first lines of 2.1 again; what good comic could resist filling those elastic spaces with what Richard Andrews calls "elastic gags"?[21]

> Nay, 'twill bee this howre ere I have done weeping: all the kinde of the *Launces*, have this very faulte: I have receiv'd my proportion, like the prodigious Sonne, and am going with Sir *Protheus* to the Imperialls Court: I thinke *Crab* my dog, be the sowrest natured dogge that lives: My Mother weeping: my Father wayling: my Sister crying: our Maid howling: our Catte wringing her handes, and all our house in a great perplexitie, yet did not this cruell-hearted Curre shedde one teare:

Note the timing of the last six colons: four very short, a fifth short colon with a ludicrous anticlimax, and a longer three-part colon with a ludicrous climax. Shakespeare's sense of timing, miraculously intuitive, affords excellent opportunities for improvisations of all sorts. Think of the opportunities for miming the maid, father, sister, and cat. There is a great deal of deictic language, giving the actor much to do in moving from one *this* to another. The actor is to use his hat, shoes, staff, and dog as props/actors impromptu. As of "Nay, Ile shew you the manner of it," Launce becomes a writer/director/producer orchestrating a dramatic rendition of his experience. Keir Elam has commented that Launce has to "decide which signified dramatis personae he must assign to his paltry set of sign-vehicles" and "inevitably discovers that the sign-vehicles are perfectly interchangeable."[22] Swapping signs, signifiers, and signifieds, Launce proposes challenges to normal ways of thinking, jogging the audience to imagine for themselves what any one symbol might be a symbol of—and then watching that linguistic and conceptual relation change. In its density, speed, and resourcefulness, Shakespeare's humor characteristically challenges the audience to *stay with* the funny characters on stage. Sociologists speak of "effectance motivation"—the pleasure we derive from having our abilities fully tested.[23] The very nature of Launce's humor motivates the audience to enjoy the exercise of its faculties. Within a system pretending unchanging authority, such training of individual faculties could tend to be subversive. Launce prefigures the mechanicals' perplexity over role and player in *A Midsummer Night's Dream*: "I am the dogge: no, the dogge is himselfe, and I am the dogge: oh, the dogge is me, and I am my selfe." Launce gets it so wrong that he gets it right: Launce is Launce playing the dog. (Launce, hilariously enough, never thinks of letting Crab be Crab.)

Some actions are clearly scripted. Launce kisses his left shoe, makes a face at its stink, and pronounces it like "my mothers breath up and downe." Many other actions, however, are left to the actor. Exactly what will he do with his staff to demonstrate his sister's "moane"? What business will take place with the hat to show it is "*Nan* our maid"? What will he do with Crab? Is Crab being carried or led on a leash? No matter what choices the actor makes, a great deal of foolish putting down and arranging of dog, hat, and staff will be necessary.

Will he keep the shoes on or take them off? Kissing of shoes, whether they be on or off, is usually comic. What will he do with the right shoe during and after the kiss? (A question to be asked. Launce says the shoe "weepes on" after being kissed. Perhaps the shoe is weeping so hard it cannot speak?) June Schlueter tells me of a performance in which the actor demonstrated a shoe with a hole in it and flipped his middle finger through the hole as he said "this is my father"—signifying the paternal penis to be fit in the hole of the other shoe, that is, Launce's mother. How slippery is the shifting qualifier *this*! If Crab was played by a real dog, and that dog acted as most dogs do on stage, a further element of the unpredictable would have been added. A live dog was not an absolute necessity; a good clown could make the audience howl just as loud with a stuffed dog, especially if he had to carry it (more fumbling with hat, staff, shoes, puppet!) or drag it along on a leash.[24] For our age, however, Crab has become a live dog's part. Consider Richard Moore's performance as Launce in the Royal Shakespeare Company's 1991–1992 production of *Two Gentlemen of Verona*. Crab was played by a real dog named Woolly. Real dogs are not written down: they are *a hors du texte*. Reviewer Paul Nelsen wrote,

> Since the real pooch used in this production is an endearing sight gag, appropriately named Woolly, that commands attention with impromptu behavior, Moore's ability to engage a crowd's hearts and minds is all the more remarkable. On the occasion of this performance, during Launce's 4.6 recounting of Crab's misbehavior at the

Duke's dinner, Woolly undertook dogged ablutions of private parts that could not be ignored by the audience. By virtue of well-timed takes and inventive connections with the text at hand, it was Moore who got the big laughs.[25]

If Moore could do it, so could Kempe. Both the writing and what it allows— the behavior of the famous Kempe, and perhaps a live dog—contribute to the world often conjured up in improvisation, one in which all relationships are provisional and subject to change at any time. Stable relationships are thrown up in the air; settled questions are thrown open; we are reminded of the power of point of view to modify our perception of reality.

Printed and dramatic fools alike call on originators and audience to collaborate in creating a forum for subversion. Such improvisation cannot but produce challenge and instability where the market of attitudes is concerned. In their book *Improvisation*, John Hodgson and Ernest Richards note that "improvisation is a means of exploring in which we create conditions where imaginative group and personal experience is possible. It is the spontaneous human response to an idea or ideas, or a set of conditions."[26] Shakespeare and Kempe set up conditions for individuals and group to imagine alternatives to the things they have been taught and think they believe.

Let me hazard some concrete referents for such instability. All over 1590s London there were such referents: a daily influx of inhabitants; haphazard, unchecked construction; filth and violence in the streets; the poor and vagrant, whose existence indicted the administrators of the Christian state; the frustrated energy of the gentry, the merchants, and other citizen classes, whose successes posed a threat to old representations of social hierarchy. Add a backdrop of religious and political groups struggling to take the moral stage. Shakespeare and his audience lived in a time of social upheaval and severe cultural dissonance. His very job—to patch together stories from different sources into a commercial product—called attention to this dissonance. He was a totalizer, a bourgeoise artisan whose practice yoked together characters, situations, and values from a plethora of different sources into a jangling congeries that resisted coherence.[27] He was literally creating emotions and ideas that had not existed before. For his efforts, he eventually got to put *"Gent."* after his name. Changing positions; new alternatives; social reorganization. I am the dog; no, the dog is me.

My point is that people were thinking hard about how life was changing, that humor was one such kind of thinking, and that such thinking begets more such thinking. Think of the generosity of Kempe's acting. He must be able to gauge the audience's desires and let them into his performance; he must modulate his own desires, his habits (what worked with Launce the last time) in tune with the conditions of the moment. He must let himself, to some extent, be guided by the concrete situation of performance. Such generosity means that his acting is a transaction with whatever audience and conditions he faced.

For Kempe, then, and for us if we are to imagine Kempe as Shakespeare's Launce, there is plenty *a hors du texte*. It does not do to claim that these conditions already implicitly exist as imagined in the text; no user of language can do that. A text for performance is a template, not a predestination. What actually happens actually happens, often quite without reference to the text, as Woolly's doggy ablutions prove. As Mikhail Bakhtin suggested, it's often what lies *a hors du texte* that counts.[28] Improvisation is a form of language that throws itself open to what is outside in order to discover possibilities latent in the act of throwing-open. Hodgson and Richards are therefore critical of "mere exhibitionism," which they decry as a "self-centered form of acting [that] in its assertion of self denies discovery, which can only follow from a more generous approach" (13). For Kempe and company, discovery is all. A subversive generosity, then, lies in the invitation to the audience to create the moment.

Michel Jeanneret writes of the tendency of Renaissance art to "put down roots in a tangible reality" in order to avoid turning in on itself and becoming a closed system. Aware of art's tendency to autonomy of function, writers sought "a dialogue and a material exchange of goods with the audience, the fusion of speech and action, the involvement of the book in the heart of experience."[29] Once again Launce appears as a token of exchange (you give us your money; we'll give you imaginative play in return), drenched in materiality (feet; dogs; tears; farts; toothless, alcoholic milkmaids), in the assertion of system (Launce as underclass idiot) and the subversion of system (Launce as smarter than his smarter masters). The Renaissance audience is laughing at and experimenting with history together. They laugh at the ways in which supposedly perpetual social order can be confused by ambiguous foolishness. They laugh at the slipperiness of words and associations, the delight when Launce, in his awkward scramble to describe the scene at home, reports of "our Maid howling: our Catte wringing her handes." People and things switch places: staffs become sisters, shoes become parents (as do flipped fingers!), foot odor becomes breath odor. *Miscere sermones*! Here is the survival of the very things the moralists appeared to hate: mixture of registers, confusion of the defined, inversion of the established, the primacy of the imagination asserted symbolically through wordplay and improvisation.

Subversive indeed is the act of "creating conditions" for such exploration, creating a place "where imaginative group and personal experience is possible." As mentioned, the theatre was created to welcome the assertion of individual imagination *en masse*. In the theatre, the imagination is made flesh, the audience, Shakespeare, and Kempe together explore their experience and ways to subvert and recast it. Money is exchanged to ensure all this continues.

Perhaps—though we cannot know—writer and audience were aware of their subversion. Public secular theatre was still a novelty. Its legal restriction to beyond the Thames was a fact not easy to forget—after all, just to get to the play you had to take a ferry or get across a bridge. (It's possible that *Two Gentlemen* was performed at the theatre in Newington Butts, a good mile south of London Bridge.) Finally, from what contemporary accounts tell us, the dramatic situation seems not to have allowed as much suspension of disbelief as does the hushed, well-behaved culture of twentieth century theatregoing. Conventions of behavior such as silence and attention were not always (if ever) at work. Andrew Gurr writes that "crowds at the amphitheatres were markedly noisier than those in the hall playhouses."[30] People shouted approval as well as clapped. They threw things in disapproval, shouted out running criticisms, sat on the stage, and sometimes disrupted performances with demands that some other favorite play be put on instead. This behavior had two effects: it strengthened the crowd's solidarity, and it prevented an easy suspension of disbelief. Gurr writes:

> Crowds strengthen their sense of identity, their collective spirit, by vocal expression of their shared feelings. The audience was an active participant in the collective experience of playgoing, and was not in the habit of keeping its reactions private. (45)

Although the Elizabethan theatre was moving towards a more illusionistic relation between beholders and actors, audiences were, by our standards, comparatively alienated from the dramatic illusion, rendered more frequently conscious of both the play as play and of itself as audience.

While he did not shout *prodeo larvatus* before entering, Kempe-as-Launce was probably aware of himself as a miscreant in the eyes of many, and of his audience as a mass accomplice. In the war between players and puritans in the mid-1590s, Kempe danced jigs aimed at the enemies of plays. (He may have done so as a member of the Lord Chamberlain's Men, and with a certain young playwright's tacit or explicit approval.) How could Kempe not be aware?

How could members of the audience? They purchased tickets for places that announced their social class to the group. They looked around to see who had come. They laughed, and looked around while laughing, to measure and compare personal and communal reactions. As they did, they were taking what Jerry Palmer calls "different subject positions" (182), creating different viewpoints from which to judge the action. They criticized the performance as it went forward. All of these people had walked, boated, and ridden here to do just this. Hard not to be aware.

6. WHAT LAUNCE MAY HAVE DONE FOR THE BEHOLDERS

Humor plays a large range of social functions. But are those functions effective? Does humor change things? To know for certain, we would need to have the original audiences, be able to poll them (in a very sophisticated manner), and then make some sense of the results.[31] But not even that would help us. Most people don't know the origins of their attitudes; they won't know whether hearing a certain joke or seeing a certain stage character contributed to the formation of this new idea or that attitude. None of us knows all of our origins; if we did, we would not be ourselves. Even if Shakespeare's first audiences were available to us somehow, in the full extent of their memory and self-knowledge, we would be left at the end of the day with only an educated guess.

And that isn't bad. My guess is that humor was an important part of the moral and cultural environment around Shakespeare's audience. People used humor as a common currency with which to exchange and test ideas. Some humor supported the dominant discourse and some did not. Since humor has many disparate origins, it could not but introduce into that moral atmosphere many values that could potentially challenge received ideas. Individual beholders of Launce could receive these new ideas and apply them to their lives in many ways. My reverence toward authority might be qualified, or my irreverence strengthened, as a result of watching Launce thwart Proteus. I might feel more comfortable letting myself be silly or exposed or vulnerable in certain situations. I might experiment with my own thoughts, cultivate my inner reality, in ways that are humanly infinite. As you can see, these speculations lead to personalism and individualism. In a dynamic social setting like 1590s England, people may have been more likely to transpose ideas and values found in the theatre to the nontheatrical, "serious" realm. Launce did not bring on the revolution; on the other hand, it was only two generations off when he came on.

A huge number of scholars, both in the human sciences and in the literary disciplines, have chosen to emphasize the socially conservative, containing forces of humor.[32] These forces are indeed strong, but they are not the only ones humor exerts. I take it that the aggregate of humorous practice in any society cannot but propose alternatives to the dominant discourse, challenging, recontextualizing, and interpellating established practices. Humor exerts pressure away from dogma and towards pluralism.

Launce succeeds through silly lack of control—over emotions, over physical things, and over language. Thus he interrogates central tenets of masculinity. Further, his part is written to confuse mastery of discourse and submission to it. Nostalgia in Launce subverts the supposed allegiance to the time, place, and system in which one lives. Improvisational space built into the part allows Launce to switch positions of jester, butt, and audience; lover and beloved; dog and man; master and servant; fool and savant. In so doing, Launce and thousands of like characters invite the audience to think in free and anarchically combinatorial ways. As sheer mental and spiritual exercise, such thinking is healthy—and, since it appears that all combinations are equally available, works against the supposed unity of culture and ideology. Ambiguity is not only a cover for dangerous ideas (for not all or even most of these new ideas will be dangerous)—it is also the medium required for the greatest possible richness in this genetic recombination.

Nor was the theatre marked somehow as a "safe" place for such thinking. If anything, theatres were marked as dangerous in 1590s London. It is ludicrous to imagine that such thinking could be contained at the theatre site or within generic or conventional boundaries—as though the margins of the play and the walls of the theatre could hold thought. People entered and left thinking in these ways, and some of the thought that left with them was new.

Shakespeare created Launce in a tradition of silly, nostalgic, extemporaneous, ambiguous comic characters, a tradition transformed in the sixteenth century, freighted with overtones of class conflict, resistance and protest. Thus the challenges Launce floats to the picture of a stable, centered social reality were both traditional and current, both part of what clowns everywhere have always done and what clowns did at that moment—near the end of a divisive, troubled century that contained vast political, religious, and social upheavals that were far from over.

Human beings have evolved humor as a survival strategy, as a way to keep human relations changing and growing. Social reorganization never ends, and humor can always be part of the process. According to our model, then, Launce may well have helped change things, some small, some great. Some of his beholders changed their minds without knowing, and perhaps a few marked the change. If I were a writer and could be sure of so much, I would be more than glad: I would be awed.

1. Stanley Wells and Gary Taylor, editors of the contentious Oxford Shakespeare (*William Shakespeare: The Complete Works, Original Spelling Edition* [Oxford: Clarendon, 1986]) write that *Two Gentlemen* "may be [Shakespeare's] first work for the stage," noting that Launce's monologues are "brilliant" and Crab "has the most scene-stealing nonspeaking role in the canon" (1). I have used the spelling and orthography of this edition throughout, especially because of the punctuation and its potential for indicating improvisational space. Because the scene and line numbering in the Wells and Taylor edition has not been universally adopted, I give the more conventional line enumeration found in *The Riverside Shakespeare,* ed. G. Blakemore Evans (Boston: Houghton Mifflin, 1974).

2. A classic statement appears in *The Riverside Shakespeare,* 145.

3. Enid Welsford, *The Fool: His Social and Literary History* (Gloucester, MA: Peter Smith, 1966), 251.

4. Sophisticated distaste for humor that was perceived as graphic and low (what we might call the Castiglione-Sidney line of attack) rises to a peak near the turn of the century and is sustained until the closing of the theaters. Hamlet's speeches against low, extemporizing fools are the best known examples. Other attacks appear in Joseph Hall's *Virgidemarium* (1597), the *Parnassus* plays (1599–1600), Ben Jonson's *The Case Is Altered* (printed 1609; written before 1599), Thomas Dekker's *A Strange Horse Race* (1613), several prologues by Marston, and Thomas Heywood's *Gynaikeion, or Nine bookes of Various History Concerning Women* (1624). By Brome's time, the "days of Tarlton and Kemp" could be depicted as an era "Before the stage was purg'd from barbarism."

5. Terry Eagleton, in *Shakespeare* (Oxford: Blackwell, 1986), finds a similar nostalgia to be a major structural element in Shakespeare's later plays. In his view, the later Shakespeare is trying to reconcile the excesses of nascent capitalism with the strong points of an idealized feudal past: "If this is what Shakespeare had in mind, then the bad news we have to break to him, in privileged historical retrospect, is that it is an illusion" (99).

6. It is important to write "feminizes" rather than "emasculates," since silliness, far from subtracting important male qualities, often adds useful feminine qualities to the character of the presumptive male.

7. Baldassare Castiglione, *The Courtier,* tr. Sir Thomas Hoby (New York: Scribner, 1953), 241–618.

8. In the past thirty years, the sociology of humor has simply exploded. Everyone recognizes the important place (and functions) of ridicule in humor. By the same token, few believe, as Thomas Hobbes appears to have done, that all or most laughter is exclusively bent toward purposely hurtful derision. Henri Bergson gave one of the strongest, and latest, endorsements of this view, when in *Le Rire* he defined humor as an unconscious form of ridicule designed to humiliate and correct others (*Laughter,* tr. C. Brereton [New York: Macmillan, 1928], 135). Since then, understanding of the roles played by situation, group perception, occasion, and framing have refined notions of ridicule and where it is "aimed." Essays by A.R. Radcliffe-Brown ("On Joking Relationships," *Africa* 13 [1940]: 195–210) and by Mary Douglas ("The Social Control of Cognition: Some Factors in Joke Perception," *Man* 3 [1968]: 361–76) study how ridicule disperses energies according to the relationships among the jokers and the structure conditioning those relationships. Thoughtful discussions appear in C.P. Wilson, *Jokes: Form, Content, Use, and Function* (London: Academic Press, 1979); in J.H. Goldstein and Paul McGhee, *The Psychology of Humor* (New York: Academic Press, 1972); and in Susan Purdie, *Comedy: The Mastery of Discourse* (Toronto: University of Toronto Press, 1994), 60–70.

9. Robert Weimann, "Laughing with the Audience: *The Two Gentlemen of Verona* and the Popular Tradition of Comedy." *Shakespeare Survey* 22 (1969): 35–42.

10. Bert Kalmar and Harry Ruby, writers, *Duck Soup*, Paramount, 1933, in *The Four Marx Brothers in Monkey Business and Duck Soup* (Letchworth, Hartfordshire: Lorrimer, 1981), 94–183.

11. *Tales and Quicke Answeres, very mery, and pleasant to rede* (London: T. Berthelet, 1535?).

12. Pierre Bourdieu, *Towards a Theory of Practice*, tr. Richard Nice (Cambridge: Cambridge University Press, 1977), 179.

13. Barbara C. Bowen, *One Hundred Renaissance Jokes* (Birmingham: Summa, 1988), xvii–xviii.

14. Louis Cazamian, *The Development of English Humor* (Durham, NC: Duke University Press, 1952), 198–99.

15. See A. J. Krailshammer's chapter on Eulenspiegel in W. A. Coupe, *The Continental Renaissance* (Harmondsworth: Penguin, 1971).

16. "Howe that Howleglas would flee from the towne house of Maybrough," in *Here beginneth a merye Jest of a man that was called Howleglas, and of many marvelous thinges and Jestes that he dyd in his life, in Eastlande and many other places* (London: T. Copland, 1528?), sig. B.iiii.

17. "How Howleglas came to the towne of Banberch and how he did eate for mony," in *Howleglas*, sig. E. ii.

18. Susan Purdie, *Comedy: The Mastery of Discourse* (Toronto: University of Toronto Press, 1993). Like all such studies (including mine), Purdie's cannot cover all the aspects of humor. Her sense that joke-telling is a form of exchange between jester and hearer, in which jesting utterances are so marked, is true for many but not all kinds of things we may find "funny." I do, however, admire her notion that we tell jokes partly to have our mastery of discourse recognized. Of course, the jokes Launce tells, if he is joking, *question* his mastery rather than aserting it.

19. For example, writing in 1612, Thomas Heywood claimed that Kempe succeeded Tarlton "as wel in the favour of her Majesty, as in the opinion & good thoughts of the generall audience" (*Apology for Actors* [London, 1612], sig. E 3). Robert Armin is named, famously, as Tarlton's heir in *Tarltons Jests*—but there are good reasons to believe that Armin himself may have written or compiled the work. See John P. Feather, "A Check-List of the Works of Robert Armin," *Library*, 5th series, 26 (June 1971): 165–72.

20. Keith Johnstone, *Impro: Improvisation and the Theatre* (New York: Theatre Arts, 1985), 72.

21. Andrews coins that lovely term in his essay "Scripted Theatre and the *Commedia dell'Arte*," in J. R. Mulryne and Margaret Shewring, eds., *Theatre of the English and Italian Renaissance* (New York: St. Martin, 1991). In this light, consider the old question of whether or not Shakespeare "gagged" his clowns. I don't see how a young playwright like Shakespeare could have presumed to "gag" an older, famous actor like Kempe. With Kempe, improvisation is what Shakespeare would have wanted. He knew that Kempe could exploit that space to get what everyone in the troupe wanted: a happy response from the audience. Shakespeare would have been crazy to object.

22. Keir Elam, *The Semiotics of Theatre and Drama* (London: Methuen, 1980), 14.

23. See Zigler, E., J. Levine, and L. Gould, "Cognitive Challenge as a Factor in Children's Humor Appreciation." *Journal of Personality and Social Psychology* 6: 332–36.

24. Kathleen Campbell, in "Shakespeare's Actors as Collaborators: Will Kempe and *The Two Gentlemen of Verona*," writes that Crab could possibly have been a stuffed doll. Philip Henslowe's diary for 1598 includes an inventory of properties for the Rose Theatre that includes "i. black dogge." Campbell immediately writes, "but the comic effects of Crab's presence in *Two Gentlemen* seem to depend on the dog's being a living presence" [present volume, p. 187].

25. Paul Nelsen, review of *Two Gentlemen of Verona*, Royal Shakespeare Company, *Shakespeare Bulletin* 9.4 (1992): 15–17; this quotation on 17.

26. John Hodgson and Ernest Richards, *Improvisation* (New York: Grove, 1979), 18.

27. Nor were the writer's materials the only aspect of theatre that embodied and created these new possibilities. Walter Cohen, in his excellent study *Drama of a Nation: Public Theater in Renaissance England and Spain* (Ithaca: Cornell University Press, 1985), 182–85, argues that the process of theatrical production itself did too. In a brilliant passage, Cohen reminds us that the public theatre was a composite mode of production, both part of the base and part of the superstructure: "The total theatrical experience meant more than, and something different from, what the dramatic text itself meant. The medium and the message were in contradiction, a contradiction that resulted above all from the popular contribution" (183). To the dramatic text, already a bricolage of jarring meanings, we must add the actual process of producing a staged drama based on that text, a process that subverts what it puts forward, changes subjects of kings into critics of kings, critics of fools into critics of reason. Humor contributes even more complexity, even more potential for new thinking and changed relations.

28. Neither the Bakhtinian nor the Saussurian/Derridean approach covers language totally; each has tempered the other. For an interesting account of Bakhtin's qualifications on Saussurian linguistics, see Katerina Clark and Michael Holquist, *Mikhail Bakhtin* (Cambridge: Harvard University Press), 1984, 221–26.

29. Michel Jeanneret, *A Feast of Words: Banquets and Table Talk in the Renaissance* (Chicago: University of Chicago Press, 1987), 260.

30. Andrew Gurr, *Playgoing in Shakespeare's London* (Cambridge: Cambridge University Press, 1987), 44.

31. See Jerry Palmer, *The Logic of the Absurd* (London: British Film Institute, 1987), 183. Palmer's excellent study is mostly linguistic and semiologic, but he admits that we must leave these methods when we come to the question of the societal functions of humor. He suggests some empirical instrument such as a scientifically controlled poll—but not even this would answer the question, for the reasons mentioned.

32. Perhaps the most influential has been Freud, with his regrettably partial focus on the aggressive and tendentious aspects of humor. Arthur Koestler memorably restated and refocused Freud's point of view for the second half of the century in *The Act of Creation* (London: Hutchinson, 1964), as did Jan Kott in *Shakespeare Our Contemporary* (London: Methuen, 1964). A recent salvo on behalf of this view appears in Peter Gay, *The Cultivation of Hatred* (New York: Norton, 1994). There, in the midst of an extremely selective "survey" of humor theory (Bergson, Kierkegaard, and Kraepelin, all of whom are similarly fixed on aggressiveness), Gay asserts that "the aggressive dimensions" of humor "must claim preeminence." While I don't question the aggression in humor, I must reject this claim to "preeminence." Humor does so much else that a single-minded focus on aggression does little justice.

Nearly as old is the notion that humor functions mainly as containment, as a cultural control mechanism to limit, circumscribe, recontextualize, or censor out-of-bounds behavior. Bergson, in *Le Rire,* wrote that "the clown functions for propriety as the villain functions for mores," and some of his viewpoint survives in more recent containment theorists, among whom we may include Michel Foucault, Stephen Greenblatt, and others who feel that, to quote Keith Johnstone, "Laughter is a whip that keeps us in line" (84). Over time, champions of containment have tended to soften their definitions and depictions of what containment and resistance are and whether there are "ways out." For most of his career, Foucault was quite pessimistic about notions of personal freedom. Only near the end of his career did he explicitly recognize the possibilities of "the undefined work of freedom." (See Alexander Nehamas, "Subject and Abject: The Examined Life of Michel Foucault," *New Republic* [15 Feb.

1993]: 27–36.) Greenblatt's work has been a true process, with the titular focus in *Shakespearean Negotiations* suggesting that containment and resistance are best understood as parts of the larger process of negotiation.

Few would argue that humor and laughter are not bound up in the myriad negotiations over different forms of power that occur momently in human societies. Most containment theory, however, tends to claim *only* this or *mostly* this function for humor, ignoring the vast arena of purely formal play and the role of humor in social change. For me, the best thinkers on this subject are not literary scholars but sociologists. In his essay "A Phenomenological Analysis of Humor in Society" (in *Humour in Society: Resistance and Control*, ed. C. Powell and George E.C. Paton [London: Macmillan, 1988]: 86–105), Chris Powell writes that "life consists of organising experience in such a way that our sense of it makes us feel comfortable in balancing" control and resistance (99). For Powell, jokes expressing resistance also conjure up control—but neither one is lost. In his book *On Humour: Its Nature and Place in Modern Society* (London: Polity, 1988), Michael Mulkay writes that "humour can be both pure and applied" and "can have positive as well as negative consequences for the structure in which it occurs" (156). Most people don't use jokes as tiny revolutions, but the potential is there: "Humour can be used to challenge the existing pattern . . . but only when it is given meaning in relation to criticism and confrontation that is already under way within the serious realm" (177). Such confrontations were all around Kempe-as-Launce, confrontations bodied forth by the playhouse itself, its location, what was sold there, and how the audience behaved. Social tensions formed an extremely strong frame for almost any joke on Shakespeare's stage; the potential for social work in his humour was therefore very great.

"To be slow in words is a woman's only virtue": Silence and Satire in *The Two Gentlemen of Verona* (1994)

Michael D. Friedman

The written texts of three Shakespearean comedies feature a significant silence by the comic heroine as she enters the married state at the end of the play. Beatrice, in the final scene of *Much Ado About Nothing*, has her mouth stopped by Benedick's kiss and never says another word. Isabella, at the conclusion of *Measure for Measure*, does not reply to the Duke's marriage proposal, nor does she ever speak again afterwards. And Silvia of *The Two Gentlemen of Verona*, in perhaps the most puzzling sequence of all, is passed back and forth between her would-be rapist (Proteus), her father (the Duke), and her lover (Valentine), all without uttering a sound. Modern feminist critics have taken these silences to connote a hierarchical subordination of these women to patriarchal authority, which has led them to question the value of reproducing such events through dramatic performance. As Kathleen McLuskie notes,

> [G]iven that feminism is a movement committed to a *change* in relations of power between men and women and to an analysis of the fundamentally oppressive character of patriarchy, it might seem that the movement has little to hope for from a drama in which marriage is a happy ending and the subordination if not the oppression of most women is a necessary element for the continuation of peace and love and quiet life. . . . Feminism, it seems, could only deplore the continued representation of women in such forms and such contexts. *(Renaissance 5)*

However, as McLuskie realizes, the indeterminate nature of dramatic texts allows theatrical personnel to shape a play's reception by spectators through unorthodox performance choices. Elsewhere, she writes that

Reprinted from *Selected Papers from The West Virginia Shakespeare and Renaissance Association* 17 (1994): 1–9.

sexist meanings are not fixed but depend upon constant reproduction by their audience. . . . [T]he text is tied to misogynist meaning only if it is reconstructed with its emotional power and its moral imperatives intact. Yet the text contains possibilities for subverting these meanings and the potential for reconstructing them in feminist terms. ("Patriarchal" 95)

Assuming McLuskie is correct, one task of feminist performance criticism might be to explore the specific means by which the subversion and reconstruction of the text's sexist meanings can be accomplished.

There are two primary strategies through which feminist productions might seek to deal with the silencing and subordination of Shakespeare's comic heroines. In 1990, I formulated these two techniques as follows:

On the one hand, [directors] may cut critical passages and use elements of stagecraft to contradict whatever evidence of the heroine's subjugation occurs in the dialogue. This strategy effectively avoids the theatrical reproduction of the sexist values underlying her enforced submission, but it also sacrifices an awareness of the social forces which prescribe her ultimate surrender. The other option, which is to foreground and problematize the notion of wifely subservience, both reveals the ideological conditions which constrain the behavior of female characters and draws upon the dramatic tension these limitations create. (Friedman 363)

In other words, productions may either remove or otherwise defuse potentially offensive material, or, conversely, they may bring the objectionable aspects of the play's treatment of women to the forefront, hoping to make a political statement by negative example. When I first approached this issue, I favored the second alternative, highlighting the text's inherent sexism, but I was aware even then that this option contained a major weakness. Foregrounding the oppressive nature of patriarchy, particularly at the end of a comedy, tends to complicate or even explode any sense of comic closure as embodied by the traditional happy ending of marriage. If Shakespearean comedies end with the celebration of a social institution that subdues women, and feminist productions of these plays push audiences to react with anger and indignation at this injustice, how can such performances retain a sense of the "comic"? Are feminist productions of Shakespeare and comedy ultimately irreconcilable?

I now believe that the answer to this question is "no," but I do think that a reconciliation requires a different sense of the comic than is usually ascribed to Shakespeare's early plays. Although scholars generally link Shakespeare with romantic comedy rather than satire, there are clearly elements of both genres in his works, and feminist directors might find success uniting social commentary and humor in the performance of Shakespeare's comedies by emphasizing their satirical aspects rather than simply subverting their emotional appeal as romantic comedies.[1] *The Two Gentlemen of Verona* contains a wealth of these satirical components specifically directed at the concept of silence of women, which the director can use in performance to ridicule the excesses of conventional male behavior that quell female voices, particularly Silvia's. A look at the performance history of *Two Gentlemen* will show how past productions have handled the issue of Silvia's lack of verbal response to her treatment at the end of the play, and a description of an alternative staging of this sequence will demonstrate how a satirical approach to this problem might accommodate a feminist perspective yet still retain a comic flavor.

Although we may think of the negative reaction to the silencing and/or subordination of Shakespeare's comic heroines as a product of modern feminist scholarship, there have been vociferous complaints, since the beginning of the production history of *Two Gentlemen*, about the way in which Silvia is treated in the final scene. The primary objections of eighteenth- and nineteenth-century critics and producers are captured in the words of Edward Dowden:

> The *dénouement* in Act V., if written by Shakespere in the form we now have it, is a very crude piece of work. Proteus' sudden repentance, Valentine's sudden abandonment to him of Silvia . . . and Silvia's silence and passiveness whilst disposed of from lover to lover, are, even for the fifth act of a comedy, strangely unreal and ill-contrived. Can it be that this fifth act has reached us in an imperfect form, and that some of the speeches between Silvia and Valentine have dropped out? (68–9)

In response to such objections, the earliest recorded performance of the play, Benjamin Victor's 1762 adaptation, altered the text by omitting Valentine's offer of his beloved to his friend and supplying Silvia with a series of passages spoken to Valentine and other characters on stage. It might be argued that, by granting Silvia a voice in this final segment, Victor staged a proto-feminist version of the play, in which the silencing of the comic heroine was not a necessary condition for the happy ending of marriage. However, by cutting Valentine's offer of Silvia to Proteus, Victor effectively side-stepped the crucial feminist issue. Silvia's silence is significant primarily in that it occurs in response to her treatment as an object Valentine might bestow upon his friend. Silvia may possess a voice in this adaptation, but in the absence of Valentine's offer, she loses her most compelling reason to use it.

So why did Victor and other later producers interpolate lines for Silvia? As Kurt Schlueter's stage history in the New Cambridge edition suggests, such alterations can be seen as part of an overall attempt to recuperate Valentine, whose questionable behavior toward Silvia in Shakespeare's version has often been condemned (18). In the Folio text, Valentine appears on the scene to interrupt Proteus's rape attempt and reprove him for violating their friendship. When Proteus repents, Valentine forgives him and rewards him with the woman whom he has attempted to violate, all without speaking a single word to Silvia. Victor, in his version of the ending, inserts an exchange between Valentine and Silvia immediately after Proteus's attempted rape has been prevented:

> *Valentine.* My dearest Silvia, [runs and catches her in his arms]
> Kind heav'n has heard my fervent prayer!
> And brought my faithful Silvia to my arms!
> There is no rhetorick can express my joy!
> *Silvia.* It is delusion all! alas! we dream!
> And must awake to wretchedness again!
> O Valentine! We are beset with dangers!
> *Valentine:* Dismiss those fears, my love;—here, I command!
> No power on earth shall ever part us more. (51)

Victor, apparently dissatisfied with the way in which Shakespeare's Valentine ignores the woman he loves in her moment of greatest distress, interpolates this passage in order to demonstrate that his hero cares primarily for Silvia's emotional well-being and only secondarily for Proteus's betrayal of their friendship. Silvia does speak at a point at which she remains silent in the original script, but her lines merely express an uncharacteristic fearfulness and provide Valentine with an opportunity to play the part of her protector; they do not endow her with the power to comment on her treatment. Overall, Victor reshapes the conclusion of the play to prove Valentine a perfect gentlemen, but he does not allow Silvia to articulate the idea that some fundamental change in the way in which such "gentlemen" treat women might be desirable.

As Victor's adaptation demonstrates, it is a simple matter to eliminate the reproduction of certain sexist values in the performance of *Two Gentlemen* if one is willing to carve out critical portions of Shakespeare's text and replace them with one's own inventions. The challenge becomes greater when a director opts to work with the original script and its built-in limitations. The text does not grant Silvia any lines to speak, but nothing prevents her from reacting in a physical or other non-verbal manner to the events happening around her. James P. Lusardi writes of the actor portraying Silvia in the 1984 Stratford, Ontario production that "her severest test comes in the denouement when, deprived of lines, she must mime a series of responses from astonishment at being given away by the highminded Valentine to delight at being dramatically reclaimed" (13). It is certainly possible for Silvia to convey her feelings about her treatment to an audience without saying a word, but the fact that she voluntarily remains silent in itself signifies her acknowledgment that it is not appropriate for her to speak out while her lover and her father dispose of her as they see fit. Other productions have avoided this inference by suggesting that her silence is caused by involuntary physical reasons. For example, in Michael Langham's 1957 revival at the Old Vic, Silvia fainted upon hearing Valentine's offer, which rendered any spoken reaction impossible. This method of justifying Silvia's failure to speak seems plausible given the traumatic events, but the objection to it from a feminist viewpoint is that it robs Silvia's silence of any significance; her passivity becomes merely circumstantial instead of an attitude imposed upon her by social norms. Like Victor's adaptation, such a production simply makes the issue of Silvia's silence go away—it does not use the textual feature to contribute to the import of the play.

Clearly, the final scene of *Two Gentlemen* can be performed in such a way that it both eliminates some of the aspects feminists find objectionable yet still retains the generic qualities of romantic comedy. However, when a production attempts to exploit Silvia's silence to make a feminist statement at the end of the play, its tone tends to become something other than comic. To illustrate, here is director Delores Ringer's description of the conclusion to her all-female production at the University of Kansas in 1989:

> Sylvia had escaped to the forest in a shiny gold cape; when Proteus raped her he ripped the cape off and it was the cape Valentine rescued from Proteus. The rape and its easy dismissal were completely dehumanizing to Sylvia—what has happened to her was of no concern to anyone else. . . . [T]he actress stood silent, shocked, in the center of the activity—no one acknowledged her, and she did not ac-

knowledge them. Valentine gave the cape, the gold loving cup, to Proteus. Thurio entered and grabbed the cape away from Proteus, then the Duke grabbed it from him. The Duke teased Valentine a bit with it, then gave the cape to him, the true victor. Everyone was happy and they all marched off to the weddings. But the actress who had played Sylvia was left, standing alone on the stage. As the lights dimmed she took the most ostentatious items of her costume off and threw them at the others. (3–4)

The major strength of this enactment, as I see it, lies in Ringer's use of the gold cape to symbolize Silvia's status as a prize, to make evident that her humanity, her ability to speak her own mind, simply isn't important to the males maneuvering to possess her. Silvia's lack of verbal interaction with the others represents the extent to which she has been turned into an object, owned and traded without her consent by the men who claim to love her. Such a staging undoubtedly strikes its viewers with an intense emotional impact.

At the same time, the tone of this enactment is dark and troubling; as Ringer herself points out, "For us, the fun was over, this was deadly serious now" (3). Instead of a threatened rape or an aborted rape attempt, Ringer chooses to allow an *actual* rape to occur on stage, despite the fact that Valentine is observing Proteus and Silvia from his hiding place all along. Aside from the deeply disturbing effect of viewing the rape itself and Valentine's failure to intervene, such a staging could prompt viewers to attribute Silvia's "shocked" silence solely to the trauma she has endured rather than to the constraints placed upon her by her society. Moreover, Ringer's conclusion leaves somewhat ambiguous the question of whether or not Silvia finally agrees to marry Valentine. Since she remains isolated from the others as they exit to be wed, then rebelliously throws items of clothing after them, the implication seems to be that Silvia will not participate in the ceremony. Ringer refers to this textually unsupportable interpretation as "a positive feminist statement which we admittedly tacked on at the end" (4), yet it seems unlikely that the "positive" aspect of this staging made the deepest impression upon spectators. Ringer's production unquestionably provokes a consideration of feminist issues, but in order to do so, it radically transforms the play's comic tone and eradicates marriage as a means to comic closure.

Perhaps, as an alternative to distressing audiences with the "deadly serious" negative consequences of patriarchal rule, feminist productions of Shakespeare's comedies could also investigate the value of turning satirical laughter against the attitudes they wish to criticize. Shakespeare's plays certainly deride various forms of folly in the relationships between men and women, and even though the tone of this ridicule is generally good-humored, a feminist director can readily employ it with satirical purpose, to scourge an inequitable society with a comic lash. Such a strategy need not involve any drastic manipulation of the tone or script of a play like *Two Gentlemen*, for the text already features clear opportunities for a satirical treatment of the notion that women should keep silent while men decide the fate of their love.

Silvia's silence at the end of the play is anticipated by several events earlier in the action, particularly in Act II. At Silvia's first appearance, she returns to Valentine a letter he has written on her behalf to her beloved, without realizing that the epistle is actually meant for him. As Jonathan Goldberg remarks, "Silvia can only speak to her lover if he speaks for her. Already she has no voice" (72). In the following scene, Proteus, departing for Milan at his father's behest, takes his leave of Julia, and the two exchange rings, sealing their betrothal with "a holy kiss" (2.2.7).[2] After this embrace, Julia does not speak again for the rest of the scene; Proteus alone swears his faithfulness and concludes their farewell:

> My father stays my coming. Answer not.
> The tide is now, nay not thy tide of tears,
> That tide will stay me longer than I should.
> Julia, farewell.
>   [Exit *Julia*]
> What, gone without a word?
> Ay, so true love should do: it cannot speak,
> For truth hath better deeds than words to grace it. (2.2.13–18)

When Julia attempts to respond to Proteus's vows of constancy, he silences her with the command, "Answer not." In performance, Proteus may physically prevent her from speaking, perhaps with a finger to her lips as she begins to address him. Unable to give voice to her sorrows, Julia bursts into tears and leaves the stage without saying goodbye. Proteus's exclamation, "What, gone without a word?" may then ironically raise laughter at his own expense, since he is the one who has been blocking her speech in the first place. His rationalization that "true love . . . cannot speak" merely shrouds in proverbial wisdom the enforced nature of the behavior he has imposed upon his bride-to-be.

This exchange, it has often been noted, is paralleled in the following scene by Launce's enactment of his farewell to his family.[3] While the entire household weeps and wails at parting, Launce berates his "cruel-hearted" dog Crab because he "sheds not a tear; nor speaks a word" (2.3.30–31). Launce's frustration at his dog's failure to utter human speech parodies his master's equally unreasonable disappointment at Julia's compliance with his command not to answer him. Later in the play, Launce and Speed read over a list of the qualities of the woman with whom Launce himself has fallen in love:

> *Speed.* "Item, she is slow in words."
> *Launce.* O villain, that set this down among her vices! To be slow
> in words is a woman's only virtue. (3.1.326–27)

In one sense, Launce's claim that a disinclination to speak is a woman's only possible positive attribute repeats and potentially reinforces a misogynist sentiment characteristic of patriarchal culture. But the fact that Shakespeare puts this ludicrous overstatement of conventional thought into the mouth of a fool both undercuts the notion itself and questions the sagacity of a society that adheres to such ideas. An actor delivering these lines on the modern stage with an exaggerated sexist attitude can easily cause satirical laughter to rebound against the male speaker rather than the women he derides.

This technique of directing laughter at the ridiculous chauvinism of the men is crucial to an alternative feminist staging of the conclusion tested at the University of Scranton under the direction of Joan Robbins. At the end of 5.3, Silvia is captured by outlaws who bind her hands and cover her mouth with a gag. When she appears in the final scene followed on stage by Proteus, who has rescued her, the gag has fallen down around her neck, but her hands remain tied as she avoids his advances. Exasperated by her disdain, Proteus elects to force her to yield to his desire: cornering Silvia, he replaces the gag and is about to ravish her when Valentine intervenes to prevent him. For the rest of the scene, as Valentine, Proteus, and eventually the Duke dispose of Silvia's hand in marriage, she struggles to speak, but none of the men pay any attention to her muffled objections. One of the advantages of this version of 5.4 is that it conveys the idea that Silvia's silence is not voluntary; it is not an acknowledgment of her subservient position but a condition inflicted upon her by men and perceived by them as nothing unusual or undesirable. Unlike other realistic justifications for Silvia's failure to speak, such as rendering her unconscious, presenting Silvia gagged and struggling provides a meaningful visual image of a woman bound and stifled by courtship practices that deny her self-determination. The other crucial aspect of this version is that it makes a feminist point without necessarily sacrificing the play's comic tone. In contrast to Ringer's staging, no actual rape occurs, and Silvia remains alert to the actions occurring around her. Silvia's impeded reactions possess great potential for comedy, although the director must take care to insure that the humor Silvia inspires is sympathetic, while any derisive laughter is aimed at the blindness of the men to their own insensitivity.

This experimental staging ends with a final outrageous instance of male folly. Valentine, standing with his arms around the muffled Silvia, looking to his counterpart Proteus, concludes the play with an appeal to the conventional closure of romantic comedy: "That done, our day of marriage shall be yours, / One feast, one house, one mutual happiness" (5.4.170–71). As Proteus embraces his bride in a re-enactment of the kiss that silenced her at his departure from Verona, Valentine also kisses Silvia without ever noticing that she is still wearing a gag over her mouth, and the lights fade to black. A feminist production of *Two Gentlemen* need not suggest therefore that Silvia refuses to wed in order to make its "positive statement." It can infer, by their conspicuous absence, the mutual respect and communication necessary for a successful and an equal marriage. In this way, the director as satirist can work in conjunction with the text to mock the sexism that prevents such unions.

NOTES

    1. For a look at the satirical aspects of Shakespeare's plays, see Campbell.

    2. All quotations from *Two Gentlemen* refer to the Arden Shakespeare edited by Leech.

    3. See, for example, Brooks (96) and Leech (xli).

WORKS CITED

Brooks, Harold F. "Two Clowns in a Comedy (to say nothing of the Dog): Speed, Launce (and Crab) in 'The Two Gentlemen of Verona,'" Essays and Studies 16 (1963): 91–100.

Campbell, Oscar James. *Shakespeare's Satire*. Hamden, CT: Archon Books, 1963.

Dollimore, Jonathan, and Alan Sinfield, eds. *Political Shakespeares: New Essays in Cultural Materialism*. Ithaca: Cornell University Press, 1985.

Dowden, Edward. *Shakespeare*. New York: Macmillan, 1877.

Friedman, Michael D. "'Hush'd on Purpose to Grace Harmony': Wives and Silence in *Much Ado About Nothing*." *Theater Journal* 42 (1990): 350–63.

Goldberg, Jonathan. *Voice Terminal Echo: Postmodernism and English Renaissance Texts*. London: Methuen, 1986.

Leech, Clifford, ed. *The Two Gentlemen of Verona*. The Arden Shakespeare. London: Methuen, 1969.

Lusardi, James P. *"The Two Gentlemen of Verona," Shakespeare Bulletin* 2–3.12–1 (Nov. 1984/Feb. 1985): 13.

McLuskie, Kathleen. "The patriarchal bard: feminist criticism and Shakespeare: *King Lear* and *Measure for Measure*." In Dollimore and Sinfield, eds., 88–108.

———. *Renaissance Dramatists*. Atlantic Highlands, NJ: Humanities Press International, 1989.

Ringer, Delores. "A Feminist Politics of Directing *The Two Gentlemen of Verona.*"
   Unpublished paper presented at the 1990 Mid-America Theater Conference.

Schlueter, Kurt, ed. *The Two Gentlemen of Verona*. The New Cambridge Shakespeare.
   Cambridge: Cambridge University Press, 1990.

Victor, Benjamin. *The Two Gentlemen of Verona. A Comedy, Written by Shakespeare.
   With Alterations and Additions. As it is performed at the Theater-Royal in
   Drury Lane*. London, 1763.

Feminine "Depth" on the Nineteenth-Century Stage (1996)

Patty S. Derrick

The emergence in the nineteenth century of Shakespearean character studies spawned an interest in Shakespeare's female characters. The critical views of Coleridge and Hazlitt, particularly views on the individuality of Shakespeare's characters and on the likelihood that readers could empathize with them, were adopted by others to analyze and illuminate the female characters.[1] Anna Jameson, for instance, sought to refute the notion that Shakespeare's women are "mere abstractions of the affections" (30) in the Introduction to her *Characteristics of Women, Moral, Poetical, and Historical* and to demonstrate "the manner in which the affections would naturally display themselves in women—whether combined with high intellect, regulated by reflection, and elevated by imagination, or existing with perverted dispositions, or purified by moral sentiments" (46). Louis Lewes expressed the same notion in *The Women of Shakespeare* when he asserted that Shakespeare profoundly depicted the "soul and mind of man" and "was equally able to explore the heart of woman to its inmost depths," by showing both what is beautiful and what is frightful ("Preface" x). Analyses such as these suggest that Shakespeare's women had been too long overlooked and oversimplified, that their intellectual, emotional, and moral complexity could no longer be disregarded. Helena Faucit Martin, writing as an actress who had struggled with the heroines' complexities, described the difficulty of playing a role like Imogen, a role that required tenderness and enduring fortitude as well as cultivated intellect and abundant emotion. How difficult it is, she explained, to "express in action, however faintly, what must have been in the poet's mind" (176). Nineteenth-century critics and actresses believed, then, that Shakespeare had invested his female characters with more than had ever been noticed, and these writers wanted to shatter old stereotypes by asserting a new perception of complexity and interiority in the women, by plumbing their "inmost depths" (Lewes). But what is the relation between the text that these writers studied and the representation that was offered on the stage? What image of feminine interiority was actually conveyed theatrically?

Russell Jackson suggests that the nineteenth-century "theatre responded fully to the demands of critical opinion for 'depth' in the characterisation of the heroines" (18). He calls our attention to the word "depth," pointing up the problematic nature of this concept, a concept that writers insisted was present in Shakespeare's women because he created women who were "true to life." Of course, the qualities of feminine "depth" are determined culturally and are based on the age's image of a "real" woman, a "real" woman being, in fact, an ideal projection of a real woman. I would like to examine two of Shakespeare's women—Julia and Silvia from *The Two Gentlemen of Verona*—to determine how nineteenth-century stage portrayals of them created an image of feminine "depth." Rather than looking at what was presented on the stage, however, I want to look at what in Shakespeare's text did not make it to the stage, what was excised or suppressed. Looking at what was omitted can perhaps reveal those elements of Shakespeare's women, with all their "depth" and complexity, that the character critics could applaud but that theatrical producers could not accommodate for the audiences. What could the critic rationalize and explain that the theatre audience, perhaps closer to the ideals of gendered thought and behavior, could not accept? *The Two Gentlemen of Verona* was staged throughout the century, by Kemble (1808), Macready (1841), Charles Kean (1846), Phelps (1857), and Daly (1895), major productions all, whose promptbooks I will use in illustrating the sorts of cuts that were made to preserve and/or promote a cultural image of "realistic" feminine "depth."

Certain topics were judged to be plainly inappropriate for women to discuss on the stage, such as Julia's consultation with her maid Lucetta regarding the masculine garb she should wear to disguise herself. Lucetta reminds her that she will need a codpiece because "A round hose, madam, now's not worth a pin, / Unless you have a codpiece to stick pins on" (2.7.53, 55–56.)[2] Kemble, Macready, Kean, Phelps, and Daly all cut this passage as apparently inappropriate for a gentlewoman to speak of, or in this case, even listen to, despite fact that Julia's response in the text is to reject Lucetta's teasing advice and insist on a disguise "most mannerly" (2.7.58). Retaining the passage as written demonstrates Julia's modesty and gives her a broader range of responses in the play, but leaving the passage in would also suggest that a proper young woman like Julia would tolerate such talk, even in a very private conversation, talk that might spur mental images of this decorative codpiece. Cutting the passage, a tradition that continued well into the twentieth century, seems to have conformed with a cultural projection of what "actual" women might speak of or imagine.

Also interesting are cuts involving "inappropriate" references to women made by men, inappropriate because they posit what might have been considered "masculine" qualities in a woman. Early in the play, Speed reports to Proteus on Julia's cold reception of his love letter by calling her "as hard as steel" (1.1.140–41), a passage that Kemble, Macready, and Kean cut. Even though Speed is referring to Lucetta, who received the letter and refused to tip him, the audience does not know this fact until the next scene so that Julia appears for a short while to possess the quality of steeliness and also to be headstrong and stubborn in refusing to tip the messenger. Silvia, likewise, is deprived of similar qualities in her letter scene with Valentine (2.1). Silvia has taken the aggressor's role by having Valentine write a letter to her beloved and then by giving it back to him, and Speed explicitly points out to the audience her manipulation of Valentine and the situation when he says in aside, "O excellent motion! O exceeding puppet! Now will he interpret to her" (2.1.94–95), a passage that Macready, Kean, and Daly all cut. The passage is difficult, its precise meaning debatable, but it seems to suggest that Silvia is in control, and she will now make her puppet speak the words she has had composed. These two cuts, referring to Julia as "hard" and to Silvia as cleverly manipulative, are too small to qualify as time-savers in a production and, therefore, must have been made for another reason, perhaps the inappropriateness of attributing aggressive motives or steely-hard behavior to women.

Anna Jameson wanted to show in her sketches that women possessed "high intellect, regulated by reflection, and elevated by imagination" (46), qualities we can assume are neccessary to apprehend and make metaphor. Often in nineteenth-century productions of *Two Gentlemen*, however, Julia is deprived of some of her metaphor-making abilities. When she petulantly tears up Proteus' letter, she immediately repents her action by saying, "Injurious wasps, to feed on such sweet honey, / And kill the bees that yield it with your stings" (1.2.103–04). The lines were omitted by Kemble, Macready, Kean, Phelps, and Daly, all five productions suppressing a metaphor whose apiary lore is obscure (the antagonism of wasps and bees) and perhaps was considered too vague to be staged, or perhaps it was considered too complex to be uttered by a young woman. It is certainly no more complex, however, than many other metaphors that remained in the play. For example, Proteus employs a canker/bud metaphor to bolster his argument with Valentine in the play's opening scene; relying on commonplace knowledge, he says:

For writers say: as in the sweetest bud
The eating canker dwells, so eating love
Inhabits the finest wits of all. (1.1.42–44)

Despite the fact that the metaphor confuses the scene since Proteus does not seem to understand his own similitude, supporting as it does Valentine's argument on the destructiveness of love rather than his own position, nineteenth-century productions retained it (with the exception of Daly who cut this passage along with the following six lines). In the case of the wasp/bee metaphor, Julia shows no such intellectual confusion. She clearly understands her comparison because she enacts it, tearing up the love letter ("the sweet honey") with her fingers ("injurious wasps"). Even a simple metaphor is excised from Julia's speech later in the play when she is disguised as Sebastian and has agreed to carry Proteus's message to Silvia. To herself she laments, "Alas, poor Proteus, thou hast entertain'd / A fox to be shepherd of thy lambs" (4.4.91–92), a passage that Kemble, Macready, and Kean all omitted. The complexity of the metaphors, then, does not seem to be the determining factor in cutting them. What is most interesting about both of Julia's metaphors is that she is alone when she voices them; she is not using metaphor or clever word-play to flaunt her wit before others, as Valentine and Thurio do when they compete for Silvia's attention, using a series of metaphors on wit and wealth (2.4.38–40), which only Daly in the nineteenth century excised. On the contrary, Julia is speaking to herself, using metaphor to understand and express the emotions she is privately feeling. Such instances seem to be ideal examples of the newly perceived "depth" that critics found in Shakespeare's women, what Mrs. Jameson called "high intellect . . . elevated by imagination," but examples that often did not make it to the stage, particularly in the first half of the century. The use of metaphor, even misunderstood metaphor, was largely reserved for men.

Since Julia wears a disguise in the last two acts, she has a few opportunities to reveal through asides the complexity of her situation and her consciousness of that complexity. The aside allows a character to reveal a sort of multiple awareness, that of an actual situation but also its layers of irony and incongruity. However, the mental quickness required to produce an aside is entirely non-threatening to the other characters; only the audience grasps the sharp perceptiveness of the speaker's private observation. But was the nineteenth-century audience ready to attribute this level of awareness to women? In Act 4, Julia/Sebastian stands in the shadows, listening to Proteus's post-serenade wooing of Silvia, and occasionally comments to herself on what she hears. When he declares to Silvia that his first love is dead, Julia sadly remarks, "Twere false, if I should speak it; / For I am sure she is not buried" (4.2.106b–07). Again, later in the scene, when Proteus requests Silvia's portrait to adore in her stead, Julia employs his own shadow-substance metaphor and privately observes, "If 'twere a substance, you would sure deceive it, And make it but a shadow, as I am" (4.2.126–27). Julia's quick use of his metaphor reveals not only her powers of empathy but also her mental acuity; she empathizes with Proteus' sentiment that without his beloved (Silvia), he is mere shadow (she too lacks her beloved), yet Julia expands the metaphor by also alluding to her present disguise, her loss of identity and gender. She comprehends layers of meaning in the shadow-substance metaphor. Her strength despite great distress and disappointment, her emotional capacity to empathize with her betrayer, her perspicacity—these qualities are all unveiled in these asides, qualities that exhibit an emotive and intellectual range in Julia, but nineteenth-century producers could reach no unanimity on the appropriateness of Julia's expressing them. Kemble omitted the asides, but Macready restored them; Kean again cut them, whereas Phelps shortly thereafter included them; and Daly closed the century by again cutting them.

A similar situation occurs in Act 5 as Julia/Sebastian listens to Proteus and Thurio quibble over Silvia's likes and dislikes in men. Julia listens and offers a series of six brief asides, often witty and sarcastic, on Thurio's foolishness. Kemble elected to cut four of them, Kean two, Phelps one, while Daly cut them all. Only Macready retained all six. In her commentary on Julia in *Shakespeare's Garden of Girls*, Mrs. Elliott points to this series of asides as evidence of Julia's complexity, her growth, her "fortitude of soul and determination of purpose" (168): "But Julia, with all her suffering, preserves a keen sense of the ridiculous in others and, during Thurio's interview with Proteus, shows how thoroughly she appreciates the humorous side of Thurio's conceit" (171). The aside allows a character to communicate interiority, as Mrs. Elliott suggests, and her specific reference to this episode in the play demonstrates that the character critic, reading in the study, was eager to accommodate these small nuances of intellectual complexity in a female character, whereas a theatrical manager, both reflecting and shaping the tastes of his audience, was less so.

The Two Gentlemen of Verona as a text presents its own problems regarding feminine complexity since Silvia has no asides and Julia has only three occasions for them, two of which I have discussed. The third occurs in the final scene as Julia/Sebastian again listens to Proteus plead with Silvia, whose response "By thy approach thou mak'st me most unhappy" is followed by Julia's aside, "And me, when he approacheth to your presence"

(5.4.31–32). This aside does not reveal Julia's intellectual quickness or perception of irony but rather mild jealousy and self-pity and must have been deemed appropriate for the stage because Macready, Kean, Phelps, and Daly all retained it. (Kemble had re-written this portion of the play and included no asides.)

For two centuries, critics and audiences have expressed disappointment with the ending of *Two Gentlemen*; Mrs. Elliott in 1885 called it a "lame and impotent conclusion" (171). Part of the disappointment for us today derives from the silence and passivity of Julia and Silvia, who are given very few lines to speak as their lives are determined by the men. In the text, just before Proteus's attempted rape, Silvia has one last show of strength when she angrily rejects his pleas and lectures him on faithless vows:

> Thou hast no faith left now, unless thou'dst two,
> And that's far worse than none: better have none
> Than plural faith, which is too much by one. (5.4.50–52)

Her fiery, pointed rebuff, after which she is virtually silent, was not heard by nineteenth-century audiences. Kemble cut it from his revision of the ending; Macready cut it along with her preceding four lines; and Kean, Phelps, and Daly continued the omission. The deeper silence of the women at the end seems to fit the image that Joseph Donahue describes of women generally in nineteenth-century drama, Shakespearean or otherwise, the image of "damsels in distress" in need of resourceful men to deliver them to safety (118). By diminishing Silvia's independent thought and speech, productions shifted the focus unequivocally onto the men, onto Proteus's treachery and Valentine's rescue of Silvia followed by his generosity in forgiving his friend's betrayal. The text itself presents a considerable problem, the sort that Alan Sinfield describes in his chapter on character and subjectivity: feminine boldness that reverts to passivity at the end of the play, generating a sense of character discontinuity. He suggests that "this sequence seems plausible in our cultures, it seems satisfactory as character analysis, but in fact it is a story about the supposed nature of women" (56). If the text itself creates this idealized, fictitious image of women, what can we say about the nineteenth-century theatrical representation of that image? These productions silenced Silvia even more than the text had done, clearly unable to accommodate her brief moment of power at the end. Her final instance of self-assurance with its dramatically resonant lines would potentially subvert the preferred cultural ideal of male-female relationships, at the core of which must be Valentine's rescue of a powerless, generally silent Silvia.

The image of women represented on the nineteenth-century stage was thought to imitate what "real" or "actual" women thought, said, and did, but, in fact, as in any age, the mimetic representation was conflated with an "ideal" of what "real" women thought, said, and did. Based on this test case of five major productions of *Two Gentlemen*, "real" women did not engage in immodest thoughts or conversations, they restricted their metaphor-making, and, even in private musings, they focused on emotions, not on penetrating, ironic insights. It would be easy to ascribe these theatrical patterns to the fact that men were managing these productions and cut the text to highlight the male roles, especially in the cases of Kemble, Macready, Kean, and Phelps, all of whom starred in their productions. But that explanation does not hold with Augustin Daly's 1895 production, which was designed to showcase Ada Rehan as Julia. She was the star, and Daly rearranged lines and scenes in order to give her as many stirring curtain lines as possible. Nevertheless, her role was trimmed in the same ways that it had been throughout the century, suggesting that a more subtle cultural imperative was at work. If Julia and Silvia as Shakespeare conceived them and as character critics found them did not fit exactly the image of "real" women to which nineteenth-century theatregoers could adapt, then the highly selective, precise cutting of the text could create the women anew.

NOTES

1. Several articles discuss the critical trends emerging in the nineteenth century: Jonathan Bate, "The Politics of Romantic Shakespeare Criticism: Germany, England, France," *European Romantic Review* 1 (1990): 1–26; Christy Desmet, "'Intercepting the Dew-Drop': Female Readers and Readings in Anna Jameson's Shakespearean Criticism" in *Women's Re-Visions of Shakespeare*, ed. Marianne Novy (Urbana: University of Illinois Press, 1990); Roy Park, "Lamb, Shakespeare, and the Stage," *Shakespeare Quarterly* 33 (1982): 164–77; Stanley Wells, "Shakespeare in Hazlitt's Theatre Criticism," *Shakespeare Survey* 35 (1982): 43–55.

2. Citations are to *The Riverside Shakespeare*, ed. G. Blakemore Evans (Boston: Houghton Mifflin, 1974).

WORKS CITED

Daly, Augustin. Promptbook of *The Two Gentlemen of Verona*. New York: 25 February 1895. (Folger 2 Gent 5)

Donahue, Joseph. "Women in the Victorian Theatre: Images, Illusions, Realities." In *Gender in Performance: The Presentation of Difference in the Performing Arts*. Ed. Laurence Senelick. Hanover, New Hampshire: University Press of New England, 1992.

Elliott, Mrs. M. Leigh. *Shakespeare's Garden of Girls*. London: Remington and Co., 1885.

Jackson, Russell. "'Perfect Types of Womanhood': Rosalind, Beatrice, and Viola in Victorian Criticism and Performance." *Shakespeare Survey* 32 (1979): 15–25.

Jameson, Anna. *Characteristics of Women, Moral, Poetical, and Historical*. New ed. Boston: Houghton Mifflin, 1911.

Lewes, Louis. *The Women of Shakespeare.* Trans. from the German, Helen Zimmern. New York: G. P. Putnam's Sons, 1895.

Kean, Charles. Promptbook of *The Two Gentlemen of Verona.* New York: 6 October 1846. (Folger 2 Gent 10)

Kemble, John Philip. Promptbook of *The Two Gentlemen of Verona* (1808). Vol. 9 of *The Promptbooks of John Philip Kemble.* Ed. Charles H. Shattuck. Charlottesville: University Press of Virginia, 1974.

Macready, William Charles. Promptbook of *The Two Gentlemen of Verona.* London: 29 December 1841. (Folger 2 Gent 11)

Martin, Helena Faucit. *On Some of Shakespeare's Female Characters.* 5th ed. Edinburgh and London: William Blackwood and Sons, 1893. Rpt. New York: AMS Press, 1970.

Phelps, Samuel. Promptbook of *The Two Gentlemen of Verona.* London: 1857. (Folger 2 Gents 13)

Sinfield, Alan. "When Is a Character Not a Character? Desdemona, Olivia, Lady Macbeth, and Subjectivity" in *Faultlines: Cultural Materialism and the Politics of Dissident Reading.* Berkeley: University of California Press, 1992, 52–79.

PART II
THEATRE REVIEWS

EUROPEAN MAGAZINE: 1821, COVENT GARDEN, LONDON

DIRECTED BY FREDERICK REYNOLDS

Nov. 29 [1821]. *The Two Gentlemen of Verona,* was this evening revived with an abundance of music, splendid scenery, and surpassing machinery. Whether this perversion of Shakespeare into melo-drame have "nothing of offence in it," may be a question; but if the offence could be palliated, it must be in the case of the present play, one the feeblest and most incomplete of all the hasty works of it's great author; so much so indeed, as to have been doubted by many competent judges, if it were really his. The love of Valentine, and the inconstancy of Proteus; the lofty resolution of Sylvia, and the gentle constancy of Julia, were to-night embellished with illuminated palaces and triumphant galleys; catches and glees in forests, and a blazing mountain! The first three acts were dull, with the occasional exhilaration of songs by Miss Tree and Miss Hallande; but in the fourth, the Carnival was displayed in more than it customary glories. The opening of the scene displayed the Ducal Palace and great square of Milan illuminated, golden gondolas on the river, and all the usual appendages of foreign gala, masquers, dancing girls, and mountebanks. The pageant then commenced, with a display of the Seasons. Spring came enthroned on a pile of unblown flowers, which the nymph touched with her wand, and the buds were turned into blooms. Then came Summer in the midst of corn, which grew into golden heads at her touch. Autumn followed, with a similar conversion of leaves and stems into melting grapes and blushing apples, and Winter closed the pomp by a view of Lapland with a shower of snow; while dancing nymphs, reapers, and shivering Laplanders, filled up the intervals. Next came the elements, Earth moved on in majesty, seated in a car drawn by lions over clouds; and Air was a portrait of Juno, attended by her peacocks.—Fire had Vulcan in his

Reprinted from Salgādo Gāmini, ed. *Eyewitnesses of Shakespeare: First Hand Accounts of Performances, 1590–1890.* London: Chatto and Windus for Sussex University Press, 1975; New York: Barnes & Noble, 1975, pp. 78–80.

forge, illuminated by showers of his own sparks; and Water was green robed, with a paid of pigmies sounding Conch shells, and seated upon Dolphins. The stage was then suddenly invaded by water, and on it's bosom rolled Cleopatra's galley, covered with silks and gilding. The Queen lay classically sofa'd upon the deck, and the Nymphs and Cupids flew and fanned about her with picturesque fidelity. This was followed by a splendid scene of the Palace of Pleasure, all gaiety and glory, which was also succeeded by a view in the Duke's gardens, with a lake, a castle, a bridge, and an artificial mountain reaching to the clouds, the explosion of which discovered a gorgeous Temple of Apollo, rich in all that is bright and brilliant; and dazzling the spectators until the drop scene covered the catastrophe. The applause which had before been most lavish, rose to enthusiasm at this spectacle, which it is but justice to say, was most magnificent. Its only fault being its too great length, which has been since remedied.

There was also rather too much music in the Play; and of this the two glees harmonized from If o'er the cruel Tyrant Love, and Pray Goody, were the most popular. Sylvia's songs, were, however, also clever compositions, and Julia's duet with Master Longhurst, displayed both to much advantage.

Jones, who bore the character which, we believe, was once played by John Kemble, threw much spirit into the true lover, and gold outlaw, Valentine. Abbott played Proteus very ably, and Farren's Sir Thurio was the "high fantastical," both in his acting and his dress. Liston was a good Launce, and his dog Crab was a fine quiet animal of the Newfoundland breed, which bore much pulling about the stage with much equanimity. Miss Tree performed and sang most sweetly as Julia, but was tasked by too many songs, and Miss Hallande both sang and acted extremely well as Sylvia. We have spoken of the general preparation of the play, which was most costly and striking; and though something more than either song or scenery is essential to continued popularity, *The Two Gentlemen of Verona,* we think, discovers all the longevity, that the managers could reasonably anticipate, for its lavish expense well deserves public remuneration. The whole play is very materially transposed and altered from the original, and many of the scenes display Mr. Reynold's blank verse in company with Shakespeare's.— What will the sterner race of critics say to this?

1895, Daly's Theatre, London

Directed by Augustin Daly

Bernard Shaw

The piece founded by Augustin Daly on Shakespear's *Two Gentlemen of Verona*, to which I looked forward last week, is not exactly a comic opera, though there is plenty of music in it, and not exactly a serpentine dance, though it proceeds under a play of changing colored lights. It is something more old-fashioned than either: to wit, a vaudeville. And let me hasten to admit that it makes a very pleasant entertainment for those who know no better. Even I, who know a great deal better, as I shall presently demonstrate rather severely, enjoyed myself tolerably. I cannot feel harshly towards a gentleman who works so hard as Mr. Daly does to make Shakespear presentable: one feels that he loves the bard, and lets him have his way as far as he thinks it good for him. His rearrangement of the scenes of the first two acts is just like him. Shakespear shews lucidly how Proteus lives with his father (Antonio) in Verona, and loves a lady of that city named Julia. Mr. Daly, by taking the scene in Julia's house between Julia and her maid, and the scene in Antonio's house between Antonio and Proteus, and making them into one scene, convinces the unlettered audience that Proteus and Julia live in the same house with their father Antonio. Further, Shakespear shows us how Valentine, the other gentlemen of Verona, travels from Verona to Milan, the journey being driven into our heads by a comic scene in Verona, in which Valentine's servant is overwhelmed with grief at leaving his parents, and with indignation at the insensibility of his dog to his sorrow, followed presently by another comic scene in Milan in which the same servant is welcomed to the strange city by a fellow-servant. Mr. Daly, however, is ready for Shakespear on this point too. He just represents the two scenes as occurring in

---

Reprinted from *Shaw on Shakespeare: An Anthology of Bernard Shaw's Writings on the Plays and Production of Shakespeare*. Ed. Edwin Wilson. New York: E. P. Dutton, 1961, pp. 200–06. [Review originally appeared on July 6, 1895, in *The Saturday Review*.]

the same place; and immediately the puzzle as to who is who is complicated by a puzzle as to where is where. Thus is the immortal William adapted to the requirements of a nineteenth-century audience.

In preparing the text of his version Mr. Daly has proceeded on the usual principles, altering, transposing, omitting, improving, correcting, and transferring speeches from one character to another. Many of Shakespear's lines are mere poetry, not to the point, not getting the play along, evidently stuck in because the poet liked to spread himself in verse. On all such unbusinesslike superfluities Mr. Daly is down with his blue pencil. For instance, he relieves us of such stuff as the following, which merely conveys that Valentine loves Silvia, a fact already sufficiently established by the previous dialogue:

> My thoughts do harbor with my Silvia nightly;
> And slaves they are to me, that send them flying:
> Oh, could their master come and go as lightly,
> Himself would lodge where senseless they are lying.
> My herald thoughts in thy pure bosom rest them,
> While I, their king, that thither them importune,
> Do curse the grace that with such grace hath blessed them,
> Because myself do want my servant's fortune.
> I curse myself, for they are sent by me,
> That they should harbor where their lord would be.

Slaves indeed are these lines and their like to Mr. Daly, who "sends them flying" without remorse. But when he comes to passages that a stage manager can understand, his reverence for the bard knows no bounds. The following awkward lines, unnecessary as they are under modern stage conditions, are at any rate not poetic, and are in the nature of police news. Therefore they are piously retained.

> What halloing, and what stir, is this today?
> These are my mates, that make their wills their law,
> Have some unhappy passenger in chase.
> They love me well; yet I have much to do,
> To keep them from uncivil outrages.
> Withdraw thee, Valentine: who's this comes here?

The perfunctory metrical character of such lines only makes them more ridiculous than they would be in prose. I would cut them out without remorse to make room for all the lines that have nothing to justify their existence except their poetry, their humor, their touches of character—in short, the lines for whose sake the play survives, just as it was for their sake it originally came into existence. Mr. Daly, who prefers the lines which only exist for the sake of the play, will doubtless think me as great a fool as Shakespear; but I submit to him, without disputing his judgment, that he is, after all, only a man with a theory of dramatic composition, going with a blue pencil over the work of a great dramatist, and striking out everything that does not fit his theory. Now, as it happens, nobody cares about Mr. Daly's theory; whilst everybody who pays to see what is, after all, advertised as a performance of Shakespear's play entitled *The Two Gentlemen of Verona,* and not as a demonstration of Mr. Daly's theory, does care more or less about the art of Shakespear. Why not give them what they ask for, instead of going to great trouble and expense to give them something else?

In those matters in which Mr. Daly has given the rein to his own taste and fancy: that is to say, in scenery, costumes, and music, he is for the most part disabled by a want of real knowledge of the arts concerned. I say for the most part, because his pretty fifteenth-century dresses, though probably inspired rather by Sir Frederic Leighton than by Benozzo Gozzoli, may pass. But the scenery is insufferable. First, for "a street in Verona" we get a Bath bun colored operatic front cloth with about as much light in it as there is in a studio in Fitzjohn's Avenue in the middle of October. I respectfully invite Mr. Daly to spend his next holiday looking at a real street in Verona, asking his conscience meanwhile whether a manager with eyes in his head and the electric light at his disposal could not advance a step on the Telbin (senior) style. Telbin was an admirable scene painter; but he was limited by the mechanical conditions of gas illumination; and he learnt his technique before the great advance made during the Impressionist movement in the painting of open-air effects, especially of brilliant sunlight. Of that advance Mr. Daly has apparently no conception. The days of Macready and Clarkson Stanfield still exist for him; he would probably prefer a water-color drawing of a foreign street by Samuel Prout to one of Mr. T.M. Rooke; and I daresay every relic of the original tallow candlelight that still clings to the art of scene-painting is as dear to him as it is to most old playgoers, including, unhappily, many of the critics.

As to the elaborate set in which Julia makes her first entrance, a glance at it shews how far Mr. Daly prefers the Marble Arch to the loggia of Orcagna. All over the scene we have Renaissance work, in its genteelest stages of decay, held up as the perfection of romantic elegance and beauty. The school that produced the classicism of the First Empire, designed the terraces of

Regent's Park and the façades of Fitzroy Square, and conceived the Boboli Gardens and Versailles as places for human beings to be happy in, ramps all over the scenery, and offers as much of its pet colonnades and statues as can be crammed into a single scene, by way of a compendium of everything that is lovely in the city of San Zeno and the tombs of the Scaligers. As to the natural objects depicted, I ask whether any man living has ever seen a pale green cypress in Verona or anywhere else out of a toy Noah's Ark. A man who, having once seen cypresses and felt their presence in a north Italian landscape, paints them lettuce color, must be suffering either from madness, malice, or a theory of how nature should have colored trees, cognate with Mr. Daly's theory of how Shakespear should have written plays.

Of the music let me speak compassionately. After all, it is only very lately that Mr. Arnold Dolmetsch, by playing fifteenth-century music on fifteenth-century instruments, has shewn us that the age of beauty was true to itself in music as in pictures and armor and costumes. But what should Mr. Daly know of this, educated as he no doubt was to believe that the court of Denmark should always enter in the first act of *Hamlet* to the march from Judas Maccabæus? Schubert's setting of Who is Silvia? he knew, but had rashly used up in *Twelfth Night* as Who's Olivia. He has therefore had to fall back on another modern setting, almost supernaturally devoid of any particular merit. Besides this, all through the drama the most horribly common music repeatedly breaks out on the slightest pretext or on no pretext at all. One dance, set to a crude old English popular tune, sundry eighteenth and nineteenth century musical banalities, and a titivated plantation melody in the first act which produces an indescribably atrocious effect by coming in behind the scenes as a sort of coda to Julia's curtain speech, all turn the play, as I have said, into a vaudeville. Needless to add, the accompaniments are not played on lutes and viols, but by the orchestra and a guitar or two. In the forest scene the outlaws begin to act by a chorus. After their encounter with Valentine they go off the stage singing the refrain exactly in the style of La Fille de Madame Angot. The wanton absurdity of introducing this comic opera convention is presently eclipsed by a thunderstorm, immediately after which Valentine enters and delivers his speech sitting down on a bank of moss, as an outlaw in tights naturally would after a terrific shower. Such is the effect of many years of theatrical management on the human brain.

Perhaps the oddest remark I have to make about the performance is that, with all its glaring defects and blunders, it is rather a handsome and elaborate one as such things go. It is many years now since Mr. Ruskin first took the Academicians of his day aback by the obvious remark that Carpaccio and Giovanni Bellini were better painters than Domenichino and

Salvator Rosa. Nobody dreams now of assuming that Pope was a greater poet than Chaucer, that Mozart's Twelfth Mass is superior to the masterpieces of Orlandus Lassus and Palestrina, or that our "ecclesiastical Gothic" architecture is more enlightened than Norman axe work. But the theatre is still wallowing in such follies; and until Mr. Comyns Carr and Sir Edward Burne-Jones, Baronet, put King Arthur on the stage more or less in the manner natural to men who know these things, Mr. Daly might have pleaded the unbroken conservatism of the playhouse against me. But after the Lyceum scenery and architecture I decline to accept a relapse without protest. There is no reason why cheap photographs of Italian architecture (sixpence apiece in infinite variety at the bookstall in the South Kensington Museum) should not rescue us from Regent's Park Renaissance colonnades on the stage just as the electric light can rescue us from Telbin's dun-colored sunlight. The opera is the last place in the world where any wise man would look for adequate stage illusion; but the fact is that Mr. Daly, with all his colored lights, has not produced a single Italian scene comparable in illusion to that by Sir Augustus Harris at Covent Garden for *Cavalleria Rusticana*.

Of the acting I have not much to say. Miss Rehan provided a strong argument in favor of rational dress by looking much better in her page's costume than in that of her own sex; and in the serenade scene, and that of the wooing of Silvia for Proteus, she stirred some feeling into the part, and reminded us of what she was in *Twelfth Night,* where the same situations are fully worked out. For the rest, she moved and spoke with imposing rhythmic grace. That is as much notice as so cheap a part as Julia is worth from an artist who, being absolute mistress of the situation at Daly's Theatre, might and should have played Imogen for us instead. The two gentlemen were impersonated by Mr. Worthing and Mr. Craig. Mr. Worthing charged himself with feeling without any particular reference to his lines; and Mr. Craig struck a balance by attending to the meaning of his speeches without taking them at all to heart. Mr. Clarke, as the Duke, was emphatic, and worked up every long speech to a climax in the useful old style; but his tone is harsh, his touch on his consonants coarse, and his accent ugly, all fatal disqualifications for the delivery of Shakespearean verse. The scenes between Launce and his dog brought out the latent silliness and childishness of the audience as Shakespear's clowning scenes always do: I laugh at them like a yokel myself. Mr. Lewis hardly made the most of them. His style has been formed in modern comedies, where the locutions are so familiar that their meaning is in no danger of being lost by the rapidity of his quaint utterance; but Launce's phraseology is another matter: a few of the funniest lines missed fire because the audience did not catch them. And with all possible allowance for Mr. Daly's blue pencil, I cannot help suspecting that Mr. Lewis's memory was responsible for one or two of his omissions. Still, Mr. Lewis has always his comic force, whether he makes the most or the least of it; so that he cannot fail in such a part as Launce. Miss Maxine Elliot's Silvia was the most considerable performance after Miss Rehan's Julia. The whole company will gain by the substitution on Tuesday next of a much better play, *A Midsummer Night's Dream,* as a basis for Mr. Daly's operations. No doubt he is at this moment, like Mrs. Todgers, "a dodgin' among the tender bits with a fork, and an eatin' of 'em"; but there is sure to be enough of the original left here and there to repay a visit.

1904, Court Theatre, London

Directed by Harvey Granville Barker

J.C. Trewin

. . . Though none guessed, it was a historic moment when Harley Granville Barker (*Candida* on his mind) took the first morning rehearsal of *The Two Gentlemen of Verona*.[1] The comedy is a Shakespearean notebook: one must hear it spoken to mark how thick the bursts come crowding through the leaves: scenes and speeches that, one day, especially in *Romeo and Juliet,* the dramatist would do much better. Few impressions of this revival have endured, though it was smoothed along gracefully, and Barker sacrificed himself as a player to the futilities of the servant Speed: in view of later events, a very apt name. The production did enchant A.B. Walkley, even if he omitted to mention Barker in a *Times* notice, for "stage managers" were not much publicised then. "I came away," he said, "under so strong a charm that I almost told the cabman, 'To Mantua—by sea.'"[2] In the next month (May 1904), Leigh had a drive at Timon of Athens in a play still less familiar, overlooked since 1856 and the reign of Phelps at Sadler's Wells. London had forgotten its scorching condemnation of ingratitude, a sin that Shakespeare abhorred. Both Timon and Alcibiades learn the falsity of the Athenians. One cries "I am misanthropos and hate mankind." The other returns to cow the Senate. What matters is the music threaded uncannily through the gale: "He ne'er drinks, But Timon's silver treads upon his lip"; "We must all part into this sea of air"; "The sea's a thief, whose liquid surge resolves The moon into salt tears"; "Lie where the light foam of the sea may beat Thy gravestone daily." The Court revival (nothing to do with Barker) made no dint at all, even upon collectors, and the tragedy would not return to a London list until 1922.

Reprinted from *Shakespeare on the English Stage 1900–1964: A Survey of Productions*. London: Barrie and Rockliff, 1964, pp. 30–31.

1. Lewis Casson, then twenty-eight, was in the Court company. He played First Outlaw and Sir Eglamour in *The Two Gentlemen of Verona*, and Servilius in *Timon of Athens*.

2. Valentine sailed from Verona to Milan—possible in those days by canal.

1910, His Majesty's Theatre, London

Directed by William Poel

Robert Speaight

. . . Poel's second production of this play was one of his most important contributions to the Elizabethan Revival. In 1910 Beerbohm Tree, who had an impresario's nose for novelty, invited him to present *The Two Gentlemen of Verona* during the Shakespeare Festival at His Majesty's. This was to ask the wolf to step into the sheep-fold, for Tree's way with Shakespeare was the popular illustration of everything Poel condemned. But he was in no mood for compromise when he led his half-trained troupe of semi-amateurs within those sumptuous and slightly vulgar precincts. The young Bridges-Adams, only recently down from Oxford, was his Assistant Stage Manager, under Nugent Monck, and he has described to me his first meeting with the great reformer.

He found Poel wrapped in a grey muffler, nibbling at a biscuit and sipping a glass of milk. In front of him a lady, shimmering with sequins and no longer in her first youth, was in an attitude of visible distress. Poel's voice was raised in querulous criticism: "I am disappointed," he said, "very disappointed indeed. Of all Shakespeare's heroes Valentine is one of the most romantic, one of the most virile. I have chosen you out of all London for this part, but so far you have shown me no virility whatsoever."

Yet the production had beauties which lingered in the memory; among them, Nugent Monck's inn-keeper nodding to sleep over his lantern. For the first time an "apron" was built out over the orchestra pit of His Majesty's and front lighting installed in the balconies. Beerbohm Tree may have smiled at the austerity of Poel's Elizabethan way, but the apron and the front lighting were retained for his own *Henry VIII* two years later. And they have now become a commonplace of Shakespearian production. It was the thin edge of the Elizabethan wedge and no one has since dislodged it.

Reprinted from *William Poel and the Elizabethan Revival*. London: William Heinemann Ltd., 1954, pp. 120–22.

The production was described by A.B. Walkley as "an entertainment of absorbing interest. The literary quality of the play, the verve of its dialogue, the lyric beauty of many of its passages came out with unusual freshness and clear-cut relief." He thought that the Elizabethan convention, for all its stiff archaic quaintness, gave one far more of the play's atmosphere—its "romantic amorism"—than could ever have been conveyed by a modern setting. And it brought to mind a number of more recent analogies—some "trifle of de Musset," some *"marivaudage* of Marivaux," or the "fervour of Cyrano de Bergerac serenading his *précieuse"* (*The Times*; 21 April 1910). This production was to be remembered. Six years later, in a letter to Poel, Prince Antoine Bibesco paid him the following tribute:

> Having been present at a Shakespearian performance given by you a few years ago at His Majesty's I realise that you are really the only man that has given an adequate idea of the way Shakespeare should be played (18 April 1916). . . .

1956, The Old Vic, London

Directed by Michael Langham

Muriel St. Clare Byrne

Michael Langham's production of *The Two Gentlemen of Verona* (31 performances) takes to itself the credit of having provided the most diverting entertainment of the season. Should one ask more of this play, or are we entitled to believe that the youthful author's intention was to poke some good-humored fun, prettily spiced with light irony, at certain fashionable attitudes then current in life and literature, in order to divert? The play's record for this century suggests that the theatre has regarded it as unsuitable for general enjoyment. Until the Bristol Old Vic company brought their successful 1952 production to London the score was: Old Vic-Stratford, 1916; Old Vic, 1923; Stratford, 1925 and 1938—not an encouraging total. It is not its artificiality which has in the past kept it out of the Old Vic repertory: *Love's Labour's Lost* can boast performances there in 1906, '18, '23, '28, '36, '49 and '54, not to mention the famous Westminster Theatre production of 1932. The trouble with *The Two Gentlemen* is that one of them isn't. The average playgoer writes off Proteus as one complete cad and the end of the play as simply silly. He agrees with Launce that his master is a kind of knave, and his instinctive reaction—like Shaw's to Imogen's predicament—is to think Valentine a fool and say, What about Sylvia's feelings, and Julia's? and to push the whole thing aside with irritation: it cannot be taken seriously and it is not funny. If the actors decide to guy the conclusion and get the audience to laugh with them they will get their curtain applause, but it will not save the play, as such.

The Bristol company got away with a straight presentation because they were beautifully produced, were carried to town on the tide of success, and delighted the select audience, largely theatrical and academic, that flocks to the Old Vic for these special limited runs, by the sheer youthful zest and

Reprinted from "The Shakespeare Season at The Old Vic, 1956–57 and Stratford-upon-Avon, 1957." *Shakespeare Quarterly* 8 (1957): 469–71.

freshness of their playing. "Do the boys carry it away? Ay, that they do!" I have spoken of this year's Old Vic company as young, but these things are comparative. It is old or middle-aged in relation to those charming young people from Bristol, to whom, we could allow, such attitudes and affectations were natural. To try to do anything of the same kind with the 1956–7 company, in my opinion, would have been to court disaster. Given these more sophisticated players, however, it was possible to underline the fact that Shakespeare was cocking a humorous eye at certain contemporary affectations and applying to them the same kind of delicately ironic treatment that delights us when we meet it in Jane Austen. To point these things for the average playgoer who does not read his Elizabethans is not so easy: he is unmoved by the debate between the rival claims of friendship and love. But he does read his Jane Austen and he has generally met his Lydia Languish and her sentimental elopement with its amiable ladder of ropes and conscious moon. Let Tanya Moiseiwitsch's decor and costumes transport us to the age of Byronic heroes and *Northanger Abbey*, and we know at once where we are. The sentiments and the clothes go perfectly together. There is an essential frivolity about Regency costume which persuades us to abandon our disapproval of Proteus and our concern for the ladies' feelings as irrelevant. If the producer can make us agree to accept it as artificial comedy, set in an age where we take romantic absurdity for granted, he can restore to the play a gaiety with which I believe its author tried to endow it and which was captured by the Bristol company with accent on youth.

The charming set, complete with practicable, ivy-mantled tower with window, amiably adapts itself in a moment to Verona, Milan and the Forest Glade, reminding us, with its subtle harmonies of green, blue and brown of a Paul Sandby gouache, properly heightened for theatrical purposes. The young gentlemen are clean-shaven, the one darkly Byronic, the other blondly Shelleyan: the Duke and Thurio are handsomely bewhiskered, the latter looking like half a dozen portraits of royal dukes rolled into one portly figure. The ladies seem to have walked out of the pages of *Ackermann's Repository* and *La Belle Assemblée*; and Sylvia at the ball is Fanny Kemble Twopence Coloured as Juliet. Incidentally, Julia as page to Proteus was becomingly garbed in a period livery, that is, genuine male costume, instead of one of the late 18th century epicene travesties that ousted from the stage the proper costumes of disguised Shakespeare heroines. The gentlemen are all extremely elegant in their uniforms or their frilled shirts, tall hats, dress pantaloons, strapped trousers and voluminous swirling cloaks. Proteus at the ball which opens Act III is a most striking figure, all in very dark red. There is much appropriate theatrical invention to divert. Thurio is groomed and

Richard Gale as Valentine and Keith Mitchell as Proteus in The Old Vic's 1956 production, directed by Michael Langham. Photograph by Houston Rogers. Theatre Museum, Victoria and Albert.

barbered and tight-laced for his proxy-wooing; Valentine's departure into exile is heralded by his luggage—this is a laugh: it is the hat-box that does it—: the Milan scenes are taken into the open air and enlivened by a display of afternoon archery, with a *vie de Bohème* artist thrown in to paint Sylvia's portrait, and by a ducal ball, complete with period waltz and sound of revelry by night, which makes a lively background to Proteus' betrayal of his friend and to the Duke's "discovery" of Valentine's elopement plans.

In such an atmosphere the play becomes a consistent whole. The preposterous ending is prepared for from the start and comes as a perfect climax, with its sensibility and its swooning and a threat of suicide with a pistol by the repentant Proteus to give a plausible period cue for Valentine's offer to surrender Sylvia. Derek Godfrey as the Duke, Derek Francis as Thurio, Keith Michell as Proteus and Richard Gale as Valentine were most stylishly and consistently within the picture; and the final comment, most effectively delivered by Mr. Michell, went right home with the audience: "O heaven! Were man but constant, he were perfect". Mr. Godfrey, quizzical and monocled, made his central scene, first with Proteus, then with Valentine, the stylistic high-light of the play. His syncopated timing, to deal with the farewells of departing guests which punctuated the scene, heightened the tension very skilfully; and the gravely sympathetic-ironic manner in which he interrogated Valentine was suggestively reminiscent of Gilbert's Mikado. If line after line in these speeches does not bear out the producer's evident belief that this is not a heavy father but the dramatist's humorous comment upon the conventional figure, then the young Shakespeare is more naive than either Mr. Langham or I take him to be. Barbara Jefford was a charming Julia, loving, sincere and natural, and at her most vivid in her scenes in boy's disguise. She and Lucetta (Rosemary Webster) made a lively affair of the letter scene, which delighted the audience. Launce and Speed were less helped by the convention than their betters. Duff, a darling plum-duff of a dog, looked as if he had stepped straight out of the pages of Turbervile. John Morris gave a charming little sketch of a gossamer but gallant and gentle Sir Eglamour (in pale grey, and steel-rimmed spectacles), who must have been in constant demand as a chaperon for young ladies escaping to forests to join exiled lovers. The company was in good fettle and very much on its toes, though there were regrettable passages when Proteus and Valentine just gabbled, nor were they the only offenders. But it was first and foremost a producer's and designer's triumph with a much neglected play. Mr. Langham has a great sense of style, a delicate touch and a sense of the theatre. We incline to be captious about stylized productions of Shakespeare. Success in this kind is a rarity, and is to be esteemed as such.

1970, ROYAL SHAKESPEARE COMPANY, STRATFORD-UPON-AVON

DIRECTED BY ROBIN PHILLIPS

Robert Speaight

. . . The last production of *The Two Gentlemen of Verona* at Stratford, ten years ago, sounded a very squeaky overture to the reign of the Royal Shakespeare Company; and there was every excuse for seeing whether sheer, irreverent inventiveness could not do for *The Two Gentlemen* what Clifford Williams had done so successfully for *The Comedy of Errors*. There was also the risk that in bringing the play theatrically to life its deeper qualities might be obscured. If one has to apologize for a play, it is much better not to produce it at all—and *The Two Gentlemen of Verona* needs no apology. Mr. Phillips deserved our applause for rescuing it from neglect and for proving its power to entertain—although I can imagine a production equally satisfying, if hardly as amusing as this one, where the emphasis would be romantic, in the neo-Platonic vein, rather than satirical. For what interests us here is the adumbration of future themes, and Shakespeare's skilful interweaving of them—with Julia looking forward to Rosalind, and forgiving the most unforgivable of Shakespearian juveniles, as, in a very different context, Helena forgives Bertram and Isabella Angelo. Mr. Phillips' production, with its flower children, its Turkish baths, and its highly contemporary costumes, was not so fantastic that Julia's heartbreak became inaudible; and indeed, if it had been less fantasticated, her magnanimity might have seemed incredible. It is a question of balance, and at the critical moment the balance held. *The Two Gentlemen of Verona* may be never so light at comedy—but like all the best comedies it is about serious matters, reminding us that in nothing are people more serious or more silly than in love.

Mr. Phillips not only broke with whatever conventions had hitherto governed the production of the play, but he challenged the current use of the Stratford stage. On entering the auditorium, I rubbed my eyes—could that really be an unmistakable flight of steps, and beside them a positive,

Reprinted from "Shakespeare in Britain," *Shakespeare Quarterly* 21 (1970): 446–47.

even a precipitous, slope? Was it possible that the action of the play would be allowed to proceed on more than one level? By the operation of what magic had Mr. Phillips secured this concession to pictorial effect? The casting was particularly happy, Mr. Richardson's playboy Proteus warning us not to take him too seriously either in his fidelity or his falsehood, and Miss Mirren maturing from flapperdom to full feminity as she discovers how "men are deceivers ever"—a gay, resourceful, and immensely enjoyable performance. Here is a Viola or an Imogen to look forward to. Mr. Patrick Stewart as Lance not only played the part with split-second timing and superb comic address—but he presided over the play with the air of a natural philosopher. One expected him any moment to exclaim, "Oh what fools these mortals be!", and if any actor needed a lesson in the art of picking up one's cue, or in the far subtler art of stealing the stage by doing absolutely nothing, he had only to watch the performance of Crab—Lance's inseparable, canine, companion. Mr. McCallin's Duke combined authority with absent-mindedness, and his exchange of courtesies, Castellas, and finally recriminations with Mr. Egan's Valentine was a dazzling example of high speed, comedy technique. Miss Daphne Dare's décor and Mr. Best's music were both attuned to Mr. Phillips' high-spirited, yet astringent, conception of the play. Stratford is all the better, and certainly the gayer, for what Bridges-Adams used to describe as a *machine de guerre*. Komisarjevsky supplied this in the 'thirties, and Mr. Phillips' secret weapon detonated with equal effect. Your could hear it both in the production and the applause.

Helen Mirren as Julia and Ian Richardson as Proteus in Royal Shakespeare Company's 1970 production, directed by Robin Phillips. Shakespeare Centre Library. Tom Holte Theatre Photographic Collection.

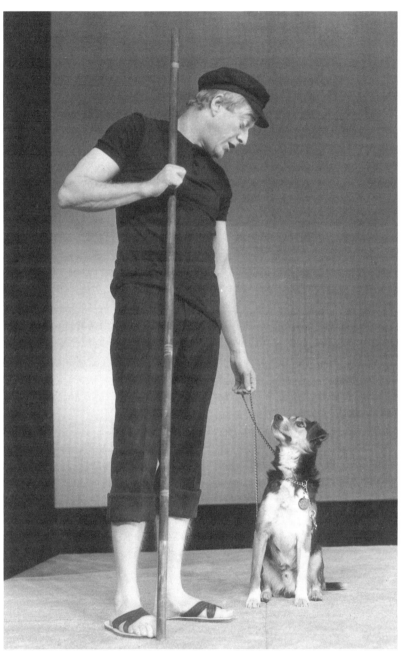

Eric Donkin as Launce with Crab in Stratford (Ontario) Festival's 1975 production, directed by Robin Phillips. Photo by Robert C. Ragsdale. By permission of the Stratford Festival, Canadian Actors' Equity Association, and Eric Donkin.

1975, Stratford, Ontario

Directed by Robin Phillips and David Toguri

Berners W. Jackson

. . . The production of the *Two Gentlemen* was full of the juice of youth. Mr. Phillips and his co-director, David Toguri, stuck faithfully to Shakespeare's text and found a tale for our time in his account of the preoccupation of the young with love and friendship. The setting was the Italian Riviera, or some place like it, where the wealthy take their pleasure amidst suntans and sunglasses, and their sons and daughters cavort in the miscellaneous finery of today's youth. A point needs to be made: this was not "modernized Shakespeare" in the usual sense of that phrase. The play was not made over to accommodate the fashions and furnishings of today; instead these things were put to the service of the play. This faithful adherence to the text in a modern setting had the effect of liberating Shakespeare from the bondage to time imposed by period costume and an attempt at period airs and manners, without subjecting his work to the kind of adjustments and ingenious inventions that are too often perpetrated in a misdirected search for relevance. We talk of the timelessness of Shakespeare. I have never been more aware of it than I was while watching this production of a comparatively slight play from his early years. The authentic voice was there, but it seemed to be speaking in our time, rather than to our time from across four centuries. The high school audiences at the spring previews recognized Valentine and his friends as their contemporaries, and kept giving the production standing ovations.

Stephen Russell, a large, dark young actor with the sort of physique that is designed for violent physical action and the sort of face that seems to welcome it, presented a dangerously volatile, restlessly physical Valentine who worked out with boxing gloves, threw a beach ball about, and displayed all the attributes of his type: frankness, generosity, impulsiveness, and a short-

Reprinted from "Shakespeare at Stratford, Ontario, 1975." *Shakespeare Quarterly* 27 (1976): 25–27.

age of acumen. Nicholas Pennell played the softer Proteus as a young man not devious by nature but grasping at duplicity as the only weapon that might serve him against such as Valentine in his pursuit of Silvia. He came to contrition at the end in the same way that Valentine abandoned his anger, almost with relief. Both the relationship and the contrast that had been established between the young men throughout the play were very evident here. Their recognition of a peril passed, and the gratitude of each to the other that friendship had survived made the scene of their reconciliation more believable than its events suggest it is likely to be.

The production was enlivened by a Silvia who was not the somewhat passive maiden of the play's tradition. Jackie Burroughs made her a capricious daughter of wealth and power who could oblige Proteus with a picture of herself by simply tearing it out of a glossy magazine, and who had been brought up in the belief that whatever she did would be commended. Beneath the softness of her filmy gown you suspected the wiry body that brought her on stage in a swirling, precarious cartwheel; behind the fluttery affectations of her manner you were aware of the quick, intuitive mind of the accomplished flirt. This was a Silvia designed to unsettle the rugged Valentine, fascinate the impressionable Proteus into forgetting his Julia, focus the attentions of the opportunist Thurio, and shamelessly victimize that aged cavalier, Sir Eglamour. A surprising interpretation, perhaps, but it worked so effectively in this production that you found yourself thinking of Silvia as the sort of girl who appropriated for herself the captain of the high school football team, or who called the Duke, her father, "daddy" when she wanted a new sports car. Miss Burroughs brought it off very cleverly. The tone of her voice—high, self-approving, with a hint of petulance in it—made the lines work for her without altering them or appearing to fight their meaning. In her final interchange with Proteus, for instance, she managed to be provocative and challenging, and then visibly excited by his advances, rather than resolute and admonitory and, finally, frightened. You felt she was enjoying herself, and that the touch of chagrin in her silence following Valentine's intervention was as much the result of being prevented from dealing with Proteus in her own way as of finding herself, for once, not the center of attention.

In contrast to this madcap Silvia there was a warm, single-minded, humorous Julia from Mia Anderson. In boy's clothes, Miss Anderson had a vulnerable, waif-like quality that made all the more appealing her determination to save Proteus from that immemorial condition in which a young man thinks he wants what he can't have and doesn't know that he wants what he can have.

Those in the supporting roles served the production strikingly. Douglas Chamberlain was a smoothly feral Duke of Milan, an updated Renaissance tyrant in velvet suitings and dark glasses, expensive, self-assured, and ruthless, designed to give Valentine and Silvia a hard time of it before he decided they should marry. Richard Curnock as Sir Eglamour in white suit and sun helmet looked like Colonel Sanders on safari as he emerged out of the dawn, equipped to meet every eventuality from butterflies to bandits while escorting Silvia on her flight to Valentine. Julia was served by Gale Garnett as Lucetta, a leggy sophisticate who tolerated the ardors and misgivings of her mistress with a mildly sardonic humor. J. Kenneth Campbell's Thurio was a handsome beach-boy, dedicated to the body beautiful, and vapidly affable in submitting to circumstance. Bernard Hopkins played Speed as a friendly lump of a boy, and made the part of that cheeky lad funnier and more agreeable than one would have thought possible. As Launce, Eric Donkin provided an ironic comment on the attachments of the young by making the lugubrious amusing, but he just managed to hold his own against Crab, a mongrel whose scratchings were impeccably timed, and who looked on the antics of the young with the same sad, speculative eyes that we see in portraits of Elizabethan notables. . . .

1983, BBC TV/Time Life Productions

Directed by Don Taylor

Harry Keyishian
Patty S. Derrick

Harry Keyishian

> *Two Gentlemen of Verona*, BBC TV/Time Life Productions. Exec. prod. Shaun Sutton. d. Don Taylor w. Frank Barrie (Sir Eglamour), Bella (Crab), Tyler Butterworth (Proteus), Hetta Charnley (Lucetta), Tony Haygarth (Launce), John Hudson (Valentine), Nicholas Kaby (Speed), Tessa Peake-Jones (Julia), Joanne Pearce (Silvia)

The major technical legacy of the BBC Shakespeare series may be its establishment of the two-shot (two heads in the "frame" conversing) as the basic mode of recording dialogue. When the television screen's borders enclose two heads—shot anywhere from waist-up to relatively tight close-ups—intimacy of expression is enhanced and formal declamation made absurd. The result is increased audience involvement.

Two Gentlemen of Verona, as an early work of Shakespeare's and relatively primitive in technique, relies heavily on "duologues" or "duets," as Bernard Beckerman has pointed out ("Shakespeare's Dramaturgy and Binary Form," *Theatre Journal*, 33 [1981]: 5–17). It therefore lends itself especially well to the use of the closeup and the two-shot and, not surprisingly, very effective use is made of these shots in the BBC's television production. The conversations between Valentine and Proteus and the comic dialogues of Launce and Speed are given special vitality and charm on the small screen.

Director Don Taylor also employs a full range of other television techniques to give life to the production. Adroit camera placement, mobile fram-

---

Reprinted from "The Shakespeare Plays on TV: *Two Gentlemen of Verona.*" *Shakespeare on Film Newsletter* 9.1 (December 1984): 6.

ing, arresting composition, and other devices were used to good effect. A few examples will have to suffice.

In 3.1, when Proteus pretends surprise at hearing of Valentine's banishment, the young friends are seated on a bench, sharing the camera frame, while Launce's figure, seated at a distance away and slightly out of focus, occupies the space between them. When they leave, Launce is seen in close-up to deliver his line of choral commentary, "I am but a fool, look you, and yet I have the wit to think my master is a kind of knave." This variation of the two-shot gives the effect of a diamond-shaped field of forces: Proteus and Valentine, the participants, form a left-right set of oppositions while the observers, Launce and ourselves, form a front-to-back one.

The intimacies made possible by close-ups also permitted effective interpretive subtexts. In a "straight" reading of the play, the Duke of Verona seems sincere in wishing to marry his daughter off to the foolish Thurio. This production asks us to understand, on the contrary, that the Duke actually views Thurio with distaste. He seems to be testing the faithfulness of Valentine and Silvia by placing barriers in their path, even as he is exposing Proteus by, in effect, tempting him with opportunities for treachery. Another example: when Proteus pretends to be reluctant to dispraise Valentine to Silvia in 3.2, the Duke conveys (to the audience) tremendous contempt for his hypocrisy. The last line of the scene, "Even now about it! I will pardon you," is divided, in delivery, so that the first part is a dismissal of Proteus and Thurio to set about their work, while the second, spoken after they are gone, is a condemnation of Proteus—saying, in effect, "a rogue like you certainly *needs* my pardon."

Surprisingly, no subtext was introduced to deal with the notoriously difficult final scene (in which Valentine not only forgives Proteus for his treachery, but gives up Silvia to him). The segment was shot in a sequence of close-ups, two-shots, and longer shots which clarified the shifting relations among the characters. Taylor calculated, probably correctly, that he had better play the scene straight and not reveal Silvia's reaction to her lover's extraordinary gesture or convey just what Proteus would have done had Julia's presence not fortuitously been revealed.

In Paul Daneman's hands the Duke of Milan was no foolish father but an effectively detached, ironic observer of the follies of the young. Tyler Butterworth as Proteus shifted from friend and lover to scheming betrayer to repentant sinner, while John Hudson gave life both to Valentine's ingenuous good fellowship, and his noble indignation. Tessa Peake-Jones, as Julia, had to move from captious flirtatiousness to tearful martyrdom; she made us feel the character's pain and disappointment. Joanne Pearce nicely fulfilled the less rewarding job of conveying Silvia's single note of highmindedness. Launce (Tony Haygarth) and Speed (Nicholas Kaby) enlivened their scenes of rapid-fire punning and quibbling. As Thurio, that fine actor David Collings was effective, though underutilized.

Patty S. Derrick

The final scene of *Two Gentlemen of Verona* includes a single line that often presents problems for the play's director. Valentine forgives the double-crossing Proteus, and to demonstrate the fullness of his forgiveness, he offers what Proteus least deserves—his own sweetheart Silvia. At 5.4.83, Valentine, who twenty-one lines before, upon stopping the attempted rape, had called Proteus a "friend of an ill fashion" and a "friend, that's without faith or love," is now prepared as a gesture of heroic friendship to offer his heart's dearest prize: "All that was mine in Silvia I give thee" (Arden). At this line, the play's theme of friendship asserts itself over the theme of romantic love, and for directors, it can pose difficulties for a coherent resolution of the plot. The action of the final scene seems to be drawing our attention to the revelation of the disguised Julia and the reuniting of the lovers, but this one troublesome line can throw that conventional romantic ending out of balance momentarily by shifting the viewer's attention to the friendship theme as an equally important focus of the play.

Many choices are available for handling this critical line from simply cutting the line to avoid any diversion of focus, to reading it straightforwardly with no stage business so that the line and its implications go unnoticed, as was the case in Peter Hall's 1960 stage production (J. R. Brown, "Three Directors: A Review of Recent Productions." *Sh. Survey* 14: 132). The BBC televised version of *TGV*, however, offers another possibility. Directed by Don Taylor and broadcast in 1983–84, this production clearly focuses on the theme of romantic love with many scenes in a Milanese garden of love filled with flower petals, courtly lovers, and gilded cupids (Susan Willis, *The BBC Shakespeare Plays: Making the Televised Canon*. Chapel Hill, 1991: 320, 212). Many other scenes, including the midnight serenade of Silvia and the decision by Julia to follow Proteus, are performed under a full, bright moon whose bluish light heightens the romantic mood. Taylor's focus on love is accomplished chiefly through scenery and lighting, not through the cutting of lines (only three lines are cut

Reprinted from *"Two Gents*: A Crucial Moment." *Shakespeare on Film Newsletter* 16.1 (December 1991): 1, 4.

from the entire text) or through the rearranging of lines or scenes (Folio scene order is followed). With Taylor's emphasis on love and its formal conventions, Valentine's offer of Silvia in the name of friendship could be quite jarring, especially to a modern audience unfamiliar with Renaissance notions of heroic friendship. But, in fact, that is not the case. Although Taylor subordinates the friendship theme throughout most of the production, the viewer has been sufficiently prepared for this crucial moment at the play's close.

Don Taylor has made a few important choices that facilitate our acceptance of Proteus' treachery and Valentine's extreme generosity. First, the actor who portrays Proteus, Tyler Butterworth, has a very youthful appearance with large, wondering eyes and a round face, a demeanor that visually emphasizes the extreme immaturity of Proteus, thus making his treachery and breach of honor less threatening and more easily forgivable.

Furthermore, as Proteus progresses into his dastardly intrigue, he never projects a soul that is entire vicious. Butterworth delivers his self-probing soliloquies in a way that shows Proteus' reluctance to betray Valentine and his true love Julia; he genuinely appears puzzled by his newfound emotions and agonizes over his dilemma in the garden of love. The camera alternates our attention (and his) between statues marked AMOR and FIDES as Proteus makes his decision and gradually appears frightened by his own desires. Surging winds and a darkening, thunderous sky scenically echo his devious choice.

A very youthful, wide-eyed Proteus who enters into treachery filled with self-dissent and tumult enables the viewer to accept his hasty and equally tormented repentance and, more importantly, to believe Valentine's immediate forgiveness. The implication is that Valentine understands the strains of first love, having earlier told Proteus, "Forgive me that I do not dream on thee, Because thou seest me dote upon my love" (2.4.168–69). Valentine admits that he has neglected their friendship in the name of love and therefore recognizes that he differs little from Proteus. Hence, he quickly forgives his friend, an action that shifts our focus squarely onto the friendship theme and establishes the groundwork for the proffering of Silvia.

The BBC production's handling of the critical line, "All that was mine in Silvia I give thee," has elicited two very distinct interpretations from reviewers. Harry Keyishian suggests that "no subtext was introduced to deal with the notoriously difficult scene" (*SFNL* Dec. 1984: 6). The scene, Keyishian believes, is played straight with the camera focusing on Proteus and Valentine, eliminating the need for a response from Silvia as she is offered to the man who had tried to rape her. Roger Warren interprets the same scene quite differently. He does not perceive Valentine's delivery of the crucial line to mean, "I give her to you" but rather "I love you as much as Silvia" (*SQ* 35: 338). In Warren's estimation, the BBC production does not include an offer of Silvia, an alternate reading that raises the question of Julia's swoon; if Valentine is not offering Silvia to Proteus, what precipitates Julia's fainting?

A third interpretation of the scene might be suggested. Like Professor Keyishian, I believe the BBC production does, in fact, contain Valentine's offer of Silvia, but I further believe that the scene is played with a subtext that allows the friendship theme to surface and intermingle with the love theme as the play concludes. In Taylor's handling of the scene, Silvia (played by Joanne Pearce) is given a very dramatic moment as she angrily lectures the threatening Proteus on both love and friendship and responds to his question "In love Who respects friend?" with a shouted, indignant "All men but Proteus" (5.4.53–4). She accepts the primacy of friendship in a man's life. After Valentine stops the attempted rape, Silvia runs to his side, and while he sadly and slowly repudiates Proteus, she hangs on his arm and gazes into his face. The camera continues to allow us a view of her response to Valentine's forgiveness; Silvia looks on with understanding and even approval as Valentine leaves her side and approaches his friend. The camera then shifts to focus only on the two young men. Although Taylor avoids the problem of showing Silvia's face at the moment the offer is made, her response to Valentine's hasty forgiveness is clear: she understands the bond of heroic friendship and evinces no disapproval. Furthermore, the actual lines in which Valentine offers Silvia to Proteus are delivered in such a way that Silvia need not feel abandoned. Valentine speaks haltingly to Proteus:

> And [pauses] that my love may appear plain [stutters, pauses] and free,
> All that was mine in Silvia [hesitates for a moment] I give thee.

John Hudson as Valentine speaks the crucial line in a way that suggests he hopes that Proteus has regained his sense of honor and will certainly refuse. When the line is spoken, Proteus clearly perceives the offer as a noble gesture of friendship, not an actual offer, because he does not even look toward Silvia but rather falls into an embrace with Valentine. Immediately Julia faints, and in a long shot of the four characters, we can see Silvia, standing aside patiently and showing no agitation over what just transpired. The implication is that Silvia maturely understands the required motions of friendship and would never intrude upon that bond.

The play's closure has been frequently altered in productions throughout the nineteenth and twentieth centuries, a testimony to the difficulty actors and directors have encountered in trying to harmonize the themes of love and friendship. Taylor's direction of the play's final scene highlights—and appropriately so—not only the rough path to true love but also the path, equally serpentine and treacherous, to proven friendship.

1984, The Young Company, Stratford, Ontario

Directed by Leon Rubin

James P. Lusardi

Presented by the Young Company at The Third Stage. Directed by Leon Rubin. Designed by Pat Flood. Lighting by Steven Hawkins. Music by Loreena McKennitt. With Robert McClure, David Clark, C. David Johnson, Maggie Huculak, Lucy Peacock, Keith Thomas, David Renton, Michelle Fisk, John Dolan, William Dunlop, Erin McMurtry, Ron Hastings, Laurence Russo, John Moffat, Kevin Anderson, Barry Greene, and Mitzi.

> *O, how this spring of love resembleth*
> *The uncertain glory of an April day. . . .*

Proteus' haunting lines might serve as an epigraph for *The Two Gentlemen of Verona*. The play is all April—the work of an April playwright about people in the April of life. But its "uncertain glory" is still glory, and it deserves to be treated with the kind of lyrical energy and imagination that suffuse it.

Such is the spirit informing the Stratford Festival production mounted by director Leon Rubin and the Young Company at The Third Stage. The charm of this early comedy is made manifest at the same time that the theme of "ungovern'd youth / Thrust from the company of aweful men" is taken seriously and suggestively realized. Rubin and designer Pat Flood risk the ire of "purists" by updating the play in costume and decor. The dress of the young principals is not merely modern but colorful new wave or "elegant punk," including the extravagances of tinted hair and flashing metal accessories; that of the heavy fathers and their retainers is, of course, strictly straightsville, subdued executive pinstripes and shining shoes. Someone like Silvia's sappy suitor Thurio hangs between, looking at first downwardly

Reprinted from *Shakespeare Bulletin* 2–3.12–1 (November 1984/February 1985): 13.

mobile in brown suit and black shoes and then absolutely paralyzed in his ragpicker's version of punk chic. The standard two-level unit set is distinguished chiefly by a tree-like stabile in gold, which projects from the right out over the stage and down toward the audience to contribute to the ambiance of stylized modernity.

Far from being gratuitous, these production values are made to serve a text that remains virtually intact, just as the incidental music composed and performed on accordion and harp by Loreena McKennit as an onstage presence enhances the comic irony or pathos of given moments. Decked in long blonde hair and long hippy-style dress, McKennit attentively observes the action throughout, her face almost as expressive as her music. Her setting and singing of "Who is Silvia?" give poignant focus to the moment in which Proteus with Thurio vainly woos Silvia, and Julia in disguise helplessly learns of her lover's inconstancy. The stage tableau at this point emphasizes the isolation of all parties, Silvia remote on the upper level, Proteus sitting disconsolately below her, the pained Julia at stage right and the thwarted Thurio at stage left, and in the midst the silver-tongued harpist, her song the embodiment of contrary yearnings.

The young principals effectively counterpoint one another. Robert McClure is a fine-featured, almost pretty, Valentine, persuasive as an idealist in friendship and an enthusiast in love. His idealism and extravagance combine, inevitably, to make him rather obtuse in dealing with his friend or his lady love or her father or his servant or anyone else who happens along, except perhaps Thurio. McClure manages to keep the character attractive through all his discomfitures and at the end to invest him with a certain anguished dignity when he makes his grand gesture of forgiving Proteus.

But in this production, the play belongs to Proteus, as it probably should in any production. Tall, dark, masculine, David Clark brings to the part not only good looks but a richly expressive voice and the physical poise of an athlete. He plays Proteus as an ebullient undergraduate whose apparently harmless self-absorption turns vicious and proves ultimately as painful to him as it has to others. One may believe in the transformations of this Proteus. Clark deepens the character as soon as he finds himself smitten by Silvia and therefore cold to Valentine and Julia. In his next scene (2.6), which consists entirely of rationalizing soliloquy delivered from the upper stage, he modulates from distraught special pleading through self-congratulation to confident hypocrisy. He becomes so plausible an opportunist that he makes easy game of Valentine (3.1) and so ardent a spokesman of the poetry of courtship that he justly holds Milan and Thurio spellbound at his recital (3.2). Clark is equally convincing in the difficult denouement, where

John Moffat as Second Outlaw, Rob McClure as Valentine, C. David Johnson as Speed, Kevin Anderson as Third Outlaw, and Laurence Russo as First Outlaw in Stratford (Ontario) Festival's 1984 production, directed by Leon Rubin. Photograph by David Cooper. By permission of the Stratford Festival.

he must first meet Silvia's resistance with desperate force, throwing her to the ground and grappling her, and then suffer the shock of Valentine's intervention and judgment. Proteus' humiliation is so complete that we accept, for the moment, his complete change of heart.

Maggie Huculak's Julia is physically commanding. Not especially sensitive to the poetry she speaks, she compensates with exuberance of expression and gesture. Since there is nothing shrinking about this Julia, her aggressive pursuit of Proteus is creditable, just as her taste for unisex apparel provides a witty rationale for her turning up in Milan looking like a fetching Boy George. As her foil, Michelle Fisk presents a dazzling Silvia, with blue eyes and strawberry hair, softly gowned in turquoise or violet and silver-slippered. The difference in acting style is as marked as the difference in appearance and character. Fisk is restrained, sophisticated, witty, speaking the verse with a sense of nuance. Yet perhaps her severest test comes in the denouement when, deprived of lines, she must mime a series of responses from astonishment at being given away by the high-minded Valentine to delight at being dramatically reclaimed.

The rest of the cast is uniformly strong, with one standout and one exception. C. David Johnson as the servant Speed, wearing a flashy black suit with white lapels and a striped jersey, is so versatile an actor, with such exquisite comic timing, that he nearly takes the play away from his masters. The exception is, unfortunately, John Dolan's Launce, who proves to be a rather tame cat with an uproarious dog.

In general, the interpretive updating in this production works admirably. Now and again, it may cause some uneasiness. For example, the tender parting of Proteus and Julia in 2.3 is played as a modern-day aubade, the two in bed together on the upper level, he half naked and she in a black slip, their "holy kiss" sealing a night of lovemaking. One may well ask whether such a steamy encounter is an appropriate expression of Julia's rather innocent sensuality. And one may well wonder at Panthino's sudden appearance on the scene. Still, altogether, this production is exhilarating and delightful. It certainly did not warrant the sour commentary of most Canadian critics, who spent so much time patronizing the play and fussing about the punk motifs in the production that they failed to respond to the charm of either.

1990, THE ACTING COMPANY

DIRECTED BY CHARLES NEWELL

Jean Peterson

Presented by The Acting Company at The Weis Center, Bucknell University, Lewisburg, PA. September 28, 1990 (1990–91 Touring Production). Directed by Charles Newell. Set by Derek McLane. Costumes by Catherine Zuber. Lighting by Marcus Dilliard. Music by Kim D. Sherman. Movement by Jim Calder. With Laurence Drozd, William D. Michie, Rainn Wilson, Diana LaMar, Trish Jenkins, Ethan T. Bowen, Mark Kincaid, Stephanie Erb, Jeffrey Guyton, Andrew Prosky, John Michalski, Dan Berkey, Ben Eric, Mark Stewart Guin, David Eichman, Matthew Edwards, and Kathleen Mary Mulligan.

There is no curtain, but the acting area is framed by a red scaffold studded with light bulbs that suggests, perhaps, a theatre marquee, perhaps an actor's make-up mirror. Actors can be glimpsed, stretching and moving, behind a diaphanous white scrim. An unseen orchestra warms up with some feisty jazz sounds—raucous drums, cool strings, impromptu trumpet riffs. As the house lights dim, two massive silhouettes are thrown against the scrim: two young men, identical in size, dress, and shape, are locked like wrestlers, gripping a baton between them for which they struggle. The scrim parts; the play begins.

The stunning visual image that opens The Acting Company's touring production of *The Two Gentlemen of Verona* is perhaps its "gestic moment." A mixture of romantic comedy, circus, musical, and farcical send-up of Hollywood westerns, this production does not merely announce its theatricality—it boldly trumpets its life as theatre. And the emphasis in this production is indeed on the two gentlemen—not on the treachery of Proteus (William D. Michie), the inconstant lover and disloyal friend to Valentine (Laurence Drozd), but on the peculiar blend of antagonism, competi-

Reprinted from "*The Two Gentlemen of Verona*," *Shakespeare Bulletin* 9.1 (Winter 1991): 33–34.

tion, and narcissism that animates this friendship between men. Engaged in a stylized tug-of-war in what could be a locker room, their identical dress proclaiming an almost interchangeable similarity, the two young men taunt each other and wrestle, apparently in fun but with an increasing edge. Their puppyish playfulness in the opening scene only thinly conceals a violent potential. Their rivalry in love arises inevitably from their fiercely competitive bonding.

Criticism has not treated *Two Gentlemen* kindly; if the major characters have been called at best two-dimensional and the comic characters accused of being barely more than cartoons, these potential weaknesses have been made the strengths of this inspiredly loony production. Thus Rainn Wilson's Speed appears in a fool's coxcomb and clown whiteface, wearing striped baggy pants and funny shoes and riding a child's scooter; Jeffrey Guyton's mournful Launce, with his Pulcinello hat and ruff, is the proverbial weeping clown. Puns, quips, and wordplay are choreographed to brilliantly executed slapstick; corny physical gags accompany verbal ones with cheerful bad taste. Rubber chickens, foam mallets, and dead fish come flying on stage at appropriate moments, supplied by an onstage clown orchestra who play minor roles, effect scene changes, provide mood music, and punctuate verbal antics and sight gags with kazoo choruses, drum rolls, and slide whistles.

Types and archetypes jostle in an amalgam of styles and subtexts: Julia (Diana LaMar) endures the teasing of the worldly Lucetta (Trish Jenkins) from underneath an enormous 50s-style hair dryer; she emerges from it in sequined Harlequin glasses, a crinoline slip, and an enormous beehive "do." The picture of Silvia (Stephanie Erb) delivered to Proteus is a life-sized cardboard cutout of Mae West. And by the time Valentine appears in Milan, resplendent in spurs and a white cowboy suit against a Wild West composed of swinging saloon doors and cardboard cacti, or when our heroes on scooter and tricycle are chased across the desert by clown bandits on pogo sticks, it all makes sense: Barnum and Bailey meet Clint Eastwood—by way of the Marx Brothers, Looney Tunes, and *The Rocky Horror Picture Show.*

The jazz that begins the show—uniting improvisation and control—makes a good metaphor for the discipline that keeps this potentially chaotic whirlwind from spinning out of control. For all its vibrant physical energy and unabashed fun, there is not a wasted gesture or an unorchestrated moment, and a dramatic logic keeps its potential excesses in check.

What more fitting environment for Julia to gossip with her maid than that time-honored venue of female confidences, the beauty parlor? Similarly, Milan as caricatured Wild West, where shootouts seem imminent and the

Rainn Wilson as Speed, Laurence Drozd as Valentine, Stephanie Erb as Silvia, and Andrew Prosky as Thurio in The Acting Company's 1990 production, directed by Charles Newell. Photograph by Irene Haupt. By permission of The Acting Company.

town ain't big enough for all Silvia's buffoonish beaux, is an appropriate setting for the final showdown between Valentine and Proteus. Unlike A.J. Antoon's nostalgic evocation in this summer's New York Shakespeare Festival *Shrew*, the play maintains an ironic distance from its Western setting: a world where exaggerated machismo and competition are made gunslingingly crude, where Silvia's smarmy father throws his weight around in the form of bodyguards that can only be described as a clown goon squad, and Proteus, following the betrayal of his friend, dresses—naturally—in black.

The extreme youth of the protagonists is wisely emphasized. Michie's appealing Proteus, subject to extremes of passion he can neither understand nor control, is simply bewildered and shaken when the sight of Silvia takes him by storm (an emotional state the stage helpfully conveys with flashing lightbulbs and choral arias from clowns on the sidelines). Youth extenuates his inconsistency and treachery. And Drozd's self-absorbed Valentine invites betrayal: he is as didactic in love as he was earlier in denouncing it, as argumentative in praising his Silvia as he is in mocking Proteus' Julia. His typically insensitive claim that Julia is fit only to carry Silvia's train unwittingly adds fuel to his friend's infatuation.

The women, in contrast, face their rivalry with mutual respect, sympathy, and dignity. Mae West is a good analogy for Erb's Silvia, an exuberant tease whose heartbreak over Valentine's exile doesn't stop her from waving an enthusiastic ovation when she is serenaded (hilariously) by clowns in sombreros—yet she shows both sincerity and courage. LaMar's Julia is both funny (dressed in chaps and buckskins to pursue her errant lover, she settles a ten-gallon hat over her mountainous beehive with aplomb) and moving—a rare combination.

And the staging of the final scene confirms the suspicion that something far more serious than meets the eye underlies the theatrical hijinks. No sooner has banished Valentine wailed his lamentations to a lugubrious country western tune ("Thou gentle nymph, cherish thy forlorn s-wain"—5.4.12) than violence—sudden, brutal, and unexpected—explodes on the stage. The attempted rape of Silvia is horrifyingly realistic. She and Proteus overturn a couch in a struggle that lasts several minutes, and, when she resists, he slaps her viciously. This rapist means business. Valentine's intervention is equally brutal—he only just resists bringing a log down on his betrayer's skull with killing force. The image visually echoes their opening wrestling bout, while the overturned couch—belly exposed, guts gaping—reinforces the sudden, visceral exposure of their friendship's violent potential. The play's ironic and sobering comment is that, in such a context, rape makes brutal sense.

The difficult reconciliations are equally well-handled: Proteus dives into self-abasement (he literally grovels) with the same intensity he has devoted to infatuation and betrayal. Valentine responds with the same grandly self-indulgent egotism he has displayed throughout. Since he is overwhelmed by his own magnanimity in forgiving Proteus, the gesture of offering Silvia seems the next logical step. And Julia's appalled, ironic response to their self-absorbed bonding gives release and expression to the audience's own. As for Silvia, in a dead faint since her rescue from rape, she doesn't respond at all; her revival moments later gives Valentine time, one presumes, both to regret his words and to be grateful she hasn't heard them.

If the hasty resolutions of the last five minutes fail to resolve the contradictions the play unleashes, this too is inherent in Shakespeare's text. Here human inconstancy and unpredictability accomplish the sudden infatuations, reversals, and equally sudden capitulations for which magical potions and supernatural beings are needed in *A Midsummer Night's Dream*. If the technicolor sunset into which the lovers promise "One feast, one house, one mutual happiness" is suitably artificial, something of substance—the limits of friendship, loyalty, and love, the human cost of masculine aggression, the boundaries of identity and theatricality—has been explored upon this stage of fools.

1991, Royal Shakespeare Company, Stratford-upon-Avon

Directed by David Thacker

Paul Nelsen
Thomas Clayton

Paul Nelsen

> Presented by the Royal Shakespeare Company at The Swan Theatre, Stratford-upon-Avon, England. April 6, 1991–January 1992. Directed by David Thacker. Designed by Shelagh Keegan. Lighting by Jimmy Simmons. Original music by Guy Woolfenden. Music direction by John Woolf. With Richard Bonneville, Barry Lynch, Sean Murray, Clare Holman, Josette Bushell-Mingo, Randal Herley, Henry Webster, Saskia Reeves, Richard Moore, Guy Henry, Terence Wilton, Peter Bygott, Lucy Tregear, Simeon DeFoe, Howard Crossley, Hillary Cromie, and Woolly (alternately Ben) as Crab.

Even as the audience assembles around the open stage in the RSC's honey-timbered Swan Theatre, director David Thacker suffuses them in the musical food of love that ornamentally plays on throughout this rendering of *The Two Gentlemen of Verona*. What is heard, however, is not sackbut and lute playing Praetorius but saxophone and piano—in fact, a seven-piece palm court combo—accompanying various cast members crooning nostalgic hit parade numbers by George Gershwin, Cole Porter, Irving Berlin, Billy Rose, and others. Couples in stylish eveningwear dance in the cabaret-light dappled downstage as songs like "Love in Bloom" issue from the bandstand in the upstage center recess, itself garlanded with blossoming trees which, with their variegated background glow, reinforce the ambience of romance. Before the dramatic action commences, the audience is put in the mood for love and transported, by virtue of the pattern of songs and fashions, to a time context readily recognizable as the 1930s.

Reprinted from *"The Two Gentlemen of Verona." Shakespeare Bulletin* 9.4 (Fall 1991): 15–17.

Although purists may be annoyed on principle, Thacker's transposition of setting to the fashionable age of Noel Coward, Frederick Lonsdale, and P.G. Wodehouse proves to be generally felicitous. Like Robin Phillips' 1970 RSC production, anachronistically relocated to a contemporary Riviera playworld with beach balls and motor scooters, the current version facilitates audience grasp of character relationships and convoluted plot by framing them in a world as familiar as Masterpiece Theatre. Here is a salon society, garbed in dressing gowns and white flannels, who bicker and banter and drape themselves on furniture in postures they would lead you to believe are signatures of breeding. Here are masters and servants; here are myriad messages and frequent trips to somewhere else; and here is intrigue motivated by ice-glazed passion, peer rivalry, and aspirations of class power. While the Outlaws of the Mantuan frontier seem oddly situated in a thirties context, and while many a problem among the silly people in the play may have been readily resolved with aid of the modern convenience of a telephone, the elements of character and conflict are coherently revealed and developed within this time-warped context.

The thirties love lyrics, sung between the scenes (and underscoring some) by chanteuse Hillary Cromie, are especially appealing and, as assembled by RSC Head of Music Guy Woolfenden, integral to the production—often offering ironic comment on the scenes. For example, Ray Noble's upbeat "Love Is the Sweetest Thing" serves as the segue from the pre-show cabaret into 1.1; Cole Porter's haunting "Night and Day" provides the musical foreshadowing of sinister actions that follow Thacker's choice of an "interval"—action resumes with Proteus' treacherous manipulation of Thurio and the Duke of Milan (3.2); Irving Berlin's "What'll I Do" effectively underscores Proteus' parting from Julia. Woolfenden's own foxtrot setting of the "Who Is Silvia" lyric, alas, pales amid the old favorites.

The musical bridges between scenes also provide cover for the several set changes. Designer Shelagh Keegan dresses settings with elegant, selective detail appropriate to Thacker's period context: wicker garden furniture, potted palms, and even a marble cistern that features at its center a sculpted cupid bearing on its shoulder a fountaining birdbath bowl. The tuneful scene transitions, however, are sometimes protracted and even seem to serialize the action in ways that occasionally inhibit developing dramatic momentum.

A clutter of suitcases and golf clubs are mounded centerstage for the opening scene. The doughy bulk of Valentine's (Richard Bonneville) figure contrasts with Proteus' (Barry Lynch) shorter and wiry silhouette as the two gents lounge on the impromptu comforts offered by the clumps of luggage. Their bumptious manners and smart haberdashery convey a prototypical image of English public school boys. The youthful sophistry of their discourse on love and the verbal gamesmanship of their banter reveal dispositional contrasts, a strange devotion to one another, and an even stranger rivalry. Bonneville and Lynch engage in residual adolescent horseplay as they boyishly wrestle on the floor in exchanges that may also suggest a dimension of latent sexuality. They also adopt postures of new manhood: Valentine gives Proteus a cigarette case as a memento of friendship and coming of age. As Valentine bids his chum "farewell," Thacker includes a bit where Proteus, in a gentlemanlike manner, extends his hand as if to shake Valentine's. As Valentine reaches for the handshake, however, Proteus boyishly withdraws his hand in an antic "fake out" gesture that Valentine seems to recognize as a recurrent jest of which he has often been the brunt. Thacker's handling of these earliest foregrounding moments engages curiosity. The relationship between these two gentlemen is suggested as somewhat more complex and ambiguous than the Italian comedy archetype.

Proteus, as rendered by Lynch, is seen as far more sullen, circumspect, and Iago-like than spontaneously passionate and protean. His manner is notably cerebral; subtext often seems remote from text. Effusive language of love is delivered in clerkish plain tones; emotion is typically repressed rather than expressed. Upon Valentine's exit from scene one, Proteus is left alone to speak the first of the play's numerous narrative monologues:

> He after honor hunts, I after love:
> He leaves his friends to dignify them more;
> I leave myself, my friends and all, for love.
> Thou, Julia, thou hast metamorphosed me,
> Made me neglect my studies, lose my time,
> War with good counsel, set the world at nought;
> Made wit with musing weak, heart sick with thought. (1.3.63–69)

Here, where the text seems to shift attention to Julia, Lynch's deconstruction sustains a resonant attachment to the departed Valentine. Thoughts of Julia seem more a consolation, which fail to brighten the shadow of Valentine's going, than a genuine attraction. "Heart sick with thought" captions this picture of Proteus.

In the subsequent exchange between Proteus and Valentine's quick-witted manservant Speed (Sean Murray), Thacker's staging further advances signals of Proteus' duality. The glib word match continues at serve-and-volley pace while Speed proceeds to dismantle Valentine's baggage heap and, in several trips, remove it from the stage. Isolated in contrasting stillness to

Speed's perpetual motion, Proteus counterpoints surface banter with an introspective concentration that suggests an envy, problematically shaded with darker desire, of Valentine—his trip, his servant, his things. With this motivational framework, Proteus' later machinations to have Silvia (Saskia Reeves) may be understood as not the product of libidinous impulses but as a compulsive extension of his complex feelings toward Valentine.

Clare Holman's attractive Julia earns respect, or at least some measure of sympathy, for her patient resolve to await Proteus' spiritual conversion from compulsive deceiver to honest man. As a fashionable and intelligent woman of independent means, she conducts her conversations in 1.2 and 2.7 with her confidante Lucetta (Josette Bushell-Mingo) on love and lovers with flippancy that mocks the dangers of obsessive romance—distanced with irony from a surface reading of text—rather than with swoons of sentimental surrender to "the fire of love." Thacker confines staging in 1.2 to an elegant patio setting and in 2.7 to a picnic blanket to allow the intimacy of friendship between the women and nuances of textual deconstruction to sustain focus. When she is disguised as Sebastian, Julia's intent seems to be more clinical—as if she wished to study the case of Proteus' compulsive duplicity, with apparent belief in the likelihood of recovery and reform—than cleverly deceptive.

What remains bewildering, however, is why Julia is attracted to Proteus. His malevolent choices and deceitful actions are deliberate—not impulsive, errant failings of youth or eruptions of Byronic appetite. We observe him engineer the treachery. While individual characterizations are interpretively comprehensible, the fabric of relationships, the nature of the love that bonds these aristocratic "friends" together, puzzles understanding.

In the climactic encounter of 5.4, Valentine stops Proteus from forcing Silvia to "yield to [his] desire" by physically wrestling him to the floor—echoing, now in desperate earnest, the playful rough-housing of act one. Following Valentine's rebuke, which Bonneville delivers with stammered intensity, Proteus stands silent and still in a suspended pause before confessing in plain, measured monotone, "My shame and guilt confounds me"—more embarrassed than contrite. Is he truly repentant or again manipulating the moment? Having witnessed Proteus' duplicitous machinations as stemming from a cerebral melancholy or even a complex psychopathy—as distinct, for instance, from roguish inconstancy motivated by sexual infatuation with Silvia—we may find such instant forgiveness of Proteus and his reunion with Julia as ponderously strange. Sympathizing with the women as victims, not objects, of desire, we receive the facile pardon and reconciliations of the love story as outrageous.

If the 1930s setting makes any sense of this non sequitur happy ending, it comes through as an extension of the sporting manners of a class whose clubby members are more concerned with preserving and entertaining themselves than they are with adjudicating matters of morality. Valentine's concluding affirmation of "one mutual happiness" has a hollow ring in the context of "what hath fortuned." Nevertheless, it summons the band to swell the finale with a toe-tapping reprise of "Love Is the Sweetest Thing."

Thacker's revisionist production is playful, and, while it occasionally flirts with going over the top in its gimmickry, it keeps a solid hold of the text. It features fluent and natural ensemble acting, several notable characterizations, and myriad inventive bits and moments. As the Duke of Milan, Terence Wilton has the look of pedigree and develops an engaging blend of mannered elegance and vindictive superiority. Thacker introduces us to the Duke in 3.1 as an amateur gourmet chef who crenellates a cantaloupe for a presentation of fruit as Proteus betrays Valentine's plan to elope with Silvia. Then, as Valentine witnesses it, this Duke de cuisine dismembers a lobster as he discredits and disowns his daughter. Guy Henry is amusingly peevish as spoiled, snobby Thurio in tennis togs. As Silvia, Reeves is attractive but unglamorous, conveying more mystique than allure, speaking with a coolly shy manner of one who is aloof but insecure. Thacker deemphasizes the image of Silvia as prize. Even the verses of "Who Is Silvia" are interrupted and upstaged by Julia's discourse with the Host (Howard Crossley).

Richard Moore's performance as Launce stands out. Moore's Stan Laurel/Buster Keaton face registers comic takes with perfect economy and total lucidity. His unaffected manner and contemplative, simple repose—seen in contrast to the dramatic writhings that surround him—invite us to delight in the humor of his earnest reflections on parents and shoes or canine crime and punishment. Since the real pooch used in this production is an endearing sight gag, appropriately named Woolly, that commands attention with impromptu behavior, Moore's ability to engage a crowd's hearts and minds is all the more remarkable. On the occasion of this performance, during Launce's 4.6 recounting of Crab's misbehavior at the Duke's dinner, Woolly undertook dogged ablutions of private parts that could not be ignored by the audience. By virtue of well-timed takes and inventive connections with the text at hand, it was Moore who got the big laughs.

The Two Gentlemen of Verona will remain in the Stratford repertory for the balance of its season. Given its popular reception, the production will certainly reappear as part of the RSC's 1992 London season.

Thomas Clayton

To the extent that *Two Gentlemen* itself is well known, its climactic crux—5.4.82–83, TLN 2206–07—is no less well known, since interpretation of the play rests on resolving it, sometimes by the facile expedient of ignoring or even omitting it.[1] "It" is the concluding couplet of the speech—5.4.77b-83—in which Valentine seems so amazingly to present his own beloved Silvia to Proteus, the very Proteus who has betrayed his sometime dearest friend Valentine, his own sometime beloved Julia, the Silvia of his fugitive affection, and withal himself. After he has rescued her from outlaws, Proteus goes so far as to threaten that he will "force" her to "yield to my desire" (5.4.59),[2] but, caught at once by Valentine, he confesses:

> My shame and guilt confounds me.
> Forgive me, Valentine; if hearty sorrow
> Be a sufficient ransom for offence,
> I tender't here; I do as truly suffer
> As e'er I did commit. (73–77a)

Valentine replies:

> Then I am paid.
> And once again I do receive thee honest.
> Who by repentance is not satisfied
> Is nor of heaven nor earth, for these are pleased;
> By penitence th'Eternal's wrath's appeased.
> And that my love may appear plain and free,
> All that was mine in Silvia I give thee. (77B-83)

Here Julia (disguised as Sebastian, in pursuit of her Proteus) not surprisingly says "O me unhappy" and [*Swoons*]," as editors beginning with Pope have had it, very reasonably, since the instant response is Proteus' "Look to the boy."[3] Whatever Silvia does, beside remain silent throughout the episode, the script does not reveal.

In the introduction to his New Cambridge edition (10–14), Kurt Schlueter discusses the fictional antecedents, the theme of friendship, and the "*alter-ego* formula," remarking in his note on the key lines 82–83 that "Silvia's silence here can only be accounted for by her absence or distance

---

Reprinted from "The Climax of *The Two Gentlemen of Verona*: Text and Performance at the Swan Theatre, Stratford-upon-Avon, 1991." *Shakespeare Bulletin* 9.4 (Fall 1991): 17–19.

from the present action or, less likely, by a theory of an abridgement of the text" (136). It is almost as if the corresponding action in the 1991 Royal Shakespeare Company's *Two Gentlemen* had been designed to refute this assertion, in a production as critically acute and theatrically stunning as any I would hope to experience of this play.[4]

Most of the reviews were strongly favorable, emphasizing especially but not only the entertainment value of the 1930s setting with a palm court orchestra seated and playing upstage as part of the set and action and a host of the classic songs of the era by Irving Berlin, Cole Porter, the Gershwins, and others, many integrated cleverly with the dramatic action. A series of these constituted a musical prologue beginning fifteen minutes before the opening dialogue, with the principals taking turns singing solos with the orchestra—as only one reviewer thoughtfully forewarned prospective spectators (Jack Tinker in the *Daily Mail*). It is less surprising that the specific performance of the endplay went unremarked by a number, since reviewing space is always at a premium and broader strokes are the order of the day; but it perhaps is surprising that those who did remark on it responded rather differently, perhaps according to what they knew in advance about the play and its notoriously difficult ending.

Some dissatisfaction was expressed by Charles Spencer in the *Daily Telegraph* (4/19/91: 489b), who wrote that "it's not all perfect . . . , and even [the director] isn't capable of making sense of the risible ending. Nevertheless, it is hard to imagine a more enjoyable production of this flawed but endearing play."[5] In the *Financial Times* (4/19/91: 490b), Claire Armistead says that

> the reconciliation of love with friendship presents Shakespeare with no small problems in this ramshackle early comedy: having sent the young Proteus off in hot and dishonest pursuit of Valentine's sweetheart, he somehow has to ensure that harmony is restored. Yet he signally fails to give Proteus a chance to redeem himself, which in turn creates no small problems of characterization . . . It is not, therefore, surprising that Proteus—in Barry Lynch's account the more naive and impressionable of the two—should find himself duplicating his friend's affections. . . . If Thacker fails to vindicate the play as coherently motivated drama, he makes the most of it as entertainment.

But Rod Dungate in the *Tribune* (5/31/91: 488d) found that "Richard Bonneville (Valentine) and Barry Lynch (Proteus) make the near-impossible ending of the play riveting and—more difficult—plausible"; and Carole Woddis notes more specifically that, "little more than a good-looking cad, he [Lynch as Proteus] swears eternal love to Julia before promptly falling, on sight, for his best mate's girl, Silvia, . . . the kind of thing that you'd think would cut him off any girl's list. But for once it is the girl's constancy in love that brings things round and Lynch anyway brings great poignancy to his regret of past misdemeanours" (*What's On*, 4/19/91: 488d). In the *Times* (4/19/91: 490d), Benedict Nightingale comments on the psychology of the repentant villain:

> Barry Lynch is certainly the kind of intense, secret boy who, with a little sophistry, can convince himself that his feelings are morally paramount. The last scene, with its hurried reconciliations, admittedly poses special difficulties for him, since Proteus must switch from a rapist to a penitent, in what good taste should prevent me calling a flash. Yet among men of a certain age is that really so unlikely? By then, the zest and humour of Thacker's production have anyway swept away most objections. This is a strong company performance.

John Peter, who "never thought" he "would ever be really convinced by the reconciliation scene," described his reaction:

> In Thacker's hands the four actors draw up their account of faithlessness, remorse and maturity and had me eating out of their hands. When it comes to clear Shakespearian speech, half the battle is to understand your role clearly. One of the reasons why these plays live and last so well is that the lines were written to be spoken. *(Sunday Times* 4/21/91: 489c)

And in the *Independent* (4/19/91: 491b) Paul Taylor captures some of the details of the telling moments:

> Caught trying to rape Valentine's girlfriend, Proteus repents so fully and abruptly that Valentine offers to hand her over. The hint of plaintiveness in [Billy] Hill's melody ["That's the Glory of Love"] keeps the subsequent shift to happiness from feeling indecently false . . . Barry Lynch brings a nervous intensity to the treacheries of Proteus and he fleshes out the character's woefully underscripted moment of shame most realistically.

Saskia Reeves as Silvia and Barry Lynch as Valentine in Royal Shakespeare Company's 1991 production, directed by David Thacker. Shakespeare Center Library. Joe Cocks Studio Collection.

In this production, Silvia's stage place, movements, and gestures are seen to be the resolution of a "crux" not evident in performance because the approach makes such perfect sense of the dialogue, the situation, and the issues that no question arose or has reason to arise in the members of the audience.[6] While the kneeling Proteus confesses, after a l-o-n-g pause, the very Silvia wronged by Proteus stands beside him, facing Valentine. Her stance and facial expression are so eloquent a mute plea for forgiveness that Valentine must be thought partly to be moved by and partly to reflect (on) it in his response, which in effect articulates the spirit seen in Silvia: "Who by repentance is not satisfied," as her unspoken imploring seemed to say, "Is nor of heaven nor earth, for these are pleased; / By penitence th'Eternal's wrath's appeased."

And Silvia goes over to Valentine and stands with him as he concludes his micro-homily with the crux, the word in action, his restored affection for Proteus made apparent in his gesture: "And that my love may appear plain and free, / All that was mine in Silvia I give thee." Love is not a commodity but demonstration: "Love hath reason, reason non, / If what parts, can so remain," according to *The Phoenix and Turtle* (47–48). That is, Valentine does not give "all" his proprietary interest in Silvia and, therefore, Silvia herself—as though the second line were syntactically independent and semantically self-sufficient, as it is often taken to be. In order that his renewed love may be plainly seen to be freely given, "all" his love that was in Silvia he gives to, shares with, Proteus, even while it remains with Silvia (and even Valentine himself), as performance demonstrated. This offer extends, restores, the affection of lover to friend, righting the wrong of friend to friend that came of excessive love of a friend's beloved, Silvia, well deserving love but not such "love" as drove the smitten Proteus to pursue it.

Behind the "*alter-ego* formula" lies the ancient and familiar notion that "the friend is another self,"[7] with its extended life in the Renaissance, when it neoplatonically embraced not only the friend (in the conventionally differential sense) but also the beloved. It is interesting but not surprising that in Shakespeare's day this duality-in-unity was more or less than a conceit of poets. It was a commonplace of ordinary discourse in accordance with Jesus' pronouncement in Matthew that a marrying man "shal cleaue vnto his wife, and they twaine shalbe one flesh" (*Geneva Bible*, 19:3).[8] In *Two Gentlemen*, there is much talk of such connections between friends and lovers, which is necessarily viewed as ironical or hollow, or sometimes both, in dark readings stressing Valentine's confusion and Proteus' treachery. But the "half-full" interpretation is at least as viable and in production easier to perform than the "half-empty" reading that accords with conceptual dark comedy, to which it is not easy to turn *Two Gentlemen* without evident strain.[9]

"You knew him [Proteus] well?", the Duke asks Valentine, who replies, "I knew him as my self; for from infancy / We have conversed and spent our hours together" (2.4.54–56). His affection for Silvia is understandably still greater than that for Proteus, and it is expressed in similar terms when he is banished upon the Duke's discovery of his plot to elope with Silvia. The Duke's last line, "But as thou lov'st thy life, make speed form hence," is the cue for Valentine's soliloquy:

> And why not death rather than living torment?
> To die to be banished from my self,
> And Silvia is my self; banished from her
> Is self from self, a deadly banishment. . . .
> She is my essence, and I leave to be
> If I be not by her fair influence
> Fostered, illumined, cherished, kept alive.
> I fly not death to fly his deadly doom:

Tarry I here, I but attend on death;
But fly I hence, I fly away from life. (3.1.170–73, 182–87)

The hyperbolic praise of Silvia by his bosom friend Valentine, who is transformed by love (2.4.121–78), is seen and heard in the script itself to catalyze if it does not directly cause Proteus' "erring love" (206), as he himself in part perceives:

Is it mine eye or Valentine's praise,
Her true perfection or my false transgression
That makes me reasonless to reason thus? . . .
Methinks my zeal to Valentine is cold
And that I love him not as I was wont.
O but I love his lady too too much,
And that's the reason I love him so little. (2.4.189–91, 196–99)

Comically radical disorientation of relationships and loss of prior identity soon ensue, with Euphuistic doubletalk and paradoxes and apt medium of expression:

I cannot leave to love, and yet I do;
But there I leave to love where I should love.
Julia I lose, and Valentine I lose;
If I keep them, I needs must lose my self.
If I lose them, thus find I by their loss:
For Valentine my self, for Julia Silvia.
I to my self am dearer than a friend,
For love is still most precious in itself. . . .
I cannot now prove constant to my self
Without some treachery used to Valentine. (2.6.17–24, 31–32)

And so it goes, until the comically obsessed and self-abandoned Proteus is exposed, relieved, and confessed in the crucial exchange.

Proteus is sometimes read and played as though he were a proto-Iachimo or Iago, but the dialogue and play seem at pains to make him a tempted and self-misguided friend in a situation such as life itself as well as fiction commonly enough affords, when best friend runs off with spouse or beloved, some of the very attraction being due to the shared values, tastes, and feelings that made the friendship and the marriage or other union in the first place. Comicality does not imply lack of seriousness; it holds gravity in solution, however, in the generic tincture that it is. In the 1991 RSC production, Proteus is played not as sinister and treacherous but initially as likeable and inexperienced. Obliged at first to stay at home when Valentine goes to Court, he quickly falls head over heels in "love" with Silvia. She becomes temporarily his obsession, from the spell of which he is freed to return wholeheartedly to his first and real love, Julia ("Bear witness, heaven, I have my wish for ever," 5.4.116), in good time for the general reunion and reconciliation (5.4.117b–69—the end).

In the script as in performance, evidence that there will ever be loose ends is not suppressed but stressed, in Valentine's intercession on behalf of the outlaws and his assuring the Duke that "they are reformed, civil, full of good, / And fit for great employment, worthy lord" scarcely thirty lines after they have arrived to see Valentine with apparent quarry exclaiming with piratical glee, "A prize, a prize, a prize!" The harmonizing of the lovers, without such deliberate comic jars, is not less stressed in the play's last lines. There punishment is commuted in Valentine's comic sentence and his proclaiming the marital and festive quaternity-in-unity to follow:

> Come, Proteus, 'tis your penance but to hear
> The story of your loves discovered.
> That done, our day of marriage shall be yours,
> One feast, one house, one mutual happiness.

The play's ultimate indeterminacies need not be denied while one nevertheless appreciates that in the Swan production, in consonance with the script, actors and director make wonderful and lucid sense in performance of dialogue, appropriate and fully prepared for, that synecdochically condenses in the play's crucial moment the very pattern explicitly identified in the play: repentance, forgiveness, reconciliation, a consummation sufficiently to be wished in irrational conflicts worldwide, at present, that it need not be referred to critical obsessions of the nineteen fifties to be understood as meaningful.

NOTES

1. In his New Cambridge edition (New York: Cambridge University Press, 1990), which I cite throughout, Kurt Schlueter provides a lengthy stage history (17–49) with detailed attention given to major twentieth-century productions (38–49), including the way in which each production addressed the crux (cf. n. 6 below).

2. Schlueter's editorial stage direction "[*He lays hands on her*]" supplies dramatic action to make sense of Valentine's coming forward and saying to Proteus, "Ruffian, let go that rude uncivil touch, / Thou friend of an ill fashion!"

3. The situation and the real or apparent problematics of a single couplet here are very similar to those at the end of *All's Well That Ends Well* centering on Bertram's

"If she, my liege, can make me know this clearly, / I'll love her dearly, ever, ever dearly" (5.3.305–06). I am grateful to Jay Halio both for confirming my recollections of the RSC performance and for suggesting that Silvia's movements in this production may owe something to Isabella's explicit intercession in *Measure for Measure*.

4. Scholarly reviews will be forthcoming in due course, but a few details are in order here. Set in 1933, the production emphasizes the upper-class and elegant adolescence of the lovers and makes extensive use of the music and dancing as well as fashions of the period. "Today . . . few directors can resist a new frame," as J.C. Trewin remarks in *Going to Shakespeare* (London: Allen and Unwin, 1978), p. 62, and this frame handsomely became the action. I saw it on May 13, 1991, in the second month of the run.

5. Page numbers are those of the photocopies in the *London Theatre Record*, April 9–22, 1991, from which the reviews are quoted.

6. As Schlueter describes them, most earlier twentieth-century productions found other ways of making sense of the offer—as "understood in the traditional way" (47)—or of glossing over it. In William Bridges-Adams' production of 1925, "Silvia buried her face in her hands and did not come to the surface again until Valentine calmly resumed possession of her some thirty lines later" (38). In both Iden Payne's 1938 (39) and Denis Carey's 1952 Bristol Old Vic (40) productions, "Valentine's offer of his bride" was omitted. In the satirical treatment by the London Old Vic in 1957, "though Valentine's offer may have been only a temporary measure specifically motivated by Proteus' threat to shoot himself, Silvia fell into a swoon on hearing it, making all further actions from her unnecessary" (43). In Peter Hall's 1960 Stratford production, the lines were spoken, but only one reviewer commented on them, writing that "Valentine's embarrassing, impossible, generous 'All that was mine in Silvia' was spoken so that it was hardly noticed" (44). In the RSC's 1970 modern-dress version, "the offer was not to be understood in the traditional way. The prompt-book reveals that Valentine kissed Silvia before speaking his two momentous lines and afterwards kissed Proteus. Valentine's offer seems to have been understood as a declaration of equality and of his acceptance of Proteus on equal terms, as balm to his deeply-felt inadequacy" (47), because "a modern-dress production will necessarily try to clarify the psychological implications or even supply a psychological aspect missing in the drama" (45). In John Barton's 1981 production, "the oft-questioned phrase was robbed of its impact by 'deliberately running it over with action' . . . The commentary in the programme did not clarify the situation; it suggested that the offer was perhaps only intended to test Proteus's reaction" (48).

The 1970 production anticipated 1991: for each, the dialogue and action had evidently been thought through in the round by director or actors, or both.

7. Tilley (F 696) cites Erasmus, *amicus alter ipse (Adagia* 14F); and, as Dent notes, Wilson adds Aristotle's *Nichomachean Ethics* 4.4 (5/1166a.32: *esti ho philos allos autos*). See Maurice P. Tilley, *A Dictionary of Proverbs in England in the Sixteenth and Seventeenth Centuries* (Ann Arbor: University of Michigan Press, 1950); F.P. Wilson, *The Oxford Dictionary of Proverbs*, 3rd ed. (Oxford: Clarendon, 1970); and R.W. Dent, *Shakespeare's Proverbial Language: An Index* (Berkeley: University of California Press, 1981).

8. For the currency of these ideas in popular usage and daily life, see the chapter on "Romantic Love" in Alan McFarlane, *Marriage and Love in England, 1300–1840* (Oxford: Blackwell, 1986), 174–208.

9. Since Schlueter capably stresses the darker interpretation in his discussion (10–14) and in his stage history of twentieth-century productions (38–49), I confine myself here to the festive face value, which seems more congruent with the tone and attitude of the script and apposite in productions conceived in conformity with Occam's razor.

BIBLIOGRAPHY

Brooks, Harold F. "Two Clowns in a Comedy (to say nothing of the Dog): Speed, Launce (and Crab) in *The Two Gentlemen of Verona.*" *Essays and Studies* 16 (1963): 91–100.

Byrne, Muriel St. Clare. From "The Shakespeare Season at The Old Vic, 1956–57 and Stratford-upon-Avon, 1957." *Shakespeare Quarterly* 8 (1957): 469–71.

Campbell, Kathleen. "Shakespeare's Actors as Collaborators: Will Kempe and *The Two Gentlemen of Verona*" [original publication in this volume].

Clayton, Thomas. "The Climax of *The Two Gentlemen of Verona:* Text and Performance at the Swan Theatre, Stratford-upon-Avon, 1991." *Shakespeare Bulletin* 9.4 (Fall 1991): 17–19.

Derrick, Patty S. "Feminine 'Depth' on the Nineteenth-Century Stage" [original publication in this volume].

———. "*Two Gents:* A Crucial Moment." *Shakespeare on Film Newsletter* 16.1 (December 1991): 1, 4.

European Magazine. "*The Two Gentlemen of Verona.*" In *Eyewitnesses of Shakespeare: First Hand Accounts of Performances, 1590–1890.* Ed. Salgãdo Gāmini. London: Chatto and Windus for Sussex University Press, 1975; New York: Barnes & Noble, 1975, pp. 78–80.

Evans, Bertrand. *Shakespeare's Comedies.* Oxford: Clarendon Press, 1960, pp. 9–19.

Ewbank, Inga-Stina. "'Were man but constant, he were perfect': Constancy and Consistency in *The Two Gentlemen of Verona.*" In *Shakespearean Comedy* (Stratford-upon-Avon Studies 14). Ed. Malcolm Bradbury and David Palmer. New York: Crane, Russak, 1972, pp. 31–57.

Freeburg, Victor Oscar. "The Female Page." *Disguise Plots in Elizabethan Drama: A Study in Stage Tradition.* New York: Columbia University Press, 1915, pp. 61–71.

Friedman, Michael D. "'To be slow in words is a woman's only virtue': Silence and Satire in *The Two Gentlemen of Verona.*" *Selected Papers from The West Virginia Shakespeare and Renaissance Association* 17 (1994): 1–9.

Hallett, Charles A. "'Metamorphising' Proteus: Reversal Strategies in *The Two Gentlemen of Verona*" [original publication in this volume].

Hazlitt, William. *Characters of Shakespear's Plays* [1817]. London: Oxford University Press, 1934, pp. 219–21.

Jackson, Berners W. From "Shakespeare at Stratford, Ontario, 1975." *Shakespeare Quarterly* 27 (1976): 25–27.

Johnson, Samuel. From his edition of *The Plays of William Shakespeare* [1765]. Reprinted in *Johnson on Shakespeare.* Ed. Walter Raleigh. Oxford: Oxford University Press, 1908, pp. 72–75.

Keyishian, Harry. "The Shakespeare Plays on TV: *Two Gentlemen of Verona*." *Shakespeare on Film Newsletter* 9.1 (December 1984): 6.

Kiefer, Frederick. "Love Letters in *The Two Gentlemen of Verona*." *Shakespeare Studies* 18 (1986): 65–85.

Lusardi, James P. "*The Two Gentlemen of Verona*." *Shakespeare Bulletin* 2–3.12–1 (November 1984/February 1985): 13.

Nelsen, Paul. "*The Two Gentlemen of Verona*." *Shakespeare Bulletin* 9.4 (Fall 1991): 15–17.

Perry, Thomas A. "Proteus, Wry-Transformed Traveller." *Shakespeare Quarterly* 5 (1954): 33–40.

Peterson, Jean. "*The Two Gentlemen of Verona*." *Shakespeare Bulletin* 9.1 (Winter 1991): 33–34.

Sargent, Ralph M. "Sir Thomas Elyot and the Integrity of *The Two Gentlemen of Verona*." *PMLA* 65 (December 1950): 1166–80.

Shaw, Bernard. *Shaw on Shakespeare: An Anthology of Bernard Shaw's Writings on the Plays and Production of Shakespeare*. Ed. Edwin Wilson. New York: E. P. Dutton, 1961, pp. 200–06.

Slights, Camille Wells. "*The Two Gentlemen of Verona* and the Courtesy Book Tradition." *Shakespeare Studies* 16 (1983): 13–31.

Small, S. Asa. "The Ending of *The Two Gentlemen of Verona*." *PMLA* 48 (1933): 767–76.

Speaight, Robert. From "Shakespeare in Britain." *Shakespeare Quarterly* 21 (1970): 446–47.

———. *William Poel and the Elizabethan Revival*. London: William Heineman Ltd., 1954, pp. 120–22.

Swinburne, Algernon Charles. *A Study of Shakespeare* [1880]. New York: AMS Press, 1965, pp. 48–49.

Timpane, John. "'I am but a foole, looke you': Launce and the Social Functions of Humor" [original publication in this volume].

Trewin, J.C. *Shakespeare on the English Stage 1900–1964: A Survey of Productions*. London: Barrie and Rockliff, 1964, pp. 30–31.

Weimann, Robert. "Laughing with the Audience: *The Two Gentlemen of Verona* and the Popular Tradition of Comedy." *Shakespeare Survey* 22 (1969): 35–42.

SHAKESPEARE CRITICISM

PHILIP C. KOLIN
General Editor